Give Sorrow Words

To my father, Samuel Woolf, who died in 1984;

to the memory of 'Robert' himself;

and to Elinor.

'… ne'er pull your hat upon your brows;
Give sorrow words; the grief that does not speak
Whispers the o'er-fraught heart and bids it break.'

Macbeth

Give Sorrow Words
Working with a
Dying Child

THIRD EDITION

Dorothy Judd

Foreword by Dora Black
New Foreword by **Jeremy Whelan**

KARNAC

First published in 1989 by Free Association Books
Second edition published in 1995 by Whurr Publishers Ltd

Reprinted 1996

Third edition published in 2014 by
Karnac Books Ltd
118 Finchley Road
London NW3 5HT

British Library Cataloguing in Publication Data

A C.I.P. for this book is available from the British Library

ISBN-13: 978-1-78049-148-6

Typeset by V Publishing Solutions Pvt Ltd., Chennai, India

Printed in Great Britain

www.karnacbooks.com

Contents

Acknowledgements

Compiling these acknowledgements has been perhaps the most enjoyable part of the task of writing this book. I shall trace the help chronologically. First and foremost, and woven into the whole time-span of the work involved, I would like to thank my husband, Denis, for his direct support, encouragement, and helpful comments, as well as his background support in sharing the holding of the domestic fort.

Then, my second analyst, Alex Tamopolsky, facilitated the process of thinking about this work and the possibility of writing something about it. Shirley Hoxter was a source of inspiration to me, as tutor, seminar leader, supervisor, and workshop convenor, at different stages of my training as a child psychotherapist at the Tavistock Clinic, and subsequently as I began to work with physically ill children.

Jeanne Magagna, Sheila Miller, Margaret Rustin, Juliet Hopkins, and Jon Jureidini all looked at earlier stages of my draft of the diary (Part Two of the book), and made very helpful comments. Later Gianna Williams helped with valuable thoughts.

A particularly significant person was Ann Scott of Free Association Books. I have been especially fortunate to have had her as my editor. Her ideas about the ways in which the diary (Part Two) could be developed into a book, as well as her encouragement and detailed comments, have been invaluable. During Ann's absence, Selina O'Grady continued confidently to nurse the book along, with great attention to detail. I am grateful, too, to Miranda Chaytor for editorial help, and to Gillian Wilce, for her very careful copy-editing.

Meira Likierman read the whole almost finished manuscript and passed on many very useful thoughts. I am particularly grateful to her for her time.

Dora Black was a source of encouragement and support throughout, in reading parts of the manuscript, allowing me to carry out some of the work, and in making herself available for interview. Thanks, too, to Grant Prentice for agreeing to my undertaking some of the clinical work, as well as to David Lee and the many nurses, doctors, and teachers in the hospital school.

Much gratitude, too, to Richard Lansdown, Sister Frances Dominica, Dorothy Jordan, and Margaret Atkin for agreeing to my interviewing them, and for permission to quote them extensively. Similarly, many thanks to Mary Sue Moore for her generous comments and insight, and to Ricky Emanuel and Peter Speck for encouragement.

I would also like to thank two colleagues, Gill Roger and Frances Gomme, for their compassionate support at different times, as well as Carolyn Lelyveld for inspiration and understanding early on. Phil Beauchamp, too, was an important and valued colleague. The ongoing work discussion group which I convene at the Tavistock Clinic has provided a valuable psychodynamic approach to illness and disability.

I am grateful to the staff of the Tavistock Joint Library for their trouble; to the typists Linda Kaufman, Jackie Lightband, Jill Fletcher, and, particularly, Linda Burkill, for their hard work.

Last but not least, there are the many children whose experiences have been the basis for all my work.

London, January 1989

Acknowledgements for the second edition

The foregoing acknowledgements are still very relevent to this book's existence in the first place, and to this development of a new and expanded edition.

I wish to especially thank Felicity Dirmeik for her ongoing considerable support, insight, and encouragement in all areas of my hospital work over the past 3-and-a-half years, without which coping would have been much more difficult, if not impossible at times.

Meira Likierman has again been very helpful in discussing some ideas.

I would like to thank the people who have given freely of their thoughts and allowed me to interview them for this edition: Robert Souhami, Anne Kilby, Jane Watson, Chris Henry, and Vikky Riley.

Others who have supported me in my work in various ways or been inspiring colleagues are Sandra Ramsden, Annette Mendelsohn, Valerie Sinason, Alexa Gilbert, David Sonnenberg, Anne Lanceley, Mike Connolly, Justin Cobb, Aleda Erskine, and Dilys Daws. Then there are the many colleagues – medical and non-medical – in the hospital setting, past and present (Pippa Chesterfield, Del McCarthy, Rosalind Brent, Anne Goodhew, Judy Walker, to name but a few), who are essential and valued parts of the whole.

My publishers, Whurr, have been a model of efficiency and friendliness.

The staff in the Tavistock Joint Library have continued to be extremely helpful and patient in guiding my clumsy attempts to master the new research technology.

And finally, I wish to express my gratitude to the patients and their families who inspire me to continue to struggle with awful issues – 'awful', both in the sense of 'causing dread; terrible, appalling', and 'worthy of, or commanding, profound respect' (*The Shorter Oxford English Dictionary*).

London, February 1995

Acknowledgements for the third edition

I would like to thank my publishers Karnac for wholeheartedly taking on this project, for wanting this book to have a new life, and for their solid support in the decisions that needed to be made.

Without the hard work and detailed research of Claudia de Campos I could not have produced this new edition. Many thanks to the professionals (Margaret Rustin, Sebastian Kraemer, Sara Stoneham, and Heather Mackinnon) who kindly endorsed the need for this edition.

Anne Lanceley, a wise friend, gave support throughout, and expert-read some of the new text.

And finally, I wish to thank my husband Denis, who believes in new editions and the effort required, especially when he finds himself looking on encouragingly, instead of being in his more usual position of writing.

London, April 2013

Foreword

Those of us working in hospitals have the task of helping children and their families cope with the effects of chronic, sometimes life-threatening, illness in children, and with the pain, inconvenience and constrictive effect of the 'high-tech' treatments now available. Multiple injections and venesections, cytotoxic drugs and radiotherapy are now routine in the treatment of leukaemia and solid tumours, but radiotherapy may involve the child being placed alone in a room inside a machine for an hour. He has to remain still and is likely to feel very sick and vomit. He will be a long way from home, especially if he comes to a regional hospital for a bone-marrow transplant. If his parents come in with him ñ and we encourage and even insist on it – they have to cope with separation from other children and home, and live in a strange artificial environment. They have to relate to many different people at a time when anxiety about their child makes it difficult to function optimally.

For the child, according to his stage of development, anxiety is moderated by the presence of his parents, but he cannot help but be aware of the danger he is in, and research has revealed the propensity of the child to protect the parents from pain and depression (BluebondLangner, 1978). This partial reversal of the normal state of things ñ the parents usually protect the, child – is often self-imposed and is rarely sought for or encouraged by the parents, but it constitutes a burden on an already overstressed child. Small wonder that the level of psychological disturbance in child, parents and siblings in life-threatening illness is between 50 and 75 per cent (Koocher *et al.*, 1980). If the price the child has to pay for recovery is a crippled mind, then the price may be too high.

In an effort to alleviate the emotional pain for children and their families, physicians are now working closely with child psychiatrists and their colleagues in some centres to provide a psychological support and treatment service. Dorothy Judd, a child psychotherapist, came to us to help develop this service, which also involves child psychiatrists, psychologists and social workers. Sometimes we are able to work with the whole family together, at other times, individual therapy may be more appropriate. Our aim is to provide time and space for children and families to reflect on their experiences, understand what is happening, adapt to the reality of the illness and treatment, enable the expression of fear, anger, anxiety and sadness and provide a safe place and person – one who is not involved in the medical treatment, and so can be the container of unwanted and sometimes frightening feelings. In this way it may be possible to bear the unbearable – the uncertainty about the future.

Doctors and nurses who have to do painful and unpleasant procedures to children, who may have to make an apparently well child sick, sometimes also have unbearable emotions. In order to carry on, we may develop defences against this pain which may make us less sensitive to our patients' emotional experiences. Child psychiatric teams can offer to share this pain and allow it to be lived with and therefore not denied ñ a process which makes us all more human.

In what follows, Dorothy Judd offers us an overview of children's attitudes to death and considers the moral and ethical issues raised by treatments for life-threatening illness in children. She allows us to share her attempt to enter into the world of the dying child, to experience with Robert and his parents the bewilderment, the isolation, the mutual pretence, the pain and anxiety that serious illness brings to families. Using her sensitive personality, honed by training and experience, she is able to make a space for this boy to make some sense of his experience – to 'live until he dies', as Spinetta has put it (Spinetta and Deasy-Spinetta, 1981). At the same time her social worker colleague is helping the parents to bear the unbearable.

Robert did not win his battle with his illness. But an increasing number do, as our haematology colleagues refine and improve their treatments, using the knowledge which they gain from their experience with many children like Robert. It is our task to make sure that they and their families have as high a level of emotional care as they do of physical care. With resources dwindling within the NHS we may not be able in future to offer the help to these families they need and deserve. I hope this moving account of a talented child psychotherapist's work with one very ill boy will help those who have to make funding decisions to understand the nature of our contribution to the care of these suffering families.

Dora Black, Consultant Child and Adolescent Psychiatrist

Foreword to the third edition

While medical advances have transformed the outlook of many previously rapidly fatal illnesses, modern medicine's continued shortcomings are all too evident whether we watch children dying from malaria on television or the still all too frequent experience of our own personal loss from diseases such as cancer. Venomous public campaigns driven through the media – such as that which recently defined the Liverpool Care pathway as 'killing patients' and a 'death pathway' for babies – add to the difficulties that both professionals and families face. Our need to prepare for, to understand, to experience death, remains fundamental. But the profound emotional complexity shared by those experiencing any death presents repeated and predictable challenges. For those whose professional life engages them as participants, effective preparation to meet those challenges is an essential responsibility.

Some twenty years ago I was introduced to Dorothy Judd's excellent text and to Dorothy herself. Before and since, in my work as an oncologist, I have shared over and over again in the experience of the death of patients, especially of young people. Even with this familiarity, in welcoming this new edition of Dorothy's work, I am convinced that I and all professionals whose work encompasses end of life care will be well served by repeatedly reflecting on their understanding of the reactions and responses of patients and families to the threat of loss of life. By so doing, they themselves will be better able to maintain effective care. In seeking that understanding, there will be few better places to start than with this analysis whatever the age group one may work with.

Despite the universality of death and suggestions that nowadays there is greater openness to discussions about dying, pretence continues to be a familiar, often dominant feature of interactions between patients, their families and professionals. So often, we can conspire to sustain an unrealistic but 'hopeful' quest for avoidance of the inevitable. Sustaining that conspiracy is such a temptation, especially for doctors, trained to think in terms of 'saving lives', and parents, desperate not to contemplate the most painful loss of all, that of a child. As so many of the interviews with professionals in this book indicate, we need never to lose sight of this. Modern multidisciplinary teams have an especially strong role to play here: to detect, confront and support interrelationships that may predict for the needs of a dying child or young person being shifted from the centre stage of care. And of course, ensuring that the support needs of staff themselves are recognized.

I was recently struck to hear 'Am I going to die?' as a question remembered by a cancer survivor 17 years after been diagnosed as an 11 year old. Also recalled was her mother's response 'I am not going to let you'. Whether spoken or unspoken, our fears of dying are powerful. This key question, whether uttered or suppressed, is of course only the opening question. Other questions must follow. How? When? Will it be painful? What will I experience? What do I need to do? Doctors, nurses and other professionals working with patients with cancer should have the skills to acknowledge and support those fears, to elicit them even when hidden by the webs of protection so ably woven by patients and their families and so often condoned by the responses of professionals.

But how should we prepare for this most difficult and exacting role? What language should we use? How will it sound and what will the effect be? The sensation of taking a discussion with a patient or family on to 'thin ice' may be familiar to the most experienced clinician or therapist. The skilful practitioner will also have more to give as a teacher and supporter of others. Here again, the insight and direction threaded through *Give Sorrow Words* is an invaluable aid. I would not hesitate in defining this as an essential text for any professional involved in the care of the dying.

Jeremy Whelan
Professor of Cancer Medicine and Consultant Medical Oncologist,
The London Sarcoma Service,
University College Hospital,
London.

Preface to the first edition

To begin at the beginning. The work which this book describes arose out of a workshop I attended at the Tavistock Clinic in 1985, for child psychotherapists working with physically ill and disabled children. It gave me support and some very early insight into my work as a child psychotherapist with a small number of physically disabled children some of whom had limited prognoses, at a special school. I began to consider basic problems concerning the chronically ill, the disabled, and the dying. When are defences useful and when are they maladaptive? How can the chronically ill child work through the normal developmental phases – particularly adolescence, with its essential bids for independence and autonomy – when his illness or disability makes him dependent on adults for basic care? Beyond which point should life be sustained by medical intervention, and how do we evaluate the quality of the remaining life for a child whose death is prolonged? Arthur Hugh Clough's caveat from *The Latest Decalogue* comes to mind:

> Thou shalt not kill; but need'st not strive
> Officiously to keep alive.

This interest led me to further work mainly with leukaemic children, in a large teaching hospital, where I was supported by colleagues and a workshop for those of us engaged in working with children facing lifethreatening illness.

When I showed my account of the work with one of these children 'Robert' (in Part Two of this book) – to Ann Scott, at Free Association Books, she expressed interest but called it 'the foothills of a publishing project'. I wasn't sure whether to feel discouraged or encouraged: only the foothills – but at least it could be considered a potential publishing project. With Ann's encouragement I developed it further.

It grew at first into many little offshoots, which somehow, almost organically; became a recognizable shape. The process was not unlike that of knitting a garment: the various parts developed, to be pieced together; details like 'pockets' were added; some mistakes were corrected and 'dropped stitches' picked up, while others remained, perhaps for ever; finally, the 'rough ends' were tidied up. Through the creative process of making this book, it felt that the painful ordeal of this particular child, and many like him, could at least lead to further thinking about crucial issues around the care of dying children.

At a more personal level, one of the underlying reasons for writing this book is that the impact of working with terminally ill children affected me deeply. Robert appeared in my life as suddenly as he departed from it: a first brief encounter, late September, with a pert little boy with a beguiling Scottish accent, so full of life and spirit that I reeled from the first meeting. I was shocked deep inside myself to think of his diagnosis – leukaemia – and the life-threatening disease in his body, destroying his blood. He occupied a pleasant side-room off the children's ward of a large teaching hospital in the North of England. The bustle of the ward seemed to take this new patient in its stride: it was only his mother's anxious expression and startled eyes that conveyed to me the seriousness of the situation.

The smell of the ward pervaded my nostrils for hours, strangely remind-ing me of a combination of talcum powder and babies' faeces. Perhaps this was evoked by the atmosphere of nurturing and cleanliness, of the appar-ent acceptance of bodily products that accompanies the care of the ill, of a powerful maternal presence in the ward, and by the helplessness of most of the patients.

This experience touched on other, earlier, more personal losses. The pro-cess of writing, firstly, the detailed account of my contact with one dying child, and then a fuller survey of the subject, was not only a way of sorting out some of my own thoughts and feelings, but also arose out of a sense of my own finiteness. For it is partly through this sense of mortality that our creativity is galvanized; that we seek to repair, create, and recreate, phoenix-like, that which has gone before – in the sense of 'happened' as well as 'lost'.

Nothing can alter the absolute loss of a child, but we need to consider the climate in which a child dies, in an attempt to allow the experience to carry its own truth. Part of this truthfulness, and of the allowing of truthfulness on the part of the child, lies in acknowledging our 'not knowing' about the meaning of death, nor when it will come, to a particular child or his family: to be able to tolerate the uncertainty that a limited prognosis brings.

In *Four Quartets* T.S. Eliot writes:

In order to arrive at what you do not know
You must go by a way which is the way of ignorance ...
And what you do not know is the only thing you know ...

This uncertainty, and the sense of vulnerability it brings, is hard to stay with, without what Keats (1817) calls the 'irritable reaching after fact and reason'. Perhaps Keats's own life-threatening illness contributed to his understand-ing of this 'negative capability', as he called it, 'when a man is capable of being in uncertainties, mysteries, doubts'.

Much of this book is factually and theoretically based, hopefully not as a way of avoiding some of the uncertainties, but as a way of providing a framework within which to reflect. I hope that alongside the research quoted and the arguments presented there is sufficient quiet and stillness, where the reader can dwell on his or her own thoughts and search for meanings.

The theoretical framework of this book is, generally, a Kleinian one: that is, I have drawn upon the writings of Melanie Klein, who, beginning in the 1920s, pioneered child analysis. Klein's perspective arises out of Freud's discoveries of the child within the adult: she developed Freud's theories further, thus encompassing the possibility of seeing the baby within the child and within the adult. At first, some of her theoretical conclusions seemed surprising even to Klein herself: 'My study of the mind of the small child brought certain facts before me which seemed strange at first sight' (1932). Understandably, some of the ideas put forward in this book may well appear strange to the reader who is new to Klein's ideas.

This perspective arises logically for me out of my training at the Tavistock Clinic, my personal analyses and supervision, as well as a continued appraisal and reappraisal of these ideas through ongoing clinical work. Inevitably, further studies by Anna Freud, Winnicott, Bowlby, Bion, Meltzer and many others have helped me, in common with many other child psychotherapists, to extend the theoretical framework.

However, although theories help to form a useful structure, it is the actual work with a child from which the excitement of discovery springs – the essential 'learning from experience', as Bion (1962) calls it. Alongside this comes the inevitable frustration of not understanding, of waiting, of continuing to look at one's own internal world, and attempting to understand one's own unconscious processes.

Recently much has been written about death, dying, and bereavement, and a great deal about children, but little has been written about the issues involved in bringing these two areas together. Therefore I address children's attitudes to death and how an imminent death affects these attitudes; ways in which adults, both professionals and parents, approach the death of children; and the increasing problems which arise when death is postponed through medical intervention and children are either living with an uncertain prognosis or experiencing a protracted dying. I have not focused fully on bereavement – on the effects of the death of a child on parents and siblings – because that is a full study in itself, but of course the book greatly concerns itself with our attitudes to loss and mourning. As the main focus is on dying children, the book aims to encompass their preoccupations and the climate in which they find themselves.

I have attempted to marry clinical experiences with theoretical concepts, published research on children's attitudes to death, and interviews with other experienced professionals.

My main focus is children with cancer, because, after accidents, cancer accounts for more deaths in children aged between one and 14 years than any other cause. Yet cancer can be considered rare. One in every 600 children under the age of 15 develops a cancer, and of these leukaemia is the most common.

The experience of working with the child whom I describe in detail in Part Two was a very intimate one, and therefore one that is not easily shared in a public way through writing and publishing the account. However, I felt that it was important to try to convey the story as I perceived it. It raises many questions about approaches to dying children, and about the support needed by the family and by the medical and non-medical professionals involved. Besides considering the appropriate psychological approach, this account raises the question of the medical efficacy of keeping someone alive where the chances of survival are very slim. The extreme physical suffering in many cases of this type has to be borne in mind when the decision to pursue medical treatment is made. It can be argued, of course, that each case can provide new medical knowledge, leading hopefully to further improvements in the future treatment of illness.

Above all, this book raises the question of whether those involved can or should ever shift their focus from one of working towards the day when the patient will be well again to one where death is accepted more openly and the impending loss is shared among all, including the patient. I can never generalize about the approach in such a delicate and painful situation, especially where a *child* is facing death, when 'where there's life, there's hope' is a necessary and understandable dictum for all those involved. In parallel with this, however, I believe there could be a place for thinking about that which perhaps is not unthinkable.

Bion (1984) describes how the infant, as part of normal development, when overwhelmed by a state of extreme helplessness, may project a feeling that it is dying into the mother. This is part of a basic psychic interplay between mother and child; the mother helps to make the infant's unmanageable experiences more tolerable through her 'reverie', her ability to take the infant's projections and anxieties 'on board'. In time, that which is thus 'processed' by the mother can be reintrojected – that is, taken once again into the infant's psyche, to become a part of his inner world.

However, if the projection of a feeling that it is dying 'is not accepted by the mother, the infant feels that its feeling that it is dying is stripped of such meaning as it has. It therefore reintrojects, not a fear of dying made tolerable, but a '*nameless dread*' (Bion, 1984, p. 116, my italics).

If the 'nameless dread' becomes something that can be acknowledged, perhaps given a form and shape, in words, play, drawings, or in a tacit calm acceptance, then perhaps fear, despair, isolation, and depression can to some extent be alleviated. Although here Bion is writing about an infantile phantasy and not a reality of dying, the feelings aroused in a fatally ill child may well be similar.

Preface to the second edition

I feel privileged to have this opportunity to bring out a new edition of *Give Sorrow Words*. Not only does this give me the opportunity to resurvey the research over the past 8 years, draw on my increasing experience, and refine or clarify some of the text of the first edition, but I have also been able to add a range of new interviews with other professionals, in order to explore more fully some of the issues and debates.

In my work in this field since the first edition, I find that there is an increasingly healthy awareness amongst nurses, doctors, medical students, and other professionals, of the painful issues around truthtelling (Weil *et al.*, 1994); consent (Alderson, 1990, 1993); the need for health workers to have more support; around the difficulties of switching to palliative care; and the need to look into our own psyches as well as attempting to be aware of those of our patients. These developments have occurred alongside pressures and changes in the National Health Service: the financial implications of treatment loom larger than ever. As treatments improve, and cure is possible for more patients, the temptation to try whatever may help is increased, both for parents and for doctors. The ethical implications explored in this book then become increasingly pertinent. Do decisions about *when* to treat have to be influenced by financial constraints? Or do we need to pay more attention to the emotional 'holding' that parents, ill children, and health professionals need, so that they can more effectively and appropriately make excruciatingly difficult decisions and keep in mind the quality of life? Indeed, the cost of the salary of a health worker who provides this holding, or thinking space, is infinitely less than many of the medical treatments that carry very slim chances of a successful outcome.

With many years' increased experience, I am now braver in speaking the unspeakable, in naming fears, when with a dying patient. Although this still takes courage, it is often rewarded by the patient's relief and increased trust. This leaves me with an awesome sense of responsibility, but in favourable circumstances the parents or other close family members can often then take on some of that intimate sharing.

In this work I find it increasingly striking that many of the normal characteristics of human nature – love, hate, guilt, a wish to repair, sexuality, hope, fear, gratitude, destructiveness, envy, despair, depression, denial – are compressed into an intense, concentrated period of time, where some, or all, of the emotions or states of mind are felt or glimpsed by those involved. This 'living nightmare', as it is often called, cannot be thought about, for the victim is subsumed by the catastrophe. Under such pressure, the predictable, meaningful, ordered world falls apart, into intense shards. The mental states that may then ensue include madness, disintegration, repression – all defences against the awful reality – or the immense task of struggling to make sense of it all, to piece together some of the fragments.

I am aware of a profound dichotomy, which, though delineated in the first edition of this book, has become more stark. How can we embrace death as part of life (which it is) and yet accept the death of a child? How can we accept the death of an adolescent girl, who cries that she will never have babies, never see them grow up? Or another, who says, 'It's worse for me than for my family, because I lose everyone, while they only lose one person'? How can we accept the death of a 12-year-old, who was his parents' only surviving child and pride and joy, after 10 miscarriages? How can we accept the death of a 2-year-old who was particularly beautiful, engaging, and zestful, despite extensive surgery and despite her single-parent mother's rejection of her? Or another 2-year-old who underwent brain surgery, chemotherapy, and radiotherapy, was particularly traumatized by the treatment, lovingly nursed through it all by his parents, and then died?

There is no rationale, so all we can do is register and express outrage, feel or try to understand the resonances in our own inner world: resonances with our own damaged internal figures (see Appendix III), and yet hope that within the bitter constraints of the short life that is left there can be some joy, some love, some hope, some opportunities to repair damaged relationships, and yet express the protest.

> … joy shines out only to reveal what the annihilation of joy will
> be like.
>
> J.M. Coetzee (1994)

In other words, death is equated with destruction, but it does not mean that our minds and our spirits are totally destroyed too, or that we lose all hope for something creative to emerge within this 'war-zone'.

The dichotomy, then, is about a struggle between, on the one hand, an acknowledgement of the death of a child as, by definition, anti-life and therefore insane, and yet, on the other hand, the need to make something hopeful out of it, without simply defending against its destructiveness. This book, and the work described therein, is one attempt to make sense of this irreconcilable tension, even though the feelings that shake us to the core do not find an easy outlet in words.

Preface to the third edition

I am very pleased to have the opportunity to bring out this 3rd edition of *Give Sorrow Words*. Although the main events it describes took place nearly twenty years ago, I feel that the book is still as valid and relevant as ever, and continues to express what I wish to say.

The body of text remains the same as in the 1995 edition. The book has a significant new Introduction, by Claudia de Campos. I am very grateful to Claudia for her careful appraisal of changes in the hospital care of children and young adults and advances in paediatric oncology which provide a contemporary context for the book.

I am also grateful to Professor Jeremy Whelan for his new Foreword. I knew Jeremy in the 1990s at the Middlesex Hospital, London, when he worked with Professor Robert Souhami, who I interviewed for this book in 1995. Recently, when I talked with Jeremy in the new University College Hospital Macmillan Cancer Centre, London, I was struck by how, after over twenty years in the field, he still appears to be in touch with the emotional weight and subtleties that this work entails.

I am aware of huge developments in the medical treatment of all cancers since 1995, and new arrangements to help increase the amount of research studies available to all patients including children and young adults. Notable, is the National Cancer Research Institute which has a 'Teenage and young adults clinical studies group'. They have instituted cancer registration; are following a survivor cohort of 15–39 year-olds; are promoting research needs for this age range; and, significantly, use clinical trial accrual as a marker of clinical care. Furthermore, international collaboration nowadays leads to improvements in treatments in just a few years, compared with, say, a twenty year span to bring about improvements in the past.

More recently, *Brightlight*, a study of 13 to 24 year-olds, is exploring if specialist cancer centres improve how well and how quickly young people recover. This research is still in its early stages. However, teenage and young adult cancer care is now considered mainstream, and not marginal.

Not surprisingly, I am aware of the fundamental similarities between the emotional problems faced in bearing the pain of working with the seriously ill, as well as the dying, child, as when I worked in paediatric oncology and haematology twenty years ago. The healthy on-the-side-of-life cannot bear the loss of this all too precious span. And so, as Ovid wrote, 'Hope prompts the shipwrecked sailor, in the midst of waves with no land in sight, to strike out with his arms.'

Thus, the main points made in this book (1989 and 1995 editions) are still relevant today: attempts to find ways of helping ourselves and others to accompany the dying child; to suffer anticipatory mourning if we can, because it may facilitate the grieving of the eventual loss; to manage our own anxieties as best we can in order to try to contain the child's, and the family's.

Yet, psychological 'work' has been resisted since Freud began to publish his theories, and before: he stated that man is generally only prepared to look outward, not inward, using a telling physiological metaphor:

> So if someone tries to turn our attention inward, in effect twisting its neck round, then our whole organization resists – just as, for example, the oesophagus and the urethra resist any attempt to reverse their normal direction of passage (1929).

On the other hand, Rilke (1925) expressed the potential enrichment of encompassing death:

> Death is that side of life which is turned away from us, unilluminated by us: we must try to achieve the greatest possible consciousness of our existence, which is at home in both of these unlimited provinces, inexhaustively nourished out of both … .

In our struggle to face resistance, language itself has its limitations. We may attempt to 'give sorrow' – or the unspeakable experience of suffering – 'words', to try to find a common language, consciously and unconsciously, but full communication is not possible. T. S. Eliot (1944) describes this struggle to express emotions that can feel overwhelming as 'a raid on the inarticulate'. In my first analysis, when bemoaning the impossibility of expressing what I felt, my analyst said, 'Yes, but words are all we have.' So, as Eliot writes, 'For us, there is only the trying.'

While acknowledging that language can feel inefficient and frustrating, or evasive, or deceptive, the interlocutor's capacity to hear and understand what we wish to convey is crucial to the whole enterprise. This harks back to the infant's need for a mother (or significant other) to instinctively make sense of, and give thoughts, or words, to something ineffable and at times unbearable.

There is the possibility, then, that the dying child is not suffering alone, if some common language (albeit inadequate at times) is found.

As some examples in this book show, children – if given the opportunity – have an impressive capacity for truthfulness. It is often adults' inhibitions, fears, and protectiveness, that leave the child alone in his or her awareness of the seriousness of their situation.

In the illustration that follows we see how powerful a child's protective concern can be. Thirteen-year-old, Michael, (Judd, 2001), had undergone an amputation of his leg and hip for bone cancer. It was this quality of truth-fulness (for example, he said 'The cancer is more likely to come back to me than to someone else') that made his task more difficult, for he was generally alone in his ability to speak the truth. My task as his psychotherapist was to try to hear and bear the truth and to wonder how best to help a boy who seemed, at the beginning, not to be defended against his own psychic pain, but sensed and respected others' defences. Thus within a few weeks he had successfully 'fooled' doctors, nurses, physiotherapists, and his own family, by appearing brave and coping, but allowed me the onerous responsibility of sharing his catastrophic reactions to the trauma. Understandably, the more extreme the condition, the more defended the family and professionals can be. In an obvious way, emotional work for the bystander begins if the patient is unhappy or protesting, but less clearly if they are aware that the protesta-tions of being 'fine' are false. However, the protective concern which Michael extended to nearly everyone he came into contact with may have been his way of splitting off and projecting the part of him which could not bear the truth. I felt that if I eroded his powerful wish for others not to know, (which I explored with him in many ways at many times,) I would be infringing the confidentiality between us which he adamantly requested, as well as the ways in which he needed to put his 'don't want to know' feelings into oth-ers. I hoped that in time his inner desperation would lessen and he would allow his outer expression to be more truthful, or at least that there would be a gradual integration between his hidden grief and his everyday outer appearance.

Several months into the treatment, with his talent for aphorism, and his capacity to find ways of expressing his despair, he said, 'The way out of unhappiness, the way to find happiness, is to understand how you became unhappy in the first place.' He concluded, 'I don't believe in God any more … it's up to me to find … to walk the last bit on my own.' In the next session he said, 'I think life mustn't be wasted … I think you only get one chance.'

In 1996 I chose not to continue to work in a hospital, but to see some adults in my private practice who were facing a terminal prognosis. I sometimes miss the privilege of working so intensively and intimately with the huge life events which this book explores. I don't think I reached 'burn-out', but I could see it on the horizon. I then had the choice to leave, a choice which tragically many of the patients and families do not have.

Dorothy Judd
London, 2013

Eliot, T.S. (1944). Four Quartets. Faber: London.

Freud, S. (1929). Letter to A. Einstein, in 'Letters between Freud and Einstein', I. Grubrich-Simitis, *International Journal Psycho-Analysis* 76: 115–122 (1995).

Judd, D. (2001). 'To walk the last bit on my own' – narcissistic independence or identification with good objects: issues of loss for a 13-year-old who had an amputation, *Journal of Child Psychotherapy, 27 (1)* 47–67.

Rilke, R.M. (1925). *Briefe aus Muzot.*

Introduction to the third edition: developments since 1995

Claudia de Campos
Child and Adolescent Psychotherapist, London

Abbreviations:

BME: Black and Minority Ethnic
CAMHS: Child and Adolescent Mental Health Service
CHCR: Calman-Hine Cancer Report
CLIC: Cancer and Leukaemia in Children
CNS: Clinical Nurse Specialist
CP: Cancer Plan
CRS: Cancer Reform Strategy
ENCORE: English National Cancer Online Registration Environment
EOL: End of Life
GOSH: Great Ormond Street Hospital
GP: General Physician
IOG: Improving Outcomes Guidelines
IOSC: Improving Outcomes: a Strategy for Cancer
IOSC/SAR: Improving Outcomes: a Strategy for Cancer. Second Annual Report
MDT: Multi-Disciplinary Team
MHC: Mental Health Commission
NCAT: National Cancer Action Team
NCIN: National Cancer Intelligence Network
NHS: National Health Service
NICE: National Institute for Health and Clinical Excellence
NSF: National Service Framework
ONS: Office of National Statistics
PCT: Primary Care Trust
QoL: Quality of Life

SAIL: Secure Anonymised Information Linkage
UCLH: University College London Hospital

I feel particularly privileged to have been invited to introduce a new edition of Dorothy Judd's ground-breaking book, which has been a good friend in my own work in paediatric oncology.

Any psychotherapist working today with children who are dying will have read Judd's book at some point for its insights. The very juxtaposition of the words *child* and *dying* at once throw up resistances and defences in the most seasoned professionals; and the humanity, courage and rigour of her work will continue to sustain those whose job it is to give words to the most speechless and unbearable sorrow.

However, since this book was first published in 1989, and since the second edition in 1995, there have been some remarkable developments in paediatric oncology, and also some important changes in attitudes to how children are treated and cared for within the NHS. Psycho-social provision has improved markedly, if unevenly. There has also been some interesting research into psycho-social care of children with cancer and their families. Notice must also be taken of the revolution in information available to people today, especially to patients themselves and their families.

In this Introduction I will look at developments in policy and practice in paediatric oncology, including some psychotherapy research and literature in the field. This will be balanced with interviews with experienced professionals and clinicians working on the ground, giving voice to their 'tacit knowledge'.

The people I have interviewed are all from University College London Hospital (UCLH) or Great Ormond Street Hospital (GOSH). This is because my own work gives me ease of access to them. However, I believe that the views expressed will be broadly representative of professionals working with children and young people with life-threatening illness in other major institutions in the UK.

Changes in health services and guidelines

When she was writing *Give Sorrow Words,* Dorothy Judd was one of the few child psychotherapists working in hospitals, as compared with the numbers of psychotherapists working in adult services. In September 2004, in its review of the National Service Framework (NSF) for children, the *British Medical Journal* observed, 'Children have been invisible in the NHS.'

That children did emerge from the shadows at that time was to a considerable extent the result of the Kennedy Report of 2001 into children's heart surgery at the Bristol Royal Infirmary, and of the Laming Report into the Victoria Climbie case. The Laming Report and the government initiative of 2003, *Every Child Matters,* emphasised the importance of joined-up care, of communication between the NHS and educational and social services. The NSF likewise focused on a broad, holistic and child-centred approach to children's health. In particular it recognised that children and adolescents have different needs from adults, and that services need to be designed specifically for them.

The Children's NSF for hospital services in 2004 emphasised that 'attention to the mental health of the child, young person and their family should be an integral part of any children's service and not an afterthought.' This document states that child psychotherapists need to be part of any Child and Adolescent Mental Health Services (CAMHS) team, to address the emotional well-being of their patients.

The National Institute for Health and Clinical Excellence (NICE) *Improving Outcomes Guidelines* (IOG) *for children and young people with cancer* of 2005 also specified a structured psychosocial assessment through the care pathway, to include ensuring that the family receives the information and practical support they need. This covered employment and education, as well as coping skills for different members of the family, especially siblings, and encouraged support groups for both patients and families. This document recognised that 'psychological services have an important role to play at all stages of the patient pathway, including after completion of treatment and into adult life,' (Section 2, p. 73,) and directed that services should be 'age-appropriate'.

The IOG 2005 manual recognised that parents/carers and professionals had identified a shortage of psychological services; the NICE needs-assessment of the same date observed that psychology services and counselling services for both patients and staff were identified by Primary Treatment Centres as having significant gaps in their provision. This substantial shortage is noted also by a survey of psychosocial support provided by UK paediatric oncology centres (Mitchell *et al.*, 2005) which declares: 'The poorest staff provision was among psychologists, where patient to staff ratios ranged from 132:1 to 1100:1.' Of 22 centres, 9 did not employ a psychologist at all. (It is probably reasonable to assume that by 'psychologists' the authors are referring to mental health professionals in general.)

Although psychological support for children and their families remains patchy, these major initiatives of the early years of this century signalled a shift in the culture of the NHS towards a more child-aware service. Their momentum has been maintained by the National Cancer Peer Review Programme, which takes an annual critical look at cancer treatment provision across the UK, and which in 2008 focussed on cancer in children and young people.

Cancer reform documents

After accidental injury in children, and circulatory disease in adults under 75, cancer is the leading cause of death in the UK (ONS 2009). A survey by the charity Cancer Research UK found that more than a quarter of people said that cancer was what they feared most, over Alzheimer's, heart attacks and terrorism. Over three-quarters of the sample said that it should be a national health priority.

The first substantial strategy document to improve cancer care, the Calman Hine Cancer Report (CHCR) of 1995, laid out the main areas of concern that would dominate policy for the following 20 years. It called for a 'patient centred' approach, as initiated by the Welsh Office, with effective local care, preventative measures and early screening, and consistency of care for everyone. It emphasised the importance of communication and joined up care, data collection, measuring 'quality of life', and addressing the psychosocial needs of patients at every stage. Perhaps the most significant recommendation of this paper was for patient care to be managed by the multi-disciplinary team (MDT). In their introduction, Calman and Hine specified the need for 'humanity' in the delivery of care.

The NHS Cancer Plan of 2000 noted that whilst certain areas of treatment, including that of children's cancer, were world class, survival rates for adult cancers were generally poor by comparison with the rest of Europe, partly owing to late diagnosis and treatment. Also the quality of treatment throughout the UK was 'patchy', amounting to a 'postcode lottery'. Out of this document emerged a programme of education and raising awareness, in particular to help prevent cancer by supporting changes in lifestyle, and increased screening. A start was made in improving local cancer services, in building cancer networks through a lead cancer clinician in every Primary Care Trust (PCT), and in providing palliative care training to district nurses. Funds were allocated for more specialised trained staff and for research, including the establishment of a National Cancer Research Network, and in particular research into cancer and genetics.

A second strategy document followed in 2007, the Cancer Reform Strategy. In its wake the National Cancer Intelligence Network (NCIN) was launched in 2008 to gather, collate and analyse information on cancer treatment in the UK, including measuring cancer awareness, speed of diagnosis and equality of treatment with regard to sex, ethnicity, region and deprivation. Following this policy document, there commenced, in 2008, amongst other preventative measures, the vaccination of teenagers at 12–13 to prevent cervical cancer.

In 2011, there appeared *Improving Outcomes: a Strategy for Cancer* (IOSC). It noted that most patients were seen by a specialist within two weeks of referral, compared with 4 weeks in 2000, but it acknowledged that if the UK were to meet average European survival rates, 5000 cancer deaths per year would be avoided.

However, a single national cancer registration system, the English National Cancer Online Registration Environment (ENCORE) is in process of development by the NCIN and is due to become operational in 2013. The equivalent of ENCORE in Wales is called SAIL (Secure Anonymised Information Linkage) which is linked to environmental data, showing any possible links between cancer incidence and pollution. SAIL is also linked to education and housing databases to provide information on children with cancer.

This database will provide a window on differences in care throughout the UK. It will enable the individual patient to chart their own treatment and test results, and see, for example, which hospital is best for their type of cancer. It will also enable researchers, both in the UK and internationally, to develop models of best practice and to identify the most effective treatments. And it will allow clinicians to track the individual patient's pathway through the shared care system, helping them to provide a holding function and to co-ordinate care more effectively (Querido, 2012).

Shared care provision

I asked Dr Sara Stoneham, clinical lead for paediatric oncology at UCLH, and consultant oncologist specialising in tumours of the central nervous system, if she thought much had changed in the field of paediatric oncology since 1995. She offered a nicely gnomic summary of the situation: 'The house is the same, but the way we live in it is different.'

The Cancer Reform Strategy of 2007 called for care to be delivered locally whenever possible, to make it more convenient for patients. Yet, as services have become more specialised, consolidated and centralised, there are fewer centres and more shared care provision. The aim of this has been greater consistency. Care is shared between principal treatment centres, which provide expert management of the patient's particular cancer, including a multi-disciplinary team (MDT), and local hospitals, known as 'shared care centres', and community services, including home visits by nurses (IOG 2005).

The National Cancer Plan of 2000 acknowledged that co-ordination of care at that time was 'poor'. As a result of the 2005 IOG guidelines and the NSF, there are now clear service specifications and more specialist nurses. So professionals all know what the patient should expect to experience as part of their care. This includes the psychological and spiritual aspects.

The administration for cancer has become much more robust, and also much more demanding as a result of these new requirements. Dr Maria Michaelinogli, consultant specialist for paediatric sarcoma (UCLH), elaborates:

'There are clear pathways to adhere to; data has to be collected, consensus for care to be secured. Things have to be more clearly spelt out, more defined. One result is that the teams are larger, and there is a broader skills mix involved in the care. Of course, this means that there is a larger number of people to be trained and supported in an emotionally demanding area.'

But as Oncology Professor (UCLH), Jeremy Whelan, says wryly:

'Nowadays there is much less informal care; and much more formal assessment of needs. Whether people actually get their needs met is a different matter.'

Dr Yen Ching-Chang, (known as Dr Chang), consultant oncologist (GOSH and UCLH), provides just one example of this kind of unintended consequence:

'Since the *IOG for children and young people with cancer* of 2005, you have to have two consultants practising Radiotherapy together in order to have a cross-over of views with the obvious benefits that come with a second opinion. However, this guideline can make it very hard for a smaller centre, as it means you have to be able to justify twice the expense.'

Dr Mark Gaze, consultant oncologist (GOSH and UCLH), also flags up the need to be alert to the problems that arise with centralised systems:

'When talking about shared care, there is also the potential for shared neglect. It is much more difficult to keep patients' records complete.'

I remarked on the difficulty of transition from one care system to another and keeping communication going through this transition. It seemed to me that this was paralleled by a domestic version of the same phenomenon, as the communication between members of a patient's family is not always reliable.

Chris Henry, Clinical Nurse Specialist (CNS) from the Royal National Orthopaedic Hospital in Stanmore, Middlesex, (who was interviewed by Dorothy Judd in 1995 for this book) develops this theme of communication:

'When the parents are separated – and this is much more common nowadays compared with the 1980s and '90s – the dissemination of information is often fragmented. With children of separated parents, unless one parent tells the other what is going on, the other parent will be looking after the child at some disadvantage. Even more confusing is when the separated parents have different opinions about the care that should be given their child. This in turn fragments the support given. Each parent needs information, which they don't usually get from each other.'

The area of transitions – especially from one hospital to another – is seen as needing work in every area of hospital treatment, but especially in the treatment of children. A new hospital always brings uncertainty and anxiety. However, Chris Henry puts her finger on the potential bottleneck:

'There are still delays in GPs referring to specialist services. Perhaps there is less listening from GPs, and a reluctance to get x-rays done. This is the biggest downfall: the delay in starting treatment. The NHS has excellent treatment for cancer, and GPs anywhere in the country can refer directly to specialist services. When this referral is received the patient has to be seen in two weeks.' A BBC health news item on 24 February 2012 supported this observation. It quoted figures from the *Lancet*, which revealed that people over 65 were twice as likely to be sent to a specialist after three hospital visits as was a 16–24 year old. Another telling statistic revealed that in a survey of 360 teenagers and young people diagnosed with cancer 47% had visited their GP four or more times with their symptoms before being referred to a specialist (CRS 2007).

Dr Gaze sees this problem as one of educating people about cancer in childhood, to see that it is different from cancer in adults:

'A diagnosis of cancer is always shocking and frightening, and delays in diagnosis often arise from prioritising reassurance. Even a specialist will constantly look for more benign causes. The word 'cancer' comes with a lot of uncertainty, and it is still a social stigma: cancer equals death in people's minds. But with childhood cancer there is generally a much better prognosis.'

It should be noted, however, that on average a GP will see 8 or 9 cases of adult cancer a year (CP 2000), but only one young cancer patient in 20 years. Together with the lack of a clear set of symptoms, 'this poses a significant diagnostic challenge' (NCIN 2010).

One area where advances in treatment have the potential to change outcomes radically is in Radiotherapy, though the provision of the most advanced therapy is still very localised. Dr Chang explains where this progress is taking us:

'Radiotherapy is always about providing a cure with minimal damage to healthy tissue from the radiation, so as to reduce late effects. 3D conformal radiotherapy, specifically intensity modulated radiotherapy, provides much more accurate dosages of radiotherapy and is now widely available. On the other hand, for an even more precise form of treatment, 'Proton beam therapy', we are still sending children abroad. However, from 2017 the UK is expected to have two Proton centres in operation.

Recent years have seen many other developments in treatment. A greater proportion of patients per capita in the UK are involved in clinical trials than anywhere else in the world, and an increasing number of trials take place every year (CRS 2007). In the last few years, research has gone into genetic variations linked to specific cancers which may be used in the future for much more effective screening and treatment (Cancer Research UK).

Owing to the centralisation of children's cancer services and close links with the Children's Cancer and Leukaemia Group, most children have the opportunity to participate in clinical trials. This is not, however, the case for teenagers and young adults; one reason for this may be that they will often be treated by adult services at generally non-specialist cancer centres (NCIN 2010; CRS 2007). Because children's cancer is so very rare, collaboration nationally and internationally is essential in order to gather information of statistical significance from which meaningful outcomes for patients may be derived.

Inequalities in cancer care

The most problematic of these inequalities is that of relative deprivation. Cancer mortality is 15% higher amongst the non-professional population than the national average (CRS 2007). This is linked to lifestyle, smoking and poor diet. It is also often a matter of late diagnosis, due to lack of awareness of the symptoms of cancer. The same is likely to apply to the children of more deprived parents. There is also less compliance in attending screening (CRS 2007). So raising awareness and screening have inevitably widened inequalities in treatment. Indeed, it was evident from the CRS document of 2007 that the attempt, initiated in 2004, to narrow the life-expectancy gap between the 'Spearhead' PCTs and PCTs in more affluent areas was having very limited impact. To address these inequalities, the National Cancer Equality Initiative was set up in 2008.

It has long been acknowledged that many people are dying of cancer because certain social or ethnic groups are not being reached by our health services. One of the main categories is the male sex. Figures for cancer in men show an excess incidence of 16%, and excess mortality of 38% (NCIN 2010).

The picture for black and minority ethnic (BME) people is inevitably more complex, but many participants at the first conference of the National BME Cancer Voice in 2012 said that BME Cancer Voice was 'much needed and long overdue'. Many said that it was the first time they had felt the NHS was listening to their experience (IOSC/SAR 2012).

Another significant area of inequality is in the treatment of teenagers and young adults. Best practice suggests that teenagers and young adults should be treated separately from children on the one hand and adults on the other. Teenage units were established in the early 1990s, though the age range was never defined – some sent children over 16 to adult wards, whereas others kept them up to 18. 'Young adults' only emerged as a separate category in 2005.

However there are still some hospitals, for example the Royal Marsden, where children up to 16 are treated in a specialist ward, but where from 16 they go to an adult ward. In 2007 it was estimated that 70% of teenagers and young adults were not treated in a setting appropriate for their age (CRS 2007). Moreover, there is no national collection of information on patient experience for children and young adults as there is for adults (NCIN 2010). It is nowadays generally acknowledged that quality of care is best shaped and measured by patient experience, and this should apply to children, teenagers and young adults.

The built environment for cancer care

As an ever more sophisticated appreciation of the psychological aspects of a patient's well-being has developed in the NHS, more thinking in recent years has gone into making the patient's physical environment support their psychological well-being. The new Macmillan and UCLH cancer centre for adults and teenagers, for example, which has been developed out of a government initiative to deliver outpatient and ambulatory care to keep people out of hospital as far as possible, does not look at all like a hospital.

There are 21 children's cancer units in the UK – that is for children under 13 (sometimes up to 16) – as well as 25 teenage and young adult units, with a further 10 teenage units in development. It is hoped that this will help to close the gap in the care of teenagers and young adults. (The 1995 edition of this book counted just 20 teenage units. Younger children were usually cared for in a non-specialist cancer unit.) As well as offering the patient comfort, there is now a consensus that building designs should be intended to provide them with some sense of control over their environment and the capacity to express their individuality (Teenage Cancer Trust, 2010).

The voluntary sector and cancer charities

Cancer care is very dependent on charities. As well as collating and disseminating information appropriately, and raising awareness, cancer charities also fund posts and research, and even cancer centres, including the provision of highly specialised instruments. For example, CNS posts in teenage cancer units are usually funded by the Teenage Cancer Trust. CLIC Sargent (Cancer and Leukemia in Children) fund social workers, who provide an invaluable source of emotional and material welfare, including financial support. They also fund free accommodation for parents and immediate family ('Home from Home'). Amongst a very broad range of activities, Macmillan provide their own trained nursing staff, and they fund posts where a gap is brought to their notice. Noah's Ark provides play therapy for patients and siblings, as well as support for parents during and after treatment. There are also a number of smaller charities, some in the name of a child who has died of cancer, which provide parents with something lasting and good to remember their child by, and which they know will contribute to the welfare of other patients and their families in the future.

Dr Gaze registers his huge appreciation of this work, but continues: 'I feel that charities could achieve a lot more if they co-operated with other charities with the same interests. Hospital-based charities are particularly resistant to coming together.'

Just as many different strands of funding are needed to address the multitude of implications and consequences, both medical and psychosocial, arising from a cancer diagnosis, so the need for holistic care is reflected in the multi-disciplinary team.

Multi-disciplinary teams

What is surprising about multi-disciplinary teams (MDTs) in the NHS is how recent they are. In 1984, the Department of Health ('Planning for the Future') recommended the establishment of MDTs specifically for the mentally ill, as 'different approaches to treatment, and the participation of people from a number of professional disciplines are required to cater adequately for the needs of the mentally ill.'

Before the early 1990s only a relatively few cancer patients had their care managed by an MDT. Most cancer patients continued to be treated and cared for by various professionals working in isolation; diagnosis would not necessarily be made by a specialist in the particular cancer diagnosed; there would be no collating of information, so there was no clear audit; there was little communication between GPs, specialists and specialist hospital facilities; and communication with the patient would be generally inadequate. In 1995 Calman and Hine recommended the MDT model of care in their report for commissioning cancer services. There are now 1500 MDTs in England alone (NCAT 2010).

The purpose of an MDT is to deliver 'person-centred' treatment and care, that 'identifies and responds to the needs of the individual' and is 'delivered in a co-ordinated way' (MHC 2006). There is little doubt that the MDT has revolutionised cancer care in the UK, not only improving decision making and communication, but also bringing an holistic perspective to treatment, so that it is the patient as a person who is treated, rather than just a disease in a patient.

An MDT will typically consist of 20–30 people, including medical doctors and nurses, CNSs, social workers, occupational therapists, physiotherapists, dieticians, play specialists (aka activity co-ordinators on adolescent wards), teachers, psychologists, psychotherapists, complementary therapists, radiotherapy specialists, and pain and palliative care staff. This list represents my own experience at UCLH, where dieticians, complementary therapists and psychologists are all relatively recent arrivals. Not all cancer centres are able to assemble all these elements, and IOG 2005 and 2008 have called for more consistency in this respect.

CNS Chris Henry is an enthusiastic advocate for an effective interlocking of skills:

'There is less of a culture of medicalisation. For example, there are more play specialists, and their role has changed to enable them to be much more involved in preparing children and young people for procedures. Where you have for example a case of parents cancelling surgery or resisting treatment it is very important that everyone is talking the same language to support treatment. The psychological input here is fundamental.'

Value for money: measuring the effectiveness of psychological services

In recent years there has been a growing pressure on government funded psychological services to provide evidence of the effectiveness of psychotherapy. In terms of funding allocation in the field of psychoanalytic psychotherapy, this pressure favours 'outcome research' over 'process research'. Outcome research finds out 'what works for whom' (Fonagy *et al.*, 2002, in Kennedy and Midgley, 2007). Process research explores 'why' and 'how' change takes place as the consequence of a therapeutic intervention and is the way that psychoanalytic psychotherapy has traditionally developed as a discipline since the time of Freud.

Following the principle of 'payment by results', introduced by the Department of Health in 2002, healthcare commissioners are less interested in the complexities of why and how; they want to know where their funding will produce the best clearly measurable results.

This financially pragmatic emphasis would appear to put the discipline of psychology in a more favourable position compared with psychoanalytic psychotherapy. However, a review of methodological issues of 2003 recommends that more clinical-based research is 'probably the best short-term and long-term investment for improving clinical practice and patient care' (Kazdin and Nock, 2003, in Kennedy and Midgley, 2007). The process of identifying the 'active ingredients' of therapeutic interventions is where the traditional strengths of psychoanalytic psychotherapy lie (Kennedy and Midgley, 2007). Moreover, whereas in the early 1990s it could be said that rigorous methods of assessment of psychotherapy with children was quite undeveloped in contrast to work with adults (Marans et al., 1991, in Kennedy and Midgley, 2007), a large body of empirical research that relates the process of child psychotherapy to outcomes has emerged in recent years (Karver et al., 2005, in Kennedy and Midgley, 2007). In particular the use of video recordings of sessions has enabled more precisely calibrated measurement of effectiveness (Kennedy and Midgley, 2007).

This pressure to make explicit, measurable and quantifiable what is implicit, unquantifiable and tacit, is generally to be welcomed. Much of the work by psychotherapists is not logged or accounted for, and work that is not down in black and white can disappear. The nuances of psychotherapeutic work, which are what make the difference, are very difficult to quantify, but it is for this very reason that they need to be recorded.

NICE guidelines recommend a 'stepped care' approach, designed to offer the least resource-intensive treatment initially. So child and adolescent psycho-analytic intervention tends to be offered to patients who have already failed to respond to briefer forms of treatment, or who present with severe levels of psychological disturbance, where results therefore will be harder won than with other psychological treatment and may take longer to achieve. However, studies have shown the effectiveness of both short and long term psychoanalytic treatment for children, and that these benefits were sustained. There is some evidence to suggest that such treatment is most effective with younger children, and that this should include parent or family work (Kennedy and Midgley, 2007).

A randomised control trial by Trowell et al. (2007) to examine the efficacy of individual psychodynamic and family therapy with children and young people with moderate or severe depression found that 74.3% and 75.7% were no longer clinically depressed following therapy. At a 6 months follow up, 100% who had received individual therapy and 81% of those who had received family therapy remained clear of clinical depression.

Psychological support for patients and families

A hospital is a complex and confusing system, where one becomes more aware of life and death and one's vulnerabilities, and where there is a loss of control and a dependency on professionals and parents. Ramsden (1999) makes the important point that 'whether the illness is primarily physical or psychological in aetiology and in appearance, its effect is most likely to be both'.

A broad range of research shows consistently that psychotherapy reduced medical service costs significantly – by 18–31% (Carlson and Bultz, 2003). However, as mentioned above, psychological support is seriously under-resourced in paediatric and young people oncology (Mitchell *et al.*, 2005).

What 'psychological support' should consist of, and who should be providing it, can at times be unclear. It should be said that while mental health professionals themselves jealously guard the differences between the disciplines of psychotherapy, psychology and psychiatry, these distinctions do not register with the wider public. My experience is that most staff – even when they have been working closely with psychological support for some time – do not really know the difference between psychotherapy and psychology. When psychological support is needed for a patient or their family, they just want someone there to address the need. The Cancer Reform Strategy of 2007 delineates four key levels of psychological support, without specifying the professionals who should deliver them (though the NCAT 2008 places psychotherapists with counsellors and mental health nurses at Level 3, and psychiatrists and psychologists at level 4).

It is interesting that psychology is the generic term used most of the time for all three mental health disciplines in the NICE guidelines. One possible reason for this is that psychology is a more numerously represented discipline than the others.

There are many crossovers between them, but the differences are significant. Broadly speaking, psychiatrists are medically qualified doctors who can therefore prescribe medication as well as recommend other forms of treatment. Psychology is concerned with the normal functioning of the mind, and with the thoughts and feelings that underlie and motivate behaviour.

My own profession, psychoanalytic psychotherapy, looks at the meaning underlying these motivations; it works with conscious and unconscious processes within relationships, both intra-psychic and interpersonal. At UCLH we are fortunate to be able to have all three disciplines well-represented, so different needs can be met most effectively.

According to Barbara Segal, (Consultant Child and Adolescent Psychotherapist, UCLH, 1997–2010), 'There has been an acceptance over many years on this teenage cancer unit (at UCLH) of the effectiveness of psychotherapy in supporting teenage patients with cancer and their families.' On the other hand, the psychologists have other very effective models of working; for example, using CBT to help patients with nausea, and short term strategies for panic attacks. At UCLH they have also developed a way of working with teenagers both individually and in a group, through the 'Beads Project', which gives the teenage patients a framework within which to put their experience in perspective using different beads to represent experiences of past, present and future. This works very well for some patients. Others seem to respond better to the psychotherapeutic approach, where there isn't a pre-conceived idea of what should be talked about at any particular time but where containment and meaning is found in the here and now between patient and therapist. This meeting may be a one-off session or it may take place over a long period, including after discharge. The effectiveness of this approach is given clinical evidence, in depth and detail, in Chapter 6 and 7 of this book.

A substantial part of the work of a child psychotherapist is with parents. 'Psychotherapy has a huge part to play in supporting parents. If the parents have a place to explore their worries and projections, they then become more emotionally available to the child rather than the child feeling they have to look after the parent, which is very common' (Segal, 2012). It can be difficult for parents to be in touch with their child's anxiety about them and how they will manage after his or her death (Langton-Gilks, 2013). It is well-established that children know more than they let on, and 'are very skilled at hearing unspoken feelings' (Brook, 2010).

Recent research (Kazak *et al.*, 2003) has shown a near universal if variable degree of distress associated with a diagnosis of cancer and its treatment both in the patient and in the family, which in some people reduces over the first 12 months. However, there is evidence that the level of parental anxiety at diagnosis is predictive of on-going distress, even after treatment ends. This has important implications in terms of targeting resources more effectively. Kazak *et al.*, conclude their survey of the research: 'Maximising care early in a family's treatment course could minimise the toll of psychosocial factors on the patient, family and healthcare team.' In particular, for siblings of a patient diagnosed with cancer, the prognosis is unfavourable; the siblings need close support until well after the death of the patient (Houtzager *et al.*, 2004).

While much has been written on the psycho-social impact and psychological implications of childhood cancer long before this book came out, psychoanalytic psychotherapy with children with cancer began to be studied only in the wake of this book.

In the last twenty years, there have been a number of clinical experimental research interventions carried out by psycho-analytic child psychotherapists (Kennedy, 2004). Psychoanalytical psychotherapy in a hospital setting is a highly specialised adaptation of psychoanalytical principles and practice. Segal (2012) suggests that what is required in this context is what Lanyado (1996) calls 'an attentiveness to the setting of the treatment' and that this 'involves a tailor-made active adaptation of the therapist's mind to the needs of the individual patient ... rather than the patient having to adapt to the classical psychoanalytic model.' Chapter 6 of this book describes some of the parameters of this context.

Emanuel *et al.* (1990) hesitate 'even to use the word psychotherapy when trying to describe the work we do ... ' In an account of their 'applied psychotherapy' on the ward, they explore the different issues arising out of their work with 20 children in a paediatric oncology ward, some of which echo the emotional reactions described in Chapter 5 of this book, though they are distinguished as general themes rather than stages: control (this includes painful picking at the skin, which is a feature of the central case in this book), denial, isolation (corresponding to Judd's stage of regression), dependency issues, contamination, abnormality, uncertainty, and cultural issues.

In the same paper, Emanuel *et al.*, describe the main purpose of psychotherapy in this context as being to 'contain the conscious and unconscious communications of the children', and 'naming the feelings and emotions which the child is communicating to us'. Adamo (2012) observes that the containment function provided by the relationship is a significantly more important aspect of the work here than the interpretative function which can be counter-indicated. Trauma can impair children's capacity to symbolise and thus make use of interpretation, as they 'tend to be overwhelmed by primitive anxieties concerning physical and psychic survival' (Rhode, 2011).

Psychotherapy has to adapt to the life on the ward, where there is no 'proper' assessment of the kind psychotherapists would make in a conventional consulting room, and where the stable boundaries and regular sessions are impossible to guarantee. The fluidity and management of these boundaries on the ward, in contrast to the tightly held boundary and task in the psychotherapist's mind, is clearly illustrated in Chapter 7 of this book. Transference and counter-transference issues are muddied by the complexities of the professional relationships in the hospital setting and the potentially catastrophic anxiety of the situation (Emanuel *et al.*, 1990). In particular, much of the work is short term, what they call 'crisis intervention'. Judd (2001) likens it to 'emotional first aid'.

A case study that offers impressive clinical evidence of the efficacy of intensive psychoanalytic treatment concerned a group of young people with 'dangerously controlled' Insulin Dependent Diabetes Mellitus. The control group received psychological/psychiatric support as part of their standard medical in-patient care. But psychoanalytic psychotherapy 3 to 5 times a week, over 15 weeks, produced a significant improvement in diabetic control, and in hospital readmission rates (Moran *et al.*, 1991, in Kennedy, 2004). A separate study of three of these young people who also presented with growth retardation found substantial increases in height, height velocity and predicted adult height in all three (Fonagy and Moran, 1991).

A study that explores a particular psychoanalytic psychotherapeutic group approach, describes a weekly 'fairy tale' workshop in an Italian paediatric oncology and haematology ward (Adamo *et al.*, 2008). This was based on workshops run for young psychotic and autistic patients in Bordeaux by psychoanalyst Pierre Lafforgue. Following Judd's observation that the trauma of being diagnosed and treated for cancer can affect a child's developing capacity to think, the project created, through the telling of fairy tales, and through the children's drawings, 'a space for expressing not only anxieties and fears, but also the psychic resources, skills and experimentation used by children, which even parents sometimes fear they must give up at the onset of the illness' (Adamo *et al.*, 2008).

This project had a positive outcome not only for the children, but also for the parents, and the ward staff. The children were able to approach their feelings of imminent catastrophe for themselves 'through a character who makes it possible to be *someone else in a different situation*.' In this, the fairy tale acts as a 'displacement and identification mechanism'. The continuity of the group – over a year – fostered a sense of solidarity amongst the participants, supporting their socialisation, free from medical interventions. The workshop also improved morale amongst ward staff, and was experienced as nourishing to both parents and nurses. The happy ending – 'and they lived happily ever after' – offers hope, but in that it is always hard won, it is a hope that does not deny reality.

Emanuel *et al.* carefully lay out this emotional balance that must be held by the psychotherapist in the context of childhood cancer: 'Nevertheless, we are working in a situation where death is always a real possibility. The therapist maintains a position of holding this possibility in mind, while working from the perspective of staying on the side of life' (Emanuel *et al.*, 1990). Segal (2012) reminds us that this perspective needs to be held as an epistemological one: 'We do try to foster hope and positivity, but there is no place for false reassurance. One might say our main task is to stay with the 'not knowing'.

The place of psychotherapy in the MDT

The child psychotherapist is part of a multidisciplinary team, liaising with the whole of the paediatric department, outpatients' clinics and wards, and developing a close relationship with doctors and nurses as well as social workers, teachers and other members of staff. All the professionals involved will try to 'hold a view of the bio-social-psychological function of the children'. A particular reason for this close relationship is because frontline staff will be the first to notice when psychological help may be needed (Ramsden, 1999).

Before 1995 the key worker, holding all the different strands of the patient care together, would have been a named nurse. After 1995 this role was taken by the CNS. Vikky Riley (also interviewed for the second edition of this book) who became the CNS for the teenage cancer unit in 1996, describes what her job entails:

'The role is to follow the patient in their journey, to make a bridge with the medical team, to advocate for the child. It is to support patients with information and advice and to liaise with community nurses. Sometimes I am seen as a translator, between the medical/technical staff and the non-medical staff, and between the medical team and patients and families.'

The CNS can also liaise with schools. Often teachers can feel frightened and inadequate about looking after pupils who are undergoing treatment, while the patient may be worried about their appearance and how they will be perceived by the other children.

This communicative responsibility clearly abuts and to some extent overlaps the psychological input. The recent change (IOG 2005, CRS 2007, NCAT 2008) in the conception and growth of the CNS's responsibilities requires some negotiation and respect on both sides, as well as training. A CNS should have the training to provide emotional containment and a basic level of psychological support (levels 1 and 2, CRS 2007, NCAT 2008).

However, Chris Henry firmly asserts an important boundary between them:

'I would say there aren't enough psychotherapists allocated – perhaps because of lack of resources – and this is problematic. It is important that the issues with the family should be addressed and supported separately from the support of the CNS. If the CNS took on psychotherapeutic tasks it would change the nature of the nursing relationship and the professional boundaries that one is working with. Nurses and psychotherapists are interdependent practitioners.'

Vikky Riley agrees with this assessment of the psychotherapeutic role, which includes introducing a psychotherapeutic awareness to the work of nurses on the wards, especially to that of the CNS:

'The teenage cancer unit at UCLH was built on the basis of psychotherapy, and to begin with psychotherapy was the main discipline for psychological support for patient, family and staff. The role of psychotherapy was a significant part of the life of the ward, and was an integral part of the MDT meeting.

'Dorothy's influence brought the question of 'What does this mean?' to the ward. 'What is going on?' And 'Whose grief is this?' If you didn't have an opportunity to discuss, you carried all these 'dead people' inside. It was very important to have Dorothy and Barbara [Segal] there. It can be a traumatic and volatile environment, and nurses and CNSs have to hold some of that without being the expert. I've learned to recognise that when there are squabbles amongst nurses for example, there is distress in the ward.'

I suggested, 'So this becomes a thermometer for stress, when things are acted out like this.'

'Yes. Sometimes a cancer ward can become a battleground. One needs armour, as it goes to brutal places. And the need for the psychological care team is invaluable there. Working as a team means not working in competition.'

Riley also appreciates the profound challenge of the psychotherapeutic role in this context, which is to handle what I would suggest might be thought of as an underlying projection arising from working with problems that cannot always be fixed – and such problems are inherent in oncology. She continued, 'A psychotherapeutic approach brings an important question: 'What is at the heart of the distress? How can a process of transformation happen?'

Patrice Guex (1994) in his standard introduction to psycho-oncology, describes this projection of the patient's internal problems or conflicts onto the teams as being like a 'cinematic projection onto a huge screen', resulting in 'interprofessional conflicts, hierarchical confusion, and sometimes contradictory attitudes in the approach to the patient'; for example, being over-familiar or over-distant.

Segal (2012) describes the containing function of the psychotherapist: 'Someone who isn't responsible for the medical care is there to address the psychological well-being of the patient, and to support their resilience, so the patient and families can cope better with the situation. *However, the psychotherapist can't take the pain away.*' The task is to support an authentic experience.

'The psychotherapist can be viewed as the one who articulates "dreaded feelings" or "bad thoughts"' (Segal, 2012). The task is 'often to contain and even experience feelings the child and family cannot bear to have ... having transferred or projected these feelings into us the child (or parent) may want to avoid or even blank us' (Segal, 2012). A similar situation is described by Lanceley (2014). Segal echoes Judd when she says of the death or dying of a patient: 'At these times on the ward there is an additional pressure on the psychotherapists and CNSs when ward staff cannot bear the sadness and helplessness.'

Segal offers an analysis of how the role of the psychotherapist has changed during her time at UCLH: 'Whilst there have been cuts in the NHS budget, the number of patients has increased. This is partly because of centralisation of services and changes in guidelines. But we also have more kinds of patient including those with tumours of the central nervous system, and haematology. The increase in patient numbers has impacted on the nature of the service provided, making it less intimate. In the past a member of the psychological team introduced him or herself to every patient on admission, so that there was no stigma attached, but simply an acknowledgement of the traumatic nature of their situation. Now the psychological support will see patients only by referral. This change has brought its own problems, as you have to rely on untrained staff to recognise the patient's needs for psychological support. In this way, educating the staff has become part of the job.'

She underlines the testimony of the CNSs, that this holding function does not stop with the patient: 'Psychotherapy offers a support mechanism over the patient's treatment trajectory which can be a lifeline for the family, but it is also a holding function for the MDT right through the team.'

Palliative care

Since 1995 evidence-based studies of psychological interventions related to end of life and bereavement have been 'extremely limited' (Kazak and Noll, 2004) and this remains an area that is very sparsely researched (Brook, 2010).

However, nowadays there is better access to palliative care, including symptom control, and this has been utilised earlier rather than later – though it may be difficult to secure the consent of the family if they haven't accepted that their child's treatment should be palliative. A major change in this respect has been the extraction of teenagers from paediatrics in the 1990s.

As Professor Whelan explains, 'This move was an acknowledgement that concepts and attitudes to death change markedly during those years. Working with a dying teenager is very different from working with a dying child. With younger children the parent and the child represent a single point of contact; the parents make the decisions. With the teenager there is a triangulation between young person, clinician and parent; the child and the parents are disassembled.'

Children and young people dying in hospital now have a distinctive End of Life (EOL) care scheme that aims to meet their particular needs and wishes, which are necessarily going to differ significantly from the needs of mature adults facing death. George and Hutton (2003) emphasise the importance of teenagers and young adults who are undergoing palliative care to have the opportunity to partake in normal activities, ranging from enjoyable social activities to more challenging ones like taking exams.

More people are now treated out of hospital in their last months. Between 2000 and 2009 39% of children and 32% of teenagers and young adults died at home, while 11% and 13% respectively died in a hospice (NCIN 2012). This is generally welcomed, though in the community they may lose out in their access to non-medical services, like physiotherapy or psychological support. According to Chris Henry, communication with community nurses has improved, so transitions to the community at the end of life is better. However, this is not universal.

Chapter 10 of this book explores the dilemma of when curative treatment should be replaced by palliative care. Professor Whelan points out that there is still work to be done in assessing this: 'Sometimes there are decreasing benefits of treatment, and then you have to consider what the patient really wants and needs. The teenager has more of a say. A five year old will have less say, and there is a danger that the younger patient gets more of this treatment than is 'good' for them.'

As symptoms of anxiety and sadness are natural responses to life-threatening illnesses and end of life, pathological anxiety and clinical depression are frequently undiagnosed and thus untreated (Theunissen et al., 1998, in Brook, 2010). Training for front-line professionals, in recognising and differentiating such symptoms so that appropriate referrals can be made and treatment given, would make a significant difference to the quality of life at that stage.

According to clinicians, the main barrier to children getting the best possible EOL care is the unrealistic expectation on the part of parents of a cure (Brook, 2010). Henry outlines the modern manifestation of the problem: 'There are a lot of alleged 'cures' for cancer on the internet, which can interfere with getting acceptance with end-of-life issues. For patients who reach that stage, parents are clutching at every straw to give them hope, but this can be disruptive and damaging, as seeking alternative treatment can make the end of life much more unpleasant, where it excludes coming to terms with this process.'

A review of the research on patient-reported outcomes of EOL care in paediatric oncology (Hinds *et al.*, 2007) noted the difficulties associated with this research: the fear of offending the already emotionally burdened family, and damaging the doctor-patient relationship; the fact that soliciting this information from the patient will confirm the patient's EOL status; and the possibility that the patient may not be capable of giving the information, either because they are insufficiently developed cognitively, or because they are sedated. However, the reviewers do not accept that not having 'reliable and valid instruments sensitive to EOL in paediatric oncology' represents an acceptable explanation for not gathering this information. Appropriate instruments need to be researched and developed (Hinds *et al.*, 2007).

Surviving and quality of life

According to figures from the USA, in the 1960s 4% of children with cancer survived more than five years (Childhood Cancer Survivorship Act Bill, 2011). Within fifty years, childhood cancer has gone from being a fatal diagnosis, to being a generally curable group of diseases, offering survival rates of 78% (Cancer Research UK). So attention has gradually turned from the issue of survival to the issues of 'late effects' and 'quality of life'. Some late effects are themselves life-threatening, including second malignancy; others cause long-term physical impairment, from obesity to cardiac and renal dysfunction; and there are significant psycho-social late effects, including learning and emotional difficulties, and even suicide.

Two thirds of childhood cancer survivors experience at least one lasting medical and/or psychological effect (Childhood Cancer Survivorship Act Bill, 2011). It has been estimated that one in 250 of the adult population is today a long-term survivor of childhood cancer (Wallace and Green, 2004).

Chapter 11 of this book explores the huge implications of these statistics, especially the psycho-social and neuro-rehabilitation needs of these numerous survivors.

But Dr Gaze feels that the message still has not got through: 'Cancer is always associated with pain and horrible treatment. It also means time away from school and from family, and serious financial burdens on the parents. But with childhood cancer, the outcome is generally better, and most childhood cancer treatment is curative. We have to educate parents in this.'

Despite many treatments being curative, in certain cancers – for example in osteosarcoma – the loss of a limb may be inevitable. Interestingly, however, a surprising finding of a study of quality of life in adult cancer survivors was that amputation does not necessarily reduce quality of life (Eiser, 1997).

Chris Henry feels that attitudes towards amputation have greatly improved: there is much more acceptance of it, and she feels some of it is to do with the higher profile of paralympic sport: 'Prosthetic limbs have greatly improved. They are much more adaptable, and the function is much better. Western young people are much happier about using their artificial limbs than before. In the past there was great concern about hiding mechanical limbs. Nowadays, some young people tend to feel proud of their 'bionic' implants – though this is a big cultural issue: it is much more difficult for people from some ethnic minorities, where a person with a limb amputated is viewed as a second-class citizen.' It should be added that military personnel amputees have contributed to the general acceptance and even normalisation of amputation, and that the NHS should be emulating the high quality army rehabilitation programmes (Spoudeas, 2013, personal communication).

Judd (2001) speaks of our atavistic terror of mutilation and the association of mutilation with punishment in some cultures today. However, her work with an ethnic minority boy ends with him looking forward to getting a 'high-tech state of the art' limb.

Dr Gaze warns that the picture is not so good later in life: 'After radical treatment in childhood, which can leave the child disabled, there is a lifetime of responsibility to look after this person. And yet there is very little support for adults. At each 'life threshold' they need support with that transition. Parents often express their deep concern about how their children will manage as adults when they themselves have gone. Although some young people do get work and become independent, for others the sequels of treatment can leave them socially isolated, and struggling to cope with the pace of work.' Dr Spoudeas adds that there is an urgent need to raise our ambitions for cancer survivors, that they need to be empowered – as far as possible – to achieve employment, independence and parenthood. 'Very little funding goes into rehabilitation and aftercare compared with the money thrown into new cures.' (Spoudeas, 2013, personal communication.)

Langeveld *et al.* (2002) found that most survivors had moderately good physical health, and good psychological functioning, but their education suffered, and they were less likely to get married and have children. This is to say, a substantial number of survivors – 60–85% – experience significant medical and psycho-social late effects: the 'price' of cure (Talbot and Spoudeas, 2010).

Quality of life (QoL) is a new concept in health care, and it is still a problematic area of investigation. Firstly, it is a broad concept that takes in spiritual aspects, as well as the psychological, medical, and physical aspects of life.

Secondly, it reflects the perspective of the survivor, and this will change significantly as the child develops into adulthood. For children this will perhaps be about body image or feeling isolated, and the cognitive implications that come with this, whereas for an adult, to lose their independence is a major factor. So on this basis one is looking at different variables from those the patient might have identified a few years previously, and certainly from those their parents might identify. Assessing younger children is particularly difficult on these terms, for the same reason that it is particularly important to do so.

Thirdly, one has to choose between generic and disease-specific measurement, and with the latter, statistically reliable results are difficult to achieve with the relatively small numbers of patients available for assessment. However, with all these provisos, QoL measurement represents an important shift of emphasis in evaluating interventions, from focussing on simple survival to identifying what individual survivors may need to support a life worth living.

One way of measuring QoL is through the 'discrepancy' or gap at any one time between what the patient feels they ought or would like to be able to achieve or experience, and what they are actually able to do or experience (Calman, 1984, in Vance *et al.*, 2004). Vance *et al*'s study (2004) of parents' ways of coping with this discrepancy in the case of patients who had had brain tumours removed identified a number of psycho-social issues that parents needed help with, including getting extra academic support, and protection for their child from bullying, whilst observing that the parents went to ingenious lengths to minimise that discrepancy.

Another study (Eiser, 2007) concludes that childhood cancer survivors need access to a broad range of detailed information about late effects, as well as practical help. It recommends psychological assessment as part of routine health assessments of survivors, and notes that when asked, survivors themselves put a high value on psychological screening and advice. The 2011 Cancer Strategy document (IOSC 2011) specifies meeting this need as one of its aims for improving quality of life: 'Reducing the proportion of people who report unmet physical or psychological needs following cancer treatment'.

Louise Talbot of the Royal Manchester Children's Hospital and Helen Spoudeas from UCLH and GOSH, in their discussion of late effects in relation to childhood cancer of 2010, draw some clear conclusions. The impact of cancer on a child's psychological and cognitive development depends on three main factors: whether or not it is a central nervous system tumour, at what age the patient was diagnosed and treated, and the type of treatment received. In many cases a subtle or partly cognitive deficit is not picked up immediately, but may become prominent over time in terms of social and educational impairment. Difficulties can often be misunderstood as behavioural or emotional sequelae of the impact of the underlying brain injury, when in fact it is cognitive in origin and the direct result of the injury and treatment. This will not be picked up unless the child has a neuro-psychological assessment to identify specific areas of cognitive impairment. Even then it does not easily fit in with the special educational needs system. Talbot and Spoudeas recommend that long term surveillance for late effects should start soon after treatment, as potential late morbidities can then be picked up and treated with appropriate endocrine or psychological support. For example, pre-symptomatic surveillance screening for hormone replacement is important for QoL. However, they note that the medium to long-term effectiveness of targeted psychological and neuropsychological interventions on survivors still awaits randomised research studies (Talbot and Spoudeas, 2010; Smit, 2013, personal communication).

Communication skills and education for professionals and patients

Professionals in the health service are increasingly aware of, and trained in, what and how you communicate.

Chris Henry observes, 'The surgeons are much better nowadays at talking to patients and families. They are more careful about giving information, and they cope better with being challenged. All professionals dealing with children with cancer have to attend a three day advanced course in communication, with actors and role play. This has made a huge difference.'

This training began in 2000 (CP 2000) and is now named *Connected*. Since it began 15,000 senior clinicians have been trained and 84% would definitely recommend it to colleagues (IOSC/SAR 2012).

Dr Spoudeas provides a succinct outline of what is needed: 'Information-giving should be 'dialectic' and 'didactic', age-appropriate and offering the opportunity for choice. And as yet it does not always happen like this in paediatric oncology.'

Even the administrative staff now have to attend training in the *In your shoes* patient awareness programme. Dr Michaelinogli explains the importance of this: 'It is the essence of team care nowadays that more people are involved in the emotional journey that the patients and their families make. The person at the other end of the phone can have a huge impact on patients' perceptions and it can 'jaundice' the whole experience if the first contact has not been right. It is about how to create an environment where someone feels contained.'

Health organisations and professionals want to make the service as user-friendly and patient-centred as possible. There is also a clear sense that the communication needs to be age-appropriate. This is especially evident in the plethora of friendly information booklets for children, from *Fighting the Big C* (1995) to *Tom has Lymphoma* (2011) (CLIC Sargent), as well as in the increasing use of videos.

In 2004, Rhonda Alexander, play specialist, and Rachel Melville Thomas, child and adolescent psychotherapist, created a 'Child's eye view' video of the journey a patient might make in the Radiotherapy department of UCLH, providing an insight to professionals and parents about what the experience is like from a child's perspective. In 2005 the video diaries of a young woman with terminal cancer formed the basis for a Royal Television Society award-winning BBC documentary *To Courtney with Love*, directed by Mark Wilkinson. In the wake of this, Wilkinson and the staff of Leeds St James' Hospital Teenage Cancer Trust Ward set up jimmyteens.tv to support new young cancer patients in working in different media – documentaries, animation, drama, video diaries – to help them understand and express their experiences. Today, supportive and inspiring videos can be easily accessed on websites and *youtube.*

A patient experience survey of 2011–2012 revealed that the most significant increase in the number of positive scores were on information and communication (IOSC DH 2012). This suggests that these various imaginative initiatives are bearing fruit.

Social media

The impact of social media and the internet on children, professionals and families is nothing short of revolutionary. In 1989, reliable information on oncology was hardly available, except from intimidating journals and textbooks in specialist libraries. Today, many patients research on the internet. They have potential access to doctors all over the world, and patients worldwide have access to our own doctors. As a result, patients may come prepared to some extent for what they will hear. But the internet can also be a source of confusion and panic. As Dr Gaze says, 'Patients can get information from here and there, and when they add it up, two and two will often make five.'

Usually, parents – understandably – like to protect and control the amount of information given to their child. However, with the wide use of the internet amongst children as young as five, it is not uncommon for a child to Google 'I have cancer'. Children can often sense the anxiety in their parents, and they want to protect them from what they may see as further worry by finding out for themselves. For their part the parents may already be feeling helpless when they find that their child has been researching about their illness. Some may feel relieved, but others may feel an acute sense of helplessness and lack of control.

Chris Henry enlarges on the virtues and pitfalls of the internet: 'The patient or carers will be given a list of credible sites, and advised not to look at others, but they will look at the other sites anyway – more mothers than fathers – and then they say, 'Oh, I did look at the other sites, and I wish I hadn't.'

'With widespread use of the internet, expectations from patients are much higher than they used to be. The internet has given them a taste for instant results for everything – whether x-rays or CT scans or even surgery. Patients expect recovery from serious surgery to be much faster than is realistic, and this actually makes the process of recovery more disappointing and more difficult. So there are some downsides to the internet.

'On the other hand, there was a case where a young person had gone to their GP, and had been undiagnosed, but who then put his symptoms into NHS Direct, and it came back with a diagnosis. He went back to the GP with this information and it was found that the diagnosis was correct. This is the internet working at its best.

'Many young people, particularly young children, want to see the CT scans and post-operative x-rays, the cross-sections of the tumours, and to see the implants in their body, as it helps them to take in information visually. I have to gauge when to show the images and when not to, but I am trusted by the Pathologist to make the decision myself; and this has only once been a problem. Patients are much more involved in the whole process of their care nowadays.'

Parents often have to come to hospital with their child for long stays at a time, leaving their other children and family behind. Easy access to communication via mobile phones, emails, skype, etc, has been of great benefit in bridging this gap, and bringing family and friends into closer contact with the parents and the child. Often, life on the ward becomes a second home, and even a second local community or neighbourhood, with different families going through similar experiences together. With little sense of physical or even emotional privacy, this neighbourly communication can develop quite easily.

Facebook and other social networks have been widely used for parents to post news of their child's development, and to keep in contact after treatment has ended. When treatment ends, it is followed by a huge relief, even euphoria; but also a sense of loss in leaving that community. But with social networks a sense of companionship in this difficult journey can continue.

It is more difficult when bad news is broken, as this can spread fear amongst this community, which feels vulnerable anyway. If another child has suffered a relapse, or death, the disease could come back for their own child. Then the chain begins to break, as people do not feel able to keep up with difficult news. This in turn can bring conflict and guilt.

Death and the dying child

Kreicbergs *et al.* (2004) found that parents who talked about death with their dying child did not regret having done so. They back up Judd's experience as described in this book. 'Evidence suggests that accurate information about the expected course of the disease is beneficial for most children, perhaps because it allows their inner lives (i.e. the awareness of their imminent death) and the outer world (i.e. the information they receive from health care workers and parents) to become congruent, thereby preventing frustration.' This study explores in particular the parents who did not talk to their children about death, and the feelings of regret that over a third of them had, together with some depression, as a result of feeling that their child had known they were dying but had been left alone with this knowledge.

Professor Whelan is concerned that there is still work to be done on the taboo around the death, or potential death, of a child: 'Children still die in the same way they died before. And the associations with it have not changed. There is a fundamental response of protecting the child from pain, but also protecting the child or oneself from knowledge of their own death. For the family and the professional, the event has the same resonance, with its tensions and difficulties. There has not been a societal shift. It is more of a secular diverse society in this country – in London especially we feel that. But general attitudes have not changed. There is more disclosure, and communicating with children has come a long way in recent years, but it is still underdeveloped by comparison with communication skills in working with adults with cancer.'

He continued, 'In the past when a patient died, Dorothy Judd would come to our team meeting and she would name someone who had died and open up a space for talking about it. Nowadays maybe this happens less often. There is always an acknowledgement of the death of a patient, perhaps by naming them in the MDT meeting, but there is no space given to taking this in, and the information usually circulates by a Round Robin email. I think this may be another omission of good practice consequent on staff being 'too busy'.

This is partly because of increased formalisation, the number of different professionals involved, and partly because of pressure of time. But I also wonder whether this is a way of distancing ourselves from this reality.

When I talked to Dr Stoneham, I shared with her a rather tasteless joke I was told by a Paediatric Registrar in oncology: 'Why do you have to nail down a coffin? To stop the oncologists treating the body.' Dr Stoneham agreed that this quite accurately, if unfairly, reflected her own training. 'The most disempowering bit is when we run out of medical options. This is when you feel most impotent, as our training is to make it better.

'Where I was trained, in South Africa, there was more of a societal acceptance of the death and dying of children. Coming to England I found that expectations were different, and many of my colleagues had a different perspective. It was a less religious society, and it had a significantly lower mortality rate. It was felt that no child patient should be allowed to die, whereas in a more religious society 'doctors treat, but God heals'. In Africa I saw a more pragmatic approach to treatment. I became much more aware of the cost of treatment, so making the decision to stop treatment was an important part of your job in such a context. Here, though, it signals your failure. We fail if we don't make it better.'

Lynda Brook of Alder Hey Hospital, Liverpool, notes what has been found to be a significant factor militating against timely adoption of EOL palliative care as being 'physicians' own death anxiety' (Barr, 2007, in Brook, 2010). She also warns that palliative chemotherapy should not be 'an opportunity for collusion between professional and family', in a way that does not address the child's best interests (Fowler *et al.*, 2006, in Brook, 2010).

There is a necessary tension between the palliative care team and the oncologist. However, the oncologist's role is not just to resist the point of surrender as long as possible. It is, as Dr Stoneham elaborates, to deliver news of the defeat, if and when necessary. 'Medicine is the smallest part of what I do. Breaking bad news is the tough part of the job. But you know you have to do it. It's like clubbing a baby seal. The patient and family become completely defenceless, and your job is to be implacable.'

Dr Stoneham's brutally frank but poignant image puts me in mind of Freud's (1920) definition of trauma, which is a piercing of the psyche's protective shield. The significance that Dr Stoneham places on this element of her work is confirmed by Woolley *et al.* (1989), who interviewed families about their experience of being told their child has a life-threatening illness. The doctor is expected to be honest, consistent, supportive, and sympathetic, but also imperturbable.

Dr Stoneham reflects ruefully on the varying responses she gets in return: 'There is a societal expectation that no child should be allowed to die. If a child does die, someone must be responsible. And in the absence of someone to blame, you cannot complain if the parents want to shoot the messenger. It is part of the grieving process that they need to express anger at some point. On the other hand, some parents and patients are very grateful for our efforts.'

She is sensitive to the unevenness of her relationship with parents and patient: 'I try to empower the family to make the decision that is right for them, and to make sure there is a real engagement in their decisions about treatment. However, one needs to get a balance between treating the family and treating the patient – and finally the duty of care is to the patient. Always one has to have the patient's best interests in mind. When this means stopping treatment it feels like you are taking away hope.'

Dr Stoneham appreciates that her work gives her a privileged place. But she adds that one should not forget that being able to leave it is also a privilege. 'You get to go home after work.'

The impact of stress on medical professionals

A qualitative research study in Canada (Dix *et al.*, 2012) found that overall the professionals working in a paediatric oncology unit describe their job as fulfilling and meaningful. However, a number of studies have explored stress and burnout in this work (Hinds *et al.*, 1998; Barnard *et al.*, 2006). It has been suggested that the term 'vicarious traumatisation' which is applied in the mental health field to therapists who are affected by their traumatised patients, may be used to refer to a possible particular stressor for professionals working in oncology, especially nurses. The trauma affects not only patients and families, but also those with whom they discuss their experience (Sinclair and Hamil, 2007). Further research and support is advocated to address this possible risk.

All the individuals I spoke to acknowledged the impact of stress in this field, but they each had their own particular view of it. When I asked Dr Michaelinogli how she came to choose oncology and how she managed the stress she answered both questions with a laconic realism: 'There is a self-selection process – people who stay in this field tend to be emotionally robust. But there is a structure of support as well, to contain the emotional overspill. And if the team is more contained, the parents will feel more contained. It can be very difficult for junior doctors and nurses as they are not much older than the teenagers they treat, and they can get too emotionally involved, which can be damaging. So there is a psychological support group for them.

'To have a cancer diagnosis is to be hit by the biggest storm anyone can imagine. You are dumped in the middle of the arena. Even as a professional we cannot help absorbing this ferocious level of stress, and we have to adopt strategies to prevent burnout, as we are always processing this stress.

'There have been moves to think about the impact on staff, like offering debriefing through particularly traumatic times, better team dynamics, after-case reviews, and even social occasions. But it is also important just to acknowledge how difficult it is.'

Professor Whelan explains, in his position as a sarcoma oncologist, that it is important to draw clear boundaries in one's own mind:

'Sometimes from the outset what you are working with is incurable. You take responsibility for what is achievable with treatment, but I do not take responsibility for people having cancer. I do not feel outraged as an oncologist. Death is certainly unavoidable. As a doctor it is important to do one's utmost to help the patient, but to also accept the limitations of medicine, and therefore your limitations as a doctor.

'This is the nature of the caring experience generally, and all the more so in paediatric and adolescent oncology. Unresolved personal issues go with it. And depending on the leadership, staff can feel unsupported when working in a team.'

Dr Gaze acknowledged the emotional toll of his job. 'It it is difficult at times to cope with some families, when one feels pushed over the edge by their demands. Trying to get a family to consent to treatment when they are clinging to any minute excuse not to come to terms with the fact that their child has a deadly progressive tumour and needs radical treatment can be deeply frustrating.'

When I asked Dr Gaze how he managed, however, he said with conviction, 'By being part of a team. The department (Radiotherapy) is well protected from burn-out in terms of managing stress risk factors. I don't work in isolation. I am able to discuss things. I also do other kinds of work – research and education, which provides variety. It is very important to have a good life outside work with friends and family.'

At the end of my interview with Dr Gaze however, he said that perhaps he should meet me every Friday, at the end of his week. Indeed, one thing that struck me about everyone I talked to about their work was that they all seemed to want to talk.

I asked Chris Henry how she coped with the stress of her work. 'On Fridays I put everything down in my diary and then close it and I switch off on the motorway home. It is very important to trust other people in their role, and also to understand when you are no longer needed. I have fostered children in the past, and I think this has helped me to accept that they may have to go back to less satisfactory circumstances, and you can't change that. It is also important to have a sense of humour.

'Being a patient advocate – putting the patient first – is fundamentally important to me, and I am careful not to get caught up in the family dynamics, or hospital politics. And this is more difficult with younger children, where you are working more with the parents than with the child. For me it is a privilege to work with young children and teenagers. The fact that they will let you help. The fact that they accept you, they talk to you, in the extreme distress they are in. You learn a lot from them every time. I will never know what it is like to have cancer at that stage of life. But if you listen, they will enlighten you. To have a life-threatening illness at that stage of life. It is very humbling to witness.'

Conclusion

The professionals working in paediatric oncology in this country are world leaders. The treatment and care of children with cancer has improved and developed in the last twenty years in ways that could not have been foreseen, certainly in many of its significant details, when this book was written. However, the reason a new edition of Dorothy Judd's book has become necessary is because the work we do has not changed in its humane fundamentals. It is and will always be about exploring and exercising our humanity in a direct meeting with the worst fears that anyone with a child can imagine.

I would like to acknowledge Mark Williams' help in pointing me towards various articles and guidelines in the preparation of this Introduction.

References

Adamo, S., Adamo, S.S., De Falco, R., Di Ciocco, T., Foggia, R., Giacometti, P., & Siani, G. (2008). Tom Thumb in hospital: The fairy tale workshop in a paediatric oncology and haematology ward, *Psychodynamic practice, 14 (3)* 263–280.

Adamo, S., & De Falco, R. (2012). The role of play in the psychotherapy of a child suffering from cancer, *Journal of Psychoanalytic Social Work, (19) issue 1–2*, 101–120.

Albett, S., & Estlin, E. (2010). Clinical trials involving children with cancer – organisational and ethical issues. In: E. Estlin, R. Gilbertson, & R. Wynn, (Eds.), *Paediatric Haematology and Oncology – Scientific Principles and Clinical Practice* (pp. 415–420). Wiley-Blackwell.

Association of Child Psychotherapy (2011). *Child and adolescent psychotherapy with children and young people in hospitals and their families*, Briefing Paper Series.

Barnard, D., Street, A., & Love, A. (2006). Relationship between stressors, work supports and burnout among cancer nurses, *Cancer Nursing 29 (4)* 338–345.

Barr, P. (2007). Relationship of neonatologists' end of life decisions to their personal fear of death, *Archives of Disease in Childhood (Foetal & Neonatal Edition.) (92)* 104–107.

Bristol Royal Infirmary Inquiry (2001). *Report of the public inquiry into children's heart surgery at the Bristol Royal Infirmary 1984–1995: Learning from Bristol.* Chairman: Professor Ian Kennedy. London: The Stationery Office.

Brook, L. (2010). Palliative Care. In: E. Estlin, R. Gilbertson, & R. Wynn, (Eds.), *Paediatric Haematology and Oncology – Scientific Principles and Clinical Practice* (pp. 392–414). Wiley-Blackwell.

Calman, K. (1984). Quality of life in cancer patients – an hypothesis, *Journal of Medical Ethics, (10)* 124–127.

Calman, K., & Hine, D. (1995). *A policy framework for commissioning cancer services*: a report by the expert group on cancer to the chief medical offices of England and Wales. Department of Health and Welsh Office.

Cancer Reform Strategy (2007). Department of Health.

Cancer Research UK: Childhood Cancer statistics. www.cancerresearcuk.org

Carlson, L., & Bultz, B. (2003). *Benefits of psychosocial oncology care: improved quality of life and medical offset,* Health and Quality of Life Outcomes, 1–9.

Childhood Cancer Survivorship Act (2011). *The Paediatric, Adolescent and Young Adult Cancer Survivorship Research and Quality of Life Act.* (Bill, 2011) House of Representatives 3015. www.opencongress.org

Department of Health (2000). *The NHS Cancer Plan. A Plan for Investment. A Plan for Reform.* London.

Department of Health (2004). *National Service Framework for Children, Young People, and Maternity Services.*

Department of Health (2011). *Improving outcomes: a strategy for cancer.*

Department of Health (2012). *Improving outcomes: a strategy for cancer.* Second Annual Report.

Dix, D., Gulati, S., Robinson, P., Syed, I., & Klassen, A. (2012). Demands and rewards associated with working in paediatric oncology: a qualitative study of Canadian health care providers, *Journal of Paediatric Haematology and Oncology.* 34(6) 430–435.

Eiser, C. (1997). Children's quality of life measures, *Archives of Disease in Childhood, (77)* 350–354.

Eiser, C. (2007). Beyond survival: quality of life and follow up after childhood cancer, *Journal of Paediatric Psychology 32 (9)* 1140–1150.

Eiser, C., & Hill, J. (2000). Examining the psychological consequences of surviving childhood cancer: systematic review as a research method in paediatric psychology, *Journal of Paediatric Psychology, 25 (6)* 449–460.

Emanuel, R., Colloms, A., Mendelsohn, A., & Testa, R. (1990). Psychotherapy with hospitalized children with leukaemia: is it possible? *Journal of Child Psychotherapy, 16 (2)* 21–37.

Fonagy, P., & Moran, G. (1990). Studies of the efficacy of child psychoanalysis, *Journal of Consulting and Clinical Psychology (58)* 684–695.

Fonagy, P., Steele, M., Steele, H., Higgitt, A., & Target, M. (1994). The theory and practice of resilience, *Journal of Child Psychology and Psychiatry 35 (2)* 231–257.

Fonagy, P., Target, M., Cotrell, D., Phillips, J., & Kurtz, Z. (2002). *What Works for Whom? A critical review of treatments for children and adolescents.* New York: Guildford.

Fowler, K., Phoehling, K., Billheimer, D., Hamilton, R., Wu, H., Mulder, J., & Frangoul, H. (2006). Hospice referral practices for children with cancer: a survey of paediatric oncologists, *Journal of Clinical Oncology. 24 (7)* 1099–1104.

Freud, S. (1920). Beyond the pleasure principle. *S E 18* 7–64. London: Hogarth.

George, R., & Hutton, S. (2003). Palliative care in adolescents, *European Journal of Cancer, 39 (18)* 2662–8.

Grinyer, A., & Barbarachild, Z. (2011). *Teenage and young adult palliative and end of life care service evaluation,* School of Health and Medicine, Lancaster University, Department of Health – Teenage Cancer Trust.

Guex, P. (1994). *An Introduction to Psycho-Oncology.* London: Routledge, 74–77.

Her Majesty's Treasury (2003). *Every Child Matters.* London: The Stationery Office.

Hewitt, M., Weiner, S., & Simone, J. (2003). *Childhood cancer survivorship: improving care and quality of life,* National Cancer Policy Board, Washington DC: National Academy of Sciences, 20–36.

Hinds, P., Brandon, J., Allen, C., Hijiya, N., Newsome, R., & Kane, R. (2007). Patient-reported outcome in end-of-life research in paediatric oncology, *Journal of Paediatric Psychology 32 (9)* 1079–1088.

Hinds, P., Sanders, C., Srivastava, D., Hickey, S., Jayawardene, D., Milligan, M., Olson, M., Puckett, P., Quargnenti, A., Randall, E., & Tyc, V. (1998). Testing the stress-response sequence model in paediatric oncology nursing, *Journal of Advanced Nursing 28 (5)* 1146–1157.

Houtzager, B., Oort, F., Hoekstra-Weebers, J., Caron, H., Grootenhuis, M., & Last, B. (2004). Coping and family functioning predict longitudinal psychological adaptation of siblings of childhood cancer patients, *Journal of Paediatric Psychology, 29 (8)* 591–605.

Judd, D. (2001). To walk the last bit on my own – narcissistic independence or identification with good objects: issues of loss for a 13-year-old who had an amputation, *Journal of Child Psychotherapy 27 (1)* 47–67.

Karver, M., Handelsman, J., Fields, S., & Bickman, L. (2005). A theoretical model of common process factors in youth and family therapy, *Mental Health Services Research, 7(1)* 35–51.

Kazak, A. (2005). Evidence based interventions for survivors of childhood cancer and their families, *Journal of Paediatric Psychology, 30 (1)* 29–39.

Kazak, A., & Knoll, R. (2004). Child death from paediatric illness: Conceptualising intervention from a family/systems and public health perspective, *Professional Psychology, 35,* 219–226.

Kazak, A., Cant, C., Merritt, J., McSherry, M., Rourke, M., Wei-Ting, H., Alderfer, M., Beele, D., Simms, S., & Lange, B. (2003). Identifying psychosocial risk indicative of subsequent resource use in families of newly diagnosed paediatric oncology patients, *Journal of Clinical Oncology, 2 (17)* 3220–3225.

Kazak, A., McClure, K., Alderfer, M., Wei-Ting, H., Crump, T., Lan, T., Deatrick, J., Rourke, M., & Simms, S. (2004). Cancer-related parental beliefs: the family illness beliefs inventory, *Journal of Paediatric Psychology, 29 (7)* 531–542.

Kazdin, A., & Nock, M. (2003). Delineating mechanisms of change in child and adolescent therapy: methodological issues and research recommendations, *Journal of Child Psychology and Psychiatry, 44 (8)* 1116–1129.

Kennedy, E. (2004). *Child and Adolescent Psychotherapy: A Systematic Review of Psychoanalytic Approaches.* North Central London Strategic Health Authority.

Kennedy, E., & Midgley, N. (2007). *Process and Outcome Research in Child Adolescent and Parent-Infant Psychotherapy: A Thematic Review.* North Central London Strategic Health Authority.

Kreicbergs, U., Valdimarsdottir, U., Onelov, E., Henter, J., & Steineck, G. (2004). Talking about death with children who have severe malignant disease, *New England Journal of Medicine, 351 (12)* 1175–86.

Lachman, P., & Vickers, D. (2004). The National Service framework for Children, *British Medical Journal, 329 (7468)* 693–4.

Lalor, G., & Talbot, L. (2010). Psychosocial needs of children with cancer and their families. In: (Eds.), E. Estlin, R. Gilbertson, & R. Wynn, *Paediatric Haematology and Oncology – Scientific Principles and Clinical Practice,* (pp. 360–366). *Wiley-Blackwell.*

Lanceley, A. (2014). The cancer nurse specialists' caseload: 'Contending with the fretful elements.' In: (Ed.), J. Burke, *Topic of Cancer – New Perspectives on the Emotional Experience of Cancer.* London: Karnac.

Langeveld, N., Stam, H., Grootenhuis, M., & Last, B. (2002). Quality of life in young adult survivors of childhood cancer, *Support Care Cancer, (10)* 579–600.

Langton-Gilks, S. (2013). Journal. In: Foreman, A., *At the moment, I'm all right, yeah!* Sunday Times magazine. 3rd March, p. 23.

Lanyado, M. (1996). Winnicott's children: the holding environment and therapeutic communication in brief and non-intensive work, *Journal of Child Psychotherapy, 22 (3)* 4–8.

Marans, S., Mayes, L., Cicchetti, D., Dahl, K., Marans, W., & Cohen, D. (1991). The child psychoanalytic play interview, *Journal of the American Psychoanalytic Association, 39* 1015–1036.

Mental Health Commission (2006). *Multidisciplinary Team Practice: from Theory to Practice*. Discussion Paper.

Mitchell, W., Clark, S., & Sloper, P. (2005). Survey of psychosocial support provided by UK Paediatric Oncology Centre, *Archives of Disease in Childhood, (90) 796–800*.

Moran, G., Fonagy, P., Kurtz, A., Bolton, A., & Brook, C. (1991). A controlled study of the psychoanalytic treatment of brittle diabetes, *Journal of the American Academy of Child Adolescent Psychiatry, 30 (6) 926–935*.

National Cancer Action Team (2008). *National Cancer Peer Review Programme*. Manual for Cancer Services. Psychological Support Measures. Department of Health.

National Cancer Action Team (2009). *Multidisciplinary Team Members' Views about MDT working*. National Health Service.

National Cancer Action Team (2010). *The Characteristics of an Effective Multidisciplinary team*. National Health Service.

National Institute for Health and Clinical Excellence (2005). *Guidance on Cancer Services – Improving Outcomes in Children and Young People with Cancer*. The Manual. Evidence Review.

National Institute for Health and Clinical excellence (2005). *An Assessment of Needs for Cancer Services for Children and Young People in England and Wales*.

National Institute for Clinical Excellence (2008). *National Cancer Peer Review Programme*. Manual for Cancer Services. Children's Cancer Measures.

National Cancer Intelligence Network (2010). *Evidence to March 2010 on cancer inequalities in England*. National Cancer Action Team.

National Cancer Intelligence Network (2012). *Place of Death for Children, Teenagers and Young Adults with Cancer in England*. Data Briefing.

Office for National Statistics (2011). *Leading Causes of Death in England and Wales in 2009*. www.ons.gov.uk

Querido, J. (2012). *Cancer intelligence: mission possible*. Cancer Research UK, 20th June.

Ramsden, S. (1999). The child and adolescent psychotherapist in a hospital setting. In: (Eds.) M. Lanyado & A. Horne, *The Handbook of Child and Adolescent Psychotherapy* (pp. 142–158). London: Routledge.

Rhode, M. (2011). What about the transference? Technical issues in the treatment of children who cannot symbolize. In: (Ed.), M. Gunter, *Technique in Child and Adolescent Analysis* (pp. 61–74). London: Karnac.

Segal, B. (2012). The unspoken reality of teenage cancer care – psychoanalytic work on a teenage cancer ward, *Institute of Psychodynamic Psychotherapy in South Africa Conference, Johannesburg*.

Sinclair, H., & Hamil, C. (2007). Does vicarious traumatisation affect oncology nurses? A literature review, *European Journal of Oncology Nursing 11 (4) 348–356*.

Talbot, L., & Spoudeas, H. (2010). Late effects in relation to childhood cancer. In: (Eds.) E. Estlin, R. Gilbertson, & R. Wynn, *Paediatric Haematology and Oncology – Scientific Principles and Clinical Practice* (pp. 367–391). *Wiley-Blackwell.*

Teenage Cancer Trust (2010). *Exploring the Impact of the Built Environment.* The Futures Company Report.

The Victoria Climbie Inquiry (2003). Chair: Lord Laming. London: The Stationery Office.

Theunissen, N., Vogels, T., Koopman, G., Verrips, G., Zwinderman, K., Verloove-Vanhorick, S., & Wit, J. (1998). The proxy problem: child report versus parent report in health-related quality of life research, *Quality of Life Research (7)* 387–97.

Trowell, J., Joffe, I., Campbell, J., Clemente, C., Almquist, F., Soininen, M., Koskenranta-Aalto, U., Weintraub, S., Kolaitis, G., Tomaras, V., Anastasopoulos, D., Grayson, K., & Tsiantis, J. (2007). Childhood depression: a place for psychotherapy. An outcome study comparing individual psychodynamic psychotherapy and family therapy, *European Child and Adolescent Psychiatry. (16) 3,* 157–167.

Vance, Y., Eiser, C., & Horne, B. (2004). Parents' views of the impact of childhood brain tumour and treatment on young people's social and family functioning, *Clinical Child Psychology and Psychiatry, 9 (2)* 271–288. London: Sage.

Wallace, W., & Green, D. (2004). *Late Effects of Childhood Cancer,* London: Arnold.

Woolley, H., Stein, A., Forrest, G., & Baum, J. (1989). Imparting the diagnosis of life-threatening illness in children, *British Medical Journal, (298)* 1623–6.

Note on conventions

Throughout the book I use the word 'phantasy' to denote what the Kleinian psychoanalyst Susan Isaacs (1952) describes as 'the mental corollary, the psychic representative of instinct. There is no impulse, no instinctual urge or response which is not experienced as unconscious phantasy ... A phantasy represents the particular context of the urges or feelings (for example, wishes, fears, anxieties, triumphs, love or sorrow) dominating the mind at a particular moment.'

I use the word 'fantasy' to denote more conscious imaginings, on a spectrum between daydreams and hallucinations.

Unless I am referring to actual clinical material, I generally describe the infant/child as 'he', although of course I mean he or she.

The 'stage' is set in Great Britain, and sometimes more generally in the western world. I am generally not relating to the psychodynamics of grief and bereavement of other cultures, although much of the theory and research would be applicable cross-culturally.

I have changed as many details as possible in the case studies I have given, in order to protect the anonymity and confidentiality of those described except where I have interviewed various professionals and gained their permission to quote them.

Robert playing and happy

Mrs Judd playing

Part I
Framework

Chapter One
The death of a child

I do not have words to express the sorrow, or the loss I felt. It left a hole in my heart that can never be filled.

Nelson Mandela (1994)

Although we know that after such a loss the acute state of mourning will subside, we also know that we shall remain inconsolable and will never find a substitute. No matter what may fill the gap, even if it be filled completely, it nevertheless remains something else. And actually this is how it should be. It is the only way of perpetuating that love which we do not have to relinquish.

Sigmund Freud (1929)

Freud wrote the above on the day his dead daughter would have been 36 years old. At the time of her death, he had written, 'Deep down I sense a bitter, irreparable narcissistic injury' (1920b).

And Mandela was writing about the sudden death of his eldest son, Thembi.

The death of a child is one of the most disturbing, shocking, unacceptable events that can occur. It is a death out of season. More than the death of an adult, who has at least to some extent 'lived his life', the death of a child is an outrage against the natural order of things, disrupting our sense of purpose, of future promise, of our progeny continuing after our death. For the parents of a child who dies, the loss that is mourned includes not only a shared past, but also future hopes. It is 'endured, rather than overcome', by mourning (Mitchell-Rossdale, 1988).

Sister Frances Dominica (Superior General of the Anglican Society of All Saints), who founded and runs Helen House in Oxford, the first hospice in the world for children, told me (personal communication):

3

I think the first thing is to be realistic, and it was important for us, soon after Helen House opened, to admit that the death of a child is an outrage. You can't explain it away, you can't make it tidy and nice, let alone give all the answers. Firstly, it's an outrage, and secondly, we don't understand why it should happen. And once you've accepted those two things, I think you're half way there.

Even to those not in the bereaved immediate family, such as those in the community, the reverberations are considerable. Feelings of shock, disbelief, and outrage are quite common among neighbours and acquaintances who hear about the death of a child, more so of course if the death is sudden. The security of the onlooker has been threatened.

This feeling, that the 'shadow of death' could as easily pass over one's own family, is only temporarily chastening. For those not directly involved, the event fades in a way that may be surprisingly rapid. We return to our everyday lives, where, we hope, 'death shall have no dominion' (Dylan Thomas, 1966). And yet, in any one year, there are approximately 5400 children living with a terminal illness in the United Kingdom, and in England and Wales approximately 1800 die annually between the ages of 1 and 14 years.

Attitudes to death and dying

In considering children's attitudes to death, we need to gauge the climate and background from which they emerge. There is still the tendency today to say 'Not in front of the children' when discussing death, and thus attempt to protect children. We need to question whether children's fears of death are a reflection of adults' inhibitions and adults' own anxieties about death, or whether children themselves have fears of death as part of normal psychological functioning.

In the west, paradoxically, there is a surge of public interest in the subjects of death, dying, and bereavement, but a continued denial of their existence in the everyday lives of most people. On the surface, it seems that the taboo around death, dying, and bereavement is being lifted, not only at a popular level in the media, but also at an academic, health care, and professional level (Parkes, 1972; Pincus, 1976). Bereavement counselling is now fairly widely available. There is the growth of the hospice movement over the past 25 years (with, in 1995, the provision of 384 home care services, 220 day care units, and 208 in-patient beds in the United Kingdom). There is also the influence of the writings of Elizabeth Kübler-Ross. The introduction of 'death education' (Willcock, 1988) in over a thousand schools in the USA, for 5-year-olds and upwards, indicates a more enlightened development that Britain may follow. Dr Robert Stevenson, one of the promoters of such courses in the USA and a national authority on death education, strikes at the heart of the taboo. He believes that silence on the subject is damaging to the child, leading to thoughts of 'What is this terrible thing I'm supposed to be afraid of, and from which I am excluded?' Inevitably, however, he has his opponents. They claim that the subject should have no place on the timetable, and they are concerned that many children will be too emotionally immature to cope adequately with the subject.

Indeed, as I will try to convey, ours is in many ways more of a death-denying society than it was at the turn of the century. Death was then a public event and often took place in the presence of family, friends, and children. In 1900, approximately two-thirds of the people who died in western countries were under the age of 50, and most died at home in their beds. Children learned to view death as part of the natural progression of life. Up to, and including, the First World War, death was very accessible (Feifel, 1962; Gorer, 1965; Aries, 1974; Stannard, 1977).

As Alan Bloom (1988, p. 192) states, in writing about the early years of the twentieth century in an English village:

> Death was much more in evidence than birth. The arrival of babies was almost furtive, but the church bell tolled for every death. And you knew from the tolling whether the deceased was a man, woman or child.

When discussing the trend away from such acceptance of death, Dr Dora Black says (personal communication):

> As Gorer (1965) writes, there was so much slaughter, death, and horror during the First World War, that the 1920s became a death-denying society in a manic way. That merged into a period of therapeutic optimism, when penicillin was discovered. The first real drug that could *cure* anything was only discovered in 1907. Before then there were no curative drugs. Salvarsan, which affected syphilis, was the first curative drug. Before that, drugs like morphine could kill pain, but not cure; and drugs like digitalis, in the nineteenth century, could help heart disease, but not cure it.
>
> Research into drugs was held up by the First World War. Then the sulphonamides were discovered; then antibiotics, after the

---

[1] It is, however, important to make a distinction between the decrease of the infant mortality rate as a result of medical advances on the one hand, and, on the other, as a result of better diet, the availability of clean water, and the proper institution of sewage disposal. The improvement of public health in general had started before the considerable medical advances in the treatment of infectious diseases. In fact, McKeown (1976), the epidemiologist, concluded that the key factors in improving health have been environmental and social, not medical. It is striking to note that over the past 40 years, life expectancy has increased in Britain by 4 years – whereas it had increased by 25 years over the previous 60 years (Forfar, 1984).

Second World War. So there was tremendous excitement that we could actually treat and cure diseases for the first time.

She believes that the 'combination of a heavy death toll by the end of the First World War and the medical treatment breakthroughs[1] led to a taboo on talking about death, for doctors considered death as a failure', and continues, 'There was also a magical feeling which still exists to some extent: I remember that my mother would never mention the word "tuberculosis" or "cancer" because to say it meant that in a sense you were giving it to someone.' These cultural taboos on talking about death shifted, if not lifted, after the Second World War, she surmises. 'Firstly, people had a more realistic attitude to what they could cure and what they couldn't, and this continued. Second, there is more openness generally about what people feel they can talk about.'

We have, then, a commonly held belief that death was far more 'out in the open' in the nineteenth century than in the twentieth, and that nowadays, in contrast, it is something which is still generally hidden away, but that we are re-emerging from a 'dark age' of repression of the subject of death.

Although Aries (1974), Gorer (1965), and others have made invaluable contributions to the body of historical and sociological perspectives, and many of their findings are beyond dispute, an important essay by the historian David Cannadine (1981) has questioned our own romanticization and idealization of death in Victorian Britain. Cannadine examines attitudes to, and the effects of, war, death, grief, and mourning, and suggests that it is extremely difficult, if not impossible, to trace the evolution of something as private as grief.

In questioning the 'beguiling and nostalgic progression from obsessive death and forbidden sex in the nineteenth century to obsessive sex and forbidden death in the twentieth', he comments that although there may be some truth at a public level about the views held by Gorer and Aries, research shows that at a private level the Victorian interest in sexuality was not that dissimilar from attitudes today (Marcus, 1966; Walvin, 1987), and casts similar doubt on assumptions about a disparity between modern and Victorian attitudes to grief.

Cannadine also wonders if the more elaborate mourning rituals were psychologically beneficial, or if their predominant value was one of commercial exploitation and ostentation. He suggests that the 'denial of death' that Aries and others attach to the 1940s onwards in fact begins before 1914; but that this was a decline in the *celebration* of death, while death continued to be *glorified*, particularly in war.

Freud, on the other hand, believed that the mass slaughter in the First World War would be bound to alter man's conventional views of death: 'Death will no longer be denied; we are forced to believe in it' (1915a: 291). Interestingly, the outcome of the widespread bereavement caused by the First World War seems to have been a turning away from Victorian mourning rituals and religion, and a turning instead to nationwide public construction of memorials.

Moving ahead to the Second World War, the horrifying use of the atomic bomb utterly changed man's views of his own power. Universal death was, and is, now possible. It is under this shadow of the possibility of global death that we all live. The effects on the individual of the possibility of a nuclear holocaust and of mass disasters are beginning to be looked at by psychoanalysts ('The Aftermath of Disaster – Survival and Care', Conference at Tavistock Clinic, June 1987; Segal, 1987), psychotherapists, psychologists, as well as sociologists and historians. Just as Freud (1915a) predicted that the mass slaughter of the First World War would make it impossible for us to 'maintain our former attitude towards death', so this nuclear age has an effect that must further alter our attitudes; even though, on the surface, we tend to ignore the threat on a day-to-day basis.

From a psychoanalytic view, Segal (1987) argues that all wars mobilize very primitive mental mechanisms (see below, p. 12) but that the existence of nuclear weapons induces these mechanisms to a far greater degree because of the threat of total annihilation that they pose. Increased threats from outside lead to increased infantile omnipotence, denial, and psychotic defences, as ways of defending against the consequences of an escalating arms race.

At a more personal level, on the other hand, dying can be judged to be easier today than it used to be, as it more usually occurs at a time that is psychologically more acceptable: old age (Cannadine, 1981). And, owing to improved pain-control and other medical interventions, it can be made more peaceful and comfortable. Derek Nuttall, ex-Director of CRUSE – the National Association for Bereavement Care – speaking at a conference on 'Bereavement: Grief and Loss' held by the Association for Child Psychology and Psychiatry in October 1988, also pointed out that more services are available to the bereaved than ever before; that people can die without pain and with more medical care. He added that there is more understanding of the bereavement process, with, for example, greater assurance now available about the normality of the emotional turmoil experienced by the bereaved.

Nevertheless, despite this greater accessibility of the subject of death, people's awareness and experience of death tend to remain at an intellectual level, unless they have been personally bereaved and are able to mourn. Many people reach middle age without a personal experience of death. As Dora Black says (personal communication):

> I was taking a seminar for medical students the other day, on death and dying, and we were doing a role play. I was trying to get them talking to the parents of a child with cancer. They found it extremely difficult to get into. They were very brusque and quite

hurtful, and unable to get any sympathetic feeling into it. It seems
they have to dehumanize themselves, in order to distance themselves. Very few have had any actual experience of bereavement
nowadays. Probably the first time they come across death is in the
hospital.

And, as Kübler-Ross (1975) writes, 'our medical schools prepared them
[medical students] almost exclusively in the *science* of medicine and
give them little help in its *art*'. Now, 20 years later, I have found that, by
and large, this still holds true. Indeed, doctors may have a particular need
to deny the fact of death – they may themselves have fears of illness and
death that are then denied and mastered by becoming doctors (Keniston,
1967; Liston, 1975; Black *et al.*, 1989). Institutional defences play a large
part in this denial (see Appendix 3 and quotation from Obholzer, p. 29).

Dr Richard Lansdown (Consultant Psychologist, Great Ormond Street
Hospital for Sick Children), feels there has been a considerable lessening of the taboo on talking about death in the hospital and the leukaemic
unit, where he works, but (personal communication):

> In society I don't think there has been any change – not that I can
> discern, and not from what parents say about the response they
> get from other people. Parents of children who have died, or who
> are dying, still have a sense of isolation, partly because they have
> cut themselves off – I think one must recognize that – and partly
> because society doesn't really know how to cope.

Black reminds us of the remoteness and rarity of child death today,
compared with the days of her grandmother, who had 10 children but
only raised two of them. It is these not untypical salutary statistics that so
greatly contrast with our present-day success in fighting death, and at
least partly explain the alienation of death as a concept and as a reality.
(The infant mortality figures in England and Wales, per thousand live
births, were 117.1 between 1906 and 1910, whereas in 1984 they were
down to 9.4. The figures for 1986 showed the first increase in 16 years:
9.6 per thousand – Registrar General's *Statistical Review*. In 1992, the
rate was 6.6 per thousand live births, which is about a quarter less than
the rate 5 years ago – *Social Trends* 24, 1994, p.94.)

It is still commonplace for us to employ euphemisms. We talk about
people 'passing away' or 'passing on', about 'losing' someone, about
people 'pegging out', 'copping it', 'pushing up the daisies', 'kicking the
bucket', 'giving up the ghost', 'ending one's days', and about pets being
'put to sleep'. We talk about funeral 'parlours', we call coffins 'caskets',
and undertakers' offices 'chapels'. All these sayings have an understandable logic and meaning, but nevertheless illustrate a propensity to deny
an ordinary straightforward description of death, and often to idealize

death. (Further on in this chapter I explore everyday ways in which death is experienced, but not acknowledged, ways in which its existence is relegated to largely unconscious parts of the mind.)

A few other factors contribute to people's difficulty in negotiating death emotionally and integrating it into their lives, despite the intellectual accessibility of death as a topic. One important one is that nowadays more people (in fact, two-thirds) die in hospital and nursing homes away from their homes. This can be a distressing and isolating experience, possibly made more strange by the use of life-sustaining technology and notwithstanding the importance of effective pain control. Another development is the expectation that the 'experts' will help with illness, death, and bereavement. In a sense, therefore, people can feel deskilled from finding their own instinctual and probably appropriate ways of negotiating death. Just as the natural childbirth movement attempts to redress the 'high-tech' approach to childbirth, so some aspects of the 'death awareness movement' aim to restore the dignity of patients, to avoid technology that is seen to be alienating, and to break down the barriers to discussing death (Kastenbaum, 1982).

Within the framework of medicine's success in saving people's lives, and against the background of there having been no world war for over 50 years, we need to question when to allow people to die if keeping them alive threatens their autonomy and dignity (see Chapter 10). Perhaps we should remember the story of Asclepius, who was so skilled in the use of drugs and in surgery that he became known to the ancient Greeks as the founder of medicine. However, so successful did he become at raising people from the dead that he was killed by Zeus for hubris.

Without death, after all, life would have no meaning. The flowers of the spring have an appeal that is related largely to their impermanence. Even the hours of the day are given meaning by the inevitability of nightfall. Similarly, if life were eternal, perhaps we would not bother to get up in the morning. The individual's impetus, zest, and appreciation are largely bound up with a span of limited duration.

The writer James Baldwin expresses a similar view thus:

> Perhaps the whole root of our trouble, the human trouble, is that we will sacrifice all the beauty of our lives, will imprison ourselves in totems, taboos . . . in order to deny the fact of death, which is the only fact we have. It seems to me that one ought to rejoice in the *fact* of death – ought to decide, indeed, to *earn* one's death by confronting with passion the conundrum of life.

> (Baldwin, 1963, p. 79)

An analogy with painting also comes to mind. Although this requires a leap of imaginative conjecture on the reader's part to consider the

subject of 'wholeness' from a visual angle, it may remind us that not only
have poets, writers and philosophers grappled with ideas of life and
death, but, more symbolically, so have musicians and painters. In painting, I am not only referring to artists' actual depictions of death in
various ways, such as Friedrich's (1774–1840) themes of temporality, and
of the passing of the seasons, but also the more abstract aesthetic experience of taking on board the darks and lights, the foreground and the
depths, object and ground, the mysterious or abstract areas of a canvas
as much as the more explicit details. This parallels our struggle to see
death as part of life. The art historian Wölfflin summarizes this process:

> If a nude in Rembrandt stands out on a dark ground, the light of
> the body seems as it were to emanate from the darkness of the
> picture space: *it is as if it were of the same stuff*. The distinctness
> of the object in this case is not necessarily impaired. While the
> form remains perfectly clear, that peculiar union between the
> modelling lights and darks can have acquired a life of its own . . .
> figure and space, corporeal and incorporeal, can unite in the
> impression of an independent tonal movement.
>
> (Wölfflin, 1932, pp. 19–20; my italics)

The difficulty in 'seeing' death as part of life is rather like the mind's
inability to 'read' both subject and background simultaneously in those
black and white illustrations of faces in profile or of vases, where the
viewer has to make a considerable effort to shift his vertex.

Linking this discourse with the psychoanalytic one to which I shall
return, I find the words of a drawing teacher I once had – 'The spaces
between objects are as important as the objects themselves' – remarkably similar to Winnicott's (1988) broad sweeps of understanding, that
the 'life of an individual is an interval between two states of unaliveness'.
And death, even before its arrival, is an 'absent presence', to quote Feifel
(1962). With resignation and acceptance, Francis Bacon wrote in the
seventeenth century: 'It is as natural to die as to be born.'

Yet this complementarity of life and death has not easily been
embraced in an appreciative way by modern western man, for an
acknowledgement of mortality and impotence in the face of death leads
to uncomfortable feelings of helplessness. Hence, one might understand
the need for religious beliefs in an after-life and for the Christian notion
of resurrection. For, as Freud (1915a) observed, the body of a dead
person can be seen to disintegrate, while memories of the person can
live on, thus creating a very understandable division of the individual
into body and soul.

While exploring man's fear of death, we need to acknowledge the
other side of the same coin: his capacity to long for death, often seen as
an escape route to peace. Freud saw protective concern as frequently

harbouring murderous feelings (1900: 145n.). Therefore, implicit in the more usual fear of death, or the life instinct holding supremacy over the death instinct, lies its counterpart or repressed side: death's attraction or appeal for man. This may be consciously or unconsciously expressed as murderous or suicidal fantasies (Freud, 1920a: 162).

The wish for death as a way of escaping from life's troubles, but then a fear of the mystery of the unknown that death might hold, is powerfully conveyed, as is well known, by Shakespeare's Hamlet (Act III)

> To die, to sleep;
> To sleep; perchance to dream: ay, there's the rub;
> For in that sleep of death what dreams may come
> When we have shuffled off this mortal coil,
> Must give us pause.

After dwelling on the many 'slings and arrows of outrageous fortune' in everyday life which could be ended by suicide, he continues to hesitate at this solution, with:

> . . . the dread of something after death,
> The undiscover'd country from whose bourn
> No traveller returns, puzzles the will,
> And makes us rather bear those ills we have
> Than fly to others that we know not of?

Dramatists, poets, artists, philosophers, and theologians have grappled with ideas around death through the ages, but, strangely, there have been few psychological and psychoanalytical investigations into the meaning of death. But Freud (1915a, p. 293) did pithily summarize philosophers' response to death: 'Philosophers have declared that the intellectual enigma presented to primaeval man by the picture of death forced him to reflection, and thus became the starting-point of all speculation.' However, he questions whether primeval man was puzzled by death, suggesting instead that the *conflict of ambivalent feelings* towards the dead person (who was both loved and hated) was the stimulus for the spirit of enquiry in man. Freud speculates that it 'was beside the dead body of someone he loved that he invented spirits', for man would need to imagine other forms of existence beyond death, rather than accept the possibility of his own eventual total annihilation. He points out that it was only later that religions succeeded in depicting an after-life that was more desirable than our present life. He concludes in the light of the First World War that, as phantasies of killing are as much in the unconscious minds of modern man as they were in primitive man and colour our behaviour, we should 'give death the place in reality and in our thought which is its due', thus taking 'the truth more into account'.

Adults tend to use a wide range of defences against looking at the finality of death, employing (as well as the religious beliefs mentioned earlier) magical thinking, the externalization of the death instinct by splitting, denial, projection, and projective identification; and delusions. The use of euphemisms described earlier is, of course, part of the denial. Yet, common though this denial is, it is psychologically costly, for the efforts made in keeping thoughts and fears of death at bay require energy that could be used for living with an awareness of our wholeness as well as our vulnerability. (It needs to be added, of course, that some denial is developmentally normal, and protects the personality from excessive anxiety. It enables people to take everyday risks, such as crossing roads and driving cars, and even allowing oneself to fall into unguarded sleep.)

In order to understand further the origins of the denial of death, we need to go back to looking at the immature ego of the infant. As Freud described it (1938), the newborn baby is exposed, from birth and perhaps before, to the extreme conflict between the life instinct and the death instinct, or between Eros and destructiveness. Freud's writings on the death instinct are, at times, at variance with each other. On the one hand, he writes about the body's tendency to return to its original, inorganic state, and on the other hand, he writes about the instinct to destroy oneself or others. The 'nirvana principle' and the destructive drive are, as Fromm (1974) points out, two 'disparate entities' that cannot be brought together under the general heading of the death instinct. I therefore find Klein (1946) more helpful for the purpose of understanding the infant's early experiences.

According to Klein, the infant is exposed to both anxiety-producing experiences, such as birth, hunger, pain, as well as life-giving experiences, such as physical closeness to its mother and feeding. When faced with the anxiety produced by the death instinct, or by negative or traumatic experiences, the infant's immature ego deflects it. In Klein's view, this process is partly a projection, 'partly a conversion of the death instinct into aggression' (Segal, 1973). This primitive splitting and projection of that 'deadly' part of itself into the main external object, the breast, gives rise to feelings of persecution. Thus, the original fear of death is changed into fear of a killing presence, which, I would add, still carries undertones of death.

In parallel with this way of expelling the death instinct, the infant is establishing a relationship to an ideal object or, in Kleinian terms, 'breast'. This comes about through the fulfilling and gratifying experiences of being loved and cared for emotionally, and fed, which are also then projected in order to create a good object which will satisfy the ego's striving for the preservation of life. Thus, from the first weeks of life, the infant relates to two polarized objects: the breast is split into a gratifying ideal object and a persecutory bad one. This ongoing splitting keeps the good object separate and safe from the bad one. 'The infant's aim is to acquire, to keep inside and to identify with the ideal object, seen as life-giving and protective, and to keep out the bad object and those parts of the self which contain the death instinct,' Segal writes (1973). Klein calls this stage the paranoid-schizoid position.

As the infant develops and natural integration occurs, an attempt to mend this massive split begins: the infant begins to recognize and appreciate that these two separate objects are indeed parts of a whole, of a mother imbued with love and hate, life and death, who comes and goes, and who can be damaged in phantasy by the ravages of the infant. At the same time as the object becomes whole or relatively whole, the infant's ego becomes integrated through introjection – that is, through taking in a whole object. Thus, feelings of concern, of guilt that his destructiveness has caused the loss or the damage, recognition of dependency, emerge in this crucial process. But, as Segal writes, this, the 'depressive position, is never fully worked through. The anxieties pertaining to ambivalence and guilt, as well as situations of loss, which reawaken depressive experiences, are always with us' (1973). Later good experiences, embodying the early primary relationship, still carry the fear of loss.

One way of thinking about this could be that until the recent partial lifting of the taboo, our society was caught up in a collective splitting process, and the individuals within it reflected this. This whole notion of death, fundamental as it is to our definition of life, was split off to the extent that it was, and to some extent still is, banished even from our vocabulary, but perhaps projected on to 'bad' forces in a global or political sense. This paranoid-schizoid method of keeping life and death separate leads to an unreal life, of idealization and omnipotence, and possibly a powerful projection of violence and then to a feeling of persecution. An illustration of this can be found in the amassing of nuclear weapons by certain nations. Although the use of nuclear weapons would obliterate life over large areas of the planet, possession of the bomb is presented as a benign, peace-keeping stance. 'We' have no intention of using the bomb, except to defend ourselves; 'they', on the other hand, can only be restrained from a malevolent use of nuclear weapons by our own capacity to retaliate.

Thus, in attempting to bring life and death into the depressive position, we need not feel persecuted by death (or by anything else onto which death becomes displaced) nor omnipotently deny its place. We can use our creative and reparative talents to attempt to restore our good and loved internal and external objects that are always under the threat of loss. These attempts to repair – both actual losses as well as, symbolically, other damage, and the anxiety of potential loss – fuel our creative drives. Anxiety of loss or the prospect of loss leads to the wish to restore, through sublimation and the use of substitutes or symbols, or directly through creative acts.

To summarize, then: in attempting to integrate death with life, we have to be able to stay with the pain of loss with which death is equated. The avoidance of this pain of absolute loss is at the root of our denial of the place of death in everyday life. An actual bereavement requires considerable emotional work to both decathect (Freud's term, meaning to extricate the energy invested in that person) and reintegrate the lost person, through the process of mourning (Freud, 1915b).

Throughout the life cycle there is growth that brings loss as well as gain. The baby loses the intra-uterine state in order to begin his own separate existence. The infant loses the breast in weaning in order to find his own identity and separateness. The toddler loses the security of the parental lap or arms, and risks falling and being hurt, in order to test out his own legs and the independence thus gained. Throughout all the changes in life there is loss and renewal. Even the finality of death can be 'the final stage of growth' (Kübler-Ross, 1975). Kübler-Ross believes death to be as much a part of human existence, growth, and development as being born, and suggests that this time limit urges us to use the time we have to live more fully. And for the survivor, involved in the death of someone close, when the mourning process is completed, the new phase of life can be welcomed as a fresh challenge to psychic growth, possibly strengthened by surviving the pain of loss.

If our lives can be seen to consist of recurrent tasks along the path from immaturity to maturity, transitions or transformations from one state of being to another, all experienced as struggles against inevitable difficulties, then the final stage, death, can be seen as the last separation, as a letting-go of life with acceptance, and as the completion of a pattern. But just as an insecure child clings to his mother (because he feels he has not internalized enough of a secure 'holding' experience), so many adults cling to life and are unable to face death with equanimity.

Fairy stories and myths give us a useful analogy to the process that I have tried to describe. As we frequently find in fairy tales, a person is dead one moment and comes to life the next, or falls into a deep sleep and is reborn. This is not simply meant to represent wish-fulfilment and an avoidance of reality, but, rather, each rebirth or reawakening symbolizes the repeated reaching of a greater degree of maturity in the face of difficulty, as well as exemplifying the link between death and rebirth, as part of the life cycle. Death is not only bound up with the actual experience of loss, but is symbolized in many different ways that are commonplace and ordinary. Death is an aspect of decay, disease, damage, and the passing of the seasons. This is exemplified in the paintings of Caspar David Friedrich (1774–1840), who symbolizes the passing of time leading to an implicit death through depictions of the wanderer, the seasons, ruined abbeys and decaying trees.

At the same time, Anna Witham (1985) has written about the way in which some ideals of the contemporary death-awareness movement point to death becoming an exalted, idealized, perhaps transcendental experience. Similarly, a note of sentimentality or drama, which belies feelings of pain or suffering, often creeps into descriptions of death and dying by those who work with the terminally ill. Witham argues, quoting Menzies Lyth (1959), that this is an unconscious defensive process, in which individuals can get caught, as part of a collective system, in order to avoid overwhelming anxiety. In choosing to work with the dying, we are attempting to heal splits in ourselves, to restore and to repair. If we idealize the experience of death and dying, Witham suggests, we are using a manic defence against the anxieties of the depressive position as described earlier in this chapter (that is, feelings of sadness, fear of loss of important people, concern, guilt, and a realization of one's own dependency) which inevitably arise when caring for the dying. The extreme pressure and demands on the psyche in that situation lead us to avoid some of the anxieties. Thus, negative feelings about the dying person, or about that which they conjure up or reflect in our own inner world – feelings of helplessness, damage, anger – are completely denied by seeing all good in the dying person, in our role as worker, and in ourselves. (For an analysis of some of the institutional processes at work in the hospital culture see Anna Dartington's [1994] illuminating paper, 'Where angels fear to tread – idealism, despondency, and inhibition in hospital nursing.')

It is important, then, to differentiate between, on the one hand, reverence and respect for death, as a major event that has inevitably throughout the history of mankind stimulated fantasies and will continue to do so, and, on the other hand, idealization and therefore denial of the reality. The former emotions contain feelings of awe, perhaps of fear, of humility, of curiosity, which idealization lacks. Kübler-Ross's writings about death as a transcendental experience may therefore be useful to some people, for whom it may bring renewed psychic growth, but if our frustrations, disappointments, sense of vulnerability, strivings, can all be pushed to one side and replaced by a view of dying as something exalted and above everyday experience, then there is a tendency to expect not only more than the health-care teams can offer, but also a possible impoverishment of the range and depth of emotions possible at this crucial time.

Kastenbaum points out the basic dilemma, in an analysis of what he describes as the 'healthy dying movement': 'Perhaps we should start to examine our underlying fantasies about what we expect. The dying-death situation is still not intimately known to many people. It is, therefore, a tempting screen on which to project aspirations and fantasies that have no other place to be displayed' (1982).

It appears, then, that for some the pendulum has swung far in the opposite direction, away from fear and avoidance of death, to, possibly, its exaltation; it has become, for some, not only an achievement to die comfortably and with dignity, but there is the added expectation that it can be a 'beautiful' and spiritual experience (Levine, 1986).

This development towards a spiritual approach over recent years seems then to be not only a reaction to the taboo on death, and to the technological approach to health care and death, but, ironically, has similarities to the denial of death. Some recent writers revere a Zen approach to death, where the 'physical death is honoured and respected as a wonderful opportunity in the passing from the body to recognize the relativity of everything we imagine to be solid' (Levine, 1986: 252). Within this approach, this attempt to transcend mortality, there is often an avoidance of the actual loss and separation that is death, and of the usually far from pleasurable experience. One has to acknowledge that certain kinds of death, such as cancer of the stomach, which lead to death by starvation, cannot be idealized. Dora Black (personal communication) believes that some experiences can only be extremely grim for both the sufferer and the family, often leading to a difficult mourning for the survivors who have witnessed so much suffering. On the other hand she feels some people *are* ennobled by death, even a difficult death, the victims more than the families; and some children seem to mature more quickly when faced with life-threatening illness.

Kübler-Ross uses the imagery of a cocoon and a butterfly: the child's ill body is like a cocoon, or chrysalis, and soon he will leave it behind, becoming the butterfly he always was, and go on. I explore children's attitudes more fully in the following two chapters.

Chapter Two
Children's attitudes to death

Every parting gives a foretaste of death . . .

Schopenhauer (1788–1860)

Healthy children are rather better at death than healthy adults.

D.W. Winnicott (1963, p. 62)

Freud (1915a) wrote that 'death was the necessary outcome of life, that everyone owes nature a death... in short, that death was natural, undeniable, and unavoidable'. He continued, though, to state that in practice it is otherwise – that in men there is:

> an unmistakable tendency to put death on one side, to eliminate it from life... the civilized man will carefully avoid speaking of such a possibility in the hearing of the person under sentence. *Children alone disregard this restriction; they unashamedly threaten one another with the possibility of dying. . . .*

Freud (1915a, p. 289; my italics)

The denial of death may be more generally understood through Freud's explanation that negation may be a stage in the process towards allowing a painful idea to be consciously accepted.

As with other concepts such as birth and sex, death is an aspect of the child's world about which he has many conscious and unconscious fantasies and anxieties. These fantasies and anxieties tend to go more 'underground' as the child grows older and is more exposed to society's mores and inhibitions, and as the child's emotionally charged early years often settle into a more taciturn relationship with his parents. Thus, a dialogue about death is probably more difficult for the adult than for the young child.

This is not to say that a young child has an uncomplicated acceptance of the concept of death which only becomes inhibited through exposure

17

to adults' anxieties. While it seems that generally children's understanding of death is not helped by adults' fears and inhibitions, the young child has many difficulties in his own right in understanding death. However, children feel themselves to be immortal in some respects: in the ways some children take physical risks and need adults to restrain them, and in the difficulty that young children have, for example, in negotiating the concept of the irrevocability of death (see p. 21).

If we try to follow the development of the child's negotiation of death, we can begin by finding much evidence in psychoanalytic studies, in infant observations, and in the uncovering of infantile layers of the personality of adults in psychoanalysis, that the young infant registers the possibility of death through a sense of the danger of death. It is a common observation that newborn babies cry if hungry or cold, or if they feel unsafe, as a way of signalling for help and avoiding death. Death, to the infant, might be an inchoate 'nameless dread' (Bion, 1984, p. 116); a primitive fear of disintegrating, of falling forever (Winnicott, 1962, p. 58). Earlier, Rank (1929) wrote about separation anxiety as being the primal human problem, equating it with a fear of death. Therefore one could say that in the infant there is a primitive awareness of death as part of a survival pattern, and that fear of separation and loss is, in origin, a fear of being totally abandoned and hence of being left to die. George Eliot wrote (1857), 'In every parting there is an image of death' (*Scenes of Clerical Life*).

Theories as to whether fear of death is a secondary phenomenon, arising from an environmental situation, or whether it is innate, are expounded in a variety of ways, making it difficult to 'take sides'. On the one hand, Winnicott (1962) describes the infant as being 'all the time on the brink of unthinkable anxiety' (p. 57), as a result of the immature ego experiencing a less-than-perfect environment. He writes, 'Death, for an infant at the beginning, means something quite definite, namely loss of being on account of prolonged reaction to environmental impingement (failure of good enough adaptation)' (1954, p. 134).

Bowlby (1960) has written extensively on older infants' and young children's reactions to the unavailability – beyond a tolerable length of time – of the mother or mother figure. He calls this reaction – from six months onwards – 'grief and mourning', and describes, drawing upon Robertson (1952), states of fear, despair, and distress in young children. He concludes that this response to separation is as a result of the young child's inability to distinguish between temporary absence and a permanent loss. Therefore, the infant feels that mother is lost, or dead.

In contrast to these environmentalist views of an awareness of death as a secondary phenomenon, Klein explains the fear of death as arising out of the infant's paranoid fear of being killed by his own projected aggression. Segal, writing about Klein's theories, states 'The immature ego of the infant is exposed from birth to the anxiety stirred up by the *inborn polarity* of the instincts – the immediate conflict between the life and the death instinct' (1973, p. 25; my italics). This polarity between the two forces or instincts leads to a dynamic interaction that Klein implies is as much a part of adults' mental processes as that of infants (1949, p. 211).

In both views, however, it seems that the baby is forced to come up against the feeling that no *good* experience can last for ever, and that this then leads to a need to negotiate a fear of something else – whether we call it a fear of death, or annihilation, or disintegration, or a state of 'not-being', or, simply, of not feeling safe.

Yet, Freud, in the quotation at the beginning of this chapter, states that children have little fear of death. Although children do seem more obviously able to talk about the subject than adults, and to deal with it in their play, it does not seem correct to deduce that they lack fear. There may not be an *apparent* fear of death, but fear of separation and loss, and thence, ultimately, of death, is a commonplace part of childhood as a survival mechanism, as well as an expression of primitive infantile anxieties, as I have explained. The use of omnipotence as a denial of vulnerability may be more apparent than fear.

If a child is confronted by an actual death, or an impending death, at close range – the death of an important family member, a loved family pet, or their own terminal illness – their understanding of death is, in a sense, enhanced considerably. They are forced into a premature grappling with the subject. This is borne out by research by Reilly *et al.* (1983). Therefore, in understanding children's concepts of death, there appear to be two rather different developmental time scales: the child with actual experience usually having a more developed-for-their-age understanding or a more developed defensive system than peers who have not been exposed in this way. This seems especially true in children over the age of 6 years (Kane, 1979).

However, this is complicated by the fact that children confronting death at close range may use denial, which then overrides any intellectual understanding they may have. For example, healthy 5-year-olds in a study (Candy-Gibbs *et al.*, 1984–1985) were most likely to use denial when they were asked about their own possible death or that of close others. It seems from this research that the child (of this age group) refuses to verbalize that which is most painful, either because they feel that the implied separation is unbearable, or because the child may think concretely that to name the possibility they will make it come true. This research does not consider children's destructive or murderous fantasies towards important people in their lives, which would also influence what they felt they were allowed to say.

In first considering the child's non-catastrophic encounters with the idea of death, there appears to be a lack of published research on the reactions of under 3-year-olds. This lack may be as a result of very young children being less verbally fluent and therefore less able to be interviewed on the subject. Another explanation is that few young children enter into psychotherapeutic treatment and therefore less has been discovered in this way; or, as I have suggested earlier, adults try to protect particularly young children from thinking about death because of their own anxieties.

Much of the research has delineated a recognizable first stage, in children of approximately 3–5 years of age, wherein the most striking feature is the denial of death as being *irrevocable* and *universal* (Nagy, 1959; Anthony, 1973; Furman, 1974; Orbach *et al.*, 1985). Kane (1979) gives a very clear and useful summary of children's concepts of death. She found that the existing literature regarding the effects of the experience of death on the child was contradictory and specifically disagreed with the findings of Nagy, who argued that the concept of death was inevitably understood by children by the age of 9 years. Kane, on the other hand, found that an awareness of death was frequently seen in children aged 6 years or more. A minimum requirement for a child to be included in Kane's study was a basic understanding of the concept of death: this awareness was ascertained by all the children being shown nine specially produced pictures of rabbits. (The children were aged between 3 and 12 years.) One rabbit was dead and one sleeping. If the child did not choose the dead or sleeping rabbit, he was not included in the study. Perhaps this is both a strength and a limitation of the research: it is clearly a way of focusing on only those children with a conscious intellectual grasp of the primary concept, but it rules out those children who have an emotional block of 'knowing' about death. Therefore, Kane's findings of the universality of death awareness by specific ages is not necessarily truly widespread as it is only about children without that emotional inhibition. Moreover, she herself acknowledges that some of her findings may be influenced by the sample in the study being limited to a specific slice of the population: white and middle class. I feel that this is indeed a very significant limitation to the research.

Ten components (later reduced to nine), or aspects, of death were ascertained by Kane in the children's responses, including irrevocability, dysfunctionality, separation, immobility, appearance, etc. Kane's conclusions are of basic stages. Young children aged 3–5 all have a basic *realization* of death, of the implicit *separation*, as well as of the *immobility* of the dead, although the immobility may be seen as partial. They tend to see 'dead' as being in a particular position: if you got into the position, you die; you could also make someone die by magical thinking or by the behaviour or wishes of others. The dysfunctionality of death is expressed as lying down immobile, with closed eyes.

Children a little older move from stage one to stage two thinking, where they add function to a structural description of death. Now they see death as an explanation for dysfunction: death induces dysfunction.

This stage is marked by reality and the beginnings of logical thought, with further development of *realization, separation, immobility*, and the inclusion of the six remaining components: *irrevocability, causality, dysfunctionality, universality, insensitivity*, and *appearance*. However, they do not always realize that the components are interrelated: initially they believe that death is externally caused, later that it could be internally caused. They realize only the most obvious dysfunctions: those of not being able to eat or speak; as they grow older, they realize that the dead cannot drink or hear. Then, as they grow older still, they evolve from realizing that dead people cannot feel cold, or smell flowers, to the more subtle dysfunction of not being able to dream or know they are dead.

Once they can interrelate the components they could be judged to have moved to stage three (at about the age of 7 onwards), when they are able to think of death in the abstract. Although their thinking is logical and recognizes reality, they can speculate rather freely. Some can consider the existential issues of life and death. This stage indicates that they conceive of death as a state of internally caused dysfunctionality; death is a definition, of which *dysfunctionality, inactivity*, and *insensitivity* are the conditions, i.e. responsiveness is not just a characteristic of life, but a requirement of life. The alteration in the *appearance* of the dead is the last and most difficult concept for them to grasp; it is only by the age of 12 years that they have a consistent notion of altered appearance: that the dead person cannot, or does not, look as though he were alive, or, on the contrary, that he may look the same.

Kane concludes by stating that her findings relate to the Piagetian three stages, 'pre-operational', 'concrete operations', and 'formal operations'. Her children first showed pre-operational thinking: they were tied to that which they could perceive, and could consider only one aspect of the situation at a time. Then they moved on to stage two, where they indicated 'concrete operations' thinking: they could consider two aspects of the situation as existing at the same time and possibly influencing each other. Then, in stage three, the children showed 'formal operations' thinking: they could conjecture, think abstractly, be logical, and consider three different aspects of the situation.

Her findings differed from Nagy's in ways other than the age at which children consistently see death as an inevitable life event. She found that the children in her study did not reify death – that is, convert the person into something material. The younger children, however, may have visualized death in some form, and she speculates that perhaps the magical thinking of younger children could have inhibited them, for to name 'death' could bring it about.

Most of the published research on children's ideas about death and dying is based on interviews. The limitations of this technique have been pointed out by Wenestam (1982): children may say things that are undigested quotations from adults. Therefore, Wenestam quotes Weininger (1979) who studied the ways 60 children played with dolls that were supposed to be seriously ill or dead. His findings confirmed some of the more obvious earlier research findings: that the accuracy of the way children understood concepts of death and dying increased with age. However, an important new finding was that there were inconsistencies between the way children expressed themselves verbally and the content of their play. The play sometimes indicated a more developed understanding than was found in their answers. It is not until the age of approximately 9 years that the content of the play and the verbally expressed concepts are more compatible.

The research carried out by Wenestam, on the depiction of death in children's drawings, concludes that the socio-cultural environment (children's books, television, comics, plus the ways in which parents and teachers talk to children about death or, more usually, avoid the subject) influences children's thinking, especially up to about the age of 9 years. The violence frequently depicted as a cause of death leads to a negative and fearful association, he asserts. Then, children in his middle age range sample (average 12 and three-quarter years) show a belief in a spiritual life. By this age, they have been exposed to 5 or 6 years of socio-cultural expectations, assertions, beliefs, and values. Wenestam suggests that while adults may tolerate divergent thinking in young children, a child over 12 years may well be subject to criticism and correction when stating his view of the world. Thus, there are 'rules' as to how the child should think, and these become more convergent as the child grows up.

Of course, this then leads to a new generation of adults whose views of life and death have been determined largely by socio-cultural expectations, and who will in turn find it difficult to talk to children about death in a way that is open to the child's feelings.

Not surprisingly, children's cultural and religious backgrounds are shown to influence their ideas. For example, these influences on the irreversibility of death are shown in a study by Candy-Gibbs et al., 1984–1985. This showed that children from southern Baptist homes in the USA reflected their exposure to the 'traditional' Protestant belief in life-after-death, whereas children from northern Unitarian homes conveyed their belief that death was the irreversible cessation of bodily functioning.

It appears that children living in politically unstable environments acquire an advanced concept of death – e.g. children in Northern Ireland (McWhirter et al., 1983) or Jewish children in Israel (Florian and Kravetz, 1985). The distinction is made in the latter study of Jewish children because it appears that ethnic minority groups there – Muslims, Druze, and Christians – lack the educational background that facilitates the early attainment of a scientific concept of death. This difference would include the differing influences of modern versus traditional societies.

A closer look at Muslim girls' understanding of death (Anthony and Bhana, 1989–1990) shows that both younger and older children spoke of God as all-powerful and providing pleasure in heaven. Cultural and religious influences lead to their belief that the dead come to life again under certain circumstances. Although this seems to lead to explicit beliefs that make it easier to think about death, as the children get older their anxieties increase as they become aware of the difficulties in meeting the expectations and requirements of leading a good Muslim life. Other research (Mahabeer, 1980) cited in the foregoing, reports that Muslim young adults showed the greatest anxiety about death, compared with Christian and Hindu young adults. The author surmises that this arises out of the exacting nature of the Koran requirements.

A conclusion drawn by Orbach *et al.* (1985) is that, while in some children distortions of the concept of death reflect a lack of knowledge and cognition, in others they reflect a defensive process – usually a high level of anxiety. Therefore, children's progressive understanding of the meaning of death is not simply linear or accumulative, but relates to experiential and emotional factors. The authors suggest that children's understanding of the death of humans is generally more advanced than their understanding of the death of animals. This is either because they have experienced the death of a pet and not of a close adult, and they may then erect more defences against death in animals because they can relate emotionally and identify with animals more readily than people, or because their cognitive development is as yet unable to apply what they understand specifically to a broader conceptual framework.

My own daughter, when aged just over 3 years, asked, 'Does coffee die when it spills on the floor?' She was clearly grappling with the concept of that which undergoes a drastic physical change, can no longer be useful in its intended way, and eventually is lost, and was questioning whether inanimate objects too can die.

A 4-year-old child (who was not physically ill) said to me in a psychotherapy session:

> 'If I put Sellotape over your mouth and your nose, would you die?' She became rather anxious, and continued, 'I saw a bird that was dead. My cat had chopped its neck. Mummy put it in the rubbish bin.' She paused, then continued reflectively, 'When creatures die, they go away and never come back. My cat died. But then it went to hospital to be maked better. I did not want it to die. It's still away. It hasn't come back yet.'

This child is struggling with the concept of the irrevocability of death: dead creatures 'never come back', she says, yet, a few seconds later, she

hopes that her dead cat will be made better in hospital, and might
return. It appears that as she has a *relationship* with the cat it is clearly
more painful to acknowledge the full implications of its loss, while the
dead bird, with whom she presumably did not have a particular relationship, she can logically assign to death and the rubbish bin. She also
recognizes the bird's altered appearance as being connected with its
death.

This same child often returned to the theme of death, perhaps as a
result of many traumatic losses she had sustained. These are some of her
musings: 'When you die, you don't get better . . . You get buried . . . What
is the colour of this "buried"?' On another occasion, she initiated a game
wherein she was 'buried'. I asked her how she got buried. She replied
'Under leaves, of course!' This would be a familiar and ordinary explanation for her, unlike the strange world of coffins and graves.

Later she told me, 'When you get buried you go in one of those red
round things that are poisonous and which can kill you if you eat them.'
She was clearly confused between 'berry' and 'bury'. Her reasons for this
confusion were not simply a cognitive problem, but were linked with
her actual loss of her mother and foster mother. This rich material
certainly provided the opportunity for further detailed analysis of her
many confusions and fantasies about death, including the causative
factors, and the part her own oral aggression played in these fantasies. In
this fantasy, she is both inside the dreaded poisonous berry while having
it inside her, leading one to speculate about the pervasively persecuting
nature of her fantasy world.

A 5-year-old pithily summarized his view of death to me, thus: 'If you
die, you never see your mum again.'

The writer, John Berger (1988, pp. 36–7) reflects on a child's view of
death: 'From the age of five or six I was worried about the death of my
parents. The inevitability of death was one of the first things I learnt
about the world on my own. Nobody ever spoke of it yet the signs were
so clear.' His understanding of his fear of death conveys a deep-seated,
almost archetypal fear:

> Every time I went to bed – and in this I am sure I was like millions
> of other children – the fear that one or both my parents might die
> in the night touched the nape of my neck with its finger. Such a
> fear has, I believe, little to do with a particular psychological
> climate and a great deal to do with nightfall.

He continues to describe his seeking reassurance through the invention
of a euphemism, 'See you in the morning', instead of asking the real
question. It seems that fundamental to his fear of his parents' death was
the fear of his own death for, if the parents die, the infant feels he would
be left to die.

When asked simply what he thought about death, a bright 8-and-a-half-year-old boy said, 'It's saddest if somebody that you know well in your family died – then it would be sad, because you knew them the best. They wouldn't have had much of their life and it wouldn't be fair on them. If an older person dies, it's not so bad, because they're none the wiser – but they're still missing out on things.' When asked what happens after they die, he replied very seriously, 'They get buried. Some people get burnt and sprinkled on flowers. And they dissolve and their bones rot and they fall to bits and they help flowers to grow.'

This particular child's only direct personal encounter with bereavement had been the death of a grandfather four years previously and the recent death of a friend's baby brother. It seems that he is able to embrace many aspects of death in this spontaneous statement, including its irrevocability; the sense of loss for both the bereaved and the person who died, as well as loss being related to attachment – that is, to whom you 'knew the best'; the difference between the death of a child and that of an older person; the truly dead state of the person who dies and therefore cannot feel that he is missing out on life; and, last but not least, a grasp of the life cycle.

Piaget's (1951) research adds an interesting dimension, when he states that the child is, early on in his intellectual development, looking for causes or motives behind every event, including death. The lack of adequate explanations from the adults in the child's life then leads the child to the conception of physical causation, such as 'killed' or 'murdered', unless the child is given theological explanations. This view is compatible, in a sense, with Klein's formulation of the working of the death instinct within the infant: 'from the beginning of post-natal life . . . destructive impulses against the object stir up fear of retaliation' (1952, p.48). In 1937 she wrote: 'A most important feature of these destructive fantasies, which are tantamount to death-wishes, is that the baby . . . feels that he *has really destroyed* the object of his destructive impulses' (p. 308). Using Klein's psychoanalytic insight into infants, one might add to Piaget's ideas above: that the child feels or fears that his own aggression has killed or murdered the dead person (or causes an absent person to cease to exist). The capacity of the child to feel guilt and concern would play a part in the outcome of these processes.

It would seem that there is in fact a contradiction between, on the one hand, the research that firmly states that children under 5 years of age do not view death as irreversible and final, and therefore have no real concept of death, and, on the other hand, the psychoanalytic findings of Freud, Klein, and Winnicott (on the role of the death instinct from birth or its inception soon afterwards), and those of Bowlby (on the child's devastation at the separation from and loss of his primary caretaker).

The available research is largely based on empirically testable data, equating the child's ability to 'understand death' with the ability to explain its meaning, and showing that in the absence of this concept there cannot be a fear of death (for example, Richmond and Waisman, 1955). This unfortunately does not always do justice to the complex topic of death, where accompanying feelings of sadness, anxiety, and a sense of loss cannot easily be measured. The language of science, describing observable data, is inadequate to describe the psychic development of the child, whether in the sphere of normal emotional development or specifically in relation to the subject of responses to death. Therefore, the mystery of the inner world and some of the child's inchoate responses can only be partly explored through questionnaires, psychological tests, and interviews. The scientist attempts to be objective, while a psychoanalytic view of infants (including their responses to death) would include some reliance on a particular kind of subjectivity. This attempt on the part of the psychoanalytic psychotherapist or researcher to look inward as well as outward is based primarily on training in infant observation where much that appears unintelligible may, in time, come to form some pattern in the mind: where there is an attempt not to form preconceptions. As Klein often stated, the infant, from the start, is involved in an intense personal relationship both with the outside world *and with his inner world*. Therefore, we, as researchers, observers, or authors, have to be aware of our subtle interaction with the subject, of our countertransference, even if at a relative distance.

We need to follow the *child's* development of an inner world and concepts in conjunction with those of their environment. Therein we can see that the young infant's reaction to loss, separation, and death is 'lost and gone for ever', and that a more sophisticated construct then develops which says that it is lost but perhaps not gone for ever. Although in this development there is a corollary with adults' use of denial, this development in relation to separation and death arises mainly out of the non-deprived child's developing capacity to *internalize the absent object*, and thus, by holding on to it mentally and emotionally, the then 'internal object', or archaic imago, is sustained in a lively way with the promise of its return. (A severely deprived child may have experienced more loss, trauma, fear, and impotence than can enable him to sustain hopefulness and a 'good enough' internal mother.)

In conclusion, therefore, the child's capacity to sustain temporary separation and loss leads to its capacity to conjure up similar hopefulness in the face of the impending or actual death of a loved one, or in experiencing traumatic separation (i.e. longer than the child's optimism can sustain). Of course the child's optimism can be truly tested and may be devastated by an encounter with an actual major loss. The child may then have to begin the complex process of mourning, as well as the painful work of rekindling or repairing the hope that may have been dashed by an early bereavement.

As I have implied, intimately bound up with the child's capacity to hold on to the absent loved one in a way that is hopeful and creative is a complex defensive structure, which uses mechanisms of denial. The task then seems to be for the developing child to integrate the fact of death, as a natural biological event in the outside world, with his own internal constructs, including that of denial, which is often fuelled by parental messages – perhaps unspoken – that talking about death is not part of the social repertoire.

Denial is a useful way of avoiding the accompanying deeply disturbing effects of being confronted by the cessation of function – for this is an aspect of death of which a young child is aware. Young children are able to grasp the difference between animate and inanimate. A 4-year-old child told me that she knew a bird was dead because it was not flying or moving its beak. Therefore, it is hardly surprising that defences quickly emerge in the form of fantasies of the possible return to life of the loved one, and so on. Although the form and substance of these fantasies are largely fed by adults' interventions, the child himself, quick to equate the death of another with his own possible death, needs to employ a range of defences. As well as the aforementioned denial, or avoidance, this could include displacement of anxiety on to some other area: obsessional ritualized behaviour as a way of attempting to ward off a recurrence or to placate, or phobias, as well as the use of cultural and religious stories and myths to explain the disappearance. Unspoken dread may be manifest in, for example, nightmares, dreams, night fears, a displacement onto fears of certain objects or people, bodily products, sounds, shapes, certain foods, or certain animals. The inevitable persecution that the child suffers at the hands of the 'bad objects' can be understood as a fear of retaliation for his projected aggression and anxiety.

Children and adults pay a heavy price in their deep repression of thoughts about death – for, as I have explained, it then becomes extensively symbolized, or persecutory. Although adults and children alike can live daily with a generally not unrealistic view that their own death is not imminent, the concept of 'not-being' is nevertheless as much a part of everyday life as 'being' or living. It is in this area that our children may be helped by adults' awareness of this duality.

I would agree with Janssen's findings (1983), which tie in with those of Wenestam, when she hypothesizes that the children categorized as having a defensive organization in their knowledge of death may have passed through a phase of discovery of death, with the difficult feelings that accompany it. Then, as their fantasies develop, there is a need for a more rigid stance in relation to death, partly as a result of adults' inhibitions. This seems much like a child's sexual development – as expressed in play and fantasies – which is turbulent, manifest, and florid in the early years, but then goes 'underground' during latency; much the same often happens with a child's creative output, as expressed in drawings. Thus one can deduce that a child's sometimes more withdrawn stance in relation to death during latency arises from the general quietening down of his emotional life through a greater use of defence mechanisms.

Tests carried out by Alexander and Alderstein (1958) bear this out. They assessed children's GSR (galvanic skin response)* as they listened to words about death. They discovered that the youngest group (aged 5–8 years) and the oldest (aged 13–16 years) gave the most emotional response, while the middle group (aged 9–12 years) responded with practically no anxiety. This probably reflects the emotional turbulence of the early and late stages of childhood, while the middle age group uses defences that lead to greater calm in the face of death.

Rochlin (1959, 1967) has carried out interesting studies of the emotional forces that influence children's attitudes to death. He clearly believes that children know about death as the extinction of all life from a very early age, but that they then utilize a range of defences in order to avoid the full implications of this awareness. As their cognitive development is not yet mature, they can more easily not only deny the meanings of death, but oscillate towards and away from a proper understanding almost from moment to moment. Thus, as Orbach (1988) summarizes, they 'reflect the duality of knowing and denying the existence of death'.

This shifting understanding is often a part of adults' behaviour, too, depending on their circumstances, situation, and emotional state, as I tried to explain in Chapter 1.

Therefore, if we come full circle, to Freud's view – quoted at the beginning of this chapter – that children, unlike adults, are in touch with the implications of death, but use defences of omnipotence, denial, and magical thinking, we can see that some of the more recent research, 80 years later, is basically compatible with his findings. I would add that the child's increased independence and ability to feel that there is a helping network beyond his prime caretaker contributes to the lessening of a primitive fear of death. In fact, the child's means of survival widens, as he physically and emotionally masters his environment – walking, talking, etc. – and in that sense he is realistically further from death.

---

*A change in the electrical resistance of the skin, related to sweating. It can be produced by a tiny electrical current and is useful as an indicator of an unconditional, autonomic response to emotion or anxiety.

Chapter Three
The dying child's
awareness of death

The wonderful thing about children is that they tend to want to get better however ill they are.

Professor Lewis Spitz (1988)

In the unconscious, there is no such concept as 'health'. There is, however, a concept of 'death', and, in our constant attempt to keep this anxiety repressed, we use various unconscious defensive mechanisms, including the creation of social systems to serve the defensive function. Indeed, our health service might more accurately be called a 'keep-death-at-bay' service.

Anton Obholzer (1994)

Bearing in mind the non-dying child's awareness of death, I shall now survey the literature on the reactions of a child with a life-threatening illness, facing his own impending death.

Early studies (i.e. pre-1962) acknowledged that only children over 6 years of age revealed anxiety or apprehension relating to their impending death (Natterson and Knudson, 1960). They concluded that the child under 6 is most concerned about separation, while the child aged 6–10 years is more fearful of physical injury and mutilation. Most studies were based on overt expressions concerning impending death. The problem when analysing these findings is that they reveal the same anxieties generally found in hospitalized children. Therefore, they fail to distinguish the specific effects of fatal illness on a child.

More recent research (Howell, 1967; Yudkin, 1967; Debuskey, 1970; Sigler, 1970; Spinetta, 1974) does manage to take into account the psychological reactions of children specifically related to the fact of having a fatal illness. Their findings conclude that the older child with a fatal prognosis can be aware of, and apprehensive about, his impending death. The authors agree with earlier research in that they state that for the fatally ill under 5-year-old, a fear of separation is the main symptom.

However, in the middle age group (6–10 years), the writers tend to base their observations on parents' and professionals' observations, rather than on direct data from the child. They feel that if the adult does not discuss the issue of the potentially fatal illness with the child, the child does not experience anxiety. Once again, one can see the mechanisms of denial operating in the researchers, as well as in the reported observations of parents and staff.

However, a number of researchers do conclude that, if not aware at a conceptual level, children are at least aware that something serious is happening to their bodies. Perhaps the most useful approach can be found in a book edited by Anthony and Koupernik (1973). In this volume, Vernick states that 'blows cannot always be softened' and exposes the lack of progress in this field of communicating meaningfully with the fatally ill child. Natterson (in the same volume) further defines the subtle approach needed when he states that 'the psychotherapist trades in life, not death', and concludes that 'working with fatally ill patients and their intimates is not helping them accept death but groping with them to find a way to live with meaning in the shadow of death.'

When discussing the final stage of a child's life, before death, Vernick observes that the patient is often very weak, sometimes devoid of feelings, and oblivious. Natterson and Vernick erroneously interpret Kübler-Ross as defining this state as 'acceptance' and therefore a potentially happy phase. Indeed, Kübler-Ross specifically states: 'Acceptance should not be mistaken for a happy stage. It is almost void of feelings' (1970, p. 100). And yet there is another problem: a seeming contradiction of terminology. 'Acceptance' here is defined as a rather numb state, whereas I would have thought that in this context 'acceptance' would mean some ability to feel a sense of loss, to grieve, and perhaps to let go. It would seem, then, that there is a difficulty in interpreting a child's weakened state, as the child is often uncommunicative. This could be a defence against a full awareness. The child would thus be particularly susceptible to the projections of those people who are involved with him, including researchers.

However, alongside a recognition of the reality of an impending death, there is a need to keep in touch with hope and hopefulness. Kübler-Ross expresses this aspect thus: 'It is this glimpse of hope which maintains them through days, weeks or months of suffering . . . In a sense it is a rationalization for their suffering at times; for others it remains a form of temporary but needed denial' (1970, p. 123). It is exactly this duality that is extremely difficult to sustain, and links with my comments in Chapter 1 about the difficulty in keeping an awareness of life and death concurrently. As with Escher's (1961) graphic images of optical illusions: how hard it is to 'read' both interpretations of his dual-meaning stairways that can also be convoluted ceilings. In fact, the psychological impossibility of 'seeing' both simultaneously is an analogy for the oscillation between hope and acceptance, or hope and despair. They cannot really be felt simultaneously.

Following the rather complex path of researchers into children's awareness of death is rather like following Freud's theories of infantile sexuality. Not only did Freud have to be open enough to what he could observe in his consulting room, but society at large had to be able to receive his findings. Similarly, with the trauma of a child facing his own death, the subjects' families, carers, researchers, as well as society at large, unwittingly limit their capacity to care and understand through their own inhibitions. Their main preconception seems to be that they do not want to frighten children, especially young children, and put ideas into their heads, by talking about death, or, indeed by really listening to *their* ideas about death.

It was not until the work of Waechter (1968, 1971) that studies emerged which showed the probability of fatally ill children aged 6–10 years being able to express an awareness of their condition directly. In a study by Spinetta *et al.* (1973), the authors conclude that

> . . . fatally ill children show significantly greater awareness of their hospital experience than chronically ill children. The leukaemic children . . . showed more preoccupation with threat to and intrusion into their bodies and interference with their body functioning than did the chronically ill children . . . The children with fatal illness also expressed more hospital-related and non-hospital-related anxiety than did the chronically ill children.
>
> (pp. 841–5)

This significant difference between the level of anxiety, present from the first admission to hospital, between the fatally ill and chronically ill, tells us that despite the parents of the leukaemic children maintaining that their child did not know that his illness was fatal, the fatally ill child's level of anxiety is markedly higher. The chronically ill child in this research study generally received the same number and duration of hospital treatments. Therefore, despite attempts to protect the fatally ill child from his prognosis, he nevertheless picks up a sense of the seriousness of his illness.

This research was able to discern the more subtle expressions of a death anxiety in the 6–10-year-olds, even though they were not always overt. Just as research into the physically well child's concept of death did not take adequate account of the inevitable denial and defences in many children, so the pre-1968 research into this area of the fatally ill child has relied too heavily on that which is easily observed and recorded or talked about in adult terms, and therefore has not necessarily tapped the actual anxieties and concerns.

A slightly later study (Spinetta, 1975) shows that awareness of their illness seems to persist with fatally ill children, even when they are not in hospital. As with the fatally ill hospitalized children in previous studies, this 1975 study indicates that the fatally ill out-patient children conveyed significantly more preoccupation with the threat to their body integrity and functioning than did a control group of children with chronic illness. Not only did they express greater anxiety, but the leukaemic children exhibited a lack of adaptability to the necessity of clinic visits, becoming increasingly anxious about the clinic both as visits became more frequent and as their illness became more protracted.

One of the means of testing that the researchers used was a projective test of a three-dimensional replica of a hospital room, as an analysis of interpersonal distancing. The authors found that the fatally ill hospitalized children repeatedly placed the four little dolls (of a nurse, doctor, father and mother) at significantly greater distances from each other than did the children in the matched control group of chronically ill children (Spinetta *et al.*, 1974). This distance increased with further hospitalizations. The authors inferred that this physical positioning and distancing of the figures by the fatally ill children reflected a growing sense of psychological separation and isolation of the dying child from the hospital and from the significant adults in his life.

In order to extract, then, how much of this distancing was hospital related, further tests were carried out, and the authors concluded that the fatally ill hospitalized children showed a greater sense of isolation than leukaemic children in remission. They also discovered that as the leukaemic child becomes older, his anxiety towards the clinic or hospital increases. Frequency of visits in the chronically ill led to a lessening of anxiety, while the opposite was true for the leukaemic children. Similarly, with the chronically ill, as the illness's duration increased, so their anxiety lessened, while with the leukaemic children the longer the duration, the higher the anxiety. The child is therefore aware that this is no ordinary illness. Even in remission, the leukaemic child is not able to live a normal life, free from concerns about the illness. An important aspect to this anxiety could be that the child is picking up parental anxiety.

This research is developed in a small study of leukaemic children, using drawings and structured interviews, by Clunies-Ross and Lansdown (1988), which reveals that they feel isolated, have lower self-esteem and poorer communication within the family when they are in hospital. Therefore despite efforts for these children to be with someone for much of the time, they still appear to feel psychologically isolated. It is not clear from this research whether this is a product of being in hospital, or of having a life-threatening illness, or both.

I have been told about a 4-year-old with cystic fibrosis, who apparently conveyed a remarkable grasp of her own impending death. Just before she died she was given a gas balloon, and her questions about this clearly conveyed her wondering about her death: 'What will happen to my balloon when there's no more air in it? Can you buy a new one?'

In considering the hospitalized dying child's awareness of death, an important matter that appears to focus the child's awareness more sharply is, not surprisingly, the death of another child on the ward. If the child who has died has the same illness, of course the link between that event and the dying child's imminent death is made more immediate. Fortunately nowadays there is a more open and truthful attitude on children's wards in most hospitals, where the event is often discussed openly in response to parents' questions, and sometimes with children, depending on the ethos of the unit.

This is not always the case, however. Some hospitals have not altered much since this account by a consultant paediatrician, Yudkin, of the approach to a death of a child on the ward, nearly 30 years ago:

> Our present method of dealing with the solemn situation that arises when a child dies in a children's ward is both ugly and obscene. There is a whispering and a scuffling behind the screens, a furtive moving of white covered trolleys in and out of the ward, usually during the night. Nurses and doctors are preoccupied and don't answer questions and are unduly irritable. Above all, there is a stupid pretence that nothing at all unusual is happening . . . But do we really think that the 'secret' is not known to every child on the ward?
>
> (1967, p. 40)

Yudkin writes that this furtive behaviour is an affront to children's intelligence and instead of helping them to regard death as a 'very sad but solemn and dignified event', characterizes death as something fearful and secretive, and deprives the child of the opportunity to talk about his fears.

Richard Lansdown (1987) of the Great Ormond Street Hospital for Sick Children, London, has summarized the stages of understanding his own death that a dying child goes through:

I am very sick
I have an illness that can kill people
I have an illness that can kill children
I may not get better
I am dying

However, the child's age, anxiety level, cognitive development, and environment would of course influence the course of that understanding. For a child under 3 years of age, the 'I am dying' concept would probably not embody a real understanding of dying, with its irrevocability, but there may be a feeling of not understanding what is happening to his body and an anxiety about this unpleasant state of being unwell separating him from his parents. In order to complete the picture of what the child may mean by 'dying' we need to understand further what is happening 'on the surface' as it were, to the body, and the attendant fantasies, in order to fully understand the causes of the fear of dying. In other words, we need to excavate the more accessible layers of the psyche before we can reach and comprehend the sub-strata.

As I explain more fully in the following chapter, the child with leukaemia feels unwell and fragile, picks up adults' anxieties and hears medical terminology more usually associated with aggressive warfare (such as 'kill', 'attack', 'wipe out', 'invade') in relation to his illness. The phantasies in the unconscious must surely abound with extreme feelings of persecution from some unseen omnipresent source, attacking the very marrow of his bones and the vitality of his blood. The Bible states succinctly, 'The blood is the life' (Deuteronomy 12: 23). In psychological terms, no illness can be more central to one's being than leukaemia, except, perhaps, heart, or lung, or brain disease. An aspect of the treatment of bone marrow transplants involves processing and freezing some of the patient's bone marrow – for possible future use – and carries echoes of Shakespeare's description of utter horror 'Would harrow up thy soul; freeze thy young blood' (*Hamlet*).

The inevitable blood tests at different stages of the illness, as well as the insertion of the central venous catheter (Hickman line, see p. 101), penetrate the skin surface. Psychologically, the skin gives the body an essential sense of being intact, of being held together (Bick, 1967), as well as being our first line of defence, psychically as well as physically, against injury and infection. The skin acts as a boundary between the me and the not-me in favourable circumstances (Winnicott, 1962). It is of course also able to receive pleasurable sensations from the touch of others and of ourselves. Yet it is repeatedly violated by the treatment, as well as perceived as having failed in being part of an effective immune system to keep out germs/poison/bad things, depending on the fantasy. Of course much depends on the child's age and maturity in understanding the necessity for treatment. (Further aspects of the *meaning* of illness for the child are described at the beginning of Chapter 5.)

Moreover, the adults in the child's life appear to the child to have failed in their protective function. Just as their own bodies (the skin, the blood, the marrow) are failing, so are the parents, in the sense that they are allowing and facilitating the treatment. This dichotomy for parents, between supporting the child's emotional state and pursuing medical treatment, exists in many types of illness. However, when there is indeed a life and death struggle, the parents may become more adamant, determined and rigid, and more detached from the child's feelings, in order to allow unpleasant treatments to be carried out. Some parents purposely absent themselves when the child is undergoing very unpleasant procedures, in order to be able to be perceived afresh by the child as a comforter and not a perpetrator. Or they absent themselves because they find it all too painful. In a way, though, it is a dilemma whatever course of action is chosen, for the parent who thoughtfully absents him- or herself or does not help to hold down a protesting child has still 'failed' the child in the child's eyes in the sense of not preventing the 'assault' or simply by not being there.

I have found that young children usefully use 'splitting' in these situations: the selfsame mother can be perceived as a 'witch' mother when she is part of the treatment team and a good mother at other times. This mechanism helps the child to feel that there is a protective, helpful mother (or father) who is not contaminated by the other 'bad' one. The older child has, in a way, the more emotionally challenging and painful task of integrating the two aspects of the one parent, but may still usefully engage splitting or projection in other ways: for example, by perceiving a particular doctor or some other person as all bad, thus again finding a receptacle for much of his anger and aggression.

The fundamental anxiety, then, underlying the foregoing phantasies and ways of coping with them, is a fear of being annihilated and therefore of dying. A 5-year-old boy who was about to undergo a tonsillectomy declared without hesitation that 'of course they cut your head off to get at the tonsils'. He then briefly muttered, 'And then you die', before adamantly changing the subject. This dramatic fantasy around surgical intervention is not all that unusual: the child can very easily feel in danger of being killed. Of course in this example the child's condition or treatment is almost certainly not life-threatening. Nevertheless it arouses similar anxieties to those that are and, as we see from the research quoted above, the persistence, degree, and progress of the anxieties

Six suns and a slide drawn by a 6-year-old with a life-threatening illness

differ in children who are actually faced by a life-threatening condition.

A 6-year-old boy with a life-threatening illness drew the picture reproduced above in a psychotherapy session. Although he was not yet ready to talk about his anxieties about dying, this drawing, which he said was of a slide, comes to a dramatic stop under the row of six suns. After talking to him about the drawing, I felt that he seemed to convey here the feeling that he was on a fast-moving downhill course, which suddenly stops, possibly leading to a feeling of falling (if we notice how the bottom of the slide is well above the ground level). Again, this confirms that the abrupt ending was ahead of him.

The sun in a picture often denotes a parental presence, or, in drawings of bereaved children, it is often placed over the dying or dead family member (Mary Sue Moore, personal communication). The ordinary or usual depiction of the sun in a 6-year-old's picture would be in a corner. This unusual display of suns here seems to carry a rich range of meanings: the six suns refer to his 6 years, which stop at the point where the slide stops; they hang over the picture oppressively, conveying both an over-protective parent as well as, possibly, marking out the *whole* slide: he was leaving no doubt that this symbol of the person who is dying truly 'covers' the area. Interestingly, this child had never really thrived: he had experienced severe eating difficulties all his life. This background seems to tie in with the oppressive suns which go back to the 'beginning', in the past – the left of the picture (Bach, 1969).

This drawing opened up the possibility of talking about his fears, and, indeed, his awareness that he was dying, but my comments on the drawing are not meant to be prescriptions or recipes for interpreting other drawings: any understanding of a drawing is arrived at in conjunction with the child's comments, the situation in which the drawing is made, and possibly the overall knowledge of the child. Wide experience of the normal developmental stages through which children's drawings evolve is also important, as a yardstick for any unusual or striking features.

For an analysis of the parents' role and responses to a young child or adolescent with a life-threatening illness see Judd (1994).

Chapter Four
Should we talk to children about death?

> Look, the dying,—
> surely they must suspect how full of pretext
> is all that we accomplish here, where nothing
> is what it really is.
>
> Rilke, 'Fourth Duino Elegy'

Recent research has challenged the 'protective' approach in relation to whether to tell the child of his or her impending death. As conveyed in the previous chapter, children sense that their illness is serious, even if they are not told explicitly. It seems from the weight of evidence that children need to be given the opportunity to speak 'about their concerns so that they can receive support in their struggles' (Spinetta, 1982).

The withdrawn or passive child may be a product of an environment that does not facilitate open communication. In an important study, Bluebond-Langner (1978) found that terminally ill leukaemic children often failed to communicate with people close to them about their anxieties. They felt despair and became withdrawn in a silent or angry way, in an attempt to 'protect' the adults around them. Thus both the adults and the child become caught up in a mutually protective falsehood. Other studies show that where families managed open communication throughout the illness, there was a high level of self-regard in the patient and a greater degree of closeness to other family members than in those families who did not use open communication (Spinetta and Moloney, 1978). Glaser and Strauss (1963), too, criticize the 'mutual pretence' communication patterns that surround the dying patient and his family. In these, each one acts as though the other does not know the truth.

It has been found that younger children – under 9 years of age – with cancer generally are told less than older children (Claflin and Barbarin, 1991) and yet younger children report similar levels of distress to that of older children. Therefore, in the study cited, the authors state that the 'protective approach' has not effectively masked the distressing aspects

of the illness. (However, this research does not address, by a compara-
tive study, whether younger children would experience more distress
than older children if they were not protected.) Nevertheless, it shows
that illness symptoms, treatments, and parental distress, 'speak louder'
than reassurance, and the lack of disclosure may convey that the disease
and situation are so bad that they cannot be discussed openly.

In considering the responses of family, friends, and health-care
professionals to the child with cancer, research shows that although
their reactions to the patient's diagnosis and illness are primarily negative, they believe that they have to remain cheerful, positive, and optimistic in their relationship with the patient (Dunkel-Schetter and
Wortman, 1982). (This research partly concerns adults with cancer, but I
am selecting aspects that are applicable to children as well.) Meanwhile
the patient himself is likely to be extremely anxious and uncertain, and
so have a greater than usual need for emotional support, as he is facing
many fears, including fear of separation, altered body image, pain, physical deterioration, increased dependency, isolation, and death (Davies *et
al.*, 1973).

This need to pretend, to act 'normal', often becomes greater as the
child deteriorates and approaches death because there are fewer
reasons to feel genuinely hopeful. With families and professionals where
there are considerable constraints on what is considered to be a safe
topic, and where there is avoidance of the subject of death and of
unpalatable evidence before their eyes, the possible conversations and
points of real emotional contact become fewer and fewer. When family
and workers assume that they have to make a concerted effort to control
their feelings and conceal their anxiety and distress, there is an increased
danger of their breaking down and betraying their feelings to the patient
(Parkes, 1979). This anxiety about saying the 'wrong thing' makes
encounters with the patient increasingly awkward and tense. In the story
of Robert, which follows in Part Two, I think that Robert increasingly
withdrew in the final stages, avoiding all that was around and inside him,
and about which his parents could hardly talk.

As an example of this kind of avoidance, a 16-year-old girl, Ruby, with a
rare degenerative illness, in the last months of her life, comes to mind. I
saw her for psychotherapy in a special school in which I worked. Her
physical condition was markedly deteriorating, and in her first meeting
with me the clearest 'message' she gave me, although she had great difficulty in talking as her breathing was laboured, was that she wondered why
she did not do computer work any more at school, when it was something
she used to enjoy. This gave me an opportunity to begin to talk with her
about the many things that she used to enjoy, and her need to address the
question as to why she could no longer do them. During the next session
she laboriously drew an apple (see page 39). She began by painstak-
ingly drawing the two little (leaf?) shapes on the right of the picture, and

then, after 'screening' them behind a line, drew, with an enormous effort, a circle. She rotated the paper bit by bit to complete it, paused, and then added a stalk and a leaf. She did not say what it was, but seemed pleased when I recognized it as an apple.

Her drawing seems to show some sense of something fragmented and weak to the right of the picture – that is, possibly, in the future (Bach, 1969). I am reminded of diabetic children conveying an unconscious sense of dying when they frequently draw decaying trees with dead falling leaves (Moore, 1994a, p. 132). The light touch with which this drawing is executed conveys a feeling of being decathected from the external world. The choice of pencil, in preference to colours, also often conveys diminished energy.

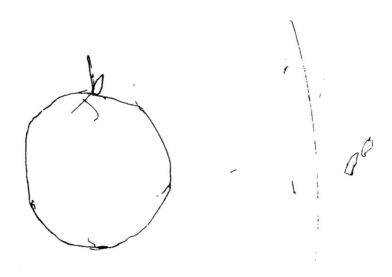

An apple drawn by 16-year-old Ruby

After further work with Ruby, and basing my interpretation on accumulated impressions, I suggested that the big solid apple – something good, that grows – represented the 'good breast' or alive Mrs Judd who feeds her 'talking food', with whom she feels in touch in the session, and yet cut off from, as I pointed at the straight line. I suggested that perhaps there was a sense that she could leave an alive part of herself with me, perhaps after her death, and I pointed to the fragments on the right. After my interpretation she relaxed, a slight smile on her face. Her eyes became unfocused, and she slumped forward, ball-like in her wheelchair, seemingly feeling relief at being understood.

Another young person with a deteriorating degenerative condition,

15-year-old James, was able to refer symbolically to his sense of deterioration and fear of death by telling me about an anxiety that the ceiling of
his bedroom was going to fall in on him, and that if he had another operation he would ensure that a nurse woke him up soon afterwards in
order to watch a favourite television programme. This distancing from
the actual reality is an understandable defence. However, James appreciated my efforts to translate his associations into the deeper level of anxiety that they represented, for later he grinningly told me that he slept
better since coming to see me, 'because it was like putting some of it on
someone else's shoulders'.

An account by a worker with patients with malignant diseases
summarizes this problem:

> The ordeals through which these people moved always contained
> elements of profound tragedy. However, the worst phase of all
> was one in which patients, families, wives and husbands did not
> talk or tell what they knew about the disease in order to 'protect'
> each other. The result was the isolation of both parties and this
> was the most devastating experience of all . . . Of course they did
> not 'escape' but only suffered greater turmoil in their isolation.
>
>   (Hageboeck, 1962)

Another way in which a child may sense that he is being left alone,
perhaps to die, is well documented in the research into the way in which
dying children receive less attention, including nursing attention, than
other ill children (Vernick and Karon, 1965; Rothenberg, 1974). They
therefore – quite appropriately – deduce that their situation is unbearable to others and they are left with a sense of isolation, loneliness and
worthlessness.

If children's awareness of the serious nature of their illness is hidden
under a veil of secrecy or even hypocrisy, their curiosity can become
inhibited, they can distrust their own senses, and tend to find everything
unreal. All this can lead to a chronic distrust of others, or even an out-of-
touch psychotic state. The former is described by Bowlby ('On knowing
what you are not supposed to know and feeling what you are not
supposed to feel', 1979) in a different scenario: that of children who
witness some aspect of a parent's suicide and are then pressurized by
the surviving parent to deny or discredit their own observations. The
less acceptable and painful feelings are shut off, in both the situation
described by Bowlby and that of children who are under pressure not to
communicate openly in other important situations of conflict.

In considering the extent to which a child with cancer picks up the
implications of the illness, it is important to bear in mind the metaphors
commonly used in descriptions of cancer, as Sontag (1978) points out.
The patient's body is considered under attack, or 'invaded' by the

disease. The language is therefore one of warfare and of military terminology. 'Cancer cells do not simply multiply; they are "invasive",' she writes. We talk about the body's 'defences' in its attempt to obliterate, wipe out, or fight the cancer. The treatment, too, uses military terminology: the patients are 'bombarded' with radiotherapy; chemotherapy is chemical warfare using toxins. Treatment, of course, aims to 'kill' the cancer, and in the process damages and destroys healthy cells.

Bearing this in mind, it would not be difficult for the child to receive messages of a dramatic and deadly war being waged within his own body. This may be exacerbated by the institution of barrier-nursing for the child in isolation – who has to be handled by people with gloves, aprons and sometimes masks – and who may feel that he is truly *contaminating* as well as – the more conscious message – *open to contamination*.

Where the problem arises of an ill child's awareness of his impending death running counter to his parents' denial, a child thus emotionally isolated may benefit from the help of a child psychotherapist, nurse counsellor, paediatric social worker, and/or other professionals to reintegrate the family, and to provide clear explanations of what is happening. (See the example of Jade, pp. 62–63.)

Research findings on the psychosocial reactions of children with cancer include a prevalence of regressive behaviour patterns, disturbances in body image, severe depression, lack of cooperation in treatment programmes, and a high level of anxiety. As some of these symptoms are part of the adaptation process, they are not entirely negative. Indeed, they may be adaptive mechanisms for negotiating loss and other unpleasant aspects of their illness. Some refuge in denial may be a way of buffering the child against the slow acceptance of what is likely to be the outcome, as I explain more fully in Chapter 5. Therefore to talk about all aspects of the illness and its prognosis is far from a general prescription.

I interviewed Dr Richard Lansdown, who has worked with dying children for over 20 years, about his views on children's attitudes to death. He says:

> I think it's quite important to get some idea of children's understanding of illness, so that their understanding of death is in context. The example I give is of a boy I saw many years ago. I first talked to him when he was 5 years. He had Stage IV neuroblastoma and I asked him when he was going to die. He said he was going to die in an aeroplane crash. On a little more probing I learned that he was going to join the RAF when he was grown up, and he thought that he would be killed in battle. He knew that he had a serious illness, but he was not equating his illness with death. It didn't then seem appropriate to encourage his parents

to talk to him or to foster a discussion with him about death, because he wasn't seeing 'one equals one'. A year later I saw him, and he talked about having a second and third tumour. He produced a marvellous phrase, 'One tumour enough, two tumours too many', which was about right. He had radiation to get rid of the tumours, and I asked what would happen if he hadn't had the radiation. He said, 'If I hadn't had the radiation, I might have died.' That was a very different story from the one the year before. It seemed much more appropriate then to get him in some sort of communication pattern [about death and illness].

This is something I think is often misunderstood in the litera-ture and by the public. People either say you shouldn't talk about dying to anybody, or you should always talk about dying to chil-dren with cancer, because there's such a taboo on the subject. Well, I think you've got to be more sophisticated than either of those views, and take your cue from the children's understand-ing. What really counts is when the child sees another child dying. It is crucial when the child knows of another child who has died of the same condition. We certainly get this on the ward. Children may be told that they may die. Their parents may say to children, 'If you don't take your medicine, you will die', but children also hear mum saying, 'If you don't tidy your bedroom, I'll kill you', and she doesn't really mean that. And granny talks about, 'I'm dying for a cup of tea', but she doesn't really mean that either. But when Elizabeth in the next bed dies of leukaemia, and she's got leukaemia like I have, then that really does hit me in the guts. That is a crucial time, a turning point in children's development and understanding of mortality.

Lansdown summarized this by saying that having that experience does not necessarily speed up the cognitive process of understanding the concept of death, but that it certainly brings it home to children, by a shift of focus about their own future and by making their attention more precise.

I then asked him to clarify the distinction between children with a life-threatening illness who may not die soon and dying children's awareness of death. In other words, whether for example, all children with leukaemia have some sense of the seriousness of their illness? He replied,

I'm not sure that they do. The literature says that they do, but I've recently been talking to a number of children in their teens. They do not necessarily remember what they felt when they were younger. How much *unconscious* fear there is is a very different matter. A lot of them very possibly do have unconscious fears of dying, which they would deny if you talked to them when they were 7 or 8.

A good example of this is a girl that I saw years ago, when she was 8. She had been told that she had cancer, but that it was not a serious illness. That is what her father told her. She told me of an old man who died in the street, aged 75. She said 'It couldn't have been cancer – I don't know what he died of, it couldn't have been cancer because that's not a serious illness.' She also had the most horrendous dreams of being put in a dark hole, and her parents looking down over her, and all sorts of very clear death anxieties. I saw her recently – she' s now 17 and she denied completely that she'd ever been worried about dying or death during that time. Consciously it may be so. Therefore, I think one is into many problems in saying whether or not a child is 'worried' or 'anxious' about death or not. What also makes a difference, as I said earlier, is whether a child has been an in-patient or not, and whether the child has come across other children who have died.

Another child who died when she was 16 had been ill since she was about 10. She had hardly been an in-patient, and hadn't come across other children who had died. It was only in the very last stages of her illness, told that she was going to die, that she said that she knew she had a *serious* illness, but she didn't realize it was *fatal*. I believe that, I believe what she said. I'm very wary indeed of the Bluebond-Langner (1978) type of generalizations that 'all children know this, all children believe that.'

Lansdown talked about the different category of very young children:

How do you communicate to a 3-year-old, or a 4-year-old, anything about death, particularly the death of a sibling or the death of a parent – before all those Kane (1979) [see pp. 20–21] concepts have really developed? I do find that immensely hard, and don't really have an answer to it. Aged 5 or 6 is a different matter; they've often got a very good idea of what death is about. But for a 3- or a 4-year-old; it is very difficult. Like George Sand, who had been told that her father had died in a riding accident. The next day she said, 'Is Papa still dead today?' It's that kind of difficulty that young children have.

He then addressed the different problems facing the approach to the older child, aged approximately 11-13 years, who is 'post-concrete' in his thinking, and who is beginning to grapple with the notion that maybe there is not an afterlife. Lansdown continued:

The child from this group says 'I don't think there is a heaven, but

I don't know.' I find this group quite hard to help. Of course it's difficult when parents don't have religious beliefs, and the child then says, 'I'm going to heaven, aren't I?' But that's not as hard as the other problems I've just mentioned, because parents can suspend disbelief in the interests of the child.

He clarified the problem of what to say to a dying child, and the issues that frequently arise:

We've never said to a child 'You are going to die.' I don't think we have a right to say this, ethically or scientifically. But we some-times say to a child 'You may die soon.' Then we're looking at the developmental stage of the child, to see where anxieties, if any, may arise. Always there is anxiety about separation – 'I shall miss you and Daddy.' There isn't always anxiety about the transition to death, but sometimes there are questions like 'How will I get to heaven?' as a 4-year-old asked. Her older sister said 'By aeroplane'. The other area of anxiety is, 'What is heaven going to be like?' Some children are worried about being lonely in heaven, and this again comes back to separation anxiety.

In an account of his own experiences with cancer, a 6-year-old boy (Jason Gaes, 1987) writes, referring to heaven: 'Once we get there we won't want to come back here. We're just scared about going to heaven because we never been there.' [*sic*]

I asked Lansdown if, in his opinion, separation anxiety is age-related, and he replied,

No, I think it goes all the way to teenagers. I don't know when it stops, if it stops at all. Like the teenage girl who was dying, and who had a sense of loss about the future, saying 'I haven't achieved anything, I haven't even done my exams yet', who was in touch with the loss of a life. She really felt that she had missed out on everything. She and I then planned her last few months, so that she could make the most of them. She made various goals as to how she was going to spend her remaining time.

Lansdown added that physical contact is also very important, partly in relation to separation anxiety, and partly as a means of communication. 'If people have been open with a child about the possibility of their dying, then non-verbal communication is going to be so much more important and meaningful for children and parents.'

I explored with him some of the difficulties around the transition from therapeutic care to palliative care (see also Chapter 10). I asked him how clearly defined was this transition for all the members of the team?

It *is* clearly made, but I think it is a difficult decision, and what is particularly difficult is, to what extent you involve the child in that decision. I mean, do you, for example, say to a 14-year-old, 'There is very little more we can do with conventional treatment. There is an experimental drug we might try. It will give you a very poor quality of life, and we don't know if it will work anyway. Would you want us to try that, or for us to give you care, comfort, as much comfort as possible?' We would certainly say that to an adult. Do we say that to a 14-year-old? Do we say that to a 10-year-old? To an 8-year-old, a 6-year old? And if we don't decide to do it by age, then what are the criteria? We recently had two 8-year-olds who said they didn't want any more treatment.

I asked if these children were asked directly? He replied:

One was asked, and one volunteered the information. I'm just speaking of the ones I know. We must have had many cases, many others that I don't know personally, because we have a great many children here – something like 120 cases of leukaemia and solid tumours a year. The general pattern seems to be that the more that children are asked, the more they opt for no treatment, but just to be made comfortable. Of course, the parents are very involved in all this, in all the decision making.

I asked Dr Lansdown whether, in his experience, the doctors are always the last to give up therapeutic treatment. His view was:

Not always; I think it's men who are the last to give up, and women who are more likely to just opt for care, as opposed to treatment that is available. Mothers more generally opt for palliative care, and tend to want the child to be allowed to die peacefully, at home. This tendency for doctors to want to try treatment to the bitter end may still be there in young and junior medical staff, but not in senior medical staff. They've been around too long to think that. They know that one has got to look after the last few months of a child's life, and that to subject them to a barrage of drugs in the hope that you might have a one per cent chance of a cure is not in the child's best interest.

I wondered whether research should play a part in this decision making, especially on the part of doctors? He replied that he thought there was an element of that, but that there is plenty of research being carried out on children with a reasonable prognosis. He went on to emphasize the place for truth:

The ethos on the Unit is always to tell the truth to everybody.

Junior medical staff, at first, sometimes find it hard to fit in with that, but after a while they pick it up and realize that it is in the interests of everybody. Sometimes the parents won't allow us to be truthful, but that's a very different matter. Mutual pretence. If the parents flatly refuse to allow us to give any information to the child, then we abide by that; we don't contravene what the parents ask. We may try to persuade them otherwise, but in the last analysis we go along with it. Sometimes children find their own way of asking, for example through a project they're doing with a teacher on the ward. One way of approaching this problem is for us to suggest to the parents that someone can work individually with their child, and then the pretence stays there, but the parents, by agreeing to somebody seeing the child, by implication are allowing the child to work in their own way on the issues.

Giving an overview of the changes in nursing ill children over the past 25 years, Lansdown emphasized:

There's much more a sense of bringing children into decision making, not only in the leukaemic unit, but also on the other ward I work on, which is plastic surgery. Also I think I've detected a loosening of relationships between children and staff: far more first-name terms, for example, and there's virtually an absence of white coats now. Oh yes, and of course, visiting hours! When I first came here some wards had visiting hours. That has completely and utterly gone.

I talked to Professor Robert Souhami, the consultant oncologist who heads the medical team on the Adolescent Oncology Unit at the Middlesex Hospital, London, in order to draw on his experience of some of these problems faced by teenagers with cancer. We began with my asking him about his approach to giving the diagnosis:

I don't really think there is a distinction between talking to an adolescent and talking to an adult as far as the diagnosis of cancer is concerned. The problems the doctor has are the same. It is a question of always judging how much information to give at any particular point and how fast to proceed. I have to do that when I first meet people without any prior knowledge of them, which is difficult. It doesn't matter whether the person is 16 or 60 – it is difficult because they are strangers. Usually, though, by the time the person comes to see me they know they have cancer. The question really is not whether or not they should know they have cancer – because clearly they should – but what the actual diagnosis means to them and how explicit to be about the disease and about the likely outcomes. It is really a question of judgements on that level that are difficult.

There is a particular difficulty, however, as far as adolescents are concerned. When they first appear they are nearly always with their parents and so you have to try to define a dimension that you don't have with older people: that is, what are the dynamics of the relationship between the parents and the adolescent? In other words, are the parents going to want to protect their child from what you are going to say? Is the child, on the other hand, going to want to protect the parents? Or, alternatively, is the child going to want to be with you on your own, not complicated by the presence of the parents? I find under these circumstances that it really is essential to have some ground-rules, and one is that I need to speak to the teenager on my own at some point. If I feel that is going to cause distress to the parents then I try to find the opportunity to say to them on their own that I would like to talk to their child on my own but that I am wise enough not to upset the child unnecessarily. They just have to trust me not to do that.

I asked him if sometimes they still put their foot down and refused?

That has happened once or twice but I have nearly always talked them out of that position. A younger doctor might find it difficult to do that because they would be, first of all, younger, and second, less experienced. But I can nearly always explain to the parents very clearly why it is that they are making a mistake. The mistake is obvious: that first of all they are imagining that they can protect their child against all things at all times, which they can't do, and, second, they're mistaken in thinking that all discussions mean bad news, which they don't. They are also mistaken if they imagine that the child might not be grateful for a chance to have a quiet word on his or her own. Of course, if the child him- or herself expresses a very strong view that they want all the discussions to be in the presence of the parents, that is a different matter. Then I wouldn't insist on seeing them on their own at all. But I would then say to the teenager, 'Look, we will have this discussion all together, but I want you to know that if ever you want to talk to me on your own, you can.'

Perhaps, with some adolescents, when we first meet they feel they are going to hear something horrible and they are not quite up to taking it without mum or dad. Mostly, I have to say, there is no expressed strong view like that. Usually when people come they are waiting to hear what I have to say about the situation and they are often calm and accepting of that approach. And if the doctor approaches the situation with a fairly calm, relaxed attitude, then it isn't very difficult or threatening.

I then asked if we 'fast-forward' to the terminal stage – then aren't you up against another set of constraints and barriers?

> You mean the barriers of how much to say to the child about their life expectation and what is going to happen to them? It is much more agonizing, not because there is a difference in principle about what your attitude should be, but simply because what you are saying can be so final and so gloomy that it might be difficult for anyone to cope with. Under those circumstances, what I normally do is take the opportunity to talk to the parents first, in order to say to them that I want to talk to the teenager about this. You might say, well, that's not right, you ought to go straight to the young person and have the whole thing out and forget about the parents, but I don't think that is realistic. Given the nature of the information (namely, that there is nothing more that can be done in a curative way, that the patient is going to die) it's absolutely essential that the parents are comfortable with what is going to be said. After all, they will have to deal with this day-by-day, hour-by-hour, at home, with their son or daughter. If, by the time the patient is discharged from hospital, the parents are full of resentment and anger about what has been said and about the position they see themselves in, then it may spoil the closing weeks of the relationship. So it is critical that the whole family is carried along as a unit and that everybody has participated in the decision-making.
>
> I may appear to ask the parents what I should say, but I actually present a view about what I think I ought to say. If I feel that they wish me to conceal too much, I tell them that this is an impractical approach which won't work out. This raises the question of what is genuine participation. Staff on the Unit and I have been in this situation countless times, while for the child and for the parents this is the first and only time and it is absolutely terrible. So participation doesn't mean leaving everything for them to decide; it means using your professional expertise to help people to decide what is in their best interests.
>
> The moment that I find really difficult is having that discussion with the parents, and telling them that the child is going to die. Then, having to walk into the room leaving the parents behind, sitting down on the bed, actually knowing that what I have to say is something . . . not cold-blooded, that would be the wrong word . . . but there is something pretty constrained about that situation. I mean, you know what you have got to say at that moment and there is no way round it and it requires a certain amount of moral fibre to deal with it.

I asked if he could say how he actually dealt with it: how he summons
. . . is it courage . . . ? Is it to some extent almost cutting off your feelings
to what you are saying, because you have to do it so often, or what?

> I can't really answer that very easily. I often ask myself the same
> question. The truth is that I know in the end certain words have
> got to be said, namely that I have no more treatment to offer. I
> know that the next question will be, 'What does that mean? Am I
> going to die?' The answer to that has to be 'Yes' and you are going
> to have to say 'Yes'. It doesn't mean that you are going to say, 'Well
> . . . ah . . . you know . . . that all depends . . . maybe not . . .' and so
> on. It is going to have to be 'Yes', and at that point, when saying
> 'Yes', I guess I have already made up my mind that I am going to
> say 'Yes'. Consequently I know what I'm going to do, and I've
> already psychologically crossed the barrier. I then ask myself,
> what is going to happen once I've said 'Yes'? What kind of
> comfort? What kind of things can one say? Not take back or
> modify the 'Yes', but to make it appear less frightening, less
> horrific than just simply somebody being given a death sentence.
> It shouldn't be like that, it shouldn't be as blunt and as horrible as
> that, but nevertheless you are telling someone they are going to
> die – and a young person at that. I might say that most of them
> know what I am going to say before I say it, but nevertheless they
> may pose the question directly. So, in a sense, getting the moral
> courage is something you have to do before you even enter the
> room. If you do it on the spur of the moment you will always
> make a mess, I've discovered.

I acknowledged his saying that he would not do it in a cold-blooded
manner, but I wondered if we could think further about how it is possible to not fudge the issue, and yet is kindly? Professor Souhami replied:

> I don't think there is a kindly way of saying it. What I meant about
> not being cold-blooded was, if someone says, 'Am I going to die?'
> and you simply say 'Yes', that would be blunt. That has a horrible
> finality about it and I don't try to modify the finality of that at all.
> But what they don't realise is what the process actually is: that
> they can nonetheless go home, that they can be with their
> parents; the small practical things; that they are not going to be in
> great pain. The actual process is something that people have no
> notion of at all, children have never seen it, and so it comes as a
> surprise that it can all happen at home, that they can go out and
> see their friends and if they are still feeling reasonably well they
> can go to the cinema and so on. They are not immediately going
> to be in a darkened room with the curtains drawn. So the idea
> that life can continue until death, as it were, is something that

needs positive explanation. It is not very hopeful, but if you don't actually say those things then you leave people with possibly a terrible kind of fantasy about what might then be going to happen to them: racked with pain in terrible circumstances. You have an obligation to try and point out that that is not going to happen. That doesn't mean that you are fudging the general message. It is actually the truth, as we know as professionals who have faced it many times. But someone only experiences their own death once and a young person hasn't an idea of what will happen to them.

I asked Professor Souhami for his thoughts about families who put an embargo on him not to be truthful about the fact that the child is dying?

That is much more common at the beginning, talking about the diagnosis. It is also common, though, for families to wish for some constraints about what is said about the terminal phases.

I wondered if this seemed to be influenced by cultural factors?

Yes, I guess it may be. Certainly in my dealings with some Asian families, I have noticed that they don't want to go as far and as fast as, say, an English middle-class family.

I suggested that this may be connected with the different emphasis on 'personhood' – i.e. autonomy and individual rights – in traditional societies (such as African and Asian) where instead emphasis is placed on a 'familial self' (De Creamer, 1983). Here, family cohesion – including the extended family – and interdependence is paramount. If, then, we think of paternalism as being an intrinsic part of that system, it is easier to understand some cultures' reluctance to give their adolescents autonomy, or to place much emphasis on confidentiality. I then wondered what was Professor Souhami's experience of Mediterranean – say Greek and Italian – families?

Yes, they are quite different and to be honest I feel slightly at sea with that because I am not of that culture. If a Greek family says to me, 'I absolutely refuse to let you say this to Katerina', I don't even try and argue against it because I feel I am treading into territory that I don't understand. It is like going back into UK medicine of 30 years ago. I think it would be very foolish for someone like myself, having grown up in my culture, to try and interfere with that. But even within Britain there are many parents who feel that they don't want their child to be told everything. The reasons they advance are usually twofold: one is that they feel they know the patient better than I do. But how do we know if they are imposing their own feelings on the child? The second reason is that they have to deal with this and if they felt it was a mistake then I am not sure that you have the right to deliberately shift the discussion between the parents and the child too far or too quickly.

I reiterated that parents will be living with this for many years to come, after the death of the young person, and in a way, therefore, was he emphasizing that the parents are the ones who are going to have to be satisfied with the way in which it is dealt? He replied with an emphatic 'Yes'. I went on to say that you could argue that the young person has an absolute right to make the most of the time that they have left and, there-fore, that should have priority over the parents' long-term view. He replied:

Yes, I think it does have priority over the parents' long-term view. But it only has priority if you are absolutely sure that the young person is taking a contrary view to their parents' view. Very often it is difficult to be sure who is right in this. Once you have said these things you can't unsay them, that's the problem. These are matters of judgement. I am quite sure that I get the balance wrong from time to time in both directions, saying too little or saying too much. All one can say is that you have to do the very best you can and be prepared to make a mistake. If you are not prepared to make a mistake, then the alternative is always to say too little. Human judgement is fallible, and mine no more or less than anybody else's. I don't believe there is such a thing as a guiding principle, in an absolute sense, in any aspect of truth telling, because as soon as you start talking about principles, there are principles which immediately contravene each other. For example, there is a principle that you shouldn't hurt people or make people needlessly unhappy, and there is a principle that you should tell the truth. These are often mutually contradictory. Truth is one principle, the aim of giving happiness and comfort is another. In the end the principles dissolve in the face of a rather messy situation which you just try to sort out the best you can, like all human relations.

I asked him if, in all this, he felt more comfortable on his own with a patient and/or the parents, or did he bring in, for example, his registrars, other doctors or nurses, or other members of the team?

You asked me that because you know I have difficulty with this. The problem is that there are certain aspects of this sort of inti-macy which I find quite difficult if people are sitting looking over my shoulder. It is stupid to pretend that having a silent third or fourth party watching does not alter the relationship between people. There becomes an element of play-acting, which is really a bit disturbing in terms of real intimacy between one person and another. So I make no apology for saying to people every now and then, 'Do you all mind leaving?' because I feel at that moment I need to have a personal contact between me and one other person. If I was ill I think I would want that; if one of my daughters were ill they would want it.

Despite that, I've got to train my junior staff, and I know that nurses have got to be there, and I know that someone has to pick up the pieces after I have left, so that in general I would like somebody there and I do want to train people. But if I think the going is getting really tough, I will tell people to go away, while I have a talk.

I asked if he thought that doctors learned best from the personal experience of having to do it themselves, first-hand?

Yes, absolutely. My position is contradictory, I realize. But, for example, the moment of relapse is an extremely serious moment for everybody. The family is feeling terrible and one has to be careful about intruding on that kind of grief. Maybe I am hypersensitive about it, maybe the parents or child wouldn't mind, but I don't believe it is easy.

I affirmed that some research (Woolley *et al.*, 1989) shows that patients prefer to have just the physician there, to which he replied:

That doesn't surprise me at all. It seems to be human nature. The question is, how to compromise, or relate that to teaching.

I asked Sister Chris Henry, of the Royal National Orthopaedic Hospital, Stanmore, Middlesex (where many teenagers with cancer come for surgery), if there is always a nurse there with the doctor when important information, such as the diagnosis, is given? She replied:

Yes, always – even if it's not bad news. Usually, but not always, the doctor breaks the news. But it is very often myself if I have been involved, particularly with my patients, because I've heard the results and I've been leading up to saying 'it's a 98% chance that you've got cancer'. So, when the actual ward round comes, it is purely a confirmation of what we have been talking about and I would certainly be there.

I asked if she meant the consultant and herself?

Yes, we just sit on their bed. They hate being taken to another room, they hate the curtains being drawn around but, if they have been prepared properly beforehand, you don't have a distraught reaction.

I clarified, 'So, you have done the preparation and led up to the diagnosis by saying that it is almost 98% likely that they have cancer?'

Yes. Then they will often ask if I will be there with the consultant and then it is just a formality to say that, yes, it definitely is. They know what the treatment is going to be, they have gone through all of that beforehand and there is not usually any extreme reaction at that stage because the process has been to very gradually work up to it.

I asked Sister Henry what she does if parents say 'If it's cancer you're not going to tell him are you? You can't use that word'?

Usually they say to us they don't want them to know until it is definite. All the parents accept that when it is cancer they have to be told and that has not been the problem. The problem has been beforehand, that that's what it might be.

'In other words,' I said, 'they don't want you to "put worry" into their child's mind?'

Yes, but the worry is in the teenager's mind already – only no one will speak to them about it. I would suspect that the parents haven't yet come to terms with it themselves, therefore can't face having to discuss it with the teenagers. What we say is that if we are asked direct questions we won't lie, and that is usually accepted. We see the parents when they first come in about what they know, and go through everything with them; and the same then with the teenagers. We haven't had the problems we used to have, I think we do it better nowadays.

I explored with a Senior Staff Nurse, Vikky Riley, who works on an Adolescent Oncology Unit, what she felt were the most difficult issues of talking to teenagers with cancer? She replied:

For the majority of nursing staff, including myself, I think the biggest dilemma is the balance of hope in all this. What I mean is, even on diagnosis, how much information should be given to the teenager and his family? Often considerable information is given to the parents, whilst some of it is given to the patient – but often not fully. We have had several people who have relapsed, or who are dying, who become very angry because they felt that they were never told the reality of the situation. Though the motives have been good on the part of whoever was conveying that information, there is still the question of – whether it's because of power or, I have to say the word, omnipotence – whether someone has the right to keep that information from the patient. How can we know what people can cope with and what they can't? Often the patient won't react there and then when they hear the information, but will come back to it in the night and will suddenly say, 'Is this what so and so was saying?' Of course this is a real dilemma, because motives for withholding information are usually good, with patients' interests at heart. Excuses are often given that they didn't think that the patient was ready to hear such information, but the important point is how information is conveyed, so that there is an opening if someone wants to ask further questions.

I can think of a patient whose disease was never controlled, and who, about 3 days before he died, had a chest X-ray and was told by one of the doctors when he approached the boy – who was dying – 'Your chest X-ray looks better.' It actually did look slightly better, but he was still dying. Of course the work he was trying to do with his parents to improve the relationship was then interrupted, as they were all confused. Hope was thrown in, in an unhelpful way.

I took up her phrase, 'the balance of hope', and wondered whether another way of putting that would be, 'the ability to be truthful about the situation'? Vikky Riley replied,

I think it is not only about how much we think they can bear, but also about how much *we* can bear. Sometimes, I think the way we practise is much more to do with issues within *us* which are just too painful, for whatever reason. I can imagine, though, how awful it must be, if you're the doctor deciding whether someone is to have more treatment or not. However, there must be a way of giving that information that can make it easier for everyone concerned. Then if the patient wants to start looking at the fact that they might be dying, they can *choose* what to do.

I often ask myself, is it easier once we know they are dying? I mean, once we know they are dying we can all have more of a sense of what our role is. We want to make it all perfect, but that's self-delusory as well, because there's a danger of denying the destructiveness of death.

I clarified that she meant that to be so positive about it was an avoidance of the pain of loss that death brings? She thought that was so, but that there are times when the truth is too unbearable, and we resort to justifying it.

Staff Nurse Riley remembered one young girl who, when the doctor walked in, had the courage to say, 'Am I dying then?' No option was given, no way out, and it led to a very – as much as death can be – special time, a time that her mother could use with great pride. The girl didn't hide the fact that she was angry that she was dying.

I asked her what thoughts she had about those patients who, when told that they are dying, can't make it a so-called 'good death'?

> That's when I think we health professionals get it wrong. This brings us to the whole question of what is a 'good death'? Some people can't ever accept it – they need the denial. That links with what I was saying about the way that information is conveyed, and the importance of picking up cues when someone clearly doesn't want to know. I'm not suggesting for a minute that everybody should be told when they are dying, but more about how the information is conveyed so that the patient can find out what he or she needs to know. If you're losing your child, no death is a good death, but there is a way that we expect people to behave when they are dying, and to become almost saint-like. That's not a good death, because at some level it's a denial of their situation.

As an example of a patient dying true to her feelings, Vikky Riley described

> . . . a young woman who died here very painfully, very tragically. She died how she felt she was living: angrily. She had had an awful life, it was all too much for her. She didn't bow to the system of having a good death. It's about allowing the patient to be how they really feel. That's what I think takes courage – to lie there with your face to the wall, angry, hurt, bewildered, distressed, and unable to move beyond that.

I discussed with a paediatric oncology consultant, Dr Anne Kilby, the ways in which she approaches young children – say, under 6 years old – and whether she is really talking to the child through the parents.

> I would only talk to the child with the parents there because I feel the parents would want to know what I was saying to the child. Usually, before I talk at any length with the child I have talked to the parents about what they have said, what they think the child already understands, and whether they wish that one of the specialist nurses is there too when I talk to the child. But of course I'm not usually on the ward when a child suddenly opens up and actually wants to talk. When the child takes the opportunity to suddenly start asking questions when the parents are not there, they probably don't want their parents to be upset.

I asked her if there were different problems for the children in the 'middle age' group – say, 7–11-year-olds? She felt that her approach was the same, and that she certainly wouldn't tell the children anything more than she thought the parents wanted them to know at each stage of their disease. She tried to answer children truthfully and emphasized that she has always encouraged parents to answer their children's questions as honestly as they can, regardless of whether it is good or bad news.

In the situation of parents who initially firmly state that they do not want their child to be told the diagnosis, Dr Kilby said that in her experience, over time, the parents always agree, so that at least the child understands that they have a tumour or a malignant disease, and can then hear what is going to be done about it. She continued:

> Parents can see that, on a mixed children's ward, the children talk to each other and would find out anyway. Parents usually develop a language of their own to talk about it and then feel able to talk to their child themselves or allow one of the staff to do so. With much younger children I try to find out the language, if any, that the parents and child have been using to describe the child's cancer before I talk to the child.

Dr Kilby talked about the much more difficult time of relapse or recurrence (in contrast to the 'easier' time of diagnosis, where there is a clearer path of treatment), where you may be wondering if it is appropriate to treat at all. 'At this stage you are weighing up the risks compared with the less clear benefits,' she said, and went on:

> Older children have got to know they have a recurrence. It's very hard for some of the parents to say to their child, 'After all this treatment the doctors have given you, the cancer has come back.' Both the children and the parents are often very angry and think, 'Well, if it didn't work the first time, why would it work the second time?'
>
> I always say to the parents, once I think the children have an understanding of the relapse and what the treatment involves, that we do have to listen to what the child's point of view of more treatment is, and not simply impose it, especially if there is a danger of our simply responding to the parents' desperation.

I acknowledged how difficult this situation is, and wondered how much detail is given to the child, of, say, possible side-effects and risks, as well as the chances of cure, so that the child is able to make an informed decision?

> I think that would very much depend on the age and level of understanding of the child. I think that for children under approximately 8, when one is treating a relapse, it's very much

the parents' view we are hearing. However, when the child hears that they are having more treatment, and if he or she is immensely distressed and says they can't go through all that again, then I think the parents and I have to listen to that and decide how much that would modify our decision about what to do, given the chances of it being beneficial.

With children aged, say, 9 to 12, they already understand enough about their disease and treatment, and are having symptoms, and therefore again I would encourage parents to be truthful. Some of these older children actually state, very clearly, what they want.

I think that if there is a good chance that you can get good quality of life for a further length of time, or even that you are still in with a chance of curing the child, then the decision is quite clear and they always opt for treatment. The much more difficult situation is of, say, a third-time relapse, where the parents may be very keen to buy time. Then, usually, you can persuade the child that more treatment might help their symptoms. I don't think I can think of a situation where the parents and child have seriously disagreed about continuing or stopping treatment.

I said how hard it was to actually know what the child wanted, when, as we know, children often go along with what the parents want in order to please them. Dr Kilby here emphasized that by the time relapse occurs, many people in the team have had intimate contact with the child, and usually know the family well, and thus they can inform her if the child wants one thing and the parents another. 'With teenagers there has to be detailed discussion with the patient themselves; they usually develop clear views on further treatment when faced with relapse or terminal disease,' she said.

I then talked about situations where we can be clear that the treatment is palliative, but that parents and children quite quickly slip into a kind of self-deluded state where they are pretending either to others, or even to themselves, that this could cure – and I don't mean the hope for a miracle that most people keep alive – but more a mishearing, that the treatment is curative. Anne Kilby acknowledged that this is a frequent problem, especially when there is widespread disease or a poor prognosis, and first-line treatment goes well. She continued, 'My response then to the parents is that this is very pleasing but that we must not lose sight that the disease might come back. I think a lot of parents choose not to hear that, or forget it very quickly.'

(See Chapters 5 and 6 for further discussion of adolescents with cancer.)

Chapter Five
The stages of emotional reactions to life-threatening illness

> . . . I wanted to know. There is no protection, unless it is in know-
> ing. I wanted death pinned down and isolated behind a wall of
> particular facts and circumstances, not floating around loose,
> ignored but powerful, waiting to get in anywhere.
>
> Alice Munro (1971) *Lives of Girls and Women*

In attempting to describe children's reactions to something as overwhelming as a life-threatening illness, I find myself faced with inchoate
terms about psychic development, leading me back to the infant's reactions to the threat of death (as described on pp. 18–25). This beginning
– although it is not really a beginning, for there are indeed some experiences of a threat of annihilation *in utero* (Piontelli, 1992, p. 218) – needs
to be borne in mind as a *sine qua non* when we try to think about the
infant's and the older child's reaction to an actual life-threatening
illness. Not only does the duality of life/death have to be carried in the
reader's mind, but also the dyad of mother and baby or mother and
child, or parents and child, for the child cannot be considered in isolation. Similarly, the duality of the internal and external world of the child
is an important constant axis within the metapsychology of the child.

Therefore, if we talk about the child's *reactions* to the illness, we
need to bear in mind the parameters of emotional growth: whether the
illness is felt to be located entirely inside him; whether it comes from
outside; whether it is 'caused' by mother or anyone else, or by bad
behaviour or events; the extent to which mother is felt to be separate
and 'out there' or a part of the child; as well as the child's level of understanding of his illness and of death. These complexities need to be held
in mind for the rest of this chapter in order to avoid a simplistic view of
the child's reactions. Just as there is no 'baby' without a 'mother' (Winnicott), so there is no illness without a patient, no child without care-
givers, and no intellectual concepts and reactions to illness without

corresponding or conflicting internal phantasies.

Psychological effects of facing a life-threatening illness depend on many factors, including: the child's age at the time of onset; the child's intelligence and maturity; the duration and degree of treatment; the severity of the malaise; the degree to which the body image is impaired; and the separations from the child's main care-giver(s) (Kahana, 1972). In charting this pattern it is important to realize that it is certainly not a blueprint: *there are considerable differences from situation to situation*. Nevertheless, a common pattern is often discernible, indicating that a distinct psychological process takes place. And, within this discernible oft-repeated overall pattern there is much similarity with the stages of bereavement (Parkes, 1972; Judd, 1994, pp. 92–93). This is hardly surprising. With both an impending death, and the aftermath of a death, there are similar physiological and psychological reactions to this crisis involving loss, fear, a state of alarm, and the human responses to dealing with it. I am basing this summary partly upon my own observations, and partly upon some of the literature (Geist, 1979; Kendrick *et al.*, 1986). Geist describes clearly the stages that children facing chronic illness go through, and many of these findings would also apply to children with cancer in the light of its course being delayed if not cured.

It is frequently stated in the paediatric literature that young children tend to ascribe illness as a punishment for their, or other's, bad behaviour (Eiser,1985). This is in agreement with a psychoanalytic understanding (see pp. 68 and 111 this volume, quoting Anna Freud, 1952) which describes the state of physical and emotional persecution that the ill child feels, not differentiating between that which is external from that which is within. This view is challenged by recent cognitive research, although the sample used is rather small (Springer, 1994). This survey suggests that preschool children with cancer are no more likely than healthy children to see illness as a punishment for misdeeds. Most children in the study saw illness as caused by material contamination, such as dirty food.

Receiving the diagnosis, and negotiating subsequent treatment, of a life-threatening illness constitutes a psychic trauma (Judd, 1994). Therefore, the patient's 'pre-disaster resources' (Menzies Lyth, 1989) – that is, the impact on inner psychic reality of the diagnosis and treatment, as well as the ways in which the inner world colours the actual external events – crucially affect their ways of dealing with the illness.

Advances in the long-term survival and possible cure of the child with cancer considerably affect the family's response to diagnosis and treatment, although there are of course still situations where even upon diagnosis there is no possibility of cure. However, generally nowadays the child and family have to live with the uncertainty that the disease and its treatment bring. This has been well described as the 'Damocles syndrome' by Koocher and O'Malley (1981). Some of the implications are addressed more fully in Chapter 11.

Psychosocial issues about which the professionals involved need to be concerned are complex. They include the need to make an appropriate assessment of the family's coping mechanisms; an understanding of the child's understanding of the illness, including their developmental level; an assessment of the sibling(s)' situation; an overview of the child in relation to school and of the family in relation to their environment/work/extended family; networking with other professionals involved. Useful early interventions are discussed by Adams-Greenly (1991).

The parents

One cannot really separate the child from the parents in this situation, for, hopefully, the parent(s) are intimately involved with the whole process. Parents characteristically act as a 'protective shield' (Masud Khan, 1986, drawing upon Freud's [1920] notion of the 'shield' that protects us from psychic trauma), thus making the experience more bearable for their child. However, the extent to which the parent is traumatized will of course affect their ability to act as a protective shield. I prefer the phrase 'protective *filter*', which implies a two-way process: the parent(s) filter that which goes through to the child, and process or translate the child's experience, both for the outside world, such as the medical team, but also for the child himself. Thus the parent acts as a container for the child's unbearable anxieties, fears and dreads, and, in time, through being able to tolerate and eventually think about them, feeds them back to the child in a modified form (Bion, 1984). Single parents can have a particularly difficult time here, without mutual support, or, without the partner/spouse sometimes acting as a protective filter or container for the more traumatized parent.

Adolescents

As the detailed case material forming Part Two of this book focuses on a young child, I will briefly mention some of the problems specifically encountered by adolescents. The parental role often differs for adolescents, depending on where they have reached in their steps towards independence. The main difficulty for parents of seriously ill adolescents seems to be in finding a balance between the inevitably altered circumstances and roles, and allowing the young adult's steps towards autonomy. Adolescents themselves perhaps have the most difficult time of all in facing the possibility of death. Adolescence, particularly with its inherent struggle for identity and independence, is totally at odds with death: it is against the grain for adolescents to accept death. Their newfound sexual capacities, steps towards independence, their physical, intellectual, and emotional growth, their ambitions, emphasis on physical attractiveness, their need for privacy and control, are all jeopardized by a life-threatening illness. Corr and McNeil (1986) address many of the issues for the adolescent. For a full analysis of their reactions, see Judd (1994); also Jamison *et al.* (1986) regarding cooperation with treatment; and List *et al.* (1991). Chapter 4 (this volume) gives some medical professionals' views of adolescents' problems.

Research suggests that children under the age of 9 years are told less about the illness than older children. However, this appears not to protect them from the impact of cancer (Claflin and Barbarin, 1991). Clearly, verbal nondisclosure does not protect them from all the physical, emotional, social, and environmental changes that the diagnosis and treatment bring, and may compound their difficulties – as explained in Chapter 4. As most medical systems nowadays do appreciate the value of a full explanation of the diagnosis and the proposed treatment for children and their parents, I am giving this summary of the stages of emotional reactions on the basis of generally open communication.

Upon diagnosis: numbness

An initial reaction of numbness can be common to both the child and parents, and links with observations of reactions to bereavement (Parkes, 1972). This numbness, or 'blunting', is an understandable protection against the shock. A feeling of disbelief and a sense of unreality can be part of this stage. Some realization of the serious implications of the diagnosis often breaks through the numbness in bursts. The psychic trauma of diagnosis and treatment for child and family is explored more fully elsewhere (Judd, 1994). Gradually a more complete awareness of the diagnosis emerges. The extent to which the parents are devastated often affects the extent to which they show 'protective concern' and are reluctant for their child to be told (Chesler *et al.*, 1986).

However, it is difficult to generalize about the impact of diagnosis, as much depends upon the way in which the disease is explained to the parents, on their preconceptions or 'pre-disaster resources' (Menzies Lyth, 1989), and of course on the way that the child is (or is not) told, as well as the severity of the condition. For many children who have felt unwell for a while before diagnosis, there may be little surprise when they hear or intuit that it is 'something serious'. There may even be some relief for the child that his malaise is being taken seriously, and relief for child and parents that treatment will begin.

Denial

Part of the numbness described above may be a more generalized denial, especially on the part of the parents, as a result of a direct or indirect awareness of the possibility of death, and is frequently part of the initial reaction. This denial can take the form of suppression (i.e. a conscious attempt to forget or deny and to avoid thinking about it) or repression (i.e. an unconscious process whereby the unacceptable and painful thoughts or feelings are prevented from coming to consciousness). It can continue to operate at later stages too, especially if the child's symptoms exacerbate.

The usefulness of denial – perhaps of the severity of the illness or of the life-threatening implications – is that it allows the patient and his family gradually to accept a change in life expectations and the possibility that death may occur, and therefore is not necessarily maladaptive. If it is an initial diagnosis and not a relapse, denial and minimization is more possible (Slaby and Glicksman, 1985). It can be a useful way of dealing with loss until there is a readiness for other more realistic responses. For some, perhaps particularly for adolescents, a degree of denial is necessary in order to continue to cope with their remaining life and to go on living (Detwiler, 1981; Corr and McNeil, 1986).

> For example, Charles, aged 14 years, had been diagnosed as having a malignant abdominal tumour. He acknowledged that he had cancer, but denied that the disease could be fatal. When another child on the ward died, and Charles heard that it was from cancer, he became extremely upset because he realized that he too could die. Thus, he was only gradually allowing reality to register.
>
> An example of a generally unhelpful use of denial is illustrated by the parents of 9-year-old Jade, recently diagnosed with leukaemia.* Her parents surrounded her with lavish presents. She presided, princess-like, seemingly enjoying the attention and specialness. Even her annoying little brothers were not there to spoil it. Her mother did not seem upset, but focused on the presents and on the money that people have raised for Jade, saying, 'It's more than I've got.'
>
> In my first visit to the family on the ward, I felt clumsy – for every time I mentioned the strangeness of all this for them, I felt that I was being inappropriate, 'spoiling the party'. It was as if 'denial is the name of the game', and any attempt to struggle with painful feelings of anxiety, loss of a healthy life, and so on, were not allowed.
>
> However, the strangeness of being stuck in a hospital bed, feeling unwell, undergoing a range of complicated and unpleasant medical tests, having a Hickman line inserted (see p. 101 for a

*This example is adapted from Judd, 'Learning from sick children', a paper given at 'Children's decisions in health care and research' Conference, Social Science Research Unit, Institute of Education, University of London, October 1993. Later published in *Report 5*, March 1994.

definition), and beginning chemotherapy, left Jade with a strange sense of de-realization: she blanked out contact, stared out of the window, effectively denied my existence whenever I visited. The nurses became worried about her not being 'with it'. The parents continued to exert a powerful embargo on any meaningful conversation, because of their fear of going to pieces if they began to feel the implications.

So I had to summon the courage to say to Jade: 'So much has happened to you in the past two weeks, it must be hard to make sense of it all.' Her dreamy eyes swam into focus as she looked at me, and said maturely, 'Yes, I don't know when I'm going home; I don't know what's happening half the time.' Clearly she had been resorting to mindlessness as a defence against an unbearable situation, which her parents were unable to process for her. The parents were acting like an impenetrable shield, attempting to protect her from the terror, but owing to their own traumatized state, where none of this could be thought about, they were not being effective in hearing her worries, making sense of them, and filtering through to her the unbearable experiences in manageable form.

My main task then was to see the parents on their own and to try to hear their state of mind; and, in a sense, to give them all permission to have feelings of fright and dread. In time, I saw Jade on her own for regular sessions with a 'therapy box', so that she could draw or play or talk and I could try to understand her immediate concerns, as well as help her to piece together the fragments of the past weeks.

This example serves to illustrate many aspects, including that of the traumatized state that children and parents often find themselves in soon after diagnosis and at other crisis points of the illness. Therefore, they are not able to think clearly or symbolically about the situation – rather they are living inside it. As people in this situation often say, it is a 'living nightmare', and states of depersonalization are understandable defences against complete breakdown.

If defences enable the child and his parents to carry on living without unbearable degrees of anxiety, then they are effective and useful (Chodoff et al., 1964). However, if the defences lead to family members being locked in a 'web of silence', unable to talk to each other for fear of breakdown, this adds to the stress and anxiety of each individual (Turk, 1964). They may continue to function without breakdown, but at considerable psychological cost.

Solnit and Green (1963) also point out that the child's lessening energy and possible eventual stupor in the last stages of a terminal illness is an incidental protection from a full awareness of the situation.

It is often hard to define how fully sensate a child or adolescent is at this stage, and I faced this dilemma with Robert (see Part Two). I wonder if some denial of the child's awareness takes place on the part of the adults involved. For example, at times with Robert I tended to want to feel that he was 'on the edge of life' rather than fully in it, in order to protect him. He then proved me wrong on a few occasions by rallying dramatically and displaying liveliness.

Some researchers have found that resistance is greater in older children, who may regard their illness as 'an inequitable breach of contract and its unacceptance is far more taxing' (Debuskey, 1970). Meanwhile, the younger child, being less aware of alternative forms of illness, may find it easier to accept the restrictions imposed on him.

The first month after diagnosis: assimilation

Children (and their families), after diagnosis, are particularly receptive to learning about their illness from many sources. Children appear to be particularly alert to assimilating relevant information from other children, doctors, nurses, teachers, parents, domestic staff, books, and television. They quickly learn the meaning of key words that relate to their illness.

Similarly, they soon learn about hospital procedures. As with their quick assimilation of the facts around the illness, this knowledge of procedures is a way of attempting to master a strange, and in many ways frightening, new environment. Part of this new understanding includes an appreciation of the necessity for treatment. Even children as young as 2 years of age are reported to adjust to submitting to painful or unpleasant treatment when they sense the urgency and insistence on the part of the adults around them.

This considerable understanding of their illness, and of the procedures, often exceeds the child's cognitive development and usual capacity, and links with the more mature concepts of death grasped by children who are facing a life-threatening illness (as has been explored in Chapter 3). This seems to be in the service of adaptation – an attempt to organize and control the experience – while *not* understanding or knowing leads to a higher level of anxiety. Research by Claflin and Barbarin (1991) shows that nondisclosure to younger children does not protect them from distress or from the salient aspects of the illness.

However, there can often be an *intellectual* grasp of what is entailed, without much emotional acceptance. For example, a 9-year-old child with a chronic renal condition had a knowledge of the working of the renal system which almost rivalled that of some doctors, but still objected to some of the treatments, protesting at the pain, and at times refused to comply with the necessary intake of fluids. This child's cognitive grasp did not mitigate his sense of outrage at what was happening to his body.

There is research evidence to show that preparing children for bone-marrow transplants reduces anxiety during the procedures themselves (McCue, 1980). My own observations of children with serious illnesses show that there is frequently a hunger for factual information. Children usually devour whatever familiarizing books, photographs, films, or information are offered to them. This opportunity to go over the procedures is as useful retrospectively as prospectively: the child needs to work through what can feel like an invasion of his body or an aggressive attack on it by doctors or equipment. A facilitator – an adult who can explain the familiarization project and listen to the child's questions, whether it be parent, nurse, play leader, psychotherapist, or doctor – is as important as the familiarizing material itself.

Regression

Alongside adaptation, regression can be found. Quite often the child adapts to the main part of the treatment, but will find a more minor aspect over which to be resistant. This, again, is the child's way of feeling he has some control and mastery of the situation.

Regression can take the form of simply reverting to behaviour that was more appropriate at an earlier stage of development, such as increased dependency, and a need for greater physical care and contact. However, regression can also take the form of the child making unreasonable demands, having temper tantrums, and being excessively irritable.

For example, a 6-year-old boy, Mark, with leukaemia, in isolation in hospital, was engrossed with a set of little hospital figures and play equipment that I provided for him. In the play he identified with the doctors giving injections. He turned their aprons round so that they became Superman, flying above all the medicines, operations, and illnesses. When I told him that I had to go in 10 minutes, but would be back next week, he called for his mother in a complete panic. When she arrived he threw the toys at her angrily. Mark had clearly been denying that he was the patient, and had used a manic defence against all the feelings of helplessness and anxiety about his illness. My impending departure seemed to remind him of his lack of control over the many comings and goings around him, as well as over the illness itself. This same boy was adept at helping the doctors with their regular checks on his catheter and their taking of blood by turning the taps on the tubing and pressing the phials with the dexterity of a theatre sister.

There are many vicissitudes, from child to child, and within each child, between passive acceptance on the one hand and angry resistance or denial on the other. Stephen, aged 14, would sometimes retort to me, 'I'm not going to be a rag doll and just sit there!' Yet, at other times, he begged to be allowed to use a wheelchair, although he could walk. When he heard about another child from his school dying, he asked directly, 'Am I going to die?'

Lorraine, aged 17, never mentioned her illness or its implications, but displaced her anxiety onto worrying about her stepfather's bad leg, or whether she had upset her mother over something apparently trivial. Her massive denial did not really seem to help her to feel less anxious, for she became extremely upset about these other situations and people.

Children who choose the path of regression with its implicit request for more mothering often seem to be those who appear not to have had, or made use of, a 'good enough' experience of being allowed to be appropriately dependent infants before their illness and who were forced, therefore, into pseudo-maturity. Jane, aged 3 years, is an example of this. Her mother proudly announced to the hospital staff that Jane had been 'clean and dry' by the age of 11 months. It was not surprising that Jane very soon used the hospital experience to regress to a stage through which she had not been allowed to go at a more appropriate pace. Indeed, she made this quite clear to everyone by smearing her faeces in her cot if left unattended.

There are parents who, when faced with an ill child, become over-protective and over-anxious. In the light of a life-threatening illness, however, this can be a very understandable reaction. Indeed, few parents do not alter their attitude to an *ill* child. But if there has been a history of a child knowing he can procure his mother's *special* attention when he is ill, being ill may well lead to a rapid submission in order to gain the desired attention: the child might feel that being more infantile than his state of health necessitates will bring extra rewards.

Besides the infantile 'gains', passive submission can also be more serious: part of a giving-up of a life instinct or life force. This may be a result of a feeling of despair, that the child has lost in the struggle against annihilating forces. These children often become mute and further lose the desire to eat. Although in some ways this makes the nursing role easier, it augurs less well for the emotional (and therefore, in the long run, physical) state of the child. It seems that the child is then giving in to dying. A little boy with leukaemia, Tommy, went through a phase of 'giving up the fight' to the extent that he would lie completely still on the bed, yet not asleep. Once his therapist momentarily thought he had died. (Tommy, as it turned out, was not in the terminal stage of his illness, for he responded well to the bone-marrow transplant and is in remission at the time of writing.)

Another type of submission and seeming acceptance on the part of the patient is prompted by the use of masochistic defences as an attempt to master the situation. So, although it may appear that there is passive submission, the child's fantasies may be more about a perverse *control* of the situation through the adoption of a masochistic defence, namely, 'I am allowing them to do this to me. I even like it, and want them to do it to me all the more.' Yet another passive response is a withdrawal into a type of mindlessness which can be a useful defence against an awful reality.

The welcoming of a re-experiencing of dependency, whether through masochism or a need to renegotiate early stages, is very different from the more widespread negative reaction of resentment found in children. Having to be looked after like a baby is an indignity to most children from approximately 3 years onwards, for it is not only the fact of relinquishing control over certain bodily functions that pains the child, but the concomitant ego development. The various developmental landmarks signify a detachment from the mother, and the beginning, at least, of owning his own body.

Having to relinquish these physical and psychological advances leads, in those children who are strongly defended against passivity, to very difficult behaviour while they forcefully oppose the enforced regression. Others, such as those described above who have not had a secure or sufficiently lengthy experience of dependence, fall back into a state of helplessness without much apparent resistance. These children may lose their perhaps precariously acquired bowel or bladder control or the wish to feed themselves.

Clearly, an adolescent suffers a different range of feelings when faced with a loss of bodily, and therefore psychological, independence. An adolescent, however, like a young child, is making considerable bids for independence and autonomy and can find enforced regression particularly humiliating. Inevitably, sensitive nursing and parenting is of paramount importance, with a respect for as much privacy as is possible.

Adolescents often view their illness – perhaps at an unconscious level – as a retaliation against their strivings for independence. Parents often report that ill adolescents who need help with toileting, washing, and eating are very difficult to please. It is hard for the parents to strike the correct balance between over-doing the care and leaving too much to the young adult. One mother related how she was snapped at by her daughter for 'hurting her' when she washed her too thoroughly, yet was told off if she did it too gently.

Increased masturbation, as a form of reassurance, is often a reaction to the anxiety and restrictions imposed by the situation (Geist, 1979), as well as possibly a wish to find pleasurable experiences in the face of so much discomfort.

Anger

Aggression, too, can be a way for the child and adolescent to express anger about the restrictions, as well as being an expression of anger towards the illness itself. Thoughts of 'why me?' and of it being unfair are common with the concomitant feelings of guilt (Geist, 1979). Adolescents are particularly sensitive to distortions of their body image: alterations to their appearance caused by drugs, hair-loss, and surgery produce a considerable sense of worthlessness and interfere with their capacity to function. They not only have to cope with their inner turmoil about the distortions, but with the reactions of society, which can be insensitive and rejecting. Anger often emerges when earlier denial and numbness fade (Kübler-Ross, 1970). This, too, links with the stages of bereavement.

Anger and aggression in younger children are often more directly expressed, especially as a reaction to fantasies of being attacked from some unknown internal or external persecutor. As Anna Freud writes, quoting Klein, the young child is often unclear as to the actual origin or cause of the pain, operation, illness, or restrictions. 'If . . . the child's fantasies are concerned with his aggression against the mother projected onto her person, the operation is experienced as a retaliatory attack made by the mother on the inside of the child's body (Melanie Klein) . . . or the operation is experienced as mutilation' (1952, p. 74).

Anger is often suppressed, perhaps unconsciously, by hospital staff and parents, in their attempts to make the environment as jolly as possible. The young person may then feel, 'How can I be angry with them when they are doing so much to cheer me up?' This dilemma appears in the detailed account of Robert which follows in Part Two. An example of this attempt to cheer up the children, perhaps taken to extremes, is the Clown Care Scheme in the United States, where clowns dress up as doctors in order to make the children in hospital laugh (as reported by Jonathan Charles on 11 May 1988 on BBC Radio 4). There may indeed be a useful role here in familiarizing children with unpleasant procedures, and perhaps in breaking down the medical hierarchy, but perhaps there is also scant attention to the children's needs and rights to *be* depressed or angry.

If the child's mixed feelings of anger and dependency towards those adults who seem to impose their will on him during treatment are expressed, it can make the roles of the carers more difficult. In the case of Robert (see Part Two), the doctors were usually kept 'good', while the nurses could be mocked or resisted. His mother was generally felt to be his lifeline, while his father went through a phase of being seen as all bad. This split was psychologically expedient for Robert, but made caring for him more difficult for some.

As an example of the anger that a parent can feel, I am reminded of one child with leukaemia, who had had a bone-marrow transplant. She had relapsed and was untreatable. She was in considerable pain and was on massive doses of pethidine. The mother had not slept for many days. The student nurses were horrified by this mother saying, 'The little cow won't even die for me, she just keeps me hanging on.' It is interesting that the mother felt that she was 'hanging on' as much as the child.

Depression

Depression is a widespread reaction in children facing a life-threatening illness and seems specifically to be concomitant with loss of autonomy, loss of control, and helplessness. The term 'depression' is often loosely used, and has both a popular and professional psychiatric meaning. The popular use describes a frequent occurrence, is a part of normal existence, and is not an illness. The psychiatric term may have features of an illness, depending on its severity. Winnicott summarizes the phenomenon thus:

> Depression belongs to psychopathology. It can be severe and crippling and may last a lifetime, and it is commonly a passing mood in relatively healthy individuals. At the normal end, depression, which is a common, almost universal, phenomenon, relates to mourning, to the capacity to feel guilt, and to the maturational process.
>
> (1963, p. 79)

Therefore, in the way that Winnicott describes it as relating to mourning, depression appears to be a part of normal existence in response to the abnormal situation of being confronted by a life-threatening illness.

Depression may be interpreted by the carers of a dying child as a giving in or a giving up, yet dying people generally fluctuate in and out of their depression. 'Sadness tends to be intermittent, and in most situations complete clinical depression is not that common' (Feifel, 1962, p. 90).

The ability of the care-givers and parents to bear the child's depression and sadness links with their own capacity to mourn the loss of the healthy child. The parents may feel guilt and depression and withdraw emotionally or even physically, thus conveying to the child that his situation is unbearable. If the child's depression is more of a depressive nature (see pp. 12–13: 'depressive position', Klein, 1940), they may feel concerned that they have exhausted their parents' tolerance or love, and this will evoke earlier feelings of having emptied out and damaged the 'breast'. Furthermore, there may be various fantasies about what the parent or parents are doing when they absent themselves from the child, leading to further feelings of envy or jealousy that may contribute to anger or further withdrawal.

If, on the other hand, the child's depression is of a more persecutory nature, he will feel that he is being punished by his illness or by his parents' negative response. Again he may feel that his illness, or that he himself, is unbearable. An attempt to jolly the child up (as mentioned earlier under 'Anger'), to lift him out of his depression, can lead to despair on the part of the child that no one can bear the pain of the loss of the healthy self and the possible loss of life. The child then is not being helped to work through the loss and the feelings of sadness as a foundation for yearning and keeping alive memories of the good missing healthy self. Of course, if the life span of the terminally ill child is crucially shortened, there will not always be time for a working-through of these feelings, although there appears to be a telescoping or condensing of the psychological phases – 'accelerated mourning' – that parallels the physical condition.

Bargaining

Kübler-Ross delineates this phase as one of the stages of grief. 'The bargaining is really an attempt to postpone: it has to include a prize offered "for good behaviour", it also sets a self-imposed "deadline" . . . and it includes an implicit promise that the patient will not ask for more if this one postponement is granted' (1970, p. 73). This form of bargaining would no doubt be much in evidence in the prayers of anyone of religious convictions, and is often a part of the parents' reactions. A child might well use superstition and ritualized or obsessional behaviour in an attempt to 'bring luck' or ward off further deterioration.

Acceptance

When considering the possible acceptance of the death of a child, the feelings of outrage, of a life not yet run, emerge, and make this stage far more complicated and difficult for the dying child and, inevitably, for his family. 'Rage, rage against the dying of the light', as Dylan Thomas (1966) writes, seems more understandable than acceptance.

However, without at least some acceptance, at some levels, it is not possible to maximize the remaining time before death. The length of illness plays a significant part in whether this stage can operate at all, with a long illness leading to a *relatively* easier acceptance of death. However, this is by no means necessarily the case, for having battled and 'won', perhaps several times, it can be felt to be worth continuing the battle: 'If we've gone through so much and carried on so long, we're not going to give up now.' Or, alternatively, there can be a bitter questioning of the months or years of difficult treatment and the hope that was offered when the prognosis becomes grim.

With some acceptance there can be a shift from active medical intervention and treatment to palliative care, thereby possibly making the patient more comfortable physically. This shift, if it does occur, on the part of the professionals involved and the family does not necessarily imply completely relinquishing hope. The hopefulness can be either for some 'miracle' to occur or, at a more ordinary level, for the patient and family to be able to make the most of the remaining time together. The child may need this time to speak of matters that are important to him; parents and siblings may wish to express their love, and to work through past difficulties, directly with the child, to the child. The dying child, or the family being left behind, may wish to express gratitude; gratitude for the times they *have* shared. This is a chance to say goodbye, directly and indirectly. Where the course of the illness makes the final stage very sudden, parents often feel robbed of this opportunity.

Although anticipatory mourning is often carried out at any of the preceding stages of an illness – on the part of both child and family – this final stage appears to be a valuable time for specifically this particular process to take root, probably then making it easier for the actual mourning to be set in motion.

From the point of view of the dying child, he can feel a sense of relief at being allowed to 'be', whether that is interpreted as being comfortable in his body or allowed to be dying. Otherwise, the child who is being carried relentlessly towards death by a clearly deteriorating physical condition can feel more tortured by parents pulling him in the opposite direction or beseeching 'Don't go, don't go, we need you', reassuring though that may be at one level.

It is often reported in the appropriate literature (Norton, 1963; Elliot, 1981) that when a child is dying, they know it. 'Every one of those kids knows what's happening to them inside, because you can feel it' (Elliot, 1981, p. 138). The writer continues, '. . . when the body is close to death, a signal goes out to let the person know.'

The child who is talked to honestly about the progress of his illness has the opportunity to build up trust, at a time when he needs a foundation of trust above all. This can be trust that those upon whom the child is dependent will tell the truth and trust that the parents are there to help the child with the last stages of their life to the best of their ability. Yet, there is a strange irony in a situation where, from birth, the parents have helped to sustain the child's life, and they now find themselves having to talk honestly to the child about the child's possible death. This 'unnatural' shift in the laws of parenting may, however, be a great relief for both parents and child, once it can be grasped and talked about. It is a bitter truth that a parent may be able to help his or her child to die. This is beautifully conveyed in *A Way to Die* (Zorza and Zorza, 1980).

A boy who had a chronic renal condition and a failed transplant, and with whom I worked, expressed this need for honesty thus: 'Underneath the clown Ronald McDonald there's a man, pretending.' He had turned to his father to tell him the truth about the proposed treatment, yet remained suspicious of the subtly differing messages he received from his father and from the medical team. There is a need to give even bad news, but to give it tenderly and sensitively, at a level at which the child seems able to grasp. Rather than cutting across or through defences that the child might need, there is the approach of asking the child if he has any questions, or anything he wishes to tell you, and responding honestly. This allows the parent or professional to find the appropriate level, which is, of course, the level at which the child is.

I will now come full-circle back to the 'Kleinian' picture of the infant, with his use of splitting and projection, as the foundation for understanding much of the foregoing. Klein believed that the infant develops through forming good internal objects. At the beginning of life, pain (in the form, for example, of tummy ache, hunger, thirst, fear, not being held) is experienced as persecution. The infant then attempts to get rid of this pain by expelling or evacuating it, probably into that which the infant feels has caused it, that is, the mother or the part of her with which he has an active relationship, i.e., the breast. This unconscious activity is an attempt on the part of the infant to preserve the 'good breast', that which nourishes, comforts, and protects, by expelling persecutory anxiety into the 'bad breast'. Thus the 'bad breast' incorporates those unbearable unwanted feelings of the infant. Therefore, in illness, and especially in extreme illness, the young child would attempt to rid himself of the pain by projecting it onto aspects of his outside world.

This splitting-off can, of course, be very useful to survival and psychic comfort. Whether the young child continues to use this primitive form of splitting and projection, or will feel that the mother, or some internal resource, is available as a remedy, depends on the child's psychological development, as well as on the capacities of the mother. However, in a young child who has had to undergo lengthy and traumatic experiences in hospital, it is very difficult for the child to sustain the notion of a good protective mother who can ameliorate the bad experiences. She has to be split effectively into a 'witch' mother who feeds him 'poison' (medicine), on the one hand, and a good mother, on the other. If this split is not adequate, she may be felt to be totally bad and persecuting (Judd, 1988). It takes some maturity for the young child to be aware that it is one and the same mother.

The extreme situation suffered by a child undergoing torturous treatment links with Bettelheim's description of concentration-camp victims. He describes how some victims of the camps would find ways of preserving a sense of autonomy, and managed not to respond with schizophrenic or suicidal reactions, even if it was a small private gesture or a way of making life a little more bearable.

> Those . . . who remained convinced they could act in their own behalf and who did act, remained free . . . of the severest pathology . . . Sometimes it was an extra morsel of food, a piece of paper to wrap around the body for extra warmth, a task successfully avoided . . . It did not matter as long as one could rightly feel that by taking action one had ever so little improved one's estate.

(1967, p. 65)

These mechanisms enabled the prisoners, who were so fundamentally restricted and brutalized, to retain some sense of control over their fate. Similarly, many of the foregoing stages and responses to a life-threatening illness and the often extreme accompanying treatment can be understood as the child's attempts to retain some degree of autonomy. It may even be worth considering the possibility that, in certain ways, some *young* children undergoing horrendous treatment and isolation are in a worse situation than a concentration-camp victim, *because the parents are necessarily obliged to be part of the system that imposes the treatment*. Thus, potentially, the child's love and trust for his parents is severely jeopardized. The 'protective shield' breaks down. The child then resorts to the primitive mechanisms of splitting, projection, and denial.

Chapter Six
Support available

'Undisclosed grief is an incurable pain.'

Fifteenth-century song title

Child psychotherapy

As Part Two of this book is written from my own perspective – that of a psychoanalytic child psychotherapist – it is important for there to be some understanding of this role. This is an expanding service, one that is fairly widely available as part of the Health Service in the London area, but is sorely lacking in other parts of Britain. Researchers have found that psychotherapy for paediatric patients with cancer markedly decreases the frequency and severity of their emotional problems (Watson, 1983).

Child psychotherapists often have had a first career in another profession, such as teaching, social work, or nursing. The child psychotherapy clinical training is specialized and extensive, taking a minimum of 4 years, after, in some trainings, 2–3 years of a pre-clinical course, as well as previous professional experience with children. The teaching throughout is linked to ongoing professional work with children. A key aspect of the training is the weekly observation, and discussion in a seminar, of a baby in his own home for the first 2 years of the baby's life. The training in psychoanalytic psychotherapy involves treating three children – a young child, a latency child, and an adolescent – three or more times per week, under weekly supervision, as well as a number of less intensive cases, including work with parents and assessments. The study of psychoanalytic theory and child development are other components. Each student has to undergo a personal psychoanalysis (of four or five times per week) in order, partly, to experience more fully the infant and the child in himself. This involves the opportunity of reworking the inevitable difficulties in the process of growing up. Thus, the

74

psychotherapist may be more able to recognize and address the patient's problems.

Perhaps I should first clarify what a child psychotherapist basically does in the more usual non-hospital setting, in order to explain the particular applied technique possible in a hospital. In essence, the psychotherapist pays attention to the child, and the understanding of the child's behaviour thus gained, in time, is fed back. This is after mood, play, speech, and actions, as aspects of behaviour, have been experienced by the therapist. Both child and therapist have an opportunity to share and explore aspects of the child that previously may not have been accessible to his conscious mind. Through this process, some integration of the less acceptable aspects of the child may, hopefully, take place. Anxieties, often originating in earlier, infantile experiences, which may interfere with the child's development, can perhaps be tolerated, understood, and in time interpreted, by the therapist to the child. This process is specialized and detailed, and requires a considerable time commitment – often years and often more than once-weekly – in order for fundamental changes to the personality to be brought about, or for a more favourable re-working of earlier stages of development.

The transference phenomenon is one of the central forces at work in any therapeutic relationship (Freud, 1905; Klein, 1952). Therein, strong feelings and impulses, usually left over from earlier childhood relationships, are transferred on to, or directed towards, the therapist or analyst in the present therapeutic relationship. This tendency for earlier relationships to re-surface (which is present in all relationships, not only in therapeutic relationships) is encouraged and facilitated by the therapist and by the setting. The transference and its interpretation becomes one of the main tools in bringing about change.

In working with a dying child, this tendency to repeat transference feelings may be kept in mind by the therapist, as part of an overall understanding. The therapist might use the transference to interpret maladaptive behaviour, if this behaviour is leading to greater unhappiness on the part of the child. For example, Tommy, a 5-year-old boy, who was dying, became extremely clinging towards his mother. This anxiety was re-experienced when the therapist left the room. The therapist then said, 'You don't want me to go, because it reminds you of when Mummy leaves the room.' The therapist had often talked to Tommy about his 'baby part' and 'baby feelings', so she was able to say, 'The baby Tommy is frightened that I, or Mummy, won't come back. It's because you need a lot of looking after now, and have worries about being so ill, that you don't want to be alone with all the worries and illness.' Through Tommy's baby needs and anxieties being understood, and 'held' in the therapist's mind, his level of anxiety and stress may be reduced.

The setting in which the therapeutic relationship takes place is normally an important consideration. Just as the therapist tries not to clutter the relationship with his or her own problems and anxieties, so an uncluttered and constant room and simple play equipment can make it easier to see what the child is expressing or bringing emotionally at any particular moment. Constancy of day and time and length of session are similarly important.

However, in a hospital in-patient setting, many of these considerations have to be put aside. It is obvious that factors, such as the unpredictability of a child's illness, necessitate that the therapist adapts to the ebb and flow of the situation. The child may be too ill, or asleep, or discharged, on the day of the appointed session. Thus, the hospital setting automatically imposes limits and conditions on the hospital therapist. One of the main limits is that contact is usually restricted to the child's stay in hospital, regardless of emotional need (depending of course on where the child's home is, and on practical considerations such as the possibility of out-patient follow-ups). Recommendations for future therapy may be made, but the therapist's task is primarily short-term intervention, focusing mainly on the child's reaction to his or her illness. In a more usual setting (say, in a child-guidance clinic), child psychotherapy aims at restoring normal emotional development. However, in a hospital setting the main focus would be on allowing the child to work through the situation that causes the child to be in hospital and the child's response to the trauma.

Of course it is also important, in the hospital setting, for the child psychotherapist to be in communication with the child's parents, either directly or through a co-worker. The parents' state of mind is clearly crucial to the child, so the child-within-the-family is, of necessity, the overall perspective for the workers involved.

Similarly, the child psychotherapist's understanding of a particular child can usefully be shared with the nursing and medical staff, particularly where the medical person's role precludes close emotional contact with the patient. It is here that the psychotherapist can be an important link and, in a way, an interpreter, between the child and the doctor or the nurses. Conversely, the therapist can learn from the medical staff's observations and experience of the child.

I will illustrate the unique contribution that a hospital child psychotherapist can make with the following example. A 4-year-old boy with leukaemia was undergoing arduous chemotherapy. His mother was a single parent. He became extremely uncooperative with his treatment and threatened to pull his Hickman catheter out (for an explanation of 'Hickman' see p. 101). The nursing staff felt extremely anxious about the child and stressed by the demands he made upon them. The intervention of a child psychotherapist, providing regular sessions, enabled this child to express some of his anger and frustration at his restricted and unnatural existence. He expressed this anger through aggressively throwing things at her, as well as symbolically in play. Some of these negative feelings could then be contained by the therapist verbalizing and interpreting the child's feelings and tolerating his rage. Containing the child's rage led to a lessening of his aggression towards the nurses and towards his already overwhelmed mother. The psychotherapist also met regularly with the mother, both to contain some of her distress, and to help her to understand her child's behaviour.

Family therapy

Family therapy can be offered alongside, or instead of, individual psychotherapy. Indeed, family therapy is more widely available than individual child psychotherapy, and is a very suitable therapy of choice in many instances. Dr Dora Black, in talking about a family approach where there is a child with a fatal illness, says (personal communication):

> One of the things that my work with families has taught me is that one can't actually look at an individual in isolation. For example, in all the families with which we're involved, where there is life-threatening illness, we're concerned about the effect on the siblings of an ill child. The whole family dynamic is very severely and constantly stressed and that diminishes the amount of flexibility that parents have. This leads to lack of spontaneity, of relaxation, and of the joys of family life. There's this kind of chronic cloud that hangs over that makes it so stressful.

Black went on to point out that the family probably has to cope with the actual absence of the mother, as she is usually the one who has to care for the ill child, and the hospital may be many miles from home: 'With the rarer childhood illnesses you usually have to go to a centre of excellence and that may be very far from home.'

Black stated that this leads to the other parent, if there is another parent, or grandparents, or neighbours, all sharing in the care of the child or children remaining at home: 'In my experience people are good at rallying round. But I think that the siblings then feel the strain. They have to be on their best behaviour.'

She continued to talk about the often considerable financial strain, despite the National Health Service paying for the actual treatment. Extra financial problems arise out of the mother having to give up her job, father forgoing promotion, or overtime, extra travel incurred, extras to keep the children happy.

I asked her about her views on the father's difficulty in having a role, when the mother is usually the main caretaker. She replied:

> Yes, I think that's often a problem. Walker (1983) writes about this. Mother and the nursing staff often form a unit, or system,

from which father is excluded. This is certainly true. Fathers are not anyway as happy in hospitals as mothers, and I think that the reason for this is that all mothers have experienced hospitals through giving birth and/or antenatal visits, whereas many fathers have never been in-patients. My experience is that a lot of men are actually very uncomfortable there. It's partly because it's a very female institution, and young nurses are not necessarily very good at talking to fathers – but then also because fathers are not involved in the day-to-day care of children.

When looking at the stress that having a fatally ill child puts on the parents' marriage, Black said that statistical research evidence shows that marital breakdown is not any higher than average, because, although the increased stress does lead to some, perhaps already discordant, marriages breaking down, this is counter-balanced by others where the illness actually brings parents together (Lansky *et al.*, 1978).

However, a later very detailed, qualitative study (Hughes and Lieberman, 1990), although using only a small sample, suggests that there are increased communication difficulties between spouses when a child has cancer. Soon after diagnosis, parents reported a loss of sexual interest, although this often reverted to normal after a few months. Their summary of parents' coping is:

> . . . the massive stress of having a child with cancer precipitates two largely separate psychological problems . . . About a third of the sample suffers psychiatric symptoms at a level which warrants further investigation and possibly treatment. A second group . . . also a third of the sample, are vulnerable personalities, rather oversensitive, difficult but not disordered . . . become isolated and angry, feel bad about themselves . . . They can be helped but probably need psychotherapeutic help and will tend to alienate ordinarily friendly hospital staff who are not trained in counselling or psychotherapy.

They conclude with 'We believe that there may be a considerable [psychiatric] morbidity in parents', and suggest the need for a large-scale randomized survey. These findings support the author's own intuitions, based on clinical experience of working with these parents (Judd, 1994).

Group therapy for parents of children with cancer

Studies have shown that other parents with leukaemic children 'were regarded by most mothers as the most important source of emotional support' (Bozeman *et al.*, 1955, p. 15). However, the provision of groups for parents with cancer is not as widespread as it could be. A recent paper (Kaufman *et al.*, 1992) in the USA offers several suggestions for this lack, including discomfort in staff when having to address difficult issues and lack of appropriate training in staff. They conclude: 'The cost effectiveness of *not* providing psychosocial services should also be addressed. Psychosocial services have been shown to decrease anxiety and nausea, which may increase treatment compliance, therefore improving survival of selected patients' (p.24).

However, one study (Hoffman and Futterman, 1971) shows that in fact mothers of children with leukaemia interact very little with one another in hospital waiting rooms. The exchanges are likely to be superficial. They suggest that this type of exposure to others could be detrimental, because it could lead to parents feeling that their own, unexpressed anxieties and doubts are unusual or abnormal. Thus, resorting to trivial subjects may be partly the result of cancer generally being a stigmatizing disease; or of a fear of upsetting others by being open about feelings.

As a way of addressing this need for a safe and structured setting in which parents of children with cancer can share their anxieties, some hospitals run support groups for parents of children who are seriously ill. I will describe in some detail a group that was run for many years during the 1980s at the Great Ormond Street Hospital for Sick Children, by Margaret Atkin (principal social worker, now retired) and Richard Lansdown (consultant psychologist).

The group was structured to run for eight meetings on alternate Saturdays. Each meeting lasted for one-and-a-half hours. The parents were self-selected. The only criterion was that they have a child with leukaemia, and this could be at any stage of the illness. Later the group also included parents of children with solid tumours. The meetings were task-orientated. Ten to 15 people frequently attended, but at times there were fewer. A comfortable room was chosen in a part of the hospital away from the wards and the treatment rooms. A crèche was provided. Parents were reimbursed for travel without question, if they asked; some parents, who lived far away, travelled for several hours to reach the group.

When the group was first set up, less effective medical treatment was available for the illness, and the improvement in treatment over the years led to a different emphasis or atmosphere within the group. In other words, there was a shift from an almost inevitably fatal illness to one with a much better prognosis, so that the parents' task generally became to live with uncertainty, rather than with the inevitability of facing death.

The parents' stress and anxiety were the main themes. A search for meaning, a turning to religious beliefs, and a grappling with the concept of suffering were some of the recurrent topics. The vast majority had recourse to spiritual or philosophical beliefs as a way of coping beyond their own resources. They came from all walks of life, but, as they all had the common factor of a child with cancer, they had similar anxieties.

Margaret Atkin (personal communication) recalls that at the beginning of the series of meetings the atmosphere was extremely tense; the coffee and biscuits would quickly disappear and the room would be filled with cigarette smoke. However, as the weeks went by the meetings became calmer, and sadder, and the coffee and biscuits disappeared less quickly.

There were often indications in the anecdotes parents brought that they were unable to cope with the day-to-day ups and downs: sometimes they were jocular, but ended up in tears. Frequent problems that surfaced were about disciplining their other children, about over-indulging the sick child, and about their sexual relationship. One father spoke about the loss of family freedom and about resenting the intrusion of the illness into family life.

'Why me? Why us?' was a frequent refrain. Atkin says that most parents feel that their child is 'special'. One mother announced that 'Our Timmy is cradled in the arms of the church'. This made it difficult for other parents who did not hold such clear religious convictions.

Some parents found that taking long walks helped them. Many turned to writing poetry, or to making things. On one occasion a father felt unable to talk about how he felt but, instead, read a poignant poem about his child. The group then fell silent.

Atkin reports that there was always a 'doctor bashing' meeting when parents felt that doctors were too brusque, insensitive, or clumsy. This often included their feelings about how they heard the diagnosis. This learning of the news nearly always seemed to remain a watershed in the parents' minds, between the way of life before and the way of life after.

It is not surprising to learn (Stein *et al.*, 1988) that parents of a child with a life-threatening illness remember vividly the way in which the diagnosis was imparted. Approximately half the parents interviewed were satisfied with the way in which they had been told. In this study parents reported that they coped better with the imparting of the diagnosis of life-threatening illness if this was divulged early, in an open and sensitive way. This was best done in privacy with both parents present. The news needed several repetitions over a period of time for it to 'sink in'.

Considerable marital strife was manifest in the group. As it was often difficult for parents to agree, it was therefore difficult for the ill child to be in a safe structure. Some parents were very outspoken. Marital tensions are not surprising at a time like this, when one thinks of the probably unconscious process of projecting blame onto one's partner. Just as the infant uses splitting and projection of dangerous feelings as a way of preserving and keeping separate that which is felt to be good, so adults, especially at times of stress, may fall back into this more primitive way of functioning. Thus, a wife may undermine her husband's efforts to deal with the ill child, as a way of locating separately from herself and her child that which she feels is worthless and helpless. This is an attempt to avoid feelings of guilt, powerlessness, and persecution. Anger, too, may well be directed towards a partner – displaced from the disease itself or even from the child for 'causing' so much upset. However, Atkin states that there was also considerable marital support within the group, where the illness seemed to bring the parents closer together.

The group could 'bring home' to parents the fact that their child had cancer. In other words, some parents had not fully digested this fact until the group met, and were then 'moved on' from their disbelief.

Some meetings focused on how they would feel if their child *did* die. Sometimes a child who had died was talked about. (If there had been a death on the ward, the nursing sister would usually have told the other parents.)

By the end of each series of meetings, an atmosphere of great bonhomie had developed, with parents finding it difficult to leave at the end of the hour-and-a-half. Parents could decide to attend a second series of meetings if they wished.

Groups have not been consistently run there – at times there are informal *ad hoc* meetings, as well as meetings on the ward.

(For an interesting discussion on the setting-up and running of a support group for Asian mothers in a children's hospice, see Muir and Notta, 1993.)

Adolescent units

There are now about 20 specialist adolescent oncology units planned for, or in existence, in Britain. The first, at the Middlesex Hospital, London, was based upon an American model of cancer care. In the USA, it was found that outcomes were better when adolescents were treated in an appropriate, age-related, environment.

Now that the pioneering Adolescent Oncology Unit at the Middlesex has been open for 5 years, I asked Professor Robert Souhami, the consultant oncologist who heads the Unit, if he could reflect on what he felt were the particular justifications for a special Unit?

Well, I think that first of all we are technically very good at what we do and I think that it's important for rare diseases to be concentrated in one Unit (see Souhami, 1993). You could do that on an adult ward, it is true, but I think that we are also good at dealing with the human aspects of these illnesses and we're not frightened by them. I think the junior staff, both medical and nursing, are actually remarkably unfrightened about the stress of

these terrible situations that arise, compared with what you
would see on a general ward, simply because they have lived
through it a lot. It doesn't mean it doesn't take its toll on them,
but it does mean that they are all familiar with what the feelings
are going to be and therefore adept at dealing with them. I think
that's of immeasurable benefit to the patients because there is
nothing that is going to 'throw' us.

On the negative side, some of the difficulties arise out of the
intensity of treatment lasting weeks and months, where teenage
patients get fond of each other on the Unit and get very upset
when they realise that one of their friends is dying. You can always
rationalize that and say that is not wholly negative, because it
gives them an understanding of what their position might be, and
if they get very ill it makes subsequent events easier to handle. I
think that is a rather weak rationalization; I think that in fact it is
distressing and there is no use denying it. As soon as you put
eight or nine very seriously sick teenagers in a room together, all
with similar diseases, you are bound to have interrelationships
between them and distress of that kind. The question is, which in
the end is better? I think you can easily answer this question by
imagining what would happen if the Unit did not exist. Then each
of those teenagers would be on a different ward and the quality of
the advice and the care that they got would be much more uncertain than it is in the Unit. I would say that the most important
thing about the Unit is this feeling that teenagers and parents
have, that they are amongst people who actually know what they
are talking about, who deal with their questions promptly, who
are consistent and coherent in what they tell you, and alert to
your feelings. That must be a comfort of a kind.

I pointed out that he had not mentioned the support that the parents
give each other and the support that the teenagers give each other on
the Unit, to which he replied that he is not able to gauge that himself as
he is not present enough. So I returned to his point about the distress
that the young people do experience when they are so close to death
and the dying of their peers, and how perhaps we need to research into
the impact that this has on them?

I think this is an extremely good idea which I hadn't thought of
before. Yes, it would be interesting to find out from the children
themselves what they actually thought about it. I would guess that
the kind of support they got would be a reflection of their own
personalities – you know, how out-going they were, and so on. I
have often noticed that some inward-looking teenagers have had
one close confidant on the ward. Of course under those circum-

stances it would be extremely distressing for the person left behind.

He went on to talk fondly about one of the teenagers on the Unit:

They're often fully-fledged individuals, aren't they? I mean, for example, Kate's Irish sense of humour is so striking and so witty, that even when she is dying, she's protecting her mother and making jokes in the most inappropriate places, which is just very funny. Yes, Kate is dying and will die in the next day or two. Her mother said to me this morning, 'She is being so brilliant about the fact of dying.' That is an extraordinary thing to say about your own child, but I know just what she means. I mean, the child *is* being brilliant about it and I think there was pride in Mrs O'Hagan's voice about her, even under the circumstances.

This morning Kate's mouth was very dry and she asked for some water and her mother didn't jump to it immediately. So Kate just looked up and said, 'What has a girl to do to get a drink?' It was a wonderful comment for somebody who may only have 36 hours to live and just wanted a sip of water.

However, some professionals have a somewhat different view on adolescent cancer units. For example, Sister Chris Henry, of the Royal National Orthopaedic Hospital, Stanmore, Middlesex, where adolescents with cancer are mixed with other teenagers in hospital, says that she feels that you need a combination of specialist units and a separate, orthopaedic and rehabilitation hospital:

I think you need a combination of both. I think teenagers with cancer should be together in a separate unit for the time they are having their chemotherapy, because it is very specialized treatment and needs specialized care. When it comes to any surgery they may need, the same applies and they equally need specialized care. I don't think that this can be given in an oncology setting. The adolescents having chemotherapy are feeling sick and are not so communicative. I find here (at Stanmore) when they come for surgery it is a relief; they have come away from a hospital where they were having chemotherapy, they have lost the smells of chemotherapy, the association with being sick and with people being ill and they have come into a different environment. Here they are having surgery like everyone else – it might be to a leg, or an arm, but there are plenty of other kids having that. But the important thing that they have all said is that they have seen people with worse things than themselves. The parents have also said, 'I didn't think that there could be anything worse than my kid having cancer but, since I've come here, I realise that there is something worse.' It is that balance that is valuable.

Also, the adolescents have to explain what is wrong with them and another young person will say 'Why have you lost your hair?' and they'll say 'Well, I've got cancer in my leg' and then the response may be, 'Well, come and play snooker'. It is a very natural level and it educates the other teenagers who don't have cancer. Very often there are teenagers on the ward that are being investigated for cancer as one of the possibilities and they have already seen the others without their hair, having treatment, and that opens the way for questions for them to ask.

I asked if she saw problems for the non-cancer patients coming up against cancer?

No. They have a different problem which they are dealing with which to them is every bit as big at the time as the others with cancer. They don't think they have cancer and they certainly don't seem to get worried by it but do discuss it. If one of the other adolescents is having a leg amputated then that is a different matter and we discuss it with them and they know before the teenager comes back what is happening. The whole ward is prepared when somebody is going to lose a limb because that is a major thing and they get quite worried about it if they are going for surgery to a limb themselves. There is always the possibility that they might think that it is going to happen to them but, if it has been handled right, it has actually been a source of support for both of them. We find that the cancer teenagers support the non-cancer teenagers and vice versa. One of the big positive things is that the teenagers with cancer make friends, often long-lasting friendships, with people who are not necessarily going to die and who haven't got cancer.

I replied, 'And that is a great relief – to put it mildly – because there is always the risk when making friends with cancer patients that some of them will die.'

Yes. One of the cancer patients said to me recently, 'I don't like to ask now how so and so is because I've known so many people who have died. I don't want to know any more.'

I think that the other thing that we offer is normality; we offer schooling – which, fair enough, they might not want – but that is part and parcel of life. Sometimes they sit together at the dinner table. They often don't eat in the oncology setting because no one fancies food, whereas here we have meal times that can be a social occasion. They play games together and they go off to the Patient Centre together.

I asked about the way in which the parents of children with mixed medical conditions interacted. Did she see it similarly?

> Yes, there is no difference. You won't find that the parents of teenagers with cancer stick together. They get involved with the parents who have disabled children – again because they feel an empathy and they often feel that they have worse problems than themselves. And they actually fulfil some of their own needs by supporting other parents. It is very much a two-way process.

I asked if some patients find it difficult to transfer to another hospital for treatment when they have already made quite an attachment to her ward?

> Yes. Initially they say that they wish they could stay with us because they know us. But we are able to say to them that they are going to a unit very similar to our own, but the nurses there are much more specialized in the treatment they are going to have so they would be safer; and that the doctors are really nice and will explain everything as they go along and that they will be coming back to us for surgery.

Sister Henry summarized,

> It is not ideal for orthopaedic patients to have surgery on an oncology ward. It is not always conducive to recovery and to integration, where people are ill and being sick. There are also infections there: mouth infections, fungal infections. It is not always the ideal situation for massive metal work to be introduced (in prostheses). It is like starting to give chemotherapy here without full expertise. Equally, we need to be aware of the chemotherapy patient and how vulnerable they are, and they need to be aware when the orthopaedic patient goes back about the specialist care required.

I commented that the transition or the change-over from one specialist setting to the other was important. Sister Henry added,

> I like the transition because I don't think we should be possessive of patients. I think we should share the care – after all we share the care in the community, we share the care out of hospital and we should share the medical and surgical care with each other and pool our resources to provide total specialist care.

I concluded that the only way in which the patient can feel secure is if we all communicate and bring together the various aspects, to which Chris Henry responded:

Yes, absolutely. And accept our limitations in the areas that we deal with.

Symptom care or palliative care teams

A significant development in Britain has been the growth and establishment of palliative care services over the past 10 years, as part of the National Health Service provision. This has come about through a clearer recognition of the different specialities of terminal care and palliative care. Although the two are closely linked, palliative care focuses on patients who may live with their disease for months or even years, whilst terminal care is clearly for those in the last or final stages of life.

The World Health Organization's definition of palliative care is:

The active total care of patients whose disease is not responsive to curative treatment. Control of pain, of other symptoms, and of psychological, social and spiritual problems, is paramount. The goal of palliative care is the achievement of the best quality of life for patients and their families.

The foregoing aims embody the approach of Symptom Care or Palliative Care Teams and are clearly important to the care of the last months of a child's life.

There are several Symptom Care Teams attached to units at Great Ormond Street Hospital for Sick Children. For example, the team attached to the oncology unit began with three people – a paediatrician and two senior nurses – whose job was to look after children and attend to their symptoms in the last stages of their lives. They are peripatetic and cover the whole of the area in and around London. They carry out home visiting, liaise with GPs and with schools, and work with parents and siblings as well. They can administer drugs and keep children comfortable and relatively pain-free. They also provide a great deal of psychological support. This facility means that many more children die at home than before, with full medical attention.

Liaison Sister Jane Watson (Clinical Nurse Specialist for life-threatening tumours of the central nervous system), who heads the team attached to the neurosurgical unit at Great Ormond Street Hospital, explains their way of working:

We are linked to the individual family from the time of diagnosis, through primary active treatment, into maintenance care. We act as a bridge between staff at the centre of treatment and local community teams. We remain attached to the family if the need for secondary treatment arises, including palliative and terminal care. Having supported the child and family through the initial crisis of having a life-threatening tumour of the central nervous system and maintaining contact, the family have instant access to support when hearing painful information and making difficult decisions at the time of recurrent disease.

With the family's consent the contact continues after bereavement in the form of phone calls and home visits for a minimum of one year, especially covering Christmas, birthday, and anniversary days. It is important that the family does not feel deserted as well as devastated after the death of their child.

For most families there comes a point during the second year of bereavement, having worked through their acute grief and loss, when they are ready to move forward within their new-structure family unit. It is important for our involvement to be relinquished at the appropriate time so as not to impede the family in their progress.

One example of our involvement was with a 10-year-old boy who, at the time of recurrent disease, felt comfortable enough to ask for more information. He said that he knew what living was, he knew what dead was, but he didn't know what dying was. We were able to have a long, exploratory discussion, before he suddenly moved on to the current football news.

I asked Jane Watson how she managed to work so intensively over many years with these very stressful and painful situations? She said that it is partly the rewards of seeing how good individual symptom control can enable young patients to use their limited energy and stamina for 'living' rather than 'coping' until they die, and partly the impressive tenacity and resilience of terminally ill children. She gave an example:

One 8-year-old girl, whose physical condition had deteriorated markedly until she could only move two fingers and her eyes, typed out on her computer: 'I feel so happy today.'

Hospices

A major development in the care of the dying has been the emergence of the hospice movement, although it is based on ancient traditions. The word 'hospice' arises out of the twelfth-century Knights Hospitallers of the Order of St John of Jerusalem, who ordained that ill or weary journeying pilgrims should be put to bed, carefully tended, fed, and given spiritual support. These original hospices, which became fairly widespread, did not have the distinctive function of terminal care, though many of them must have provided it. It was often the religious orders who cared for the dying, particularly the victims of leprosy and plague – diseases that inspired such fear or disgust that the sufferers were shunned by their families. During the centuries when few illnesses could be cured, monks and nuns offered shelter to the terminally ill in a way that anticipates the work of the hospice today.

Again, a definition by the World Health Organization, of 'palliative care', is relevant to modern hospice care, as it is more accurate than 'terminal care':

> Palliative care . . . affirms life and regards dying as a normal process . . . neither hastens nor postpones death . . . provides relief from pain and other distressing symptoms, . . . integrates the psychological and the spiritual aspects of care . . . offers a support system to help the family cope during the patient's illness and in their own bereavement . . .

The first modern hospice to be opened in England was St Christopher's in Sydenham, in 1967. The first hospice for children was Helen House in Oxford, which was founded in 1982. As with St Christopher's, and many other hospices that have opened all over the world, there is a religious orientation. The Director of this Anglican hospice's multi-disciplinary team is Sister Frances Dominica, who founded it, but it makes no discrimination in serving people from all religious denominations, as well as the agnostic and atheist. (There are now seven other children's hospices in England.)

The main groups of children whose condition may cause them to die slowly are: those with progressive neurodegenerative disease; those with major congenital malformations; and those with malignant disease or major organ failure for whom treatment is not possible. It is these children and their families who may need support over a prolonged period. This support is most often respite care, but can also be emergency or terminal care.

There is not always a choice between hospice and hospital for respite or terminal care for children. The child and family may feel safer returning to a known hospital, rather than forming new relationships in a hospice. Much would depend on the medical condition as well as the family's awareness or acceptance of the child's impending death. One writer (Murphy, 1992) gives a very striking description of hospitals, which makes important points even though there are many exceptions to this description:

> The hospital environment is a sterilised container of technology designed principally for the supposedly efficient carrying out of procedures. Over-lit, noisy, and inhumanely institutional, hospi-

tals have little room for quiet or for friendly interaction, and this affects equally patients, families, doctors, and nurses . . . Technology has overwhelmed medicine and science has suffocated the art of healing . . .

(p. 16)

However there has been criticism of the special provision for dying patients in hospices from those who believe that the existing hospital system is adequate (as elaborated by Kastenbaum, 1982). Anxieties have been expressed about the quality of medical care available in hospices. At another level the public is often anxious about many dying people being put together to die, and whether this becomes too macabre or gloomy for the workers, the patients, and the neighbourhood (Lamerton, 1973).

These questions, and others, were answered for me by meeting Sister Frances Dominica in July 1988. Not only were some of the hospice myths dispelled, but many fresh insights were gained. Her face was alert, readily opening into a broad smile, her body tall and graceful in long blue robes. Her voice sounded vigorous, matching her energetic manner and mind.

Helen House was purpose-built, in the grounds of a convent. Most of the rooms open on to beautiful gardens, where I watched a dog trot, doves nest, and fountains play. Two children rushed joyously behind the shrubbery. Despite their odd gait, it was hard to believe that they must have a terminal or degenerative illness.

Sister Frances showed me the rooms. Immaculate pastel-coloured walls, clean carpets, sturdy attractive modern furniture; all with the children's needs in mind. Cots, mobiles, pictures, appliqués on the walls, gates to keep the children safe; signs on doors designating their use, decoratively adorned with hand-painted pictures in a way that evoked a home rather than an institution. I heard a piano playing 'This is the way we . . . on a cold and frosty morning'. Rooms for parents and children; rooms for parents; rooms for siblings; laundry room; sluice room – all the rooms that a large family home or children's home would have, plus a treatment room for drugs, dressings, and equipment, and a small room that can be made very cold so that children who have died can be laid there until the funeral, and parents can be free to be with the body, if they wish.

I asked Sister Frances whether Helen House was not necessarily for dying children, but primarily provides respite care for children (and their families) with chronic illness. She replied:

That's right. We provide for children with chronic life-threatening disease – but they do have to have degenerative illnesses. Otherwise the floodgates would open, and if you decide to specialize in something, you've actually got to stick to the criteria, otherwise you're just going to offer false hope to people. In the early days, when we weren't anything like fully booked, it was tempting to say 'yes' to all sorts of families when they had a severely handicapped child, but whose handicap was not life threatening. Then we recognized that, as we became better known and it seemed we were providing a useful service, more children with a progressive disease would come, and we would then disappoint the others by having to give the children with progressive illness the priority.

So, I asked, you have many, many families on your books, and they call upon you when they want to?

That's right. At any time there are probably about 90 families on the books with their child still living, and there's room for eight at a time. It just about works out. There are peak times, like summer holidays, when we have to limit the length of stay, and sometimes we have to juggle dates a bit. That figure doesn't take account of the bereaved families we have in continuing contact. We do keep in touch with all our bereaved families for as long as they wish.

I wondered whether the whole bereaved family still came to stay sometimes?

This again is difficult because we don't have elastic walls, but quite often the bereaved families will come and spend a day or part of a day with us, and occasionally they come overnight. More often members of our team visit the families in their own homes. We don't have a defined catchment area, so we travel widely. We feel it's very important. To go to the family's own home alters the relationship completely, because you're then accepting their hospitality, and we feel it's good to do that. Even if all they've had is the opportunity to offer us a cup of tea or something, you've gone to their place and seen them in their environment, and accepted their hospitality.

I asked Sister Frances whether fund-raising was a constant worry, as Helen House receives no state funding.

No, it isn't, and in fact we spend very little time on it now. Obviously at the beginning a lot of time and energy was spent on it, but we were in the extremely fortunate position of never having to initiate any fund-raising. People heard about the plans, and very quickly word spread, and all we did was produce a little leaflet and then try desperately to keep up with answering invitations to go to talk to groups. We have to be careful financially, and not be irresponsible in any sense – it is other people's money after all. We've been very fortunate. I hardly ever go to talk to a group just because they want to fund-raise for us. I confine my speaking now almost exclusively to professional groups, because I feel we've got a lot to share: groups of people involved in health care, or sometimes clergy groups.

I then asked her about the criticism levied at hospices, especially hospices for children, as being inappropriate from the medical care point of view, as well as taking children out of the familiarity of home or even a hospital that they may have grown to know well.

Until people understand why we're here, then we are a target for criticism. Initially when we were trying to set up Helen House, we encountered a lot of adverse criticism, particularly from paediatricians saying 'How dare you!' and 'This is all wrong thinking'. You see they were thinking that the children who would come here would almost exclusively have cancer or leukaemia, and in fact very few of our children have malignant disease. I think it's 20 per cent of all the children who have been here, and I think that's because a child who is going to die of malignant disease is probably – and this is generalizing – but is probably going to be cared for, able to be cared for at home, because the tendency is to treat right to the last, and so probably the time of palliative care is going to be relatively short. In our experience, people will rally round in a short-term crisis, and a variety of support and help at home is available. If that's what the family chooses then I think that's what should happen. An alternative is, of course, for the family who doesn't feel safe or secure at home to go back to the hospital where they've received treatment while they were still hoping for a cure.

But there are a few children, for example, with slowly growing inoperable tumours, where it's not going to be a question of days or weeks – it's going to be months or possibly years, and therefore we can offer the kind of respite care that we offer to the other children with slowly progressive diseases. I think it's important to recognize that the number of families needing this type of respite care, where the child has a degenerative disease, is small, thank God. Most of the children who come to us have rare diseases so the numbers are quite small in the UK, and even of those families, not all of them will need this type of respite care. Some of them will have built-in support systems anyway, whether it's extended family, or good neighbours, or friends. Or they may have negotiated some sort of private scheme, whereby their child might go for respite care to another family, or they may be in the fortunate position of being given adequate support in their own home.

It's important to remember that the public usually define 'hospice' as a place where you go to die. We prefer to define it as a place where hospitality is offered to those on a journey. We still think we can justify calling ourselves a hospice, but it needs to be explained.

However, there is a controversy over the place of hospices for children. At a symposium in 1987, sponsored by the Help the Hospices charity with the assistance of the Royal College of Physicians of London and the British Paediatric Association, the question of ways in which the needs of dying children and their families might best be met was discussed. The conclusion was that the widespread development of hospices for children was unnecessary, as the number of such children is small – estimated at approximately six a year in each health district. However, this estimate was probably an incorrect understatement. An article in the *British Medical Journal* (Chambers, 1987) points out the need for health districts to review their services for dying children, whereby 'provision would be made within the child's home or as close to it as possible'. The author argues that if a family prefers hospital care, the existing wards may not cater for the 'more measured pace' required by the dying child. He concludes that institutional arrangements are second-best, and that professionals should be offering more domiciliary support. He emphasizes the importance of domiciliary night nursing, as 'sleeplessness is most destructive of parental morale'.

The book *A Way to Die*, by Rosemary and Victor Zorza (1980), gives a very moving account of the authors' daughter's illness and death. It is particularly illuminating on the type of care a hospice can offer, with its skill in managing physical pain. Once the physical care of the patient was eased by the experienced hospice workers, the parents and the patient herself could relax and even enjoy the remaining time. Where chronic pain cannot be eased by hospital doctors, it seems that the highly experienced hospice doctors and nurses can often succeed.

In conclusion, it seems that hospices and the special qualities that they offer can be fully utilized only once a family and patient have accepted that the 'war' on the disease is over, that further curative treatment is not appropriate, and that palliative care is needed. If the family can gain support from each other, from friends, relatives, and their family doctor or contact with the hospital that treated them, and help from a Symptom Care Team, they may not need hospice care. I do not wish to imply that hospice care is only where these other networks fail, because, of course, it can work well alongside these supports mentioned.

Part Two
Robert, aged 7-and-a-half

Chapter Seven
Diary of my work with Robert over 3 months

No need to be so scared of words, doctor.
This is called dying.

Luigi Pirandello on his death-bed (1936)

To live a half life half dead, a living death

Milton, Samson Agonistes

Background

This is an account of my work with a 7-and-a-half-year-old boy whom I shall call Robert. He was diagnosed as having acute myeloblastic leukaemia about 2-and-a-half years before I met him.

I introduced him briefly in the Preface. His large eyes, with their enquiring look, conveyed more vigour than the rest of his thin body. Perhaps the size of his eyes was emphasized by his lack of hair. His scalp was bald and smooth, covered by a very fine down, reminiscent of a young baby. The beautifully curved dome of his head seemed to invite gentle stroking.

Before proceeding with his story, and how I came to know him, I will convey some necessary background. Inevitably, many of the details that follow are bound to be painful for the reader. Perhaps this is unavoidable in an attempt to gain some understanding of the situation surrounding one particular child and others like him, as well as raising important issues over the ways that we approach illness, death, and, more specifically, the death of a child.

Childhood cancer is rare (with an overall incidence of 1 in 600 over the total span of childhood and adolesence in Britain), yet it constitutes the second greatest cause of death, after accidents. My focus will be mainly on leukaemia, the causes of which are generally unknown.

Environmental factors

Some known external causes of leukaemia are radiation (such as atomic bomb survivors, and people exposed to certain X-rays *in utero*), and mutagenic drugs and chemicals.

There appears to be increasing evidence that some leukaemias and non-Hodgkin's lymphoma are caused by living in close proximity to nuclear power stations. A report published in June 1988 by Comare (the Committee on Medical Aspects of Radiation in the Environment) concluded that the 'raised incidence of leukaemia near Dounreay, taken in conjunction with that relating to the area around Sellafield, tends to support the hypothesis that . . . nuclear plants . . . lead to an increased risk of leukaemia in young people living in the vicinity' (*Guardian*, 21 July 1988). Another report has uncovered a raised incidence of childhood leukaemia in the area around Hinkley Point, an Electricity Generating Board nuclear site (Milne, 1988). There is another theory linking living in the shadow of high-voltage electrical power lines with above-average rates of leukaemia (Sadgrove, 1988).

However, there is a newer theory (Kinlen, 1988; Kinlen *et al.*,1993) about the clustering of cases, which does not refute the link between radioactive materials and leukaemia. It proposes that sometimes childhood leukaemia is caused by an infection, for we know that viruses can cause leukaemia in animals. Kinlen suggests that children living in isolated rural areas are not usually exposed to whatever virus causes leukaemia. When a nuclear plant is built in a remote area the construction workers and the workers in the plant may bring the virus into the community. Kinlen relates this theory to other influxes of new populations (such as new towns; evacuees during the Second World War) and he finds that indeed leukaemia was nearly 50 per cent more common in areas where there has been a large influx of new people.

Robert's mother showed me a photograph of the pleasant rural surroundings in which they lived, commenting on the many large electrical pylons spoiling the landscape. Even though I realize how many different risk-factors play a part in every leukaemia and in Robert's illness, I could not help wondering about the possible connection between the pylons and Robert's leukaemia.

In order to confirm some of the factual medical details that follow, I had to contact one or two overworked hospital doctors in order to show them my rough notes. One of them caught sight of my description – on another page of my writing – of the hospital as 'encapsulating' and its atmosphere as alien for these parents. He became very disapproving of my seemingly emotive language. This reaction demonstrated the distance between many of the doctors and myself, as a child psychotherapist, and, as I observed, between the doctors and the rest of the team. The considerable work-load that the doctors face can only partly explain this. The extreme pressure provides them with an inbuilt 'escape clause' – 'there's not enough time to get involved' – as a way of avoiding some of the emotional implications of their work. This phenomenon is similar to that described by Menzies Lyth (1959) in her research into the ways in which the hospital system colludes with nurses' denial of painful feelings (see Appendix 3). These difficulties are part of a much wider debate, but the problem has relevance to the various situations that I describe later.

As I mentioned in Chapter 1, referring to the training of medical students concerning issues about death and dying, there are fundamental residual obstacles preventing some doctors from embracing a psychodynamic understanding. I see this partly as a result of the intensely hierarchical system within the hospitals, which, at least in some respects, may arise from the methods of selection of medical students and from their training. I suppose it was partly this 'divide' that perhaps explains the unavailability and impatience of many doctors for discussion of issues arising from the first edition of this book. However, there were one or two exceptions.

It is important to add, however, that the preceding paragraph was written in 1987, and that now, in 1995, I am aware of a gradual shift over the past 8 years. There seems to be a more thoughtful, sensitive approach on the part of many medical students, despite the psychological/psychodynamic input in their training being minimal. Perhaps the increase in the numbers of female medical students has contributed to this development. Many junior doctors are extremely concerned about, and want to think about, the emotional care of their patients – despite being very over-worked – and are pleased that there are child psychotherapists on the team. Some senior doctors are accepting, and sometimes welcoming and appreciative, of a psychodynamic component in the care of their patients. The different contribution and ways of thinking between a counsellor and a psychotherapist are, however, not understood by many.

Leukaemia

The facts and figures that follow are gleaned from many different publications; from my researching into bone-marrow transplants for a hospital familiarization project for children; as well as from some very helpful communications from Professor Judith Chessells of the Great Ormond Street Hospital for Sick Children, London.

'Leukaemia' comes from a Greek word, meaning 'white blood'. It is commonly known as cancer of the blood. The word describes a group of malignant disorders that arise in the blood-forming cells. One of this group is acute myeloblastic or myeloid leukaemia (AML), which is the type that Robert had. As with all types of leukaemia, it involves the production of abnormal, immature white cells in the bone marrow, which results in the excessive accumulation of white cells both in the bone marrow and in the blood stream. Therefore, it is really a bone marrow disease that appears as a blood disorder.

This type of leukaemia, AML, accounts for approximately 35 per cent of all diagnosed leukaemia cases in western countries but is not common in children. It accounts for about 20 per cent of childhood leukaemias. Thirty years ago, the outlook for AML was so grim that it was questionable whether patients should be treated at all. Bone-marrow transplantation (BMT) for the replacement of a patient's own bone marrow with that of a suitable donor was pioneered in the 1960s. Treatment of children by BMT has only been carried out in Britain since the early 1970s, but recently there has been an 'explosion' of this technique in Europe. Considerable advances in treatment over the past two to three decades have led to remission being possible in approximately 80–85 per cent of children with myeloid leukaemia. Despite this initial remission, most patients eventually relapse. Prolonged survival now seems to be possible for up to 30–40 per cent of those treated.

BMT is offered to some patients who do not respond to chemotherapy, who have relapsed, or who are at high risk of relapse. It has been discovered that BMT is more likely to succeed in patients who are in complete remission, rather than in those who are in partial remission or relapse. Therefore, it is usually recommended that AML patients receive transplants during the first remission. The perfect situation would be one where a sibling with a perfect tissue-type match can donate bone marrow. Fewer transplants are carried out where the donor is not a perfect match because of the increasing availability of well-matched volunteer donors.

To convey the background, Dorothy Jordan, a paediatric sister in a large teaching hospital, described the set-up for the leukaemic children:

Most of our deaths are from the children with leukaemia. These children are sometimes in hospital from 3 to 4 months. We also get to know them quite well because they come back again. Because medicine, and the treatment of leukaemia, have improved so much, parents now have to deal not only with the statement that 'your child has got leukaemia', and therefore their whole life is turned upside down, but with the drugs and the régime that we use. For some it is relapse, remission, relapse. So for the parents, you can imagine the strain that they are under. As a paediatric nurse I would stress that when you're treating a child it involves the whole family unit, and obviously support for parents is needed.

I think we could do better here than we do. Many times, when off-duty, we take parents out to get them off the ward, take them for a cup of coffee, and sit and talk. We tried to form a support group for the parents, but it's never materialized. A helpful factor is that parents of children with leukaemia do support each other. Because of the way the ward is – that we don't just have children with leukaemia, and there are many other demands on your time – we don't have time to give more. In an ideal situation, I'd like to give them much more support than I do.

However, many units would try to ensure that children with leukaemia, who have reached the stage of care and not cure, die at home whenever possible. The crucial issue, of the approaches to this final stage, I will explore more fully on pp. 148–149. Certainly social work support should generally be available for families, thereby relieving the nursing staff of this responsibility. Many of the designated social workers are funded by the Malcolm Sergeant Fund for Childhood Cancer, and one post by CLIC (the Cancer and Leukaemia in Childhood Trust).

Robert received chemotherapy after the diagnosis, and had been in remission for about 2 years when he relapsed. He then received further chemotherapy, leading to another period of remission when he had no physical complaints. About 6 months after this relapse, and during this second complete remission, he was admitted to a large hospital in the North of England for BMT. This is a potentially life-threatening and highly sophisticated rescue procedure, where the patient is given new bone marrow. It was to be a mismatch (that is, of a different tissue type) allogeneic transplant. 'Allogeneic' means that the donor's marrow is genetically different from the recipient's. His father was to be the donor. Donors are usually siblings, since the chance of finding an acceptable tissue type match is one in four for siblings and much lower for anyone else. However, Robert's father's bone marrow was found to be the most suitable.

Under these circumstances, Robert's chances of a successful outcome were probably around 5 per cent. There was some doubt in the care team over whether the doctors, in fact, had told the parents that his chances of success were around 10 per cent. Parental consent was of course received, but it is debatable as to how *informed* this consent was. This ambiguity indicates either the doctors' own difficulties in really facing some of the implications, or the parents' need to believe in a more optimistic prognosis. The confusion itself reflects the lack of a cohesive care team. (See comments by Senior Staff Nurse, Vikky Riley, pp. 53–55) The divisions, at times, in the care team reflected the division between the parents themselves, and their oscillations between approaching the reality and withdrawing from it.

It is important to point out that this type of transplant, which could be called an experimental one, is very unusual, and would probably not be considered by most paediatric bone-marrow transplant centres today.

Therefore, it does not serve to illustrate the more typical pattern of BMT treatments in paediatric oncology. Nevertheless, it raises significant moral and ethical implications as to whether this type of treatment or research should be carried out at all (see Chapter 10), and the extent to which parents and the patient should be fully informed. It probably accounted for approximately 10 per cent of paediatric BMTs at the time that the first edition of this book was written (1987/8). However, was that 10 per cent too many? It also highlights dilemmas common to all terminally ill children and their families: can the quality of the remaining life be the main priority and focus, rather than an attempt to cure that which is probably incurable, through treatment which is particularly aggressive and invasive?

I knew Robert for the last 2 and a half months of his life, from his admission at the end of September to his death in mid-December. He had visited the hospital a few weeks earlier for tests. He arrived with his parents, Mr and Mrs Campbell, from their home in the Highlands of Scotland, for the transplant at the end of September. He spent the first day in a hotel, going to the hospital, going for a walk in the park with his parents, and visiting a toy shop. These were his last acts of freedom and health – although no one realized this at the time. Mr and Mrs Campbell had resolutely wanted everything medically possible to be tried for Robert even if the chances of survival were slim. Without a bone-marrow transplant the chances of survival would be even less. So, although the consultants did not hold great hopes for the success of this treatment, the parents wanted this attempt to be made. When Robert was admitted, his medical notes stated that he was well, had no specific complaints, and had a good appetite. He was taking no drugs.

Robert had an 11-year-old sister, Julie, who was staying with an aunt back home in Scotland. The family came from a rural part of the country, and were involved with farming. They had rarely visited big cities, and had never before stayed in this part of England. In time I gathered that not only did they feel totally out of their usual environment and away from their support systems and extended family, but the encapsulating air-conditioning of the modern hospital with its hermetically sealed windows exacerbated their feeling of landing on a threatening, and at times alien, planet.

On the day after Robert's admission, some of his own bone marrow was harvested. In this procedure, under general anaesthetic, some bone marrow was removed from the pelvic bones, using special needles. The marrow obtained in this way was then processed and frozen. In the event of the bone marrow graft from his father failing, this could then be used instead, for an autologous, or 'self-transplant'. At the same time, he had a lumbar puncture, in order to see if there were leukaemic cells or infection in the spinal fluid, and to inject a drug to prevent the recurrence of leukaemia. A programme of intravenous cytotoxic chemotherapy was commenced, in order to obliterate the existing bone marrow, which would contain many leukaemic cells. He also received total body irradiation to compound the effect of the chemotherapy, as well as to get rid of his own immune system and thereby reduce the likelihood of rejecting his father's bone marrow. Total body radiation is frightening for many young patients. For Robert it required an hour of immobilization alone in a shielded room. Both the chemotherapy and the total body irradiation induced nausea and vomiting as predictable side-effects. (Total hair loss is another inevitable side-effect of this treatment, but this is temporary; permanent sterility, as a result of radiation treatment, is yet another.) These treatments alone would be lethal without the transplant, which would eventually repopulate Robert's bone marrow, and then his blood, with healthy cells.

The transplant itself, which then followed, was quite a simple procedure. This central event is, paradoxically, brief and uncomplicated. The bone marrow was harvested from Robert's father in exactly the same way as the back-up bone marrow was taken from Robert. This was then processed so that only cells necessary to repopulate the bone marrow remained in a very small volume, and were then given to Robert directly into the Hickman line, like a blood transfusion.

The Hickman line is a central venous catheter via a skin tunnel from the chest into the superior vena cava of the heart, to give ease of access for the blood, blood products, chemotherapy drugs, antibiotics, intravenous feeding, etc., and for blood sampling for laboratory tests.

The transplanted, or transfused, cells would then find their own way back into Robert's bone marrow spaces, where they would multiply, mature, and engraft. In 2 or 3 weeks, the then mature cells from the marrow would spread into the blood stream. Until then, Robert would have no cells of his own to protect him from bleeding, bruising, and infection. Once these cells have spread into the circulation, these risks would decline. The risk, once the new marrow begins to 'take', or grow, is of graft-versus-host disease developing. This is a phenomenon whereby the implanted cells attack those of the recipient, and is potentially fatal.

The detailed consecutive diary, forming the rest of this section, conveys the way in which notes, made after the meetings, are used as an aide-memoire and as a way of thinking about the situation. Theoretical understandings often emerge later, with the help of notes. Minute detail gives the reader an opportunity to get close to the actual events, and to evaluate and apply the foregoing chapters. It is also a way of putting the reader through one part of the ordeal, thus experiencing, albeit at a distance, one family's tragedy. It is salutary to remember that if this diary is, at times, almost unbearable to many readers, it reflects only two, and occasionally three, meetings per week with this child. This is little compared with the almost constant deep involvement of the parents over this period, plus the preceding build-up of 2-and-a-half years of illness – let alone the experience for the child himself. However, the parents and the patient can and do use necessary defences, while the therapist, and perhaps the reader, can 'afford' this intense pain because the contact is not constant. The mother of another child (who had a brain tumour and was hospitalized for a year of treatment) said to me: 'I feel that he was put through Auschwitz, and then they did experiments on him.'

In the account that follows, the reader will see the many occasions when my own courage failed, when I avoided what perhaps I should have said, when the team of professionals was divided, as well as when family members were at odds with each other. But perhaps through reading this, others facing similar situations, personally or professionally, will find some useful guidelines, warnings of possible pitfalls, rather than hard and fast prescriptions. And those who read this after experiencing the death of a child may find that it helps to compare and thus process their own experience.

First contact

30 September (Thursday) 3 pm. I am taken by Dr Simmons, a child psychiatrist, to meet Robert for the first time. I see an attractive child with a bald head lying on the bed. He looks at me with large eyes. I feel slightly shocked by the baldness. I naively had not anticipated it. It is the result of previous chemotherapy. To those unfamiliar with leukaemic children who have lost their hair, this baldness seems to give them a 'sameness' of appearance, making it more difficult to discern their age, sex, and (until one gains familiarity with leukaemic children) even their individual facial characteristics.

I am introduced to his mother, Mrs Campbell, and to Robert. Mr and Mrs Campbell have already agreed to my seeing their son regularly. My role as child psychotherapist has been briefly explained to them (see Chapter 6 for a description of this role). Robert was referred to me because of the isolation of this family from their normal environment as well as the grim prognosis. It was anticipated, therefore, that they would experience extreme stresses. Peter, the paediatric social worker, was to keep in touch with the parents regularly, and liaise with me. Robert was also to receive frequent visits from the play specialist, and from a particular teacher from the hospital school assigned to him. Unfortunately, owing to limited resources, only a few children in hospital have the opportunity to receive psychotherapy.

I decided to plan to see Robert regularly twice weekly. This seemed to be the maximum time that I had available, and, I felt, was the minimum requirement of a child in his situation where continuity was important, and where inevitable physical fluctuations, such as being too unwell or asleep during therapy session times, necessitated frequent contact. Moreover, to a child in hospital, unable to escape from bed, and being nursed in isolation – as I explain further – even one day can seem like a very long time.

Mrs Campbell sits between Robert and us. She is a pretty, delicate looking woman, slim and bright-eyed. By answering for Robert, she seems to be acting sensitively as a buffer between her son and the outside world. She seems thus to be percolating the myriad strange experiences that her son is having to face. I notice a worn-out little yellow teddy bear on Robert's pillow, and ask him about it. Robert tells me its name is Sunshine.

I leave, telling Robert that I will have my first proper meeting with him next Tuesday, and then on Thursday, and so on, each week.

4 pm. I see Mrs Campbell and Robert going down in the lift. Robert is being carried by his mother, his large head again so reminiscent of a baby's. Mrs Campbell's lips seem to brush the downy surface. Robert looks bright and happy.

A few days after I met Robert, I began writing a diary of my visits to him.

Second meeting

2 October (Tuesday) 11 am. The blinds are drawn on Robert's door. Unsure if it's the right room, I knock and enter, recognizing his bright red dressing-gown hanging up before I see him.

He is in bed, slightly curled up, his father sitting on his bed, showing him cards he has just received in the post from his school friends back home. I introduce myself to Mr Campbell, who is a large man with a gentle manner, and remind Robert who I am. Robert just looks at me. I talk about all the different people they must be meeting, and how muddling it must be. Mr Campbell agrees, but smiles and says, 'It's not too bad. I'm getting it all sorted out.' He invites me to sit on the bed as he moves to a chair.

I explain to Robert that I am not a doctor or a nurse. Mr Campbell quickly interjects, 'So she doesn't have to do any horrible things to you . . . but you're not afraid of doctors or nurses, are you, lad?'

I explain that I am really here for Robert to talk to if he wants to, and that I will be bringing some play things that will be specially for when I am with him. Mr Campbell quickly and attentively says, 'That will be nice, won't it, son?' Robert seems to half shake his head, looking at me. I say to him that it must be difficult, all these strange people, and a strange hospital, and not knowing me.

Mr Campbell then talks about the strangeness of it all. We exchange comments about the hospital being a world of its own. He talks about a need for him and his wife to get out sometimes – 'to take it in turns.' (Weeks later I realize that this is *his* strong need – to escape from the claustrophobia of the hospital – and not, at least overtly, his wife's.) Mr Campbell asks if I have met his wife, who is out at the moment. He conspiratorially mimes something about what his wife is doing, which looks like ironing. He talks rather breathlessly as if he is overwhelmed by it all, and somewhat shocked. His eyes are full of feeling, his face flushed, yet I feel that he is holding back in Robert's presence. He talks about a lovely walk the three of them had in a park a few days ago.

He shows me a card made by several of Robert's school friends, quickly explaining that of course Robert hasn't been to school much for the past 2 years, but his friends still remember him, 'Don't they lad?' I read out some of the names on the card. When his father and I cannot decipher one name, Robert calls out in a loud, definite voice.

Meanwhile, he is fiddling with a card depicting a picture of Jesus. I ask him if he'd like me to fetch the toys now. He shakes his head. Mr Campbell volunteers that he's not feeling too bad today as he didn't have to have treatment [radiotherapy] today. He adds that tomorrow would be the last one. Robert shakes his head. Mr Campbell repeats, 'You have your last treatment tomorrow, Friday, Bobby.' He seems to hit out at his father with his hand. I say, 'You don't want to talk about some things? I'm wondering, Robert, if it's your Dad saying that it's the last treatment you disagree with?' He seems to nod.

I say that I know that he would be having the transplant next week. Mr Campbell says, 'Yes . . . on Monday. He has more radiotherapy, and then the bone-marrow transplant.' He adds that he has to 'go in' on Sunday evening as the donor, and has to 'starve' himself before the anaesthetic. Robert looks round and fixes his eyes on father for the first time.

I say something to both of them about this being one of the things a Mum or Dad does for their children. Mr Campbell nods in agreement.

I say that today I am really introducing myself, and that I wanted also to say that sometimes boys and girls find it easier to talk to someone who isn't their Mum or Dad about any worries they might have, because sometimes they don't want to upset Mum or Dad. I say that I am saying this in front of Dad so he would understand too about Robert having me as someone who won't tell Mum and Dad everything. 'It's because Mum and Dad are such important people in your life that sometimes it's useful to have someone else who's separate from them.'

Robert is still bending the card of Jesus. Mr Campbell asks him to stop. He continues. Father says, 'It's a special card; Agnes gave it to you at the airport.' He takes it from Robert, straightens it, and puts it on the ledge with other cards.

As if to cheer Robert up he says, 'I telephoned Julie [Robert's sister], didn't I, Bobby? She's glad to know you're OK, and you're glad to know she's OK.' He then tells me that Julie is staying with her aunt, and continues, 'I was saying to Robert that when we get him on his feet again, he could trot along and give her a ring.' He gives me a big wink. 'That would be nice, wouldn't it, Bobby?'

Robert is fiddling with his ears, twisting them, and now bends them over, as if to block off any sound. When Father talks about Robert getting on his feet, I feel he is inviting me to join him in his denial of the possibility that Robert will not be 'on his feet'. I feel trapped between his wishes and Robert's needs. Robert seems to be feeling not only doubt about whether that was the last radiotherapy treatment, but also anger when he seems to hit out at him and then attack the religious card. But I do not at this point feel able to say much more to both of them. I need to wait until I have built up more of a relationship with Robert on his own.

As I leave, saying, 'See you Tuesday', Mr Campbell says, 'Don't work too hard!' (I wonder if this is a covert expression of his resentment at my going off for four days, leaving them with the distress of the next few days.)

6 October (Monday). Robert is given the transplant. During the preceding radiation treatment he was apparently extremely silent and some of the medical staff express concern about his emotional state. They notice that he is withdrawn, and sense that he may be depressed. As they know he is being given psychotherapy, they appropriately pass these worries on to me.

The psychotherapy begins

7 October (Tuesday). He is now being barrier-nursed, in isolation, so anyone entering the room has to don mask, gloves, and plastic apron in order to reduce the dangers of infection. If I feel very cut off behind the mask, what must it be like for Robert to see only the eyes of everyone, I wonder.

10.30 am. I go in and find him very perky and smiling. He is sitting up, wearing smart striped pyjamas. He shows playful aggression towards the nurses, openly criticizing the big nose of one of them. This spirited rapport between Robert and the nurses seems a denial of anything serious. Mrs Campbell seems tired. I ask about Mr Campbell – he, apparently, is 'sore', recovering from donating the bone marrow, and is on another ward. Robert tells me that he thought Daddy would be recovering with him, and not in another part of the hospital. Both Mrs Campbell and Robert refer frequently to Julie as a missed member of the family.

I introduce the box of play equipment, which includes a miniature hospital set. Robert examines the tiny figures and objects. He calls the little television in this set an X-ray machine. (Another hospital patient had thought this same little television was 'an ambulance kit' – instances

of the unusual distortion of the lives of children who have lengthy exposure to hospitals.) He attempts to get the tiny vase of plastic flowers to
stand up. Its repeated toppling, and his repeated attempts to right it,
convey to me something of his precarious state, and his wish for greater
stability.

As Mrs Campbell is there, I feel that it is not a 'proper' psychotherapy
session – so I am unsure about some possible interpretations in
mother's presence. As I leave, Robert says to Mrs Campbell that he is
'starving for a cheese sandwich'. His Scottish accent makes his speech
particularly attractive.

Later, I hear one of the sisters describing Robert as a 'really cheeky
delightful child'.

9 October (Thursday) 11.30 am. I arrive on the ward with Robert's box
of play things. All the senior nursing staff seem very busy, so it's not the
right time for me to explore with them the possibility of making the
sessions a little more 'private' – there are innumerable medical check-
ups each time I am with Robert and I wonder if non-essential ones could
wait for half an hour or so. He is bed-bound, tied to his Hickman
catheter. Because of the catheter, there is no possibility of my taking him
into another room. I look for someone to tell me more about bone-
marrow transplants. But it can wait.

I ask Dr Fish (Robert's senior house officer) in passing if he has done
his ward round yet (hoping to time my session around this) but he says
amicably, 'No . . . but never mind . . . I'll just pop in.' In time, I learn that
I have to try to work around and with the environment.

Through the blind on Robert's door I can see Mrs Campbell. I don
the mask, gloves, apron, spray the toys and the box with sterilizing fluid,
and go in. Robert immediately tells his mother that he wants the bedpan.
Mrs Campbell lifts him on to it. He seems so full of lines leading to the
Hickman. Later a nurse calls it Spaghetti Junction. Although Robert
seems not to mind my presence while he defecates, I look out of the
window, but have noticed his thin white body. Mrs Campbell says something about Robert's trousers being dirty. She wipes him and then makes
him comfortable under the sheets, and takes the bedpan out.

Robert then says something quietly to his mother, who then asks me
about leaving the toys in the box here for Robert. I explain – with difficulty – that it is important for me to bring them each time as part of my
sessions with Robert, so that they remain special, and Robert and I can
try and understand each time what meaning they have for him. Robert
replies to his mother, 'It was you who wondered about it!' Mrs Campbell
says that she had thought that I took them away each time because I had
to use them with other children. I said that I could see that it must be
frustrating when I take them away each time – but no, they are only for
Robert's use.

Mrs Campbell asks Robert if she should show me the letter from Julie received today. Robert is silent. I say, 'You're not sure.' Robert then nods to his mother, giving permission. Mrs Campbell shows me the letter, and we talk about their wish for Julie to be here, and how feasible this might be for a few days. Robert interjects, 'Not for a few days, for a week !' Robert shows me a card from a school friend. The name looks like hieroglyphics – and then I realize it is 'Stevie' backwards. Robert smiles brightly and says, 'Oh yes, he always used to write backwards!'

I've left the therapy box a little way from the bed, and am sitting on a chair by Robert's bed. Mrs Campbell says, 'You've got to take your medicine. Come on, Bobby.' He sullenly sits there. Mrs Campbell hands him a cup. He refuses. Mrs Campbell says, 'If you don't, maybe Mrs Judd will have to go.'

Robert still sits there. I say, 'Is it horrible? He nods. Robert takes little sips of it. Mrs Campbell praises him, but tells him to finish what is left at the bottom. Robert refuses. I ask how often he has to take this? Twice daily. Mrs Campbell tells Robert kindly but insistently that the doctors say it's important. I feel tense, caught between the opposing pull of the mother (and the doctors) and Robert's assertion of some autonomy. She relents, with the retort, 'I'll put it down the sink and that won't do much good! And I'll have to tell the doctors!' as she tips it away.

A student nurse comes in, to take nose and throat swabs. Robert protests. Mrs Campbell appeals to him. The nurse suggests that Robert does it himself. No. The nurse then gently carries out the simple procedure, Robert acquiescing, but he seems to feel very invaded and upset. The nurse asks to have a look at his dressing (around the Hickman catheter). Robert sulks. The nurse gently lifts his pyjama top. He cooperates by removing the sticky strips himself, then looks down at the plastic tube entering his chest. (I wonder to myself what it must feel like to have a hole in your chest so near the heart.)

Mrs Campbell watches, close by. Robert says something to his mother and then mimes with his hand a pumping action, meaning he can feel his heart beating. The nurse wipes his skin with a swab. Robert flinches. I ask if it's cold, or does it sting? He tells me it's cold. When the area is wiped further, Robert squirms more than before. My questions indicate my need to become familiar with the *many* procedures he has to undergo, and to begin to sense what their impact is on Robert.

The nurse then has to dress the site – and as we all wear gloves, we cannot peel the sticky tape, so Robert volunteers, struggles, and succeeds; then helps to stick the strips down. He pulls off more tape, beckons the nurse towards him, and sticks some across the nurse's mask, half on the bridge of her nose. The nurse jokes about it and leaves. I think how sensitive some of the nurses are to Robert's need to attempt to control some of the procedures.

Mrs Campbell asks her son if she can go off for a while. He nods, adding, 'But only to the coffee lounge.' I say that I can be here until one o'clock, depending on how Robert feels. Mrs Campbell says, 'Oh, in that case, I'll go and get Dad to come and have lunch with me . . . he's still quite sore', and leaves.

I take up with him the question of my taking the box away each time. He interjects conspiratorially, 'I often think that if you have a toy or something all the time, you get bored with it.' (I do not link this to any feelings he may have about my coming and going, partly because it is early in the relationship. But perhaps the difficulties in working in an unsequestered setting, as well as the feeling that Robert's death may be imminent, explain my difficulty and reluctance to encourage a deepening of the transference. With hindsight, he may have been helped more had I not felt this inhibition.)

I clear Robert's bed-table surface, and open the therapy box. He peers in, takes out a new box of plastic figures, opens it, and then skilfully constructs the family. As it is new he has to assemble many of the parts. He finds a little piece of foam rubber and exclaims, 'This must be the soft pillow.' He seems to enjoy the process of organizing, making, deciding for himself. When I voice this observation, adding, 'especially when you have to have so much done to you these days', he nods wisely.

He then tries to get the mother doll to push the little pram, but mother's hands are stiff, so he uses the father doll instead, adding, 'He's too little!' Interestingly, although he could make father's feet touch the ground, he leaves him as seemingly too little, thereby conveying a weakened father. This clearly relates to his current perception of his father, now debilitated by the donation of bone-marrow, and may have further-reaching implications of his feelings. But at this stage I do not interpret, as it is too early in the contact. These are simply some of my thoughts and understandings at the time.

He says that they are on an outing, ' . . . to the *park*', the last word said with great enthusiasm. He takes out the box of animals, and asks me which ones would not be in a park. I comment on there being wild animals and farm animals. He leaves the two lion cubs (calling them puppies), takes a baby kangaroo, and says that Skippy must be in a park. He then enacts what he calls a hippo (but is really a rhinoceros, perhaps thus defusing the fierceness of the animal) fighting with a tiger, the tiger hitting the 'hippo' and the 'hippo' then charging at the pram and knocking over the baby and the mum and dad. The mum then rides on the 'hippo' to tame it, and order is restored.

I comment that at first he seemed to want to keep the wild animals separate from the peaceful scene in the park, but they soon attacked everything. I say that I wonder if Robert sometimes feels very angry, like the hippo – angry at having to be like the helpless baby in the pram. (I also wonder – to myself – if the hippo represents the disrupting invasion of the illness, upsetting the family triad. Although there is a fourth member of the family, it seems that Robert's focus is on those who are with him in hospital.)

By now he has placed two little lambs on the baby's pram. I ask what he feels about this. 'They're horrible,' he says expressively. I say that although they look gentle, they're frightening to the baby ' . . . like the horrible things you have done to you . . . things that may look gentle as a lamb but are very upsetting'.

Now he gets the mum to push the dad, while the dad pushes the pram. I comment on this being like his family at the moment – 'You're like the baby, lying down a lot and having to be looked after. Dad helped you with the transplant, and so pushes you along, in a way, but he is now weak like this Daddy – and Mum has to look after both of you.' He listens to this with interest.

And then he takes out the Plasticine, looking at all the colours. He wonders aloud which one would be skin coloured, and chooses white, although there is some flesh-coloured plasticine. (This choice not only seems to reflect Robert's very pale skin, but may also reflect his having probably heard talk about the important part that white cells play in leukaemia.) He models a head, and adds two brown eyes. He wonders how to make hair. I ask him what ideas *he* has? He proceeds with the body. I say, 'You seem to be leaving it without hair, perhaps so that the little figure is like you?' (See photograph of Robert's plasticine man, page 110.)

He darts a look at me, and then nods. I say, 'You must miss your hair.' He nods emphatically. I say, 'What colour was your hair?' 'Reddish brown,' he replies feelingly, with pride. Then he adds arms and ponders the problem of how to add legs.

Dr Fish comes in, and chirpily holds up one of the animals, asking, 'What's this?' Robert says, 'Hippo!' Dr Fish bursts forth: 'No, it's not! It's a rhinoceros! Javanese . . . or Sumatran . . . very rare . . . only about a dozen left in the world . . . that's its armour . . .' Robert just looks at him.

He asks Robert how he's feeling and looks in his mouth. Robert is ultra cooperative; then he listens to his chest. He asks if he hasn't eaten because he feels sick or because he's not hungry? Robert just shrugs. He asks where Mum is. I explain. He says, 'Dad's very sore, he's got lots of holes in his back, like a tea-bag.' Robert stares at him.

He goes. I feel, through a strong identification with Robert at that moment, as if the hippo (or rhino!) had charged over me. I say to Robert, 'It's difficult being interrupted when you're busy with something.' He nods. After further doubts about how to add legs to the figure, he succeeds and shows me how it can stand up.

I feel that his difficulty in executing the legs reflects his present helpless bed-ridden existence, where his own legs are out of action and not much use. The upstretched arms also convey helplessness and an appeal to be comforted or picked up. The exceptionally large eyes, and the exclusion of any other facial features, emphasize the need to look and to take in through the eyes. This seems to reflect Robert's own scrutiny of his environment, for literally vital information.

Later, when I look at this figure, I feel that it is like a little ghost. This is confirmed when, months later, I photograph it and then photocopy the photograph. The photocopy is also ghost-like and the head looks skull-like.

He then methodically packs up the Plasticine. I say, 'You seem to have had enough.' He says, 'No – now I'm going to play with the hospital set,' and sets it up. Again the tiny vase of flowers topples over. He is more resigned this time. The same student nurse comes in, shows an interest in the toys, and asks Robert to remember to do a specimen of urine in a special container next time. Another nurse gaily comes in. A porter pulls faces at Robert from the door. He pulls faces back.

Robert's Plasticine man

Suddenly, he says, 'I feel sick!' I quickly fetch a vomit bowl, and he is very violently and copiously sick into it, remaining stoical throughout. I find my role immediately has to change to a more maternal one.

When the vomiting is over, I talk to him about my now really seeing some of the awful side to being ill. He continues to play with the hospital set, making a little boy doll get out of bed, put on big slippers belonging to the mother doll, and then enacts him eating his dinner. He then makes the little boy go back to bed.

Most play sequences are very rich and complex in meaning, and the child psychotherapist often attempts to deal with only some aspects of that which is revealed at any particular moment. I will give a detailed analysis of the foregoing sequence as an example, to illustrate my understanding – some of it with hindsight – of this last passage of material, although I did not attempt to tell Robert much of what I understood. The therapist stores and processes the child's information and feelings. This is rather like the way a mother might hold a crying baby in her arms and feel responsive to, and think about the baby's mood, without actually crying with the baby, nor, necessarily, saying much to the baby.

If we look at this last sequence, it seems that Robert, using the little boy doll as a symbol for himself, shows this doll becoming a coping mother: the child literally steps into the mother doll's large slippers. Perhaps Robert feels the mother doll is able to walk around and cope at this point because I became the coping mother helping him when he vomited, and also because of repeated experiences of his own coping mother. This little-boy-inside-the-mother can now take in good food in this sequence. Interpretations that I give him may indeed feel – to a more infantile part of Robert – like 'talking food' or 'food for thought'. He has literally evacuated the 'bad stuff' in his stomach, now feeling symbolically able to leave the sick-bed, sit at a table, and eat good food. With a child who is actually ill, and who actually vomits as a side-effect of some of the medicines he has been given, the situation cannot be understood simply at a symbolic or psychological level. However, although the cause of the vomiting may be predominantly or entirely *physical*, there are nevertheless accompanying psychological processes. It is the understanding of these processes that is my focus, while at the same time I acknowledge the purely physical aspect. Anna Freud adds to one's understanding: 'The child is unable to distinguish between feelings of suffering caused by the disease inside the body and suffering imposed on him from outside for the sake of curing the disease. He has to submit uncomprehendingly, helplessly and passively to both sets of experiences' (1952, p. 70).

So, to a child undergoing chemotherapy, as Robert is, the *repeated* experience of diarrhoea, nausea, and vomiting links with early infantile experiences of defecating, feeding, and being sick. Of course, in a healthy baby, as Robert seems to have been, good experiences hopefully outweighed the inevitable tummy pains, moments of feeling unheld, and infantile rage and distress. These earlier good experiences would help to mitigate some of the unpleasantness now encountered.

Therefore, if we try to understand how Robert feels, perhaps the vomit, or 'bad stuff', at a psychological level, is an angry violent expulsion of what is happening to his body and of what feels like the poisonous medicine invading him. He cannot express this anger directly to the nurses, doctors, or parents; there seems to be a need, on the part of the staff, for him to be happy, even though there is much more for him to be angry than happy about.

As an illustration of this, at this point a doctor with a Scottish accent puts his head round the door and calls out, 'Come on, smile! I must teach you to speak Gaelic! Can you see what I'm doing under my mask?' Robert correctly deduces, 'Putting your tongue out!'

A nurse comes in again. I tell her that Robert has been sick. She says breezily, 'First time today!' I ask her about a bell for when I have to go. She places it near Robert and leaves the room.

I tell Robert that I will have to go soon, and that I will be here again in a few days. I ask him if he remembers my days here? 'Yes, Tuesdays and Thursdays.' I confirm that I will see him next Tuesday at 2 o'clock.

We pack up the box. I feel he is being bravely self-contained. I ask him if he wants me to pass him anything before I leave. He shakes his head.

I leave. He does not turn his head in my direction. A few minutes later I pass his door and glance through the glass panel. He is lying still, looking straight ahead.

After this session, I wonder for whose sake Robert has to be cheerful. And the doctor's emphasis on the damage to his father seems an unnecessary burden.

14 October (Tuesday) 2.00 pm. I arrive to find Robert fast asleep, his mother sitting by him. Mrs Campbell tells me Robert has a high temperature. An electric fan is on by his side. Mother says he has been sleeping most of the day. He is wearing hospital pyjamas instead of his own smart ones. The hospital name is printed largely on the chest. It seems to indicate part of a general loss of individuality and autonomy. Loss of health, loss of home, loss of hair, loss of freedom of movement . . .

After waiting a while, I write a brief note to Robert, telling him I visited and that he was asleep, and that I would see him on Thursday.

16 October (Thursday) 10.30 am. I look through the door and Mrs Campbell shakes her head at me. To warn me? To keep me away? I had seen in the medical file that his condition had deteriorated considerably in the past 12 hours. The file mentions jaundice, haematemesis (vomiting up blood), pyrexia (fever), extreme bruising, liver dysfunction, oedema (swelling due to fluid retention), diarrhoea, poor platelets rise

(poor response to platelet infusion), rash. Robert's rash, skin colour, jaundice, and general condition indicate that he has graft-versus-host disease. This occurs when the new, donated marrow reacts against the recipient's body. This disease may slow the growth of the new marrow and immune system and can in itself be fatal. Medication is given to fight this disease.

Mrs Campbell comes to see me at the door with tear-stained eyes. I say that I gather Robert is very poorly today. She tells me that he is much worse. I ask if I can still see him, and she agrees.

I am confronted by a shocking sight when I see Robert. There are reddish blue patches around his eyes and mouth, his face is swollen, and the rest of his body is covered in a bizarre red rash. Even in the muted darkish room he appears in technicolour. Mrs Campbell understands intuitively that Robert wants to say something, approaching her son who then whispers in her ear. Robert wants Coca-Cola. Mrs Campbell says to me, 'Last night, do you know what he wanted to have with his medicine?! Tell us, Bobby!' Robert croaks, 'Vodka!' Mrs Campbell says, 'Next thing you'd be singing . . . and the doctors won't know what's going on when they come to take blood!' All this jollity seems bizarre in the face of Robert's appearance, but understandable as a defence.

Apparently Mr Campbell is giving platelets for Robert at this moment.

Robert very forcefully rejects the medicine that Mrs Campbell tries to give him. Anna Freud explains this, referring to Klein:

> For some children the taking of medicine presents a major diffi-culty. Though the taste or smell of the drug is in the foreground so far as the child's conscious reasons are concerned, analytic investigation discloses invariably behind these rationalizations the existence of repressed ideas of being attacked by the mother through the symbol of the drug (Melanie Klein), of being poisoned . . . by her.
>
> (1952, p. 74)

He rejects other interventions. Mrs Campbell beseeches him. The nurse seems very sensitive to Robert's resistance. Robert still has a very high temperature. I feel that his very powerful rejection of medication is para-doxically a sign of his strength and his wish to live: he seems to be saying that he is not passively going to give in to all this paraphernalia, but is going to fight it in his own way. He is showing some autonomy when there is little enough of that now in his life.

Suddenly and unexpectedly he evacuates his bowels before he can ask for a bedpan. Mrs Campbell and I perform a major change of sheets, while Robert is very cooperative. His little body is so hot when I help to lift him. He peers to see his mother come and go through very puffy eyes. He does not want to wear pyjama trousers any longer.

A bed is then moved into the room for Mrs Campbell to sleep in at night, instead of the parents' shared room a little way away.

When Robert falls asleep, Mrs Campbell cries, saying to me, 'It's so sudden . . . he was so fine . . . did we do the right thing, bringing him here?' I try to acknowledge these doubts now that Robert seems worse, but add that if they had not tried this treatment they might have had regrets too.

Meanwhile Robert wakes and sleeps fitfully, biting his nails, shivering, and fiddling with his teeth when awake.

Then suddenly he is sick, very sick, vomiting in a projectile way. Momentarily Mrs Campbell recoils at the vomit all over her, and then quickly rallies and goes forward to help him. We both hold him. He vomits up a big clot of blood, and then says that now that 'the thing' at the back of his throat has gone, he feels better. Mrs Campbell tells me that she used to 'hate vomit and that sort of thing, but if it's your own child, it's different'. The Catholic priest puts his head round the door and asks how Robert is. Mrs Campbell says, 'Not too good, not too bad', and pops out to have a word with him in the corridor.

I say to Robert, 'This must be the worst you've felt so far . . .' He shakes his head. I ask what was worse? 'Radiotherapy,' he whispers. I say emphatically that that tells me how awful the radiotherapy must have been. (Yet radiotherapy is usually considered by patients to be less unpleasant than chemotherapy.)

When Mrs Campbell returns, I have to go. I feel that Thursday to Tuesday is such a long time when Robert's condition is so precarious, so I decide to come in again on Saturday. I say to Mrs Campbell (Robert is asleep), 'See you Saturday.' She shrugs, saying, 'Maybe, see how it goes . . .' She has tears in her eyes. She adds, 'You don't normally come in on Saturdays?' I say, 'No, but I will be this Saturday.' Mrs Campbell says, 'Thank you.' I feel that indirectly we have both acknowledged the gravity of the situation.

I speak to one of the ward sisters about Robert. She seems very understanding of Mrs Campbell's present situation. She talks of mother's need for a place to cry and says that she tries to provide this, by talking to mother alone. She says that Mr Campbell does not seem to know how seriously ill Robert is. I suggest that he cannot bear to acknowledge this; and with the exception of the support of the staff, Mrs Campbell is left alone with the realization of the severity of Robert's illness. Sister seems very sensitive to Mrs Campbell as Robert's most important person. She is aware that Robert appropriately demands mother as his nurse, but that mother is becoming totally drained, as she is at Robert's beck and call practically all the time. Sister seems very supportive of my involvement, as indeed I am of hers.

Later, I think back to this session. I feel outrage at all this happening to a child. Then, on further reflection, I observe a regression in Robert from the baby that he seemed when I first met him, with his bald head, being cradled in his mother's arms, to this foetus-like state: his large head, his red colour (as if his skin is transparent), his curled-up half-naked posture, his dependence on sustenance from the 'umbilical' tubes entering his body. It is as if he is taking a path back into the womb, yet not towards life but towards death. 'In my beginning is my end' (Eliot, 1944).

Am I becoming over-involved? What do I mean by that? I find myself waking up in the middle of the night, confronted by the dreadful vision of Robert. I compare him with my own child of the same age: they have the same 7-year-old little shoulders, the same big new teeth, and yet set on such different paths. My child's robust physical health seems so precious, and makes Robert's state more poignant. Perhaps this pain I feel is a part of what is of value to him and to his mother: that I can, albeit peripherally, begin to comprehend and share some of their nightmare.

18 October (Saturday) 11.30 am. I feel faint as I leave the lift and walk towards the room. I tell myself that this is ridiculous. The hospital has enough to worry about without an over-involved child psychotherapist collapsing in the corridor. I feel worse. I tell myself that I can always leave, turn around and go home, tell people I have a cold and should not see Robert. This 'escape clause' relieves the faint feeling.

Through the door, Robert looks even worse: more swollen and purple. Positioned outside the room, Mrs Campbell seems resistant to my going in to see him, saying something about not disturbing Robert. (Why? I quietly wonder if she feels fearful of my reactions to her son in this grotesque state? Or fearful that she would break down and cry if I gave her permission? Or anxious that I would talk to Robert about death?) I wait, walk off to see one of the other children on the ward, and then return, and look through the door. I see Mrs Campbell repeatedly stroking Robert's forehead through her rubber gloves. It seems a pity that there is this barrier, as well as the mask and plastic apron, between mother and child.

Eventually, I enter the room when a nurse enters and disturbs the peace anyway. I stay for only a few minutes, when Mrs Campbell and I exchange a few words. I say to Mrs Campbell that the important aspect is that Robert has her with him. I think to myself about Mr Campbell hardly being around, so I ask Mrs Campbell about religion – does she find sustenance in that? She says she tries to pray but cannot.

After a few minutes, I say that I will be back on Tuesday. She says, 'I hope we'll still be here . . .' and breaks down and cries. I put an arm around her.

21 October (Tuesday) 2.00 pm. I gather at the haematology meeting that Robert has deteriorated further. There is a note in his file not to resuscitate him in the event of cardiac arrest. He has been bleeding, and is on morphine to control the pain. The paediatric social worker and I wonder if we should talk to the senior house officer about whether barrier-nursing (especially masks and gloves) could be dispensed with now, in order to give Robert and his mother closer contact. (The effectiveness of barrier-nursing is scientifically debatable, and aspects of the practice vary from hospital to hospital. For example, masks can only effectively keep germs at bay for a couple of minutes.) In the meeting, anxiety over Mr Campbell is expressed: he seems so 'out' of all this, possibly feeling guilty over his donations of bone marrow and platelets not helping. He goes to the chapel frequently, wanders around the hospital and goes to the pub, while Mrs Campbell is with Robert all the time. Yet Robert so clearly needs his mother, checking up on her presence all the time. Mr Campbell was going back home to fetch Julie but that is felt by the parents no longer to be appropriate while Robert looks so dreadful. Apparently, when Robert's appearance suddenly changed, Mr Campbell could not face him.

On my way to seeing Robert, I meet Mr Campbell. He says his son is somewhat better, and asks me how *I* am. *He* has just given another batch of platelets, and looks shell-shocked, 'petrified by such misfortunes' (Ovid). He goes off to find his wife, as they are both due to meet with the paediatric social worker.

I don mask, gloves, and apron, and go in to see Robert. He is on his own, lying there, still, his eyes open. He looks grotesque. His head seems so large. I angrily retort to myself that I thought they said in the file that they had reduced the swelling! He is a deep purple colour. His eyes are now affected: they are bloodshot, the pupils look grey and clouded, and the puffy lids make it difficult for him to open them properly. He is lying on his side, awake, quietly poking his fingers into his nostrils. The pillowcase is smeared with streaks of blood. His fingers look so frail in contrast to his head. I say, 'Hello, Robert, Mrs Judd has come to see you.' After a while, I ask if Mum has gone to lunch? He nods. He coughs an awful rattling cough. He seems so approachable in spite of everything.

I lean over towards him and talk about remembering when he played with the toys I brought . . . the little hospital scene, and I briefly recount some of the play he had enacted. He seems to listen intently. A nurse comes and checks the drip and gives Robert a drink, and then goes.

I hear his mother's voice in the corridor. He seems to be listening too. I ask if he can hear Mum's voice. He nods. Mrs Campbell enters, saying to Robert immediately, 'You've been picking at your nose again! I wasn't too long, was I?' Robert points to his cup. 'Drink?' asks Mrs Campbell. 'I'll get you some fresh . . .' 'No! That is fresh! I already had a drink!' Robert bursts out, loud and clear. I tell Mrs Campbell that the nurse gave him one a few minutes ago.

Then Robert says, 'I want to go!' and Mrs Campbell smiles and fetches the bedpan. She uncovers Robert whose abdomen is now plump and swollen, purple all over except for whiter-than-white speckled areas on his thin legs and hands. I wonder to myself what he feels about the state of his body.

I offer to help but they have their own routine by now. Robert hangs around Mrs Campbell's neck and lifts himself onto the bedpan. He suddenly burps loudly, saying 'Pardon me!' Mrs Campbell says, 'Of course, my love.' Robert urinates and defecates copiously. His arms look strong as he leans back on them. Mrs Campbell wipes him, while Robert beseeches, 'Quickly!' As he lowers himself back onto the bed, he complains violently about the pain. Mrs Campbell acknowledges this pain 'in the tummy', as Robert settles down on his back now with relief. I say, 'It must feel better now you can tell when you need the bedpan, Bobby.'

He beckons to his mother, whispering in her ear. Mrs Campbell duly announced, 'You don't want to be called "Bobby", only "Robert".' I say, 'Of course . . . perhaps you feel "Bobby" is a little boy's name, and Robert is a big boy's name?' He nods. Mrs Campbell says, 'When you go home we'll have to tell Julie that . . . she'll have to stop calling you "Bobby"?' He nods.

The sister comes in to check Robert's drip and lines. Mrs Campbell says, 'Where would we be without it?' (She is referring to the almost constant infusion of medicine and food via the Hickman catheter.)

In a little while Mrs Campbell calls him 'Bobby' and then checks herself. I say, 'Perhaps only Mum can call you that . . . it's Mum's special name for you.' He nods.

He says his eyes are itchy, and Mrs Campbell wipes the lids with tissues. Robert begins to fiddle with what seems to be his genitals under the sheets and then demands, 'Cotton buds!' Mrs Campbell gives him one. Robert pokes repeatedly into each ear, examining closely the substance on the cotton-wool. Mrs Campbell remarks that Robert has always liked poking into his ears. I do not have to wonder long to myself about the significance of that – for Robert gives Mrs Campbell the cotton bud and demands another. She says reproachfully, 'What for?' Robert says, 'You know well enough what for!' Mrs Campbell resignedly gives him one. Robert pokes around under the sheets. She says, 'They're not for bottoms!' Robert replies, 'Well this one is!' I think to myself that for someone who is on morphine, he is remarkably alive. Or perhaps the morphine disinhibits him.

(Clifford Yorke (1985) writes about a seriously ill girl focusing on a stye on her eye to the exclusion of a recent amputation she has undergone. He writes, 'Does the displacement of her anxieties to the comparatively trivial matter of the stye have a defensive and, in the circumstances, adaptive function?')

Mrs Campbell looks exhausted. Robert continues to be very busy under the sheets.

I say to Mrs Campbell, but also to Robert, that perhaps it is important for Robert to get different, maybe pleasurable, sensations from his body at the moment, when there is so much *dis*comfort; perhaps this reassures him in the face of feeling so uncomfortable.

Mrs Campbell nods half-heartedly, as if it is the least of her worries what Robert might be up to. Robert then brandishes a soiled cotton-bud, which Mrs Campbell wraps in tissue and disposes of.

(Greenacre has written about children who are hospitalized and kept immobile for long periods of time: '. . . prolonged early restraint, producing a condition in which stimulations to the body far exceeded possible motor discharges, also resulted in an increased general body erotization' [1980, p. 105].)

I feel quite surprised and, in a sense, relieved by his liveliness and mischievousness. It is a delicate situation, where he is engaged in an activity that should be allowed to be private, and yet he is carrying it out in front of his mother and me, albeit under the sheets. As he has scarcely any privacy, it may be erroneous to deduce that this is a direct communication to us.

However, upon reflection later, I realize that I am caught up in his denial, and am avoiding the underlying meanings of his activity and his mood. With hindsight, I ponder the possible accompanying masturbatory phantasies of passive and active identifications with either parent. He may have phantasies of getting inside his mother's body, in order to fuse with her. The sense of triumph he conveys suggests this, with its avoidance of any sense of loss or damage. It may carry a wider meaning of an omnipotent attempt to wipe away all his sickness.

These thoughts, and others, remain at the back of my mind. In this setting with the many interruptions and intrusions, I cannot really attempt to analyse much of the material with Robert to the level at which I might take it in long-term psychotherapy.

I say I have to go soon. Robert then pipes up, 'I'm bored' I ask him and his mother what he does in the long hours of lying here? (There is a tape recorder and a television in the room.) Story tapes? Music? Mrs Campbell says, 'Yes . . . and I read to him.' I mention that Lorraine, the teacher, is away this week, as it is half-term. Mrs Campbell said she had not realized that. (As Lorraine visits Robert several times a week, I feel it is important to spell out the holiday, in case Mrs Campbell feels that the teachers have given up on Robert.)

Mrs Campbell seems deflated in the face of Robert asking for further input. So I say, 'When I come on Thursday, I'll bring the toys . . . even if you cannot play much, we'll see what you can manage. Goodbye.' Mrs Campbell thanks me. (I leave wondering if perhaps I should have brought the therapy box this time.)

I think back upon his condition today: he is invaded by tubes, ther-mometers, needles, swabs, and now he pokes into most of the orifices of his body. I wonder if this is an attack on himself, or an exploration at a more infantile level. Perhaps some of his exploration would not be noticed and would be a 'normal' part of his life if he were well, and not being scrutinized and monitored. He has scarcely any privacy left. Whose body is it now?

I also wonder about his self-image now. He still looks grotesque. I hope he has not seen himself in the mirror, but he is, of course, aware of the great changes to his body and limbs. In a sense, an infant sees himself reflected in the mother's eyes. 'What does the baby see when he or she looks at the mother's face? I am suggesting that, ordinarily, what the baby sees is himself or herself. In other words the mother is looking at the baby and *what she looks like is related to what she sees there*' (Winnicott, 1974, p. 131). I feel that the foregoing applies to the older child as well, especially to one who has regressed to a more infantile level and finds himself utterly dependent upon mother and other care-givers.

I then think about Kohut (1977, p. 76) who writes about the parent, usually the mother, who responds to the child who 'seeks confirmation by the mirroring self-object'. The child may then encounter a 'joyful, prideful parental attitude' or, if not experienced as an aesthetic object, a rejecting one. This inability to respond to the child as a whole or even as a collection of part-objects leads the child to feelings of fragmentation and depletion.

This leads me to wonder further about the serious disease that invades Robert's body and makes it impossible for his parents to have a positive attitude towards his whole self. Winnicott (1972) uses the term 'personalization' to describe the existence of a satisfactory working arrangement between mind and body: 'Healthy feelings of personaliza-tion have their origins in, and are based upon, positive parental attitudes towards the child's body. When these are not present, the child's resul-tant attitude toward his own body will be critically impaired.'

Therefore, one can see how both parents and child have to keep in mind the healthy body that once was, in order to retain hopefulness for a return to that state.

So I wonder what Robert sees now when he looks into his mother's eyes. We know that, understandably, his father avoids being in his room for long, as he seems to find the sight of him too painful. How difficult it must be for either parent to feed back anything optimistic in their eyes, especially when they try to use denial and yet their underlying feelings show through.

As well, he is draining his mother with demands, thus contributing to a vicious circle of a depleted 'breast', or mother, which cannot satisfy his needs. This perhaps symbolizes what the whole of life has become for him.

23 October (Thursday) 10.00 am. Peter (the paediatric social worker) and I meet. He has talked to Mr Campbell about the possibility of Robert dying. Apparently the parents cannot talk to each other or share any of this. Mr Campbell cannot look at Robert and feels that it is not the child he knows. He prays a great deal. Later, one of the ward sisters describes Mrs Campbell praying to St Rita, the Patron Saint of 'desperate cases' and Mr Campbell saying, 'Oh well, sister, God wants him.'

We go off to the ward together. The 'protective isolation' sticker has been peeled off the door. Masks, gloves, etc., are no longer outside the room. So Peter's and my discussion with the doctors on barrier-nursing being lifted was effective. We wonder, though, if the parents (and possibly Robert) will read this as a sign of the hospital giving up.

We enter the room. There is a peaceful atmosphere: as it is a dull day, a sombre light pervades the room. There is a sense of normality about seeing both parents sitting in the room, and both without masks. Mr Campbell is sitting on a chair where his view of Robert is obscured by the locker, perhaps intentionally. Mrs Campbell looks very thin.

Robert seems to be sleeping. They tell us that he is much better: they are pleased with the blood count – the platelets are helping. Mr Campbell will be donating more platelets on Saturday. They say Robert is brighter in himself too. Peter says, 'So he's better in himself, even if his body isn't very well?' Mrs Campbell says, 'Yes – and the blood count *is* better – let's hope he'll be able to start making platelets himself now.'

Robert half opens his eyes. Mrs Campbell goes up to him. He opens his mouth. 'Drink?' He nods, and sips the chocolate milk, struggling to swallow. 'Enough,' he says. He tells Mrs Campbell about a 'kind of little bottle . . . in the advertisement'. His voice is as clear as a bell. Mrs Campbell listens attentively.

Peter invites the parents to have a coffee and a chat. Mr Campbell accepts, while Mrs Campbell says she would rather stay with Robert.

Robert requests the bedpan. He leans back on strong arms. His enormously swollen, shiny, distended belly appears to me to be almost obscene on this little boy.

I think I am momentarily in touch with a deep instinctual biological reaction to the trauma or shock of what I see: to withdraw, avoid, or shun that which seems to have gone beyond a reasonable chance of survival. This brief awareness is in conflict with a predominantly nurturing instinct, and may indeed be felt by most of those who encounter the severely ill or profoundly disabled. It is an aspect that may be less shameful if more openly shared and understood.

Mrs Campbell then decides to go and have some lunch – so Robert requests, via his mother, that I read him a story. He specifies *Snow White*. Mrs Campbell leaves.

He seems to listen intently, even though his eyes are shut. The story seems particularly poignant – the drops of blood on the snow are the vital fluid that create Snow White – and seems to link with the emphasis on blood in Robert's illness and treatment.

The 'mirror, mirror on the wall' aspect of the story reminds me of my earlier thoughts about mirrors and mothers' eyes. Robert looks into his mother's eyes/mirror. Can mother reflect back, and if so, what? And, of course, this is a story about the extreme and destructive envy of the wicked step-mother Queen, when Snow White is aged 7 years – exactly Robert's age. I wonder to myself about Robert's possible underlying anxieties and phantasies of his infantile wish to have mummy all to himself, leading to fears of an attack or retaliation for such phantasies by his mother or father in the form of this illness.

I pause, and ask him if he wants me to continue reading. He nods. I say, 'Seven years old, like you. And you made a little white figure in plasticine, perhaps like Snow White.' I take it out of the box. Robert doesn't want to look at it. I say, 'Perhaps you don't want to think about when you were able to do more.' His breathing is laboured.

Nurses pop in and out throughout. Some, who have been away, seem puzzled about who I am and what I am doing there.

I ask Robert if it is difficult to breathe. He nods. There is a long silence. He is struggling, giving little moans, his eyes closed.

I say, 'I wonder if there's anything you want to try and talk about . . . any worries you might have.' There is a silence. I go on ' . . . about where this is going to lead?' He does not respond. I do not know what he is hearing. He makes little twitches and occasional grimaces. I find myself having to summon courage to put thoughts into words beyond the point of comfort. I continue, ' . . . whether there may be things you can't talk to Mum or Dad about, because you don't want to worry them, or upset them.' He nods. Further silence. Then I say, 'You must sometimes wonder how long this will go on for, and if you *are* going to get better.' He gives another little nod. I feel immensely sad.

I stroke his forehead for the first time. It's so soft and silky and warm. He seems to like it. I feel relieved that we no longer have to wear gloves. Dispensing with this rubber barrier parallels what feels like the more important removal of an emotional barrier between us.

I stay a little while quietly by him and then have to go, and put the bell by him. He has hardly opened his eyes since his mother left. I feel he reserves that way of actively 'holding on' with his eyes for when she is in the room.

I say goodbye, and mention to him that we can carry on with the story book next time if he wants. I tell him that the bell is by him. I leave, and tell one of the nurses that Robert is alone.

Later, in talking to one of the sisters in the corridor, she expresses her upset at the 'grotesque appearance' of Robert. 'Bloated, absolutely awful, absolutely horrendous,' she says. 'And he's conscious of what's happening to him, and so aware that his body is not functioning properly,' she continues. I feel relieved that this sister, with her many years of experience of this work, including similar leukaemic cases, is also in touch with what we agree is 'torture'. I come across a saying by Hippocrates: 'Extreme remedies are most appropriate for extreme diseases' (c 460–357 BC). I wonder about that. Perhaps that attitude, which still seems to be around today, needs to be reappraised.

That evening, on the telephone, Peter tells me that Robert's lungs are in a bad state. Apparently, the medical team is surprised by the improved blood count.

I have the fantasy of cooking wholesome soup for Robert's mother and bringing it to the hospital. They must be tired of the hospital diet. But, of course, I am prompted by my feelings of frustration and impotence: if I cannot 'feed' Robert more, perhaps I could concretely nourish his most important care-giver.

25 October (Saturday). I telephone the ward to ask how he is, and hear that he has been moved to the intensive care unit, mainly because of difficulty breathing.

27 October (Monday). I hear that Robert is back in his own room.

28 October (Tuesday) 2.00 pm. I go to the ward, and on my way to reading his medical notes, I hear terrible yelling coming from Robert's room. I ask Carol, his special friend (an auxiliary nurse), who is walking by, if Robert is alone. We both go in. Robert is alone, and he's screaming, '*Mummy!*' His bloodshot eyes look redder than ever and are very wide open. Robert seems caught in the grip of severe anxiety – possibly separation anxiety. Underlying the fear of separation in a young child is the fear of complete abandonment and thence of being left to die, as I explain in Chapter 2. Indeed, I feel that Robert's terror at this moment has the raw primitive quality of a fear of death.

Carol countermands, 'What you screaming for? What do you want? Why don't you use the bell? You'll hurt your throat. Want the bedpan?' Robert nods. So Carol helps him; now Robert hangs around Carol's neck, as he's no longer strong enough to support himself on his arms.

While in this 'embrace' Carol lovingly caresses Robert's swollen body, calling him 'Little Prince'. Then she wipes him, asking each time, 'Enough?' Robert says, 'Not quite', each time. Carol seems amused and continues until Robert is content. Carol is also Scottish. This seems to contribute to a special closeness with the family.

Then she covers Robert who says he is cold. Carol says she will fetch another blanket.

Robert is now less red, and looks less swollen than previously. He has an oxygen supply, pumped out in puffs near his face. Carol asks Robert if he would like toast and he nods. 'With marmalade?' He nods again.

While Carol is out I ask Robert if he would like the box of toys. He nods. I take out the family he has used before, with the pram and the baby. I feel he is too weak to play actively, but he looks at it with great interest.

Carol brings the toast, and Robert nibbles tiny bits. He seems to dislike the marmalade, so Carol says, 'OK. I'll get you jam', and leaves.

Robert tries to spit out the shreds of marmalade. He accurately eliminates the lumps one by one for me to wipe off his tongue. I am reminded of an infant who has not yet accepted lumpy food. Moreover, I have the increasing impression that symbolically Robert is pushing out 'dirt', or bad stuff, or the illness, at others, as his way of actively trying to spit out or evacuate it.

We continue with the toy family. Robert seems to look intently at the baby. I talk about previous times when he more actively created the play: how he had said this was the strong Mummy who helps the Daddy and the baby, and how he must feel like that baby now that he feels weak. I begin to explore this further with him: about him needing Mummy so much, and crying out for her. At this point Mrs Campbell arrives.

She seems bright and well, and immediately shows interest in a letter that has arrived for Robert from their doctor in Scotland. Mother says that she must try and telephone the doctor as she finds it hard to write. She asks Robert if he would like a drink. He shakes his head. I fill Mrs Campbell in a little about Robert calling out for her, needing the bedpan, and getting toast from Carol.

Mrs Campbell senses that we are busy, so says, 'I'll leave you.'

I get out the box of assorted animals. Robert seems particularly attentive to the baby kangaroo that fits in the mother's pouch. I refer to him being in a sort of pouch, or inside-place, now: the bed, being fed by tubes. He looks at me and then handles the two baby lambs. There is a pause. I ask him if he remembers playing with them before. He shakes his head. I leave his possible defence against remembering that the baby doll had thought these lambs were 'horrible' and frightening in a previous session. He picks up the hippo, as he still calls it (which is really a rhinoceros). I say 'This is the animal that was angry before . . . and perhaps you too feel angry at all that is happening to you.'

He picks up the white Plasticine little figure he had made before, and stares at it. I say, 'Perhaps you're remembering how we talked about this little boy that you made not having hair, like you?' He nods.

He asks for the hospital set of figures. We put the other toys away. But he does not play with the hospital set. I become aware that I might be feeling that I have to inject life into him – sensing an over-energetic streak in me that *wants* him to play.

So I sit quietly. After a while I talk to him about him having some worries and some questions that he might not want to talk to Mum or Dad about. He nods. There is quite a long silence. I say that it seems hard for him to talk, so does he want me to ask the sort of questions that I think might be in his mind? He nods. I go on, 'Perhaps, you wonder if you *will* get better.' He nods, opens his eyes more fully, and looks at me. I say, 'Of course, no one can know the answer to that.' He tries to say something, but cannot manage it. His tongue is moving against his teeth. I go on, 'These are big questions in your mind. Rather than you feeling all alone with them, we can share them.' Again he tries to talk. (I wonder whether his brain is affected by the stress or the drugs. The teacher had said that Robert could not talk easily. How much of his inability is emotional? Perhaps, the dread and anxiety are too much for him to formulate?)

His tongue movements, and failure to enunciate, lead me to feel that there is a 'nameless dread' I have to try to talk about. Robert is now very still, his eyes closed. Carol comes back with the requested jam. Robert opens his eyes. Carol leaves.

Robert asks for the *Snow White* story again, so I continue with that. He seems very interested in the illustrations. I think to myself about the sensory privation of being in a hospital bed, in a small room, for so long, and how his eyes seem to feed on the extended vistas opened up by the pictures and the story.

When we reach the part of the story where Snow White recovers a second time from near-death, I pause to say that perhaps Robert wants to hear this story because it is about a child like him, who nearly died three times and then gets better each time. He seems to listen to what I am saying, but does not react.

Soon after that I have to go. I show him the bell. He is very still and quiet as I leave.

30 October (Thursday) 10.30 am. I see from the medical notes that Robert's blood pressure was considerably raised the day before.

I go into the room. There are fresh flowers in a vase for the first time. This is one of the advantages of him not being barrier-nursed, as flowers were not allowed then. (Besides the restrictions to normal life that I have already mentioned, before the platelet level has risen and therefore while there is a strong risk of infection, leukaemic children cannot eat anything that is not sterilized by first being put in a microwave oven. Chocolate is not allowed at this hospital because it cannot be sterilized. Animals or pets would not be allowed. The danger of infection being transmitted by pets is considered by many hospitals to be serious enough to recommend that when the patient goes home, they are not brought into contact with pets for a while.)

Mrs Campbell tells me, 'I don't think he'll be up to much. He's been awake all night. The oxygen kept him awake.'

Robert looks grey now that he is less red and purple. I ask Mrs Campbell if she too was up all night. She nods. Yet, surprisingly, she looks pretty and bright today.

Mrs Campbell asks Robert if he wants to be more upright? 'No.' So Mother leaves the room, telling us where she will be.

The television is on loudly. Robert seems to be avidly watching a programme about a child flying a kite. We watch together. I ask him if he has ever flown a kite? 'No.' 'Has Julie?' 'No.' I suggest that by watching this, maybe he would like to be able to fly high in the sky like the kite, and in that way get right away from all his worries, away from the hospital and from being ill.

He nods, looking serious. When the programme ends he asks me to make him higher, so I crank up the back-rest, thinking that he has thus perhaps affirmed my interpretation.

He asks to play with the hospital set. I get it out. But as he seems too weak to play actively, I ask him if he wants to tell me what to do with the figures. He instructs me to put the doll's tiny hat in the locker. This is something he had done the first time he played with the set. I say that this seems to be his way of keeping alive the hope that the little boy doll and he, himself, will get better: if the outer clothes are kept in the locker for when he can leave the hospital. He then designates the lady doll as the mother and the man as the priest. He denotes the latter by turning his collar round.

I comment that he does not want him to be the Dad, perhaps because he feels angry with his Dad.

He places the little boy in the bed, and tiny plastic flowers in a vase by the bed. Meanwhile, he is picking his nose, and shows me brownish stuff in his mouth. He grunts as if to tell me to do something about it. I mop up his mouth with tissues. He grimaces. I ask if it tastes awful. He says, 'Yes', and fiddles with the mucus on his hands from his nose.

Again, I feel he tries to project into me his disgust with his illness. He seems to act out a phantasy that the whole of his inside is full of dirt and contamination – which is not far from the truth.

I comment on his feeling so full of so much bad stuff coming out of his nose and mouth, and I wonder if it comes up now when I talk about his not wanting the Dad in the play. 'You can keep the Dad out of the play, but you can't help what's happening to your body.' He continues to fiddle with the mucus. I say, 'Perhaps, it's important for you to be able to do this, when you have so much done to your body . . . *this* is something you have control over.'

He seems disinclined to play further with the toys. I ask him if he wants Plasticine? He nods. I ask him what colour? He says emphatically, 'Dark pink.' He first uses one hand, then both, and soon has fashioned a shark. I ask him what thoughts he has about this shark? He seems too exhausted to contribute more. So I say that a shark is fierce and biting. He nods. I say, 'Maybe you feel like a red angry shark, wanting to bite: angry about not being well for so long . . .' (At another level perhaps Robert feels at the receiving end, assaulted by the shark/illness.)

He then asks me to make something. I comply, although I think to myself that I probably would not do so in a 'normal' psychotherapy setting, where it may be preferable to avoid adding my own fantasies or creations, as this could complicate what the child is bringing. Am I, like Carol, wanting to grant him any wish? This feels very understandable if someone's life is limited. I make him a tiny yellow bear, like his special 'Sunshine', and ask him if he knows who it is. He guesses correctly.

He requests more of the *Snow White* story. We carry on from where we left off. Again he is very interested in the illustrations. Meanwhile, nurses pop in and out, taking blood-pressure, etc. One of them seems very interested in my role and later wants to share thoughts about Robert.

I have to leave. He asks me to call his mother. I leave my version of Sunshine with him, and he agrees to my packing up the shark in the same little box within the bigger therapy box where I keep his previous plasticine model.

Later, I see Peter, who has spoken to the parents while I saw Robert. He says they are 'poles apart': Mrs Campbell is talking along the lines of, 'What if Robert dies . . . what if I saw him in a coffin . . . what would it feel like . . .', while Mr Campbell is unable to listen and distracts with his conversation. However, Mrs Campbell says that overriding *hope* has kept her going.

Now that Robert has survived the intensive treatment crisis and is a little better, perhaps Mrs Campbell can now talk about her fears. And perhaps, simultaneously, she is distancing herself somewhat from Robert – preparing herself for his death – for she seems to be in Robert's room less.

I talk to one of the ward sisters, who feels that Robert picks his nose for attention: the resultant bleeding creates the fuss he wants. She says all leukaemic patients do this. I put forward my thoughts about the nose picking, and the other intrusive things he does to other parts of his body, as perhaps the result of frustration and anger that he feels about being ill and in such a closed-in world, where the only outlet, and way of mastering and controlling the situation, is his own body. She seems interested in my thoughts.

We talk about his mother seeing less of Robert these days. Sister says that, nevertheless, his mother is still doing most of the nursing. She adds that she is very aware of his father hardly being there, and that it is a pity that mother and father do not share much with each other.

4 November (Tuesday). I hear at a meeting how much better Robert is, in spite of frequent profuse nose-bleeds even when nose-packs are in.

2.00 pm. I go in. Mrs Campbell is reading letters and cards to Robert who is *sitting* up in bed, wearing over-large hospital pyjamas. The play leader has apparently been in to see him earlier: a large dressed-up teddy is on the bed. Robert sits on his bent legs beneath him. Mrs Campbell hardly says 'hello', and carries on reading. Again, I feel she resents my visit, especially after I have not seen Robert for 4 days. Robert too barely acknowledges me.

Robert complains about his eyes, so Mrs Campbell gives him a tissue. Robert is then busy fiddling with a loose tooth. I comment on what he is doing and Mrs Campbell tells me that the tooth is hanging on a thread. I think about all the normal bodily processes that 7-year-olds go through and which, of course, are still happening to Robert in spite of everything.

Mrs Campbell says she has to see Peter about a refund on a plane ticket (this was intended for Mr Campbell to fly home to fetch Julie, but Robert's recent crisis forced a cancellation). Robert whines, 'Don't go.' Mrs Campbell suggests Robert plays with the toys that I have brought, and tells him to be a good boy. She leaves, Robert watching her with bated breath.

I say, 'It's difficult when Mum goes out . . . when you need her so much . . . and perhaps you don't want me in here?' He shakes his head. I say, 'I'm not sure what that means. Perhaps I talk about things you don't want me to?' He replies, 'No . . . you don't.' Meanwhile, he is poking into his nose, examining smears on his fingers.

I talk to him about how busy he is with his nose, and how important it must be to be the one who decides now about poking in, when doctors and nurses have to poke in a lot these days, in different ways. (Later, I think that my arrival in Robert's room probably felt similarly intrusive to Mrs Campbell and possibly to Robert.)

The drip, which gives him his basic nutrients, suddenly makes a loud gurgling noise. I say, 'The drip is deciding to feed you. Even your tummy isn't deciding when it's hungry . . . It's being automatically fed every few minutes.' He nods.

After a pause, I ask him if he would like to do a drawing (see p. 20). He nods. I get out the thick felt-tip pens, and he non-verbally asks for help with the stiff lids.

He draws a layer of sky, then the sun, and then six big birds, like the letter 'm', forming a further layer. Then a purple figure, smiling. There is no ground line. He adds orange hair. I wonder to myself about the purplish skin he has, but only comment on the hair being like the hair Robert had when he was well. He nods. I go on, 'And like the hair you'd like to have again.' He nods again. He leans back and looks at the picture. It seemed quite an effort. I ask him if he wants to tell me more about it. He is quiet. I comment on the birds being like 'm' for Mummy, forming a sort of blanket above the little boy Robert, 'protecting you, like Mummy does'. I tell him that I will keep the drawing safely in the box. He agrees.

And then he blurts out, 'I want my Mummy. Will you ask her to come here please?' I say that he seemed to want her when I talked about the mummy birds. I then ask if there is any particular reason why he wants her (thinking it may be a need for the bedpan). Robert says, 'I just want her.'

I go out to find Mrs Campbell and discover that she is meeting with Peter, so I return and explain to Robert that she is busy talking to Peter but will be back in a little while.

He begins a second drawing, now sitting up much more. He seems more able to express himself through drawing than through talking. He draws a blue neat sky, filling in any spaces assiduously. A nurse comes in to take his blood pressure while he is drawing and Robert reluctantly allows her to interrupt. He suddenly asks me in a shrill voice, 'Can you leave the pens here with me?' I say, 'Yes, of course . . . and the pad of paper. You may want to draw when I'm not here, and you could show me your drawings, when I come again.'

The nurse leaves. I expand further to Robert that the drawings he does with me we are understanding together, so it is important for us to keep them in the box to look back on – whereas, of course, it is up to him what he does with the drawings he produces when I am not here. He nods emphatically in agreement.

He then draws green grass, and a careful row of eight trees or plants. He inserts a smiling figure between the sixth and the seventh tree. I think to myself about the eight trees, about him being eight next birthday, and about him becoming ill between six and seven. I ask him who the person is. He says, 'You!' I ask what I'm doing in the picture. 'Playing.'

I ask if he has any thoughts about anything else in the picture? He does not respond and seems tired. We look at the two pictures, side-by-side. I say that he made one of himself and one of me, perhaps telling us about his times with me being a time to look back to when he was well, to remember the fresh air and the green grass and the trees in these summer pictures, and all the things he misses. I comment on this second picture perhaps showing him, too, as he was, playing and happy. (I think to myself that perhaps this too is an attempt to integrate his present state with his pre-illness state, as well as a representation of a Mrs Judd who carries on living after he dies.)

He seems to want to stop. As I put the tops back on the pens he tells me in his characteristically emphatic way that grey is his favourite colour. I say, 'Mmm . . . it's very different from a bright colour, like red . . . perhaps you're saying that grey is more like how you feel now . . . sort of sad or dull.' He nods.

We sit in silence for a while. I say, 'You've shown me often how much you notice colours . . . how they can fit in with what you feel . . . like . . .' and I show him the white Plasticine figure he had made. 'Your skin was white then.' He nods, making direct eye contact with me. I then talk about the red shark he made, when his skin was looking red and angry, and perhaps he felt angry.

There is a silence. I say, 'You're letting me know that you don't feel like being happy, or smiling. You feel fed up much of the time. Perhaps it's hard for you to be cheerful and smiling for other people.'

He nods meaningfully.

I say that I have to go now, and that I will be back the day after tomorrow. I tell him that I will try to find his Mum. I forget my handbag – this obvious reluctance on my part to leave is no surprise to me – and return. He is fingering the box of felt-tips, and seems to be taken by surprise at my re-entering.

Later, I look back on those pictures, and have further thoughts: in the first picture, the layer of birds not only adds to the encapsulating quality of the hair and purple head but also keeps the sun and sky away. It seems to reflect the present hospitalization as well as, possibly, echo the previous well child aged six (the six birds). The lack of a ground-line suggests a feeling of not being held, echoing his earlier play with the toppling vase of flowers. Perhaps this is exacerbated when his mother goes out.

In the second picture the firm ground-line possibly conveys a feeling of now feeling held by my attention. Again the six trees are emphasized by the positioning of the figure – registering the onset of the illness – and although he designates this figure as 'Mrs Judd playing' it embodies Robert in protective identification with a living, playing me. In other words, he wants to put himself into me and thereby be saved and go on living. I think the years stretching ahead are my years, not his. Perhaps – if these *are* trees – the larger-than-life figure reaching upwards to the sky conveys an awareness of his impending 'journey' to heaven, which may be his way of conceptualizing death. (Indeed, his little Plasticine figure also had upstretched arms.) (See Appendix 1 for further analysis of these drawings.)

6 November (Thursday). The playleader tells me Robert enjoyed squirting 'silly string' all over the room the night before, as it was Bonfire Night, and he had made 'hair' for himself. I notice that the medical notes state a marked improvement: his blood-pressure is more stable, and the bruising is described as 'old'. Sister tells me that Robert has a mouth infection.

I ask sister about the possibility of some undisturbed time with Robert with perhaps a sign on the door – except, of course, for really necessary medical procedures. Sister is dubious and suggests I ask the doctors.

10.30am. When I enter the room, two radiographers are just leaving with their equipment, after taking X-rays. Robert is intently watching a television drama about boys and girls. He remains absorbed, while I sit by him, and watch it with him. Nurses come in and out. Robert seems to be vicariously joining in the TV lives of gardens, boy- and girl-friends, and dancing.

When it ends I suggest that I should turn the sound off. He nods. He has been busy pulling at scabs on his lip. I comment on what he is doing. He nods and continues. His fingers look bloodstained.

We are both silent. I notice some drawings that he has done in my absence and ask him if I can look at them. He nods. One is very colourful, of the sun, coloured birds, a big tree, and a row of flowers. Another is a night sky with coloured shapes in it, and the third is of a big black cloud, with grey sky, rain, and lightning. I describe them aloud. He nods. I ask him if he has further ideas about these pictures? He looks at me and then at the pictures. I ask if perhaps the happier one was before he was ill? He nods. I suggest that he sometimes feels fed up and very unhappy, like the black cloud in a grey sky, and perhaps angry like the flashing lightning – but that he has also shown a brighter colourful side, with the sun shining.

He asks for the box. I open it, and he takes out the box of animals. He examines the crocodile's opening and closing mouth avidly, opening the jaws as wide as possible. Then he inserts the foal's legs, and closes the jaws on them, thus lifting the foal; then feeds the giraffe to the jaws as well. I talk to him about the crocodile's biting teeth and jaws being like his own angry and biting feelings, like the shark he made before. He repeats the scene, perhaps needing to repeat because he has not been fully understood. I suggest that when he picks at his lip he is attacking himself rather like this crocodile attacks the helpless baby horse, and at the same time he feels rather like the helpless foal, being attacked by the illness. He leans back and seems to relax. We are silent. Then I say that he seems to feel tired, that playing takes quite an effort. He nods.

He looks down at the Hickman catheter that enters his chest. I ask him if he can feel it. He says, 'No.' (I think to myself that at this moment he is calmly acquiescing to the treatment.)

He seems to be listening to all the sounds . . . of voices, footsteps, other TVs, machines, his drip machine. He turns to look at the door when footsteps approach. I ask him what he is listening for? 'Mum.' I say, 'You feel you need Mum almost all the time?' He nods in a rather desperate way, and then rubs his eye. I ask if it's itchy. 'Yes.' I think to myself about the irritable eye as a reminder of a needy uncomfortable part of him. There is silence. I talk about Robert feeling 'grey', not wanting to be cheerful. He nods, looking very depressed.

I say, 'We can share your sad feelings. Perhaps you're not only sad about being ill, but also sad about being away from home, away from Julie . . . I wonder what you miss most . . . Now that your body seems a bit better, it seems you feel more fed up than when you were really ill, and sleeping a lot.' He seems to take all this in.

He then looks at me beseechingly and says, 'You tell Mummy I want her! ' I say, 'Yes . . . but I wonder why . . . is it a feeling that you need something special, or what?' 'No, I just want her!' he replies desperately.

I think to myself that Robert feels that his mother is distancing herself, leading to fantasies that he is abandoned or unwanted. Perhaps my emotional availability stirs up this pain in him. Again, this is so unlike an 'ordinary' psychotherapeutic relationship where I may have stayed with the child's anxiety in order to understand it further, rather than rushing to relieve it.

I go to find Mrs Campbell. She has her coat on, ready to go out, and comes back to Robert's room, with Mr Campbell. Mr Campbell asks Robert how he's feeling. 'Leave me alone!' he growls. Father sits down and reads the newspaper.

Mrs Campbell decides not to go out. There is an exchange between mother and son about mayonnaise making him sick the night before, while Mrs Campbell spreads cracker-biscuits with mayonnaise and Robert devours them hungrily.

Meanwhile, Mr Campbell talks to me about Peter being away this week, adding that he was always very busy anyway. (Doubtless, Mr Campbell has a great need to talk to someone about Robert's rejection of him.)

He asks Robert if his legs still feel weak. He snarls, 'Leave me alone!' I comment on seeing this anger directly for the first time, and suggest that Robert needs to put bad feelings into his father, but that it's hard for him. Father nods feelingly while making a pretence of reading the paper.

My understanding of this process, in more detail, is that Robert is at times overwhelmed by death anxieties. These are not necessarily conscious, or clearly formulated, but perhaps more akin to Winnicott's (1962) view that the infant is 'all the time on the brink of unthinkable anxiety', relating to an innate awareness of a potentially annihilating force. If this is part of normal experience (Likierman, 1987), Robert's actual illness would surely exacerbate this fear. In order to relieve this unbearable state, he expresses it through destructive behaviour towards his father. Thus, through attempting to expel the experience, or to project it into his father, he becomes bad in Robert's eyes. Mr Campbell's actual avoidance of contact with Robert must be contributing to this view of father.

With Peter away, I feel I have to try to address the family difficulties further. I say something about it not being surprising that Robert does feel fed up and angry. Mrs Campbell interjects that Robert used to talk to the doctors, to *tell* them what was wrong, but now they cannot get anything out of him. She continues insightfully, 'Perhaps that's understandable, because I think he wants to *control* what people say or do to him – and if you think about it, he hasn't much control over things at the moment . . .' gesturing towards the drip. I agree with Mrs Campbell and say that Robert and I sometimes have a quiet time together, where nothing is expected of him. Mrs Campbell says, 'I don't say much to him – I just do things for him.' I acknowledge this, and then add that of course it *is* difficult for Mr Campbell to know what to do when Mum has the job of looking after Robert.

I have to leave. I feel inadequate and wish Peter was around to provide family therapy.

I leave a note for Peter, for his return from leave, putting him in the picture and hoping he can address the problems of Robert's rejection of his father, of Mrs Campbell not seeming able to facilitate a role for father, and telling Peter of my anxiety that if Robert were to die now, there would be *so* much unfinished business.

Later in the day, driving around, I find myself taking the wrong road back to the hospital.

11 November (Tuesday). I gather he was worse over the weekend, with the doctors saying that maybe the transplant had not taken, and that he had the last rites administered. Mrs Campbell was apparently in a bad way yesterday, saying Robert should have died three weeks ago. Clearly she cannot, at times, bear the fluctuations of his condition. There is a possibility that the blood count is not good because of infection, so there is a decision to return to barrier-nursing. I hear from one of the teachers that before the weekend he was 'very bright' and was busy on the computer. The medical notes mention that he is very withdrawn and not eating.

2.00 pm. I put on mask, apron, and gloves, wondering to myself if this is emotionally a retrogressive step, in the sense that we are returning to further barriers between Robert and the people who are important to him.

He is alone, lying on his back, playing with his fingers. His hands have a marked tremor. His face looks swollen. I say, 'Mrs Judd is here again. I've brought the box of toys. I don't know if you want to see them, though.' I sit by him. A nurse enters to check the drip, and then leaves.

After a silence, I talk to Robert about our being back to wearing masks, gloves, and aprons, and ask him if he knows why? He nods. He is fiddling with a finger-nail very intently, pulling at any rough bits. 'Your illness must feel like one big rough bit . . .' He seems to listen, looking straight ahead, and continues to pick at his fingers. I comment on his shaking fingers making it harder for him to manage to do delicate things. He seems very tense. I comment on that too, and then gently hold his arm. He seems to relax, and stops fiddling with his nail. He gently strokes his own bare neck and chest with his free hand. I comment on him now seeming to find his skin soft and comforting.

Nurses come and go. Dr Fish comes to take blood via the catheter. Robert seems to breathe more quickly as he comes in.

When he leaves, I talk to him about seeming sad today. He is lying very still. I talk about him feeling fed up . . . perhaps wondering if he *is* going to get better . . . how long this will go on for. He listens to me. He seems to feel deflated, and I wonder if he is discouraged perhaps by the recent relapse and return to barrier-nursing. I say that I wonder if he feels he is going to die. He looks at me with wide eyes and nods slowly.

A nurse pops in, asks Robert where his Mum is. Robert shrugs. She goes out.

There is a silence. I hold his hand. I comment on the rubber gloves between us. I say, 'We can share feeling sad.' I feel both a heavy sadness, and yet loving towards him. I long to kiss him as one would one's own child. He coughs. His eyes look frightened. 'And frightened,' I add. He seems to agree. I feel that at that moment he is frightened of dying.

He asks for the toys, and takes out the box of animals. He finds the crocodile, and makes it bite the foal, as he did last time. This time I feel that there is a different communication: I suggest to him that the crocodile is killing the helpless foal, and that perhaps Robert feels like the helpless little foal being attacked by death – the illness.

He lies back, coughing. After a silence he asks me to go and find his Mummy. I talk to him about being angry with his Dad last time. I suggest to him that he feels that Daddy is all bad, like a dustbin, to put all the bad feelings in, and that he seems to feel Mummy's all good. 'Perhaps that way you can feel there's a place for all your bad feelings to go . . .' (With hindsight I think my comments were not on the right wavelength at that point. I think his coughing again leads to a fear of dying there and then, perhaps choking to death, and he needs his mother to be with him.)

I say I will try and find his mother and then come back to say goodbye.

I find Mrs Campbell in her private room. She comes along with me, and I ask how Robert has been today. '*Fed up*. Terrible over the weekend – it was bad news – but now we're holding thumbs . . . He's just fed up.'

A nurse is taking his temperature and blood pressure when we return. Robert indicates non-verbally to his mother his wish to use the bedpan.

He sits on it for what seems like a very long time, leaning back on strong arms. He looks like a statue. I am becoming more used to his large hairless head, purplish skin and frail limbs.

I say goodbye, and that I will see him on Thursday.

13 November (Thursday) 10.15 am. Peter is still away. I look through Robert's door. Mrs Campbell shakes her head at me. I had heard from the play leader that Robert (and therefore his mother) had a bad night.

Perhaps Mrs Campbell feels that I am only there to 'play' with Robert and if Robert is not well enough, there is little point in my seeing him. Again, I wonder if she resents my reappearance after two days away, while she has to do *so* much. Nurses and doctors can be seen to be helping in a practical way all the time, unlike psychotherapists.

Mrs Campbell comes to the door to tell me that Robert is very unwell, and that they are busy changing the bed linen. I say I will come back in a little while.

I return half an hour later. Two doctors and several nurses are in the room. Robert has just had a body-scan, and is due to have more platelets as soon as possible.

I stay in the background, after greeting Robert, and watch the many procedures. His temperature is taken; the fluid in his chest is measured twice; nose swabs and throat swabs are taken; he urinates in the special bottle; Mrs Campbell washes and dries him after he has vomited; his bed linen is changed; he is weighed by being lifted into a special chair (he weighs 19 kilos); he has his mouth cleaned with mouth-wash and swabs; cream for his sore dry lips is applied; his blood pressure is taken; his Hickman site is cleaned and the dressing changed; drips are checked; the bed is lowered and raised; clean pyjamas are put on him; new student nurses come and go – and all this within the space of half an hour!

It all seems a considerable ordeal, except that he cries out for more mouth-wash swabs as he finds this procedure very satisfying. He is remarkably tolerant of all that has to be done, only complaining once or twice while shivering at being washed.

I comment to Mrs Campbell on her expertise (for she is the one who carries out most of the nursing). She tells me that she is used to it, as she's been doing it in one way or another for the past 2 years, on and off. Mrs Campbell does indeed have a competent way of doing everything conscientiously and sensitively for Robert.

I notice how skeletal his limbs are. His puffy face and swollen abdomen belie the shrunken state of his limbs. I gather he has a temperature and has been vomiting since midnight.

During one of the complicated procedures to measure the fluid in his chest, during which he has to hold up an arm for a long time, he complains that his hand feels cold. Suddenly he calls out, 'I want Mrs Judd to hold my hand!' The sister, who is new, says, 'Who's that?' I stand up and step forward, and hold his little hand. He calls out, 'And stroke my forehead!' Mrs Campbell stands on the other side of the bed and holds Robert's other hand. Robert seems to calm down and stop shivering. I feel gratified at his ability to ask for me, and my ability to give the warmth of physical contact, albeit through rubber gloves. As I have taken 'a back seat' during all these procedures I feel especially touched by his acknowledgement of something I can offer. I then reinforce Mrs Campbell's contribution when Robert clamours for his Mum to clean out his mouth again, by saying, 'Yes, your Mum knows just how to do it.'

I think to myself that there comes a time when words are not enough, and where physical contact is the most helpful contribution.

Mr Campbell appears at the moment when his son is sitting shivering in a chair while his bed is being made. Robert brushes his lips along the red dressing-gown over his bent knees, seeking comfort. To my surprise he beckons his father to him, with raised eyebrows and a slight tug of his head. Upon his third gesture, Mr Campbell notices, responds, comes across the room, and kneels by him. Rather guardedly, Robert requests, 'I want you to go and buy jellies: orange and lemon jellies.' Mr Campbell agrees. He tells father to hurry up. Sister jokes about Father being given his orders. Mr Campbell's forehead, pouring with sweat, conveys his anxiety.

I pop out of the room to speak to him briefly about Robert's angry feelings. He says, 'It's much better since you talked about it on Tuesday, and the wife's been helping . . . Oh, it's not so bad now! Much better . . .' I suggest to him that it was easier for Robert to feel that his father was bad, including the marrow and platelets he had donated, rather than that Robert had made them bad or useless and was then full of badness. I also refer to the loving feelings for him that he still has underneath the anger, and which seem to be surfacing again now. He says he knows about the loving feelings, and understands that he's serving a useful, but difficult function. He goes off on his errand.

I return to the room. There is a new large Paddington Bear from Carol, the auxiliary nurse. Mrs Campbell tells me, 'If Robert picks his nose and makes it bleed, Paddington Bear goes back, back to darkest Peru, doesn't he, Bobby?' Robert nods seriously.

Carol arrives with a big box of ice lollies which she has bought, and which she will freeze. She calls Robert 'Prince' as usual, and seems to personify my instinct to indulge Robert's every whim. She also brings orange and lemon jellies, duplicating Mr Campbell's order. She asks Robert for a kiss and bends down, bestowing kisses and being kissed, and then leaves.

I say to Robert that I should go now, but could stay a little longer. He shakes his head. I say I am not sure what he means. He says, 'Stay here.' I say, 'Fine. I'll stay for another quarter of an hour.'

Once all the procedures are over, Mrs Campbell and I step back, thinking Robert is dropping into an exhausted sleep. He grimaces. Mrs Campbell immediately interprets this correctly, fetching a vomit dish, into which Robert is copiously sick. Mr Campbell arrives and holds a new bowl while Mrs Campbell disposes of the first one. He seems at last to have a nursing role, and to be as involved as his wife. Eventually, Robert lies back exhausted.

He then begins to shiver dramatically, because platelets are being given in the drip. Apparently this is a usual reaction. His father covers him with two blankets. Mrs Campbell briefly disputes this as too many, and then concedes.

Meanwhile, I have decided that Thursday to Tuesday is too long a gap (from my point of view anyway) and that I will visit on Saturday or Sunday. I tell Robert that I will be working on Saturday or Sunday, and will see him then. He nods. Mr Campbell says, 'That will be nice – thank you. See you then.'

Later I wonder if my proposed extra visit is a response to his more apparent appreciation of me. Am I becoming an 'auxiliary' mother to Robert, in order to spare his own exhausted mother?

He feels perhaps that I can acknowledge his sadness and his anger, and therefore feels me to be more resilient at the moment. Hopefully this, plus Mr Campbell's increased involvement, could spare Mrs Campbell from having to bear everything alone.

Mr Campbell's previous distancing himself is not unusual. The tendency for fathers to abandon the family psychologically during serious illness, by spending increased amounts of time away from home, is reported by Lansky (1974). 'The more a father is separated from the situation . . . where the mother may shut him out emotionally, the more a father may feel jealous, threatened, and certainly unprepared for a possible death' (Elliot, 1981, p. 117).

16 November (Sunday). I gather from sister that Robert has had a severe nose bleed earlier today from picking his nose, but that he is not so ill and is accepting his drugs more easily.

When I enter the room, Robert is watching *Worzel Gummidge* on television. He seems very withdrawn into a world away from the hospital and away from me as he watches with big eyes and furrowed brow. He is sitting up in bed, his knees up. Characteristically, he is fiddling with his fingers.

He virtually ignores me. Perhaps he needs to reject me; perhaps he is letting me know about *his* feelings about when I go away and 'reject' him.

The only time he talks is to ask his mother plaintively for a nail file. In spite of his trembling hands, he uses it deftly to poke and scrape at his nails and cuticles, his mother meanwhile warning him to be careful. I feel aghast at Robert's ferocity in this activity.

Suddenly, Mrs Campbell calls out, 'Robert!' in a pained panic. He has pulled off a big chunk of dried skin from a finger tip; his mother holds this bit of discarded skin, saying, 'You'll go septic!' and then gives up and goes back to her chair.

I think to myself about the removal of *rough* bits again: his wanting to rid himself of the roughness of illness and to find an inner undamaged unblemished smoothness; wanting to feel some physical sensation, even pain, which *he* can control; wanting to attack the surface of himself to mirror the disease deep inside, possibly as a way of externalizing it. He cannot or does not attack his father any longer – so where is all the 'bad' now situated? I also think about the apparent conflict in Mrs Campbell between (predominantly) a fight for life and (to a much lesser extent) resignation about impending death, in her brief reaction to this incident.

A nurse comes in to make the bed, bribing Robert to cooperate with an ice lolly. Robert watches the bed-making avidly from the chair even though he must have seen it countless times. Of course, he is constantly wired-up to the drip and has to be carefully lifted in and out of the chair. His blood pressure is then taken. He seems to examine his painfully thin arms after the pressure cuff is removed.

When I leave I say, 'See you on Tuesday.'

Outside the room I look at his weight charts. He is steadily losing weight. I think about his quietness: it seems he is conserving his energy for vital (in the true sense of the word) matters only.

18 November (Tuesday) 2.45 pm. When I arrive Robert is on the bedpan. The television is on, showing a programme about plastic surgery, which he seems to be watching.

Mrs Campbell says she is going off to do various things. Robert makes a slight protest, but allows it. We watch television for a few minutes, and when the programme ends I say, 'We could do something now – can I turn the TV off?' He nods.

I show him a new set of a family of little soft dolls in his box. He seems to feel helpless about relating to them. I ask him if he wants to do anything with them. He shrugs.

Then he asks, 'Can we play with the hospital?' So I pull up a table and he gets the set out, meticulously setting up first the food trolley, with tiny plates and cutlery, then the little boy in bed, then, significantly, he changes the priest-collar on the man so that he's a Daddy again.

He sets up the vase of flowers and hat in the locker, and then spends a long time fixing crutches on the man, as well as a plaster cast on his leg and his arm. He makes the little boy similarly attired with plaster casts and stands them both up. At that point a nurse comes into the room to check Robert's drip, and he seems to freeze, and to proceed with the activity the moment the nurse leaves, conveying, I sense, that he feels involved in something significant.

He tells me the man is Daddy, and looks at me. So I say, 'It's like Robert and Daddy – Daddy when he gave the marrow and the platelets, and perhaps wasn't very well.' I see him give me the first glimmer of a smile that I have seen since knowing him. I smile too, under the mask. He looks hard at my eyes. I ask him if he can tell that I am smiling. He shakes his head. I tell him that I was smiling just then.

He sets up the tiny toy television and radio, and then slumps back. He removes the plaster cast and crutches from the little boy and the man and starts to pack up. I comment that today the Mummy was not in the play. 'Perhaps she's resting, like Mummy can rest now when I'm seeing you.' I go on to talk about him seeming pleased just now to make a scene with the Daddy and the little boy in hospital together, both not well – 'Perhaps you feel a little happier when you think of your Dad really sharing all this with you, even sharing being unwell.'

I think to myself about Mr Campbell showing considerable emotional pain and distress and wonder then if the analogy, therefore, is at an emotional as well as a physical level.

He clearly does not want to play with anything else. Then, in a little voice, he says, 'Feel sick.' I quickly get the vomit bowl. He is copiously sick: a bloody and mucus-like substance. He seems *so* resigned and stoical. I wipe his mouth. Then he calls out, 'Want bedpan!'

I quickly fetch it, and propping himself up on his arms he produces dark blood-coloured diarrhoea. Characteristically, he sits there for a long time. His limbs are so thin that I am reminded of concentration camp victims, and I feel angry that this can happen to anyone.

He tells me he has finished. I wipe him repeatedly as I have seen his mother do. He gets off the bedpan. His undersheet is stained. I ask him if I should change it. He nods. So I do. He is very cooperative throughout, and I feel somewhat clumsy.

He lies back on his pillows, exhausted. And then the relentless nausea causes him to ask for the bowl again, and he vomits again.

When this is over he asks me to read him a story. I ask which one, and he shrugs, so I pick up the first book that comes to hand, which is *William Tell*. He listens to the whole story, looking at the pictures. I ask him if he thinks that the people in the castle should have been killed and he nods. He also seems to agree with William Tell slaying the cruel governor.

I am aware of feeling some resistance to reading to him. My reasons are complicated. Partly, I feel that the story is a defence against any spontaneous talking we might do. Mrs Campbell, as well as the teacher and play leader, all read to Robert, so I feel that my particular role is being blurred. I ask myself if this is rigidity on my part. I remind myself that this is one of his coping mechanisms (and is not being used to the exclusion of all else). But the weight of awareness of our limited time together is nevertheless a continual pressure on me – a pressure which I try to resist – to use each moment for 'important issues'.

He leans back, his eyes closing. I stroke his forehead, and ask him if he wants the bed lower. He nods. He wants it right down. I rest my hand on his shoulder. He seems to drop off to sleep, opening his eyes the moment I remove my hand. I tell him I will stay until his Mum returns. He then falls into a deep sleep. Mrs Campbell returns 10 minutes later.

Looking back on the present situation, I think about Robert once again rallying, playing with the toys. After all the critical phases of the illness that he has endured, I find it difficult to know what to think or feel. Is he dying? He probably is, but of course in an unpredictable pattern. I sometimes long to talk more to the doctors, in an attempt to have some answers about his physical state, even though I know the fallibility of prognoses. The medical notes are helpful. I feel I have to remain in touch with the probability of him dying and, at the same time, the hope of remission.

Robert himself seems to bob up repeatedly after being punched down by the illness. What can this feel like to him? It seems he has a very powerful life force that continues to resurface, like a cork on a stormy sea. I feel that this is reinforced by his parents' love, concern, and attention. Yet, at times, he has seemed so exhausted and unwell that this life force seems to be wearing very thin. I am reminded of Shakespeare's:

Vex not his ghost: O, let him pass! he hates him
That would upon the rack of this rough world
Stretch him out longer.

(*King Lear*, V, iii)

Throughout I have to continue to remain emotionally present through the reverberations of the buffeting of the illness which I feel. I see this as my main task. At times it seems incredibly difficult to continue, especially when my role is not clearly understood by some of the other professionals, nor, perhaps, by the parents.

I wonder about Robert's fortitude, which seems to appear alongside his resilience and life force. The stoical resignation with which he appears to tolerate so much, repeatedly – interspersed with some angry protests – may be a result of his keeping his limited energy for basic survival tasks. But I feel this tacit tolerance is more of a helpless depression, a withdrawal, in the face of such overwhelmingly unpleasant experiences.

20 November (Thursday). When I arrive the notice about protective isolation has (again) been removed from the door. The television is on and Robert seems half asleep and his mother is in the room. The notes had said that he was a little better. I wonder why the doctors have decided again upon this shift from barrier-nursing.

He opens his eyes and looks at me. Mrs Campbell says she is going to do a few things. I sit by the bedside. Robert opens his eyes and looks hard at me. I talk about not having to wear a mask, and his being able to see my face now. I turn the television sound off.

We sit quietly together. After a while I say, 'Perhaps there's something you would like to talk about?' He looks at me expectantly. I say, 'I wonder what you think about during the long hours that you're lying here . . . do you dream . . . remember your dreams?' He shakes his head. I say, 'I wonder if you feel lonely sometimes . . . I know your Mum is nearly always here, and Dad, and the nurses . . . but I wonder if you sometimes feel that you're all alone in being ill . . . no one can really know what you're thinking and feeling. Do you know what I mean?'

He gives a little nod and closes his eyes, lying very still. He opens his eyes, tries to speak, and then says, 'I feel sick.' I fetch a vomit dish, and lying weakly on his side he brings up two bowls full of what seems like mucus, blood, and bile. And then he requests the bedpan, which I help him onto, again producing some blood-like substance. He seems weaker. After wiping him and tucking him up I comment on how tiring this must be for him.

As Robert talks so little with me, I often feel there is a danger that I, in putting forward what I feel he is thinking or feeling, may be colouring the picture with my own fantasies and emotions. His nods or shakes of the head are a helpful guide here. Nevertheless, I worry about becoming too much of a thinking or feeling part *for* him. Being appropriately sensitive to him is an integral part of the present relationship. I can only attempt to monitor if and when I am projecting too much of my *own* feelings through self-analysis and discussions with colleagues or my analyst.

He lies there, soon requesting the bedpan again. While he is on it, his mother returns, with the haematology consultant and the senior registrar. Mrs Campbell, who has been anxiously awaiting this ward round, exclaims, 'You *would* be on your throne when they come in! They'll come back later', as they withdraw for a moment. Mrs Campbell wipes him and I report to her about the vomiting.

Soon the consultant, senior registrar, and sister return. The consultant is very friendly; he seems not to know what is causing the vomiting and diarrhoea. More platelets are due. Apparently, Mr Campbell cannot donate platelets at present, as he has a cold and has been ill in bed for two days. It seems the blood count has gone up and both sister and the consultant refer to this as 'good news'.

Robert is passive while being examined: neither cooperative nor unhelpful. The consultant's comment upon leaving is, 'Try and get some weight back on you!'

Robert looks hard at me after they have left. I feel his searching eyes are saying, 'Why is he talking about things getting better when I feel weaker and weaker?' I do not address this searching look, perhaps because Mrs Campbell is in the room. I just say, 'He's going to try and help the vomiting. And the blood count *is* up.'

Mrs Campbell reinforces this, and says, 'And we could do with some platelets . . . been waiting since Tuesday.' She adds, unconvinvingly, 'I suppose it's not an emergency.'

Robert grunts, looking at his mother. Mrs Campbell says, 'Bobby, I know what you want, but you can tell me, can't you? Is it the bedpan?' Robert nods. Mrs Campbell says, 'Really Robert, you're just getting lazy about talking!' as she fetches the bedpan. Robert seems less ready to make the effort to get onto it, so we both help him.

Then he lies back, half asleep. I tell him I can stay for another quarter of an hour. He nods. Mrs Campbell and I sit quietly: I sit by Robert, Mrs Campbell behind me on her bed. After a while, Mrs Campbell talks about the cold weather and the dark evenings. When I leave, I say 'Goodbye, see you on Tuesday', to both of them. On this occasion Mrs Campbell seems warm and friendly.

There was a new drawing by Robert on his wall this time: of a smiling little boy holding a red balloon. He is encompassed by big 'm'-shaped birds, and a layer of colour in a cocoon shape around him. I feel it conveys his feeling encapsulated by the hospital, the bed, and particularly his mother, like a young baby. The red balloon may signify many things. It may have unconscious associations to a placenta – linking with Robert's regressed and dependent state; or the redness can reflect, as Bach (1969) states, 'an acute . . . consuming state of illness, or psychologically, a "burning" problem'.

I wonder about his mother's understandable attempt to resist some of the regression (for example, in requesting him to speak up more) and how this may represent a necessary part of the fight for life, growth, and development, in spite of such a grim situation. And yet Robert's utter exhaustion may make it very difficult for him to make the effort to talk.

25 November (Tuesday). At a ward meeting before I visit Robert, I gather that he has had a very severe nose bleed the day before. The charge nurse really thought he was dying. The nursing staff seem to be questioning the fact that the care of Robert is not *terminal*, and are wondering what is best for Robert and for his parents. It seems that there is a lack of communication between the nursing staff and consultant: the nurses wishing to indulge Robert more and make this a more positive phase in the sense of acknowledging openly that he is dying, and that, therefore, everything should be as pleasant as possible for him – possibly withdrawing drugs which cause vomiting. However, the doctors' approach seems to be 'Where there's life, there's hope', right until the patient draws his last breath.

2.30 pm. I go in to see Robert. The television is on extremely loudly. He is sitting up, for once unsupported by pillows, slowly eating a dry cracker biscuit. He looks at me, and then ignores me. Mrs Campbell says that she is going now; and does Robert want anything from the shop? Robert does not answer, for he is busy poking at the back of his throat to remove bits of biscuit. I comment on his red nail varnish and ask who painted his nails? I speculate to myself that it is an attempt to stop Robert from picking at his nails. Robert says, 'It's a secret.' As his mother leaves Robert tells her not to be long.

Robert agitatedly picks at his teeth. I comment on him seeming to want to poke into his mouth, as he did his ears and his nose before, and that he seems very busy, perhaps to let me know that as I have not been here since last Thursday he wishes to keep me out.

I ask if I can turn the television sound down. He nods. I bring up a chair. Now he is picking his fingernails, and trembling. Suddenly he blurts out, 'Can you get me gum in the back of my locker?' At first I do not understand his pronunciation of 'gum'. Then I ask if he is allowed to have it? He nods. Eventually I find it. He unwraps the chewing gum with some difficulty, curling it into a roll. His lips are scabby. He bites into it as if it is too big for his mouth, totally absorbed in the experience.

He suddenly asks for the bedpan. I fetch it, commenting that perhaps having the gum, like an enjoyable feed, makes him want the bedpan. He produces blackish diarrhoea. I wipe him and wash my hands. I like the smell of the hospital liquid soap, so I hold out my soapy hand for him to smell, responding to an impulse to increase his range of sensations. 'Yuck,' he says. I say 'I like it . . . you prefer your spearmint gum smell.' He nods.

And then he asks me to read him a story. 'Which one?' *Paddington Bear*, and he directs me to the last story in the book. I feel a pang when I see its title, 'The Last Dance'.

I read to him, battling with a sudden headache and a feeling of exhaustion that I did not have before. I feel that I am carrying the threat of death alone today – a threat which Robert with his bizarre scarlet fingernails and mouth full of sweet gum is pleasantly denying. He seems to scan my face avidly as I read, as if devouring the details, especially my mouth, with his wide eyes.

He asks for a tissue, to dispose of the gum. After a while I say that the story is very long, and I cannot read all of it – so I mark the page and talk to him.

I ask him if he has seen his Dad lately? He shakes his head. I ask if he wants to? He nods. I say, 'It's because of his cold . . . but it's important for you to see him . . . even if he stands by the door, with a mask. I'll try and arrange something.'

I ask him if there's anything else he would like very much? 'For Julie to come over,' he states emphatically. I acknowledge this, saying I will speak to Peter and to Mum and Dad, to see what we can arrange, 'Because, of course, it's important for you to see her, and for her to see you.'

His eyes begin to droop. I ask if he would like to lie back. He nods. I remove a pillow and make him comfortable. After a quiet time I say, 'I'm thinking about you not being so angry with your Dad these days, about things being better between you and him, and also your need for him to be here to share things with Mum, and to give Mum support.' He gives the most emphatic nod so far, and closes his eyes.

I ask if he wants me to stroke his forehead. He nods. As I stroke his forehead and his slightly furry head, he relaxes more. Occasionally his mouth turns down at the corners, or his brow furrows, or he suddenly grimaces.

I think to myself about him dying, about how he would look – perhaps peaceful like this. I feel we are understanding each other, perhaps he knows I am acknowledging a moment of peaceful acceptance of death, without fear or tension.

I stop stroking his head and rest my palm on his head. He seems to fall asleep, then half opens one eye. I tell him that I will have to go soon, but that I will be back as usual on Thursday, and would do what I could about Daddy visiting, and about Julie.

I leave the bell by his pillow, and leave.

Later, in a workshop, we discuss Robert, and it is decided that Dr Green (the consultant child psychiatrist) will see the haematology consultant, to discuss the nursing approach to Robert, including whether Mr Campbell should be allowed in even if he has a cold. It is also decided that I am to discuss with Peter the possibility of arranging for Julie to come over. There is a strong feeling that I should do all I can to sort out these practical things as well as to sense what is best for Robert as regards talking about death: how explicit to be. Everyone is very supportive, especially Dr Green.

Later, Dr Green hears about another dying child I may be taking on and asks me if I am sure I can take it. I say, 'Just about.' She says, 'You have got some healthy patients somewhere, haven't you?'

Their difficulties seem momentarily insignificant.

27 November (Thursday). I receive a letter from Dr Green letting me know that Robert's consultant is abroad, so it is hard to gauge Robert's medical condition and the overall approach to him. Dr Green says that she visited Mrs Campbell, who seems optimistic about Robert's condition.

I see Peter, who reports that the senior house officer is trying to get Robert to eat more; his liver is functioning badly and he has a temperature. Apparently, Julie cannot come over because she has been in touch with shingles, and there is a danger that she may import chicken pox to Robert. Peter says that he gathers that Mrs Campbell was surprised by Dr Green talking to her about the possibility of Robert's dying.

I enter Robert's room. Mrs Campbell gives a little nod of acknowledgement at my arrival. The television is on loudly as usual. Robert sits in the chair while his mother makes the bed. I sit quietly by Robert for a while. He is busy picking his lips and trembling grossly. He requests to return to bed, so Mrs Campbell puts slippers on him. I see Robert 'walking' the few aided steps to his bed for the first time since before the transplant.

Mrs Campbell then helps him to rest his head back on the pillow as one would a young baby whose neck is not yet strong enough. Robert lies on his side and seems cold. He asks for a bedpan. Mrs Campbell helps him onto it. He produces diarrhoea and then wants to be sick. We both help him. He vomits dark slimy stuff. Mrs Campbell rubs his back seemingly roughly throughout. (Tropauer *et al.* [1970], writing about children with cystic fibrosis, found that parental hostility was conveyed to the child by the strength of the mother's pounding during physiotherapy sessions.)

I hold his forehead and the bowl. His mouth is then full of mucus. I ask him if he wants a mouth wash. He nods. Mrs Campbell resignedly fetches a sterile mouth wash kit. Robert cries out in pain at the substance being rubbed on his gums: his mouth is full of ulcers. This is the procedure that he used to welcome. Finally, Mrs Campbell puts ointment on his very sore lips. He lies back, exhausted. And then needs the bedpan again. Mrs Campbell seems fed up. This time Robert does not produce anything in the bedpan.

I talk about the problem of Julie coming over. Mrs Campbell says categorically that she cannot, and that she does not want to plan ahead, because the last time they bought air tickets for Mr Campbell to fetch Julie, he could not go (because Robert had suddenly deteriorated). She says that perhaps, with Christmas approaching, the planes would all be booked up anyway, and adds, 'Everything is against us.' (I think to myself about her determination *not* to make plans for Julie's visit, and feel that it is part of her denial that her son is dying.)

Eventually, she leaves the room. I turn the television sound down, with Robert's permission, and sit by him. He seems to be looking intently at my silver bracelet, and shivering, as he has a temperature. He then concentrates on his hands and nails, picking at them. I say, 'You're busy with your fingers . . . perhaps because they don't go away, like Mum, or Dad, or Julie, or Mrs Judd . . . they're always there.'

He is focusing on them at close range, picking at the dry skin, and rubbing the dead bits on the sheet. I repeat what I have said to him before, about being ill being like the rough bits . . .'You know, people say, "I feel rough" when they're not feeling well.'

He starts to poke his cuticles with his nails. I say, 'Perhaps you're poking into yourself, when you're fed up, and cannot poke into anyone else.' There is a silence. He looks hard at me.

Then his mother returns. I say to Mrs Campbell, 'It seems Robert would like his Dad to pop in more, to see him, if possible.' Mrs Campbell says, 'Well, he was in here yesterday, wasn't he, Robert?' And then she tells me how much her husband hates the hospital air-conditioning, how he gets claustrophobic, phobic about hospital procedures, and how she used to be too, 'about sick, and drips . . . I used to feel faint . . . But when it's your own child . . .'

Mrs Campbell seems, once again, to be bearing all the actual contact single-handed while all the anxieties are located in her husband. I wonder what Robert is making of this conversation.

He is lying passively on his side. He asks his mother for a nail file. She gives him one, saying, 'If you've got any nails left to file!' I notice Robert sticking it far up inside his cuticle, and feel appalled. I find myself stopping him, by clasping his hands in mine. I worry that it will bleed and

bleed; I also worry that by talking about his depression and hopelessness, he is feeling more self-destructive than ever. His mother dismisses
what he is doing by saying, 'Oh, he's just getting off the old dry skin.'

Again Mrs Campbell and I seem to be responding in an oscillating
and polarized way: previously she was appalled at the implications of
some of Robert's activities while I resignedly tried to accept or understand them. Perhaps the acknowledgement of an impending imminent
death is often something that is so awesome and overwhelming that we
shy away from it if someone else can be felt to be carrying some of that
awareness for us. I also feel that she is showing me *her* anger at having to
go through all this.

It is time for me to leave. I say, 'Goodbye, see you on Tuesday', feeling
helpless. Mrs Campbell, as usual, is more friendly when I leave than
when I arrive. Is she pleased to see me leave? Or can she only value me
when she re-experiences me as helpful and involved? I feel that in my
absence, I become remote and useless to her.

2 December (Tuesday). Robert is in the chair, the television is on
loudly, and the play leader is reading him a story. I say, 'Hello', and that I
will return in a little while. While I am looking at Robert's notes, the play
leader comes to tell me, 'He's all yours'.

I go in. His eyes are glued to the television. Nurses come in and out. I
ask Robert if I can turn the sound down – he nods – adding that it seems
I am to feel left out, especially when it feels to him that I have been away
for a long time and have been ignoring him.

He seems to look a little better, his colouring seems more normal,
and he is calm. But he does not look at me. I ask him if the programme is
important to him. He says, 'No!'

I talk again about it seeming like a long time since I was here, and
wonder what he's been doing? 'I guess lots and lots of nurses have been
in and out . . . and doctors . . . and Mum . . . What about Dad?' He nods.
'As much as you wanted him to?' He nods again.

His eyelids begin to droop. I ask if he wishes to return to bed? He
shakes his head. His eyes are still fixed on the television. I think to myself
about watching television being a necessary defence. We sit quietly
together. More nurses come in and out.

After a while, I say, 'Last time you felt really fed up . . . and now, again,
perhaps you just want peace. Your body seems more comfortable today.'

He then asks if he can go back to bed. I carry him, with his arms
around my neck. He seems so light (17 kilos now); I worry about the
many tubes getting in a tangle, but we manage. He lies back, seeming
comfortable. I cover him up and stroke his forehead. His eyes droop.
And then he opens them, and looks hard at me. He grimaces slightly as
he moves his tongue around his mouth. I comment on him having had
such a sore mouth last time, and ask if it is still so sore. He nods. I say,

'That must be awful – I guess every time you eat or drink it stings.' He
nods. I say, 'Mouths should be places that feel nice and comfortable,
where food tastes good.' He nods.

His eyes close, and he falls into a deep sleep with my hand on his
head. Nurses come in and change the drip, talking very loudly. He does
not seem to stir, but I wonder about this restless atmosphere.

I notice a new photograph on the wall, of Julie and Robert taken
perhaps a year ago, each holding a little puppy. Robert wears a peaked
cap (perhaps to hide his hair loss) but looks well and happy.

4 December (Thursday). I go into the room, to find that the bed and
drip are not there. Mrs Campbell is asleep in the chair. I feel shocked.
Has it happened? Has he died? His toys are still around the room.
Bundles of dirty linen are in plastic sacks on the floor.

I go out and find sister, and gather that Robert is in theatre, having a
bowel biopsy under general anaesthetic. She tells me that the anaes-
thetist insisted upon a venous injection when he could have given it via
the Hickman. Robert had protested. Sister had felt very upset.

I wait a while. Sister goes back into the room to tell Mrs Campbell
that Robert is on his way back from theatre. Mrs Campbell seems
displeased to see me, but perhaps is just sleepy. However, I go in and
talk to her about Robert. She seems to take this new procedure of the
anaesthetic and biopsy in her stride, saying that she did not feel that
Robert really minded the injection.

Soon Robert is wheeled in, in his bed, asleep, and apparently all
right. Mrs Campbell gets up to see him, strokes his head, and Robert half
awakens. Mrs Campbell seems very pleased to see him. The nurses take
his blood pressure, pulse, and temperature, all of which are normal.

Mr Campbell comes in, and there is no exchange of words between
husband and wife. He looks extremely anxious as he looks at Robert. I
tell him that apparently he has taken the operation well.

He asks me how I am. I say, 'Well, how are you is what I was going to
ask!' He sits by me on the spare bed, seeming very keen to talk. He says
he is fine. I ask about the hospital atmosphere. He says he does not want
to complain. He feels Robert is much better. He tells me about Robert
hugging his old doctor from Scotland who visited him recently. I
acknowledge that he does seem more comfortable in his body.

He then tells me that Robert cried for Julie, but that they do not want
to risk chicken pox. They feel it would be a 'marvellous tonic' for Robert
if Julie visited. He goes on to talk about him anecdotally: about his liveliness, his always putting Julie first when he was well. (I think to myself
that he is mentioning the qualities that Robert is so markedly deprived of
by his illness, and therefore perhaps it is all the more understandable
that he should want us to remember them. This idealization of Robert
seems akin to the frequent idealization of someone who has already

died.) Mrs Campbell interjects that all leukaemic children in remission are hyperactive, thereby dismissing Mr Campbell's appreciation of his son's lost liveliness. I ask if he has always been active before he was ill? He says, 'Yes . . . never needed much sleep . . . even now . . . it's 11 pm before he settles down.'

Meanwhile, he is sleeping deeply. Nurses come and sort out the drip and Mrs Campbell helps. Her husband comments, 'She could have been a nurse.' Mrs Campbell denies this, saying that she is still squeamish, unless it is her own child.

I leave soon after.

9 December (Tuesday) 2.30 pm. For a reason I do not understand I do not bring the therapy box to Robert's room today. I enter his room, where the television is on loudly, and Mrs Campbell looks very drawn. She greets me and tells me that 'Robert won't be up to much today . . . he is asleep.' I notice that Robert's hands are covered in large bandages, like boxing gloves. Mrs Campbell says it is to stop him picking his lips, since this morning.

He sleeps peacefully, breathing deeply, his 'paws' up near his head. Mrs Campbell says that things have been much the same, but they are trying to get a new antibody from Birmingham. The biopsy confirmed that he has graft-versus-host disease, and Mrs Campbell thinks that this new antibody is, possibly, to combat this condition. I ask Mrs Campbell how *she* is? 'Oh, all right.' She looks pale and exhausted. She tells me that she has had disturbed nights as usual.

She goes to the hospital shop, leaving me with Robert, who continues to sleep for about 20 minutes. In his sleep he repeatedly feels his swollen sore lip with his tongue. Then he groans, opens his eyes which are filled with tears, looks at me, frowns, moves his position, and goes back to sleep. He is half awake again, busy with his tongue.

I stand by his bed, stroke his soft forehead and bald head, notice his lack of proper eyebrows as well, and say hello. I quietly tell him that I saw him last time, asleep, after he had the anaesthetic. He looks at me, then closes his eyes, and opens his mouth, revealing a yellowish substance. I talk about him seeming to be uncomfortable. He sticks out his tongue, as if to request help for the stuff on it. I wipe it with a tissue. Even his tears are yellowish.

I talk about his bandaged hands – that it must be very uncomfortable. He nods. I say, 'I guess you know why . . . to stop you picking at your lips and nose . . . making them bleed.' He nods. I acknowledge how fed up he must feel, though, to have bandaged hands, 'Because when you're lying in bed for weeks and weeks it seems one of the few things you *can* do is to use your fingers.' He nods.

I hold the bandaged hand, and say, 'It's not the same as holding your hand.' He nods again. I go on to say, 'But I can still stroke your forehead.'

His tongue is busy. Then he tries to say something. I don't understand. I ask him if he wants a drink? He calls out, 'Bedpan!' I quickly
fetch it. This time he has difficulty in sitting on it in his usual way by
supporting himself on his arms, because the bandages prevent him from
bending his wrists. I lift him, but cannot get the bedpan beneath him.
Fortunately, a nurse appears at this moment and helps. He has diarrhoea
again. 'Finished,' he tells me. I wipe him. He lies down on his other side.

I wash my hands, and then come over to talk to him – to tell him that
I will have to go soon. I tell him that on Thursday, the day after tomorrow, I'll be back. I stroke his forehead. I say, 'I know it's difficult to talk,
but is there anything you want to say, or to ask me . . .?' He is silent,
perhaps asleep. Then he says he's cold. I find an extra blanket. He
appears so tiny when I cover him. (I wonder how much the coldness is
part of his physical condition and how much a response to his awareness
of his situation. I wonder if my leaving evokes a dread of the ultimate
separation.)

I put up the cot-sides of the bed, which is what the nurses and Mrs
Campbell seem to do. He asks for his mother. I say that she will be back
soon. Robert seems half asleep. I realize that with his heavily bandaged
hands he cannot ring the bell. So I try to rig it up with tape so that he can
push it with his 'paws' but I don't know if it will work.

3.00 pm. I attend the haematology meeting. Dr Fish is there, talking
about the consultant's approach to Robert, 'Where there's life there's
hope.' Apparently, they always go on to the bitter end with transplant
patients. He explains that the awaited antibody is to counteract something in Robert from his father's marrow. His transplant has 'taken', but
there are now these complications. The consultant apparently admits he
is dying but cannot say when. The nursing staff express their feeling that
there is a lack of communication between them and the doctors. They
feel that, in their ongoing nursing of him, it would be more appropriate
to acknowledge that he is dying and to alter some of the nursing –
perhaps disturb Robert less, in order to make him more comfortable.
Sister even wonders if Robert and his parents should be flown back to
Scotland for Robert to die there. Dr Fish acknowledges the lack of
communication, but feels the doctors cannot alter their attempts to fight
for Robert's life.

This situation leads me to think further about the issues around
home care. While active treatment is still being given, home care could
not really be considered. It is this switch to palliative care that is the
crucial and difficult decision, especially for the doctors. Home care for
dying children has been advocated by many authors (Lamerton, 1973;
Lauer and Camitta, 1980; Martin, 1985; Martinson *et al.*, 1978). Of
course most children prefer home to hospital or hospice. If home care
can be combined with the support of a palliative care team (see pp.

86–92) or other specialist agencies, clearly the child and family are more likely to be able to manage at home. The advantages of home care are summarized by Martinson *et al.* (1978), where they describe not only the child receiving the security and love he needs that can usually be found in the home environment, but also: 'The parents may derive satisfaction in fulfilling their child's wishes to remain at home. This may help allay the sense of guilt that frequently follows death.' Research shows that, through home care and therefore improved family satisfaction, the child's psychological state is improved. At home there is often less confusion, less pressure, and fewer negative stimuli on the dying patient and his family. Psychiatric symptoms in parents are then often reduced (Lauer and Camitta 1980; Stein and Jessop, 1984). Home care enables the parents and sometimes siblings to be essential and active in aspects of their child's care, and not observers. (For a fuller analysis of home versus hospital care, see Dufour, 1989).

Although Mrs Campbell is very active in nursing Robert in hospital, and this can deepen the relationship, this is not always the case. As the experience of home care can be terrifying for the parents if there are unexpected medical crises, clearly, expert emergency medical help and palliative care support has to be readily available. 'Because serious childhood illness is rare, GPs are not that comfortable about offering support,' says Dora Black (personal communication).

It is characteristic of this phase that the transition to a terminal state is not recognized simultaneously by all those involved. In this ward it is often the doctors who are last to give up hope for the child. This conflict between members of the team signifies the differences in role, style, timing, and emotional response. As nurses are most constantly physically in touch with the child, and with the suffering, it is not surprising that they are often keen to prevent unnecessary suffering if it is indeed unlikely for a child's life to be saved through further efforts. This is not always the case, though. (For further discussion on this see Chapter 10.)

To return to the story: after the haematology meeting I meet a volunteer who has just met Mrs Campbell. She tells me that Mrs Campbell is devastated at finding a leaflet in the hospital chapel which states that Robert has died, and that the community should pray for him. Apparently, Mrs Campbell is being comforted by Carol, to whom she is very close.

At Dr Green's workshop which follows, for those working with terminally ill children and their families, we relate this appalling mistake. She asks Dr Simmons, the child psychiatrist, to find the chaplain, and says she will bring the matter to the administration, in order to try to prevent unvetted literature entering the hospital. Apparently the leaflet is produced by a local church.

I talk to the workshop about Robert again. They feel that the family should be helped to bring Julie over, in spite of the anxiety about chicken pox.

I talk about the bandaged hands. They feel that cotton gloves would be better. The meeting confirms my feeling that this is the removal of one of the few sensations left to Robert. I agree to try to talk to the nursing staff about alternatives. Dr Simmons returns to join us, telling us that the chaplain has apologized to Mrs Campbell.

I feel greatly encouraged and supported by this workshop in confronting some of the issues more actively, as well as in carrying the pain of Robert's condition. I go and see sister about Robert's hands. She feels he picks at his lips and nose as a way of getting at his mother. He seems to do it all the more when Mrs Campbell asks him not to. I say that I still wonder about cotton gloves – so he can use the bell, for instance. Sister suggests I speak to Mrs Campbell about this.

I go to see Robert and his mother, and find him sitting up, being fed marshmallow biscuits by his mother, because, of course, he cannot hold anything with heavily bandaged hands. His eyes are half closed. I say that I have been wondering about the bandages, and whether Robert could perhaps wear gloves instead. Mrs Campbell replies, 'No, he'd still pick at himself. It will be just for a few days, until his sores have healed. Already, after *one* day, it's a bit better.'

I comment then to both of them that perhaps it helps for Robert to know that the bandages will come off soon. Mrs Campbell interjects, 'Oh, he knows that all right! Last night we bought him this robot-car, which he could have if he didn't pick, but he didn't keep his promise.'

I say that I do not think he means to pick at himself to be naughty. Perhaps when he is frustrated, his body is all there is to have a go at.

Mrs Campbell says that he never used to, when he was ill before. (She is not prepared to realize that this time the illness is different, more serious.) I comment that the nurses have said that picking at the body is very common among leukaemic patients.

(Repeated picking of the nose and cheek was observed by Bowlby *et al.* [1952] as characteristic behaviour of a 2-and-a-half-year-old hospitalized girl. Anna Freud suggested to them that that behaviour may have been connected to the child's attempts not to cry and to wipe away her tears. The authors conclude that while face-fingering may be connected with attempts to control crying, nose-picking appears to be more of a masturbation equivalent.)

Mrs Campbell has left the new remote-control robot-car by Robert on the bed. He looks grotesque: like an injured boxer, with half-closed eyes, sitting up, trying to push the button of this new toy through heavily bandaged hands.

I have to leave soon.

11 December (Thursday). His notes say that he has deteriorated generally over the past 36 hours. He has a persistent fever and a chest infection.

10.30 am. I arrive, to find the blind on his door closed. I tentatively enter the darkened room. Robert is sitting in the chair while Mrs Campbell is busy cleaning the room.

I say hello and go to him.

His eyes are closed. I tell him I am here. There is silence, except for Mrs Campbell vigorously wiping everything she can reach in the room with sterilizing fluid. I talk to him about having his eyes closed for much of the time these days.

Mrs Campbell says, 'Oh, it's because of the eye ointment – since last night.' But I think to myself that he has been increasingly withdrawing for many days. There appears to be an actual eye infection as well.

His hands are not bandaged. His eyes are running, and I do not know if they are sad tears or simply watering eyes. He begins to drop asleep, his head drooping. I ask him if he would like to return to bed? He nods, so I ask Mrs Campbell who replies briskly, 'Oh, he must sit up . . . mustn't be in bed the whole time.' Robert seems to accept this. (Mrs Campbell is clearly making a great effort to get Robert back on the path towards health, and her cleaning activities seem to be her way of wiping away the illness.)

Eventually, Mrs Campbell comes to transfer Robert to bed. He seems too weak to push his feet into the slippers that mother holds out. At this point a nurse comes in to weigh Robert who is transferred to the weighing chair. He then 'walks' backwards to the bed, Mrs Campbell supporting him, and telling him to 'straighten up'.

In bed he lies on his side in a foetal position with eyes closed, seemingly exhausted.

Mrs Campbell is still bustling about the room, and comes to bandage Robert's hands, who passively accepts this. Robert half opens his eyes, to say, 'Read me a story.' I say, 'Sure, which one?' He does not answer. I fetch *Snow White* and two others, and read the titles to him. He shakes his head with tiny movements, as if economizing on the effort. I then fetch the story of *Thumbelina*, to which he nods. His eyes are closed throughout: he no longer seems willing or able to make the effort to see the pictures, as he used to.

As I begin to read it to him, Mrs Campbell leaves the room. I find the story increasingly poignant. Thumbelina is nursing the swallow:

As she covered him up, she felt his heart still beating.
The swallow was not dead. He was still alive but very weak.

My voice trembles, but I carry on until the end. Robert seems to be asleep. I sit quietly until his mother returns. A nurse takes his temperature, which is quite high, so she uncovers him except for a sheet. Robert continues to sleep.

Mrs Campbell returns, saying that he sleeps on and off all the time because he is always disturbed by medical check-ups during his sleep.

She tells me that her husband is still asleep.

I say I will pop back later.

I think about the burden Mrs Campbell is carrying, and how it is not surprising that she should be using so much denial. I pass the auxiliary nurse, Carol. She beckons me, to talk with her. We go into the milk kitchen for a brief chat. She tells me that Mr and Mrs Campbell had a row last night in front of Robert and Carol. Mrs Campbell impatiently asked her husband to leave Robert alone when he was busily trying to do things for him. Carol feels awful about the fact that she is going on holiday on Monday. Apparently Mrs Campbell and Robert are both very upset about this. Carol feels Robert to be worse. Carol tells me that Robert has pleaded with her to try to arrange for Julie to come over, and that Robert has said to Carol, 'That's why I'm fighting.' We both share our feeling that he may indeed be holding on for Julie – and what if she does come over – will he then give up?

Later I return to the room. Robert is vomiting lots of mucus into a bowl, while his mother is patting and rubbing his back (perhaps too hard?) Robert needs the bedpan at the same time. It is awful to witness his extremely weak body being wracked by the violent muscular spasms of his stomach, his throat, his bowels.

Eventually, he is finished. Mrs Campbell leaves the room. Robert looks at me more penetratingly than he has done for weeks. I stroke his forehead, and try to talk to him about how awful he must be feeling. Tears stream out of his eyes. I say, 'Watery-eye tears, and sad tears.' He begins to feel sick again, and to cough. He chokes. I fear he will die there and then, and sit him up. He vomits a little. He feels hot. He complains with a weak moan and then lies back.

Again he starts to cough. He looks at me with startled eyes beneath their swollen lids. I say, 'Perhaps you're frightened that you'll choke, that you won't be able to breathe.' He nods, holding on to me with staring eyes.

A nurse comes in, so I explain to her about Robert choking. She tries to get Robert to sit up, but Robert complains, and will not, or cannot, cooperate. The nurse gives up and leaves.

Mrs Campbell soon returns. I tell her about the choking – she says she knows and that they are going to give him medicine for his chest.

Sadly, I have to leave him. I talk to Mrs Campbell and to Robert about Carol being away from Monday, and how difficult it will be for them. Mrs Campbell replies matter-of-factly, 'Oh, yes, indeed.'

I go and see Peter to brief him. He has been snowed under with other urgent cases. He agrees to see the parents about Julie coming over. I tell him I will be 'on call' over Christmas, if necessary.

15 December (Monday). The first good news for a long time! Peter rings me at home in the evening to say Julie came over on Saturday. This arose out of a meeting Peter arranged on Friday between the parents, Peter, and one of the doctors who informed the parents of the grim outlook.

16 December (Tuesday) 2.00 pm. I go into the room and find Robert alone. I turn the television sound down. He is lying on his side, propped up on pillows, picking relentlessly at his bottom lip, which is a dark purply red. Bits of skin and blood are on his fingers and on the pillow-case. A medallion of the Virgin Mary is pinned to his pillow.

I say hello, and sit by him, taking the cot-side of the bed down. His eyes are streaming with yellowy liquid. Again I say that I am not sure if they are sad eyes, or watering eyes, or both. He looks at me, continuing to pick and squeeze his lip with trembling bony fingers. I tell him I did not bring the box, as I thought his hands would be bandaged. (This is not the only reason. I am avoiding the truth: that I thought he would be too ill to take an interest in it.)

I talk about him picking his lip, and wonder aloud if it is his way of getting at something, when all he can attack is himself. He nods slightly. I continue to say that I have heard the news about Julie being here. He nods. I ask if they are all having lunch at the moment, and he nods again.

I talk about this being what he has wanted so much for a long time. I ask if Julie has spent a lot of time with him, and he shakes his head. I say, 'Perhaps you pick your lip all the more when Mum, Dad, and Julie are out, and you want them here with you?'

I try to hold his hand to calm him down. He allows it, but then carries on picking. I say, 'You're hurting yourself. Perhaps you feel you have to be punished . . . that it's your fault you're ill?'

He looks hard at me and nods. I ask him in what way he thinks he has caused it. He does not answer. I say, 'People often wonder, "Why me, why am I the ill one, why not my sister, or someone else", and they think it's because they've been bad.' He gives a hacking cough, and cries a little.

I say, 'You feel you're full of bad stuff, but you know, it isn't anyone's fault when they are ill – and no one can know why it happens to you . . .'

He is picking and pulling his lip in an awful way. I say, 'You're wanting me to know what it's like to see you pulling at the rough skin. The roughness is like the illness. This way, by showing me, I can share it with you. But you may make it bleed a lot – shall I read you a story, or tell you a story, instead?'

He blurts out, 'I want the box!' 'The box with the toys?' I ask. 'Right . . . I'll get it. I'll be a little while . . . have to go in the lift.' I put up the bedside bars. I dash off, cursing myself for not bringing the box, but pleased that Robert so actively requests it.

When I return, a few minutes later, he is in exactly the same position, picking at his lips. I make a little table out of the box lid, and hold up the various collections within. Animals? He shakes his head. Hospital set? He shakes his head. Soft little dolls? He nods.

I put them out. He seems unable to play with them, so I hold them up, and ask if this is the Mummy, Daddy, and so on, to which he nods each time, correcting me that 'Granny' is 'Nan'. He agrees that the little boy is Robert and the bigger girl, Julie. I ask if Mum or Dad are busy with the children? He shakes his head. I say, 'So are they like this, busy with each other?' He nods to my positioning the parents as if talking to each other. I interpret his wish for Mum and Dad to get on well together. I go on to talk about this little boy doll being left out now, now that Mum and Dad are busy '. . . perhaps how you feel when Mum and Dad and Julie go out and leave you? And now that Carol has gone away, it must be very difficult.' He looks at me.

(I do not interpret that the imminent death leaves him feeling excluded from his parents. Nor do I interpret his feelings that I too come and go, and leave him, like they do. I am not sure why I avoid saying this. Perhaps the imminent death is like an inevitable sudden separation or ending that makes me instinctively avoid the impact of *my* close relationship with him. But for whose sake? Mine or Robert's?)

I ask him what he wants me to do with the dolls now? His face puckers. 'I want Mummy!' I stroke his forehead, saying, 'Mummy will be back soon. You feel upset when I talk about Carol going away.' Then, feeling bolder, I say, 'And I go away too, between Tuesdays and Thursdays and Thursdays and Tuesdays.'

(With hindsight – and now much more experience, 8 years later – I feel that at this moment Robert is gripped by fear of dying without his mother. I would now talk to a child about this, specifically.)

'Bedpan!' he blurts out.

Just as I am about to lift him onto it, his sister Julie and his parents walk in. I say, 'Your Mum is much better at this than I am', and hand over the role to Mrs Campbell. Mr Campbell helps too. Robert suddenly cries, as if in pain. Both parents expostulate about his lip, especially Mr Campbell, saying that it is much worse now. Apparently, they had asked a nurse to sit with him. Mrs Campbell clears up the mess impatiently, but is verbally resigned, for when Mr Campbell continues to complain about the state of his lip, she says philosophically, 'He won't stop . . . no point in going on about it . . . nothing we can do . . . even if his hands are bandaged, he'll rub the bandage against it.'

Meanwhile, I talk to Julie for the first time. She seems a pleasant, polite, sensitive girl. She appears rather plump, but perhaps that is simply in contrast to the state of her brother.

Suddenly Robert calls out shrilly, 'I want Mrs Judd to lie me down!' His mother seems to show some difficult feelings about this in her way of saying, 'Oh, all right.' Doubtless, they feel angry with me for 'allowing' the lip-picking. I step forward to help Robert, saying, 'Well, you don't see much of me.' Feeling rather guilty about the lip-picking, I say to the parents that perhaps he feels fed up and feels he has to pick at *something*.

Robert asks for the bedpan again. Mr Campbell tells me he wants it 30 to 40 times a day. I comment on how exhausting this must be for him and for them.

Mrs Campbell continues about the picking, 'We can't stop him . . . if he doesn't want to take his tablets now, I don't force him.'

I wonder to myself about the extent to which Mrs Campbell has given up the struggle. She talks with slight bitterness at times, exhaustion at others. Her shift of attitude does not seem one of a peaceful acknowledgement of the inevitable, a wish to make it as calm as possible. Perhaps not surprisingly, after the months of an agonizing struggle on her part, she cannot give in gracefully at this point. As part of her acceptance there seems bound to be some outrage at what is happening. (This links with my comments on the phases people approaching death go through in Chapter 5.)

Julie's arrival seems to be an appropriate gratification of Robert's overriding need to see her, and Julie's need too to see Robert. The family unit is completed at this point of crisis. But, in a way that I had not anticipated, it seems to stress the situation further. The parents are more anxious and exhausted than I have ever seen them. I feel this is mainly their response to Robert's deteriorating condition, but Julie's presence must lead to conflicting pulls in them to protect the older child on the one hand from the dreadful situation, while, on the other hand, to help her prepare for Robert's death. But can they manage any of the extra parenting Julie requires when they are both so fully stretched by Robert?

Mr Campbell and Julie then set off for a walk. Robert calls out to me, 'I want the hospital set!' I am supposed to attend a meeting at this point, but I decide not to. So I set up the table over his bed and take out the hospital set. He is propped up on pillows, and, in spite of his heavy-lidded eyes, he appears interested. Mrs Campbell leaves the room. I tell Robert that I will just pop out to tell people that I am not going to a meeting and that I will be back soon.

I return very quickly. He seems to expect me to somehow facilitate his play, so I ask him how I should arrange the little figures. He wants the little boy on the bed, the mother and father by his bedside, the hat in the locker (as he himself has arranged it previously). He seems to appreciate my talking about the things *he* did with all this when he was not so ill. I wonder aloud if the hat in the locker is for when the little boy goes home. He wants the little boy to get up and have food at the table, and to then go back to bed. I do not talk to him about his need to experience the normal aspects of life through play, as his way of re-living and re-gaining a lost or dormant aspect of himself. The mere enactment of a more well little boy seems sufficient.

Mrs Campbell returns, and Robert requests the bedpan. While he sits on it he says his back aches. His mother gives him a close cuddle while rubbing it, and then leaves again.

Robert requests the little family of soft dolls. Again, he seems too weak to play with them himself, so I ask him what he wants me to do with them for him. I make the mother doll cuddle the Robert doll, describing the actions, and ask him if that is what he wants me to do. He nods. I ask him, 'And the Dad? To cuddle too?' He affirms, so I do this. I then enact Dad and the Julie doll going off for a walk and talk about Robert struggling here, for such a long time, to get well, while the others can go out for walks.

He blurts out, 'Want Plasticine.' (His requests today have an almost feverish quality, as if he wants to play with everything for the last time. I wonder if this is the efflorescence that can precede death.) I ask him what colour he wants? 'Pink.' So I soften some for him. He tries it out and asks me to make something for him. I remind him that I will have to go soon, and make him a little car, perhaps connected with my coming and going, but more consciously because of Mrs Campbell often telling me about Robert's liking for toy cars. He watches my hands intently as I work. I put it in front of him. He asks me to make something else. I ask him what? He says, 'You choose.' I tell him I will make something for him to guess, and fashion a little mouse. He shakes his head at the finished product. I am not sure if it is a poor representation, or if he has a block to knowing what it is. Anyway, I tell him what it is, adding that perhaps he reminds me of a little mouse today: quiet, but busy. I put the mouse and car on the little shelf with the Plasticine Sunshine (teddy bear) I had made before.

He asks for the urine bottle. After using it he lies back, exhausted.

Mrs Campbell returns. I pack up the toy box and say that I have to go now. For the first time he cries out plaintively, 'Don't want Mrs Judd to go!' I stroke his forehead, and say that I will be back on Thursday, the day after tomorrow.

This turns out to be a false promise, as I *am* back on Thursday, but not to see Robert. I find myself holding out the expectation of the usual pattern of visits even though I know that this may well be broken by his death. I continue to hope that there will be another day – even though, in a way, Robert himself seems to have reached a stage of awareness of the imminent ending and where he needs peace above all.

(Robert seems to be showing a growing attachment to me, as someone important to him. Needless to say, the corollary to this is that he occupies a central position in my thoughts and feelings. The volume of painful feelings that I carry reinforce my awareness that I have to try to keep a balance in my life between this kind of work and other work.)

Mrs Campbell comes and stands by Robert's bedside, sympathetically. I say to both of them, 'Robert feels upset at my going, especially after Carol left to go on holiday yesterday.'

Mrs Campbell nods, adding, 'But Carol is going to send you a card, your own special card, isn't she?' She continues to stroke Robert's forehead as I leave, as if to facilitate my going. Later I try to arrange for someone else in the department to see Julie on her own. I realize that today is the only day that I have 'forgotten' to write a note on Robert's ward file about my session with him.

17 December (Wednesday) 12 noon. I receive a phone call at my other place of work to phone Miranda urgently, the head of the hospital school. I do so. She says, 'I have sad news for you. Robert died this morning.' Apparently, it was at about 10 o'clock, and she recounts to me that the parents are weeping, wandering around the hospital looking very lost; everyone is relieved that Julie is over here. She says they are going back home tomorrow or the next day. I tell her that I will try to arrange to come to the hospital today.

Fortunately, a colleague agrees to see a family without me, so I can leave the clinic. The intervening meeting and interaction at the clinic have a strange, unreal feel. Later, I realize that I was in a state of numbness. I feel some conscious relief as well. I have an oppressive headache which lifts soon after I arrive at the hospital.

I think about Robert dying only four days after Julie's arrival. It seems that he really was 'holding on' until seeing his sister again. (Kübler-Ross [1987] writes about similar situations of dying people, beyond the point where they can be helped medically: not letting go until some crucial issue has been resolved. Research by the University of California bears this out: it suggests that dying patients enter a 'bargaining' phase in which they ask their god to allow them to survive until the arrival of an important occasion [Brindle, 1988].)

3.20 pm. I arrive at the hospital and go up to the children's ward. Straight away I see Peter with the parents and Julie in the parents' lounge, talking to them with another Scottish couple. Mrs Campbell is crying, pale, and red eyed. Mr Campbell immediately comes up to me and blurts out how much he had tried '. . . everyone had tried . . . how we all did what we could.' His speech flows on in a stream: 'Everyone gets impatient sometimes . . . fed up . . . I know I did . . . feel I could only give so much . . .' I try to talk to him about Mrs Campbell having a definite role with Robert and that it was hard for him not having this clear role. I also talk to him about him feeling so much, right from the start, and that perhaps because he felt so upset, and felt it so strongly, he had to go away a little each day.

I notice Julie sitting there, crying. So I go and put my hand on her shoulder, and say how important it is for her to be here. She nods.

Peter has to go with Mr Campbell to sort out the death certificate and then to arrange tomorrow's journey with the undertaker. The plan is that after all the arrangements have been made, we will go and see Robert's body. I decide to wait with Mrs Campbell and Julie, and then to go with them, for my sake as much as theirs, to see the body.

The Scottish couple are, apparently, from a charity that helps to raise money for leukaemia, and they seem to be here to befriend the parents. Tonight, the parents and Julie will sleep at their flat, and the next morning they will fly up to Scotland.

I take them down to the hospital canteen for tea. (I sorely feel the lack of a more private place to be together.) The visiting Scottish lady seems to counter my attempts to allow Mrs Campbell and Julie to cry, with comments like, 'Robert wouldn't want you to cry. He's happy now, in heaven. He's up there', pointing to the ceiling. Mrs Campbell and Julie, though, seem very open in their feelings of loss and utter misery. Mrs Campbell cries, and talks copiously about Robert's special qualities.

Mrs Campbell tells me that this morning he had been breathing with difficulty since about 5.00 am, so they provided oxygen. At about 10.00 am. Robert asked for the bedpan, but was too weak to lift himself up, and soiled the undersheet. Mrs Campbell tells me how he held out his little arm, which mother took, 'And it felt strange. He just looked at me with those great big eyes. I rang the bell. Mike [the charge nurse] came, and then I went to get my husband. I think he was "gone" by the time we got back.'

Mrs Campbell reproaches herself for the times she has been impatient with Robert in the middle of the night, saying, 'Not again, Bobby!' when Robert wanted the bedpan for the umpteenth time. I notice that she is wearing Robert's little blue watch. Apparently, Mrs Campbell had asked Julie to put it at the right time earlier today, before the death. Robert has not worn the watch since he has been in hospital.

Mrs Campbell eats a sandwich slowly, as if force-feeding herself. She chokes on it once. Julie begins to cut away at the table top with a plastic knife, so I acknowledge her feeling so angry that this has to happen. More tears spring to her eyes, prompting the Scottish lady to ruffle her hair and tell her that Robert would not want her to cry. I put forward my belief in the value of crying, as a very normal and healthy response. This is risking the alienation of the Scottish lady, but my main concern is clearly with Robert's family.

Mrs Campbell then cries desperately at the prospect of going back home without Robert, going into Robert's room, seeing his little bed, and wonders what to do with all his toys and possessions. I talk about her doing it in her own time. She says she has decided to give the hospital all the toys that are new here, and to take Robert's little Communion Book, and a neck chain with a cross, which she is going to put with Robert. She also has two little bottles of holy water from Lourdes, and 'relics'.

Eventually, Peter and Mr Campbell return. Mr Campbell is extremely agitated, and cannot bear to sit with us while Peter telephones the undertaker. The husband of the Scottish lady rejoins us.

After a long delay, we all go down to see Robert in a strange underground – or should I say underworld – part of the hospital, through various locked doors, escorted by a young man.

Robert's body is in a little room, lit only by a candle-bulb. An iron cross stands next to it. He is covered up to the neck in a royal blue shroud. His bald head rests peacefully at last. His eyes are closed, behind pinkish lids. The rest of the face is pale, except for dark red lips. Are they painted, or is it purplish bruising? He wears the smart striped pyjama top he wore before he became desperately ill.

His parents touch his forehead. Mr Campbell exclaims, shocked, 'How cold he is!' as if he should warm him or do something to remedy it. Mother is overcome with crying, touches Robert, hugs Julie, who cries too. The blue shroud becomes stained with their tears. Peter and I stand back a little.

I say, 'How peaceful he looks.' Father readily agrees. I touch Robert's forehead and am shocked at the coldness. I remember my father's dead forehead: that lifeless quality. I cry too.

Mrs Campbell searches frantically for Sunshine, the teddy bear. It does not seem to be there. Julie joins her in the search. They then find it, tucked far down. Mrs Campbell adds the mementoes she has brought. Mrs Campbell's desperate need to place Sunshine with Robert seems to be her way of easing the separation between Robert and herself. Sunshine represented mother for Robert in the past and now Sunshine once again is to bridge Mrs Campbell's separation from her son. Similarly, Robert's little blue watch on Mrs Campbell's wrist may help to ease the separation.

> This small forgotten object, that was ready to signify everything, made you intimate with thousands through playing a thousand parts . . . This Something, worthless as it was, prepared your relationships with the world . . . you experienced through it, through its existence, through its anyhow-appearance, through its final smashing or its enigmatic departure, all that is human, right into the depths of death.

Thus Rilke (1914, *Gesammelte Werke*, IV) described the importance of that which Winnicott (1951) much later termed a 'transitional object'. In describing its symbolic potential Rilke encompasses the possibility of including the 'depths of death' in its range. Although Rilke did not mean it literally, it serves to illustrate what he describes in his Fourth Elegy as 'the gap left between world and toy': the significance of this toy/doll/teddy bear/object that usually represents the absent mother.

I am reminded of hearing from a health visitor about the death of a young baby. The mother wished to place some of her breast milk on the baby's lips, as her last gesture, when saying goodbye to her baby. This seems to epitomize the wish to continue to provide for the baby after death and to ease the separation for the mother. And, as we know, the ancient Egyptians attempted to assure the happiness of their dead children in the after-life by burying with them the toys with which they had played (Puckle, 1926). Similarly, another mother insisted upon changing her dead daughter into a new track-suit, after the child had already been laid out.

Peter asks about the holy water that Mrs Campbell has not used yet. She makes the sign of the cross on Robert's forehead with it, and on his chest, and gives some to Julie to do the same, then puts the bottle of holy water with Robert.

The Scottish lady says, 'He's not there, that's not Robert, he's in heaven.'

The parents look at his seemingly long limbs stretched out under the shroud as if to take stock, before leaving. Mrs Campbell kisses him, saying, 'Good night, my pet.' Afterwards, she says, 'I kept wanting him to open his eyes.'

Julie and Mrs Campbell are crying as we walk along the corridor away from the mortuary. I put an arm around them, feeling helpless, saying, 'It's awful for you. Robert had a few happy years, and lots of love. . .'

We all go up in the lift, to the children's ward, for the parents to pack their bags. I say goodbye to them, and Mrs Campbell begins to cry again. We hug each other, and she thanks me. I say that I will be thinking of them, and that I feel grateful to have known Robert. Mr Campbell and I shake hands warmly. I say goodbye to Julie, and shake hands with the Scottish couple. Mrs Campbell's eyes follow me beseechingly to the lift, as if searching for her son through me.

Outside the hospital, the darkness of the night is regaled by the Christmas lights. I curse the Christmas trees and the Christmas lights. I feel so angry with this season of jollity. I can now fully understand why the word 'Christmas' had made Mrs Campbell cry earlier today.

Tomorrow they fly home 'with' Robert.

Later, at home, I feel the need to care physically for my healthy 7-year-old. I look at him, stretched out in the bath, and gain succour from his health, while feeling a shiver of shock at the coffin-like surround of the bath. I have to begin my own process of mourning Robert.

18 December (Thursday). I go into the hospital as usual on Thursday. I feel deeply touched by the warm support I receive from colleagues. Robert's family will not need to return to the hospital today. I go up to the children's ward to add my last notes to Robert's medical file.

I read the medical notes for yesterday. These are some extracts:

7.15 am. Very weak.
7.30 am. Fairly rapid deterioration. Pneumonia.
9.30 am. Very unwell. Morphine prescribed.
10.10 am. No spontaneous respiration. No pulse. Certified dead (by the Senior House Officer).

I wander into Robert's empty room, feeling that if I postpone this step it will become more fearful. The door is wide open for the first time. And the room is indeed empty. Very empty. Some of the posters are still on the walls. I find the little Plasticine version of Sunshine I had made for Robert still sitting on a shelf. I feel irrationally hurt that it has been left there. I remove it.

At a staff meeting the next week, one of the staff nurses who knew Robert brightly tells me that she and the other nurses were 'really pleased' when Robert died. At first I think I have misheard her, and ask her to repeat herself. I then realize that she does mean what she says, and that she is referring to the understandable relief the nurses felt that the long and painful struggle was over. Nevertheless, it leads me to wonder about some of the nurses' difficulties in really feeling loss at Robert's death. Their training and work, with its emphasis on nursing people to health, does not seem to have sufficient place for thinking about, and staying with, the pain of terminal illness. But then, can anyone repeatedly *experience* this in an exposed way? (Again, I think that there has been a development in the past 8 years, and many nurses nowadays are more in touch with their feelings if they are in a climate that allows it.)

I realize I have to spare myself too frequent encounters with death through my work: to balance it with all the other work as a way of gaining equilibrium. To really share the process with the dying and their families, I have to find a balance: somewhere between the raw pain that they are feeling, and the defended state of some of the medical team, in order to be most useful to them.

Without the support of colleagues, of Dr Green's fortnightly workshop for those working with terminally ill children and their families, as well as that of my husband and analyst, I probably would not have coped.

Weeks later, I go back to Robert's medical file, and see that someone has written in the date of his death under the 'date of discharge' column, and then inscribed, in big letters, 'RIP'.

Chapter Eight
Postscript

> . . . the emotional pain of loss, the pain that has broken a heart.
> Such pain fills the space of an entire life. It may have begun with a
> single event but the event has produced a surplus of pain. The
> sufferer becomes inconsolable. Yet, what is this pain, if it is not
> the recognition that what was once given as pleasure or happi-
> ness has been irrevocably taken away?

> John Berger, *And Our Faces, My Heart, Brief as Photos*, 1988

Five months after Robert's death, I heard from Peter, the paediatric
social worker, that Mr and Mrs Campbell and Julie would be revisiting
the hospital in a few days. This seemed to be in order to see the hospital
staff again and to go over some of the events by re-experiencing the
place.

I left a note for them, so that they could contact me if they wished.
Mrs Campbell telephoned, sounding jovial, and I arranged to meet them
at Carol's flat, with whom they were staying.

I was warmly welcomed by Mr Campbell who seemed to have put on
weight and looked extremely well. He told me that the airline company
had – after Mrs Campbell had complained – offered them free tickets as
compensation for the 2-hour delay they had endured at Aberdeen
airport when they were taking Robert's body back home. Julie, now in
the same room as her father, continued with her absorption in a television computer game, barely acknowledging my visit. Understandably,
she had more engrossing matters to attend to.

Mrs Campbell then came in to meet me. She looked pretty and delicate, her gentle manner harmonizing with the pastel shades of her
jumper and make-up, reflecting the warm early summer weather. I felt
relieved at the apparent health of all three of them, and moved by the
keenness and openness with which both parents talked about their feelings upon revisiting the hospital. It seemed that through this nostalgic,

painful, and pleasurable journey they were sharing memories with the many people who knew Robert. It seemed a very understandable part of the mourning process: to face the hospital ward (and most of the people involved) that had been the centre of their life for 3 months, to express gratitude for all the concern and care Robert that had received, and perhaps to begin to work through some of the agonizing questions, particularly in Mrs Campbell's mind. She conveyed that she repeatedly questioned every aspect of the past few years, feeling guilt and self-reproach at some decisions and ways she behaved.

Julie continued to play with the computer game throughout my long visit, interjecting with occasional comments. I gathered she had had an outing the day before, alone with Peter, so I felt her avoidance of me now may have been her way of giving her parents, and particularly her mother, their 'turn'. Her manner was pleasant and calm, and she was looking forward to a shopping trip that afternoon.

A very detailed account was then given to me of the 3 years since Robert's diagnosis: from the initial tummy pains, to the sore throat, to the numerous copious nosebleeds, to the body rash – until the diagnosis was made. And then the first treatment, followed by several healthy months in remission, then an ominous nosebleed and the realization that he was relapsing. This time Robert was very close to death, and yet, with the chemotherapy, he re-emerged for a further remission; and then began the final phase at the hospital in the North of England.

Mrs Campbell showed me an album of photographs of Robert, from babyhood onwards. He did indeed seem to have been an active, spirited, and robust child. It is hardly surprising that the home was described as being very quiet and empty nowadays. It seems that the remaining family members were very conscious of the gap left by Robert. Mrs Campbell found it difficult to enjoy her increased leisure now that she did not have a boisterous little boy – nor an ill little boy – to care for.

Mrs Campbell recounted how Robert, even as a very little child, had a precocious awareness of death. She gave several examples of her son's down-to-earth (if I may use that expression) understanding of the process, including the 3-year-old Robert's own word for coffin, which was 'bury-box'.

Mrs Campbell cried freely at many points in her story. Both parents were still raw in experiencing their pain. It seemed that now their religious beliefs were helping them in their mourning: some feeling of a divine being that has an all-powerful plan seemed to help them to relinquish Robert.

I felt there was a possibility that this tragedy of Robert's death could actually leave them with a greater awareness of life's pleasures as well as its pains. 'The deeper that sorrow carves into your being, the more joy you can contain' (Gibran, 1926). They seemed to have so much humility, love, and compassion, in their accounts of their son and of their involvement with others who had helped them. Although there were reproaches, mainly self-directed, but also towards possible delays in the doctors diagnosing the illness, there was no bitterness.

Mrs Campbell said that she had one or two further administrative matters to sort out regarding Robert's death, which she was consciously postponing. It was as if she did not yet wish to complete the 'burial'. Yet, of course, this child will live on in the minds of many of us.

We talked about the many times that I sensed Mrs Campbell's ambivalent and, at times, negative feelings towards me. She acknowledged that this had indeed been the case: she had often had appallingly disturbed nights with Robert and then the next morning they would be in the midst of various medical procedures, when I would arrive. Of course, my appearance with a box of toys for Robert, who could barely move, seemed singularly inappropriate! Mrs Campbell felt, moreover, that I would be judging her if she felt exhausted and did not face Robert's demands with resilience. However, she warmly conveyed that she now saw it all differently: 'You were there for Robert, and he valued you. That's the important thing.'

Chapter Nine
Brief retrospective analysis

> . . . but I think people always die alone . . . with or without rela-
> tions. I was a little girl then. And I remember asking her one time
> . . . how does it feel to die? – Only a little girl would ask such a
> question . . . She said – It's a lonely feeling.

Tennessee Williams, Orpheus Descending

Reflecting upon my inhibition in really using the transference in my
work with Robert, I now feel that it would have been more useful to him
if I had 'gathered' it more fully. Limitations within the setting and my
own countertransference responses, at times, of overprotectiveness,
played a part in this. Eissler writes 'It is conceivable that through the
establishment of transference, through an approach which mobilizes the
archaic trust in the world and reawakens the primordial feeling of being
protected by a mother, the suffering of the dying can be reduced to a
minimum' (1955, p. 119). I would add, however, that equally the transference relationship would be the place wherein anxiety, grief, anger,
guilt, and other painful emotions can be experienced – once the 'archaic
trust' is established.

Given the widespread anxiety about facing death *alone* – alone externally as well as internally – an established relationship with a therapist
can provide a sense of inner 'holding', which mitigates the pain, fear,
and impending loss. This is something that has rarely been established,
owing to the unusual time commitment and flexibility required on the
part of the therapist. In situations where there are emotionally available
family or friends it is less necessary. I would argue that as family and
friends have, understandably, a greater emotional vested interest in the
survival of the patient, even when medical science appears to have little
further to offer, the therapist, although still struggling with his own
inner feelings of grief, anxiety, guilt, and anger, may be better able to
facilitate (and I do not mean *instigate*) a process of anticipatory mourning in the patient (Eissler, 1955, p. 181). Thus, as we often see, the

patient gradually detaches from his loved ones before death, as a way of easing the separation. A transference relationship to the therapist can then provide a substitute, or 'safe place' arena for relinquishing the ties.

I touched on the question of compromising my usual analytic technique at various points during writing the Diary of my work with Robert. Perhaps it is important to realize that the dying patient, whether child or adult, usually has no awareness of 'normal' therapeutic settings. The contact is beneficial if the patient feels understood and is thus helped to understand himself better.

I feel that my ability at times tacitly to accept Robert's impending death (even though part of me railed against it) was probably of considerable benefit to him. To sit with him, quietly, but thinking about him and his situation, seemed to give him the opportunity to 'be'. There is an irony in a situation which, by allowing the child to be dying, actually seems to validate him and in that sense allows him to be alive. The alternative would be to deny him the life he is still living, albeit a dying life, by attempting to force him backwards towards health, or by denying his sadness.

Winnicott (1972) writes: '. . . it is not unhealthy, but indeed a sign of health, that the child can use relationships in which there is maximal trust, and in such relationships at times disintegrate, depersonalize, and even for a moment abandon the almost fundamental urge to exist and to feel existent.' Although he is not necessarily writing about a child with a terminal illness here, his comments describe the way in which Robert and other dying children can use trusted relationships.

As the reader will have noted, I hardly spoke to Robert directly about death. This was, sometimes, the result of my own inhibitions; at times the parents' denial made it difficult to really pursue this; and, at other times, Robert and I seemed to communicate to each other non-verbally that he was dying. In fact, generally, he was very communicative in his nods and facial expressions.

I do have some regrets about the lack of communication between individual members of the team. This problem ties in with the other main difficulty: that a clear decision to switch to palliative care was not made. Therefore, Mr and Mrs Campbell did not have a final stage of relative acceptance (admittedly with a dying child it would be rare for there to be absolute acceptance) and thus Robert did not have the opportunity of sharing his *dying* with anyone other than myself and possibly Carol (the auxiliary nurse). Above all, he may well have suffered unnecessarily with various treatments and medical investigations right until he died.

I need to add that Peter (the paediatric social worker) was considerably over-worked during those 3 months owing to an unusually heavy and demanding work-load, partly as a result of a curtailment of social services resources. This led to less contact between him and the family, and between him and myself and the rest of the team, than he, or we, would have liked.

Each of us who is closely involved with a dying child has to negotiate our own individual sense of guilt and failure. This arises not only out of understandable regret at not having somehow increased one's efforts to save and repair the child, but also out of feelings that we have played a part in bringing about this death. For we have underlying primitive phantasies: when frustrated we tend to hate that which frustrates, leading to aggressive impulses to destroy the 'breast' or mother (Klein, 1937). These basic conflicts unconsciously colour the emotional life of adults: not only may we feel at times that our anger may have caused this death (see the Freud quotation in Chapter 2, 'children . . . unashamedly threaten one another with the possibility of dying . . .') but past impulses of hatred towards someone we love contribute to our now feeling guilty when faced with death.

In a case with which I have been involved, the parents of a 5-year-old girl, Polly, became emotionally unavailable to her owing to their uncertainty about her survival. Polly became increasingly rejecting of them when they did appear. The hospital staff attempted to encourage them to participate more in the everyday care of Polly, but did not have much success.

However, Polly was then seen twice weekly by a child psychotherapist, to whom she developed a very strong positive transference. Although Polly showed considerable distress at the gaps between the therapy sessions, the therapist was able to use this positively by helping her to get in touch with her anger at her parents' frequent unavailability. The parents were able only up to a point to use the support of a social worker, and they found it difficult to remain present as much as possible and to bear, and survive, Polly's onslaughts. They were helped, separately, to express some anxiety and grief.

Until her death 5 months after her BMT, Polly continued to use the therapist as a reliable and resilient figure, finally mourning her too by becoming very detached from her and from everyone else in the last week of her life. She seemed to accept and appreciate the therapist's calm presence as sufficient.

The psychotherapist's work generally goes against the grain of this process of detachment. Therefore, the distancing mechanisms can be talked about with the patient: 'How painful it feels to get attached at such a time.' This ability to *stay* with the detached patient (contradictory though that sounds) and survive the apparent rejection is important.

Perhaps in the light of having looked at the death of a *child* any discussion about an acceptance or death, or a working towards death, seems inappropriate. Perhaps some readers feel that they (or I, if it were my child) would rail against death until and beyond the last breath, and possibly for ever. I feel that this *protest* does and must exist, but that alongside, or interwoven with this, the therapist, in the special position of being both involved yet not totally personally immersed, can at times swim with the patient who is being carried along by the tide of the illness.

Part Three
Survival or death

Chapter Ten
Prolonging dying?

... the doctor should obtain the patient's freely given consent after the patient has been given a full explanation. In case of legal incapacity consent should also be procured from the legal guardian ...

The doctor can combine clinical research with professional care, the objective being the acquisition of new medical knowledge, only to the extent that clinical research is justified by its therapeutic value for the patient.

> Wolstenholme and O'Connor, *Declaration of Helsinki Code of Ethics* (1964) of the World Medical Association

... it [medicine] is to do away with the sufferings of the sick, to lessen the violence of the disease, and *to refuse to treat those who are over-ministered by their diseases, realising that in some cases medicine is powerless.* (my italics)

> Hippocrates *The Art c.*330 BC.

In considering the complex and controversial issue of sustaining the life of a dying child, we need to approach the dilemma from the points of view of all those involved: the patient; the patient's family; the medical team, which includes doctors, nurses, students; as well as the paramedicals, such as social workers, teachers, psychotherapists, clergy, and others. It is interesting that the core issues have not changed much since Hippocrates, nearly 2-and-a-half thousand years ago.

First, in defining 'terminally ill', we mean a state of disease that is characterized by irreversible and progressive deterioration. Inevitably, therefore, there are varying degrees of impairment of function, and the patient's survival is severely time-limited. With modern technological developments and new therapies, life for the terminally ill can be prolonged. However, looked at from a slightly different angle, *dying then becomes prolonged*. Therefore, there is an increasing need to concern ourselves with the moral and ethical implications of prolonging dying: the quality of the remaining life and dignity of the patient needs to be considered.

Ethical committees of professional and lay people are attached to all National Health Service teaching hospitals in Britain. They are actively debating these issues, often in a thoughtful and caring way. Their main role is to consider all proposals for clinical research, thus providing peer-group supervision. Clinicians submit their protocols, and although the committee's approval is deemed important, there is no legal obligation to respect it. The basic guidelines are the Nuremberg Code (1947), which, prompted by Nazi medical crimes, lays down 10 standards to which physicians must conform when carrying out experiments on human subjects (see Appendix 2); the Declaration of Geneva (1948), which is a modified form of the Hippocratic Oath; as well as the Code of Ethics of the World Medical Association Declaration of Helsinki (Wolstenholme and O'Connor, 1964). There are also guidelines published by the Royal College of Medicine.

Some of the research proposals include plans for trials of new therapies or drugs for children that may affect the life (and death) of the terminally ill. I gathered from Reverend Peter Speck (Trust Chaplaincy Team leader, Southampton University Hospitals NHS Trust, previously Royal Free Hospital Chaplain) that at the Royal Free Hospital, in respect of every protocol, the clinician responsible writes a one-page synopsis in lay terminology, which is attached to the protocol, and which comes before the Ethical Practices Committee. This synopsis is supposed to carry details not only of potential therapeutic benefit, but also of possible side-effects and risks.

The British Medical Association's ruling states that from the age of 16 years a child's informed consent must be sought. However, some physicians and some ethical committees respect the involvement in the decision-making process of some 14- and 15-year-olds. In Speck's experience, below those ages it seems that *parents'* decisions are sought. The BMA, in its attempt to clarify this grey area, adds the proviso that if the consent of under 16-year-olds is sought, you have to demonstrate that the child is capable of this decision. This seems to lead to a further grey area: how do you prove this kind of capability? I explore this further under 'Children's consent' (see pp. 177–9).

In parallel with the work of ethical committees, individual consultants have to make clinical decisions about, for example, the shift from cure to palliative care. These are decisions that do not depend on committees. It is here that there is an attempt to teach medical students through the involvement of clinicians in the teaching programme, thus hopefully opening up a dialogue on issues such as when to pursue *cure*. Speck says (personal communication) that students' questions during 'ethics seminars' within a clinical attachment can be useful as part of a self-questioning process for doctors. Inevitably, the majority on ethical committees are doctors, and they are deeply committed by their training and vocation to *save* people's lives and primarily to *cure* illness. This may be an obstacle to the objectivity required, and the same reservation applies to the consultants who, against the background of ethical committees, are making major decisions.

However, Judith Chessells, Professor of Haematology and Oncology (Great Ormond Street Hospital for Sick Children), herself a chairman of a joint ethical committee, says (personal communication) that her unit does not find problems in switching its emphasis from cure to care; nor, in her experience, do patients always opt for treatment. She explains, 'In our institution, when treatment has failed, there is a very open discussion with the parents involving various members of the caring team, and we try to reach a communal decision about what is the right thing.'

In discussing these concerns there seem to be two separate problem areas: one of economic moral questions (considerations of financial cost) and the other of non-economic moral questions (the quality of life and human dignity). The former inevitably becomes a political issue, with governments primarily deciding upon the allocation of resources. The moral approach to this is that the decision as to who should be kept alive and who should die should not depend on governments, for it runs the risk of creating situations of totalitarianism. Therefore, these decisions should be part of non-political health councils, ethical committees, and medical research councils.

Looking, then, at the non-economic issues, there are those who believe that there are situations where death can be hastened – not just allowed to run its course. Those who believe this are not denying the value of medical intervention to prolong life where it is meaningful (and this needs very careful definition) but are saying that there are times when the vitality, purpose, and meaning of life have broken down, cannot be repaired, and life becomes non-life. They are not in favour of killing, but, as Phillip Miller (1987) writes, on occasion willing 'to take an active role in the process of death'. He continues that they must do this 'to stop suffering . . . to protect autonomy, and to replace technology by real people in dying situations'. He writes that, if he were breathing his last breath, he would prefer to be 'touched by a hand than violated by a tube'. However, in attempting to define 'suffering', and the issue of the dignity of the patient, we are up against the differing perceptions of the patient, the observer, the family, and the professionals. (These issues reflect the similar debate between those who wish to 'unmedicalize' birth and allow it to be more natural, and those who favour technological innovations.)

The conflicting view of, on the one hand, those doctors who believe in a compassionate easing of dying or, at least, in an allowing of dying, and, on the other hand, those who believe in a sustaining of life, are expressed in these two quotations (Crispell and Gomez, 1987):

> It should be stressed that treatment that prolongs pain and suffering by patients and relatives and only prolongs the physiologic process of dying benefits no one, least of all the patient.

While another doctor says:

> Perhaps philosophers and theologians can resolve these perplexing problems, but the medical profession must follow a one-track course favouring life with a humane and sensible therapeutic approach.

I do not for a moment propose that there is the intention on the part of those who wish to prolong life at all costs to undermine the patient's dignity or autonomy. I believe that they are acting to the best of their knowledge to do all that they can for the patient. And indeed, often the patient's dignity and autonomy are enhanced by being granted more time or fewer symptoms, both frequently gained by second-line or third-line chemotherapy. *However, a distinction needs to be drawn between that which is therapeutic and that which becomes research*. By 'research' I mean trying some new method or practice in order to gain knowledge and in the long run hopefully benefit other future patients. This is an important issue, which needs to be openly debated between the parents of a child, different members of the professional team, and possibly the child himself, depending on his age, understanding of the situation, and physical and emotional state. The issue of whether or not a child is capable of giving informed consent is crucial to this debate.

As stated previously, all this is complicated when considering the ethical issues around sustaining the life of a terminally ill *child*. In this area we are not considering someone whose life has run its course. We are up against a tragic curtailment of life and many other issues mentioned in Chapter 1. This makes any moral or ethical debate more fraught, and makes the polarized views expressed above perhaps even more opposed.

Sam Ahmedzai (1993), a doctor and medical director of a hospice, clarifies this debate by understanding the changing role of the doctor in the process:

> . . . in this society . . . at present only doctors are empowered to make important decisions about curability or need for palliation. This may be appropriate soon after diagnosis when complex and rapid choices need to be weighed up – and offered to the patient for final consent. When the stage of illness enters the palliative or

hospice care domain, it would be quite unacceptable for the decision making to be seen as largely or entirely a medical matter . . .
Towards the end of life, the patient and family need to have
increasing power of autonomy, guided by the professionals.

When considering the issue of when the medical team switches from
treatment to palliative care, the paediatric sister quoted earlier, Dorothy
Jordan, made the point that this decision is more readily and easily
reached in a specialist children's hospital than in a paediatric ward of a
general hospital. This is because the doctors in a general hospital are not
necessarily *paediatricians*, and therefore find it more difficult to
embrace the child's emotional state. She describes the situation in a
general teaching hospital:

> It's because the doctors are so dynamic. You can understand,
> going to the bone marrow transplant meetings, listening to those
> doctors, and their fight to get a cure for leukaemia – you can only
> feel admiration for them. But if the white-cell picture looks good
> – it doesn't matter what the child looks like – they think they're
> better, and you know, it takes a while for them to understand, to
> begin to understand what the child *really* feels like.

I talked to her about the difficult position she, and other nurses, are in,
as somebody who is closely involved with the child on a daily, indeed
hourly, basis: who is in touch with the child's distress, and who then is
told to administer a drug that will actually make the child feel worse. I
asked her how that left her feeling?

> Obviously you do feel frustrated, but also don't forget that when
> the doctors are saying there's this new drug to try, they've got the
> consent of the parents, and the parents are desperate. One mum
> said to me she'd go to the top of this hospital and jump off the
> roof if that would make her child better from leukaemia. So, if
> we're saying, which we have done, that we've got this new drug,
> it's still on trial, but we're willing to try it, of course the parents
> want to try that . . .

I questioned this statement about parents always opting for treatment.
She replied that in her experience in this particular hospital, over the
past 15 years only two parents have taken their children home:

> And that was very early on, probably about 1980, when of course
> the treatment wasn't as good as it is today. There was a 2-year-old
> with myeloid leukaemia, and the parents took him home without
> treatment. And, sometimes, we are in a situation where we have
> no treatment to offer the children, and the parents then take
> them home.

I asked Dr Anne Kilby, a consultant paediatric oncologist, how much patients and their parents are told when a drug is experimental – say, when it's a last attempt?

She replied:

> When we use drugs which are experimental, or haven't been tried very much before, the parents would always be aware and usually have requested this in the first place. For example, often they have read the newspapers and then suggested this or that, and this can drive the doctors forward. If you can't provide this they will then often take their child to the States or some other centre, to see if they can get it there. So if one is using rather experimental drugs or treatment, then I would always explain to parents first. Indeed, even when we are using palliative treatment, when we know we are very unlikely to cure a patient, but are still continuing to treat, I make it very clear to the parents, and also to older children. I explain that if the treatment becomes worse than the cure, then there is no point in pressing on with it. In other words, in second-line or third-line treatment, if we are not achieving good quality of life, then we need to rethink what we are doing.

Many of the issues around current guidelines for research on children in Britain, and some of the moral dilemmas arising, are delineated in the detailed report of the Institute of Medical Ethics working group, on the ethics of clinical research investigations on children (Nicholson, 1986). Important distinctions between therapeutic and non-therapeutic research are explored, as well as between invasive and non-invasive treatments. They conclude that '. . . the distinction has to be that *therapeutic research* is research consisting in an activity which has also a therapeutic intention, as well as a research intention, towards the subjects of the research, and *non-therapeutic research* is research activity which has not also a therapeutic intention' (p. 33). When considering the problems of using 'controls' for the purpose of comparison, their committee examined the extent to which a control group should be subjected to non-therapeutic research in order to benefit at least some of the children in the project.

They quote the example of the treatment of acute lymphoblastic leukaemia, or ALL, where the control children may receive what is considered to be the best treatment regime, while the subject children receive a new regime which *might* be an improvement. As the cure rate for ALL is greater than 50 per cent (and is in fact now over 70 per cent), one could conclude that both groups are receiving therapeutic benefit. This trial could be considered to be therapeutic research. However, 20–25 years ago, when the cure rate for ALL was less than 10 per cent, a trial of treatment regimes often led to death before the trial was finished.

Therefore, those children in the trial did not benefit, but future children with ALL may have benefited. It is this type of issue which is still relevant to children with other cancers today, especially those with poorer prognoses.

Some research projects question established treatment, and can lead to a re-evaluation and a change. For example, children with ALL were routinely given 3-monthly bone marrow examinations while in remission in order to detect relapses. A research programme (by Watson *et al.*, 1981) established that the incidence of unexpected relapse was only 0.4 per cent. Therefore, as this is a traumatic procedure, it was concluded that it was unnecessary, and it was abandoned.

Children's consent

Whether or not children can or should give meaningful, informed consent to treatments which are proposed is another issue debated by the Institute of Medical Ethics. Basing their research on studies by Piaget (1932), Kohlberg (1976), Weithorn and Campbell (1982), and others, they conclude:

> Before the age of 7 years (by which is meant the developmental age of an average 7-year-old, rather than a precise chronological age that would apply to all children equally) attempts to obtain a child's assent (by which is meant the permission given by the child that does not, however, have the legal force of consent) are likely to be meaningless, and it is more important simply to tell the child as much as possible, using his level of language, what is going to be done. From the age of 7 upwards, it becomes important that an investigator should try to obtain the assent of a child subject. The nearer the child is to 14 years old, the more important does his assent to a research procedure become.

> (Nicholson, 1986, pp. 150–1)

They add, however, that, as the young person between 7 and 14 years will still have an immature moral judgement, in some instances refusal of assent would have to be overridden. They conclude that over the age of 14 years young people are as competent as adults to decide, and that therefore their views should carry as much weight as those of their parents. A refusal to give consent, therefore, should be binding – whether to therapeutic or non-therapeutic research procedures.

Many of the salient issues around non-disclosure of a fatal prognosis are well explored from a moral, ethical and philosophical angle by Leikin (1981). He reminds us (p.41) that of course a very sick child is dependent on his parents. Therefore the parents need to be in agreement with the disclosure. He goes on to argue that the parents' 'right' to be responsible for their child is complicated by the fact that health-care professionals also have a responsibility and expertise in the care of sick children. Moreover, the two parties can be at odds with each other. Given these and other elements which make up the truth-telling dilemma, the only true indicator of what to tell the child is the child himself, and the only way that this can be discerned is through the sensitivity of the professionals and the parents. Alderson (1990, 1993) has researched issues around children's consent, parents' consent and legal issues very thoroughly.

I asked Dorothy Jordan to what extent she thought that the children themselves should be brought into the decision-making process about continued treatment, say, after relapse when there may be little chance of a cure?

> It depends of course on the age of the child. You can say to the 4-and-a-half-year-olds and the 5-year-olds, 'We're going to do this, we're going to do that' and they can say 'Yes, that's all right'. Then when you come to it, they change their minds. I don't know how much we should be saying to them, 'You're going to die if you don't have this treatment'. But I think maybe the 12-, 13-, and 14-year-olds should be consulted. But then you've always got this horrible feeling that they are going to say 'Yes' but when they have all that chemotherapy that makes them so ill, their hair falls out, and so on, then they might change their minds. It's a terrible dilemma.

Of course the parents also have to give their consent. She emphasized the importance of this, and how the haematology consultant is adamant about this, 'because we've had situations where a child has had a bone-marrow transplant and it's gone wrong, and the parents then say it's our fault. So the consultant makes it quite clear to parents that their *consent* is sought.' (It is interesting that here the reason for seeking parents' consent seems to be primarily legal rather than psychological or ethical – although the two are linked.) She continued:

> However, although parents are told what the chances are, what they *hear* and what they *retain* are often very different things. If you say to them we are offering you 75 per cent for a lymphoblastic leukaemia, 75 per cent chance of becoming disease-free, but 25 per cent die because of the bone-marrow transplant – they don't hear that. They don't hear that, about the 25 per cent who die. Maybe it's just human nature; maybe you don't want to listen, do you?

In considering what we mean by 'informed consent', therefore, we find it difficult to arrive at a proper evaluation when, understandably, parents' decisions and consent are so coloured by their emotional state.

It seems that one way in which parents manage to continue to opt for treatment, even when this is extremely unpleasant if not horrendous, is by distancing themselves from their own child and from what is happening to him. Sister Jordan confirms this: 'Looking back to all these deaths, and all these children, I think nearly all the parents say, *that's not my child.*' This denial seems especially understandable in the light of the external, visible signs of the illness, or the reaction to the drugs, altering the child's appearance dramatically, as well as a defensive way in which the parents cut off from their utterly painful feelings if they were to stay in touch until the end. Inevitably, however, there are serious emotional dangers for the child in this situation, of feeling abandoned and not heard. I wonder if the withdrawn state quite frequently observed in children who are terminally ill is a defensive response to their parents' emotional withdrawal.

Yudkin (1967), speaking from the point of view of a doctor, pleads for the dying child to be allowed to die peacefully:

> I am not, of course, referring to an acute crisis in illnesses which can perhaps be cured but, when the end is inevitable, although we feel the death of a child to be out of time, must we rush around with tubes, injections, masks and respirators? Someone said recently that no one nowadays is allowed to die without being cured. Perhaps we do it only for the parents' sake; but perhaps we ourselves cannot accept our limitations.
>
> (Yudkin, 1967, p. 40)

Chapter Eleven
Those who survive

In order to arrive at what you do not know
You must go by a way which is the way of
ignorance . . .
And what you do not know is the only thing
you know . . .

T.S. Eliot, Four Quartets

As increasing numbers of children survive treatment for life-threatening diseases, we need to consider the physical, psychological, and social effects on these children and on their families – who often live under the shadow of the possible return of the illness. This has been well described by Koocher and O'Malley (1981) as the 'Damocles syndrome', where children and their families do not know whether to mourn the loss of life or risk hoping for sustained remission or cure. It is this difficulty in balancing a fear of death with hopefulness that makes it particularly problematic for parents to manage normal parenting, including limit-setting and consistency. Some parents feel that if they curb their child's difficult behaviour they are squashing the child's liveliness and spirited will to live.

Whilst previously the prognosis after relapse was generally poor but clearly defined, now patients and their families are having to struggle with more uncertainty about the effects of new treatments and the eventual outcome. However, for those who survive 3 years, nowadays the prospects are good. Studies show that for most of the childhood tumours, over 80 per cent of those surviving 3 years are alive 10 years later (Hawkins, 1989).

In the light of the marked improvement in prognosis for childhood cancer over the past 30 years, some recent literature does show a considerable shift of emphasis from a position of preparing for death, to one of preparing for living with a life-threatening illness. As this is a relatively new field, a great deal of research into the psychosocial needs of children with cancer still needs to be carried out. Spinetta (1977) describes a series of coping tasks (originally described by Lazarus, 1976), which are: tolerating or relieving distress associated with the illness; maintaining a sense of personal worth; maintaining positive personal relationships with parents, peers, and care-givers; meeting the specific requirements of particularly stressful situations; utilizing the resources available.

However, for many surviving children the quality of life inevitably suffers in a major way. The adverse effects seem to remain for a long time in some instances: 25 per cent of unmarried adult survivors of childhood cancer thought that their illness experience was a hindrance to marriage (Holmes and Holmes, 1975). No doubt, here the long-term effects of infertility and in some cases mutilating surgery would be significant factors.

Physical side-effects of bone-marrow transplantation

Bone-marrow transplantation (BMT) is a life-saving procedure for an increasing number of children and young adults. As greater numbers of patients undergo this procedure, and are cured of their underlying disorder, increased attention must be paid to the side-effects, some of which do not appear for several years. In this section I shall briefly describe some physical side-effects to be borne in mind, as a background to the psychological effects of BMT.

Immediate or short-term implications

Among the relatively minor restrictions upon remission and discharge from hospital is a prohibition upon going into crowded public places. The depression of a child's immune system presents a constant concern because of the greatly increased susceptibility to all kinds of infections (Koocher and Sallan, 1978). Hygiene between members of the family would have to be strictly observed. Over-exposure to direct sunlight would have to be avoided. Clearly, exposure to common childhood illnesses would have to be assiduously avoided. Special oral hygiene procedures are often recommended, because as a result of total-body irradiation (TBI) the salivary glands have changed and are no longer as effective at washing bacteria from the mouth. Persistent dryness of the mouth is therefore a likely symptom, as well as an increased tendency to develop dental caries and mouth ulcers. Contact with pets may not be allowed for a while.

The psychological implications of having to be wary of, and vulnerable to, infection, may lead to a feeling that the world is a very hostile and attacking place. In other words, this could well accentuate underlying infantile phantasies of persecution. (See earlier chapters mentioning

Anna Freud's and Melanie Klein's theories of the development of infants.)

Long-term side-effects

With the improvement in the treatment of childhood cancers over the past 30 years has come an increasing number of long-term survivors at risk of a range of side-effects. These include delayed growth and physical development (or, possibly, in younger children, a delay in overall growth) due to multiple factors such as chronic graft-versus-host disease, pulmonary dysfunction, general ill health, steroid therapy, endocrine deficiencies, and the effect of radiotherapy or TBI on skeletal growth (Bender-Götze, 1991). TBI almost always affects growth (Sanders et al., 1986).

After chemotherapy and TBI, nearly all girls who undergo BMT before or during puberty show primary ovarian failure, lack of menstruation and lack of secondary sexual characteristics. Hormone therapy, however, can often remedy this. Boys undergoing the same treatment at the same stage of life appear to develop normal secondary sexual characteristics, but sometimes with delayed puberty and usually with reduced sperm count. Sperm banking therefore should be considered before TBI – but that can be an upsetting, demoralizing experience if the boy is not able to produce viable samples (Bender-Götze, 1991). However, fertility would depend on many variables, including the type of malignancy, the age at time of treatment, duration and combination of chemotherapy drugs, and the site and strength of radiation. Therefore it is difficult to predict definitively.

Intellectual functioning seems to suffer from the disease and treatment, although here the research (Cousens et al., 1988) on IQ decrement is inconclusive as to the part played by cranial irradiation and that played by the emotional impact of the disease and other treatments administered. However, it appears that younger children suffer more of a deficit than older children, perhaps because their brains are more vulnerable (Stehbens et al., 1983) or because their intellectual growth is arrested at a younger age and therefore they have longer to fall behind their non-affected peers who continue to develop (Twaddle et al., 1983). I would add that the emotional trauma of facing a life-threatening illness, the irradiation treatment and chemotherapy – as described earlier – must play a considerable part in arresting the child's cognitive growth. This can be assessed through the developmental level of children's drawings, which can become 'frozen' at the age of onset of traumatic experience or traumatic medical treatment (Moore, 1990).

Other problems may include dramatic weight gain or loss, mouth ulcers, muscle spasms, skin rashes, skin discolorations, scars, and, depending on the type of cancer, organ losses and amputations

(Koocher and Sallan, 1978). Psychological preparation is of course help-ful for all these, but ongoing problems in adapting to physical changes and treatment arise.

Continued loss of hair (including eyebrows and eyelashes) is a side-effect for those children on maintenance chemotherapy. Many children report being teased by other children at school, and being called 'Baldie' or 'Skinhead' (as shown in *I'd Rather Stay at Home*, 1986, a film by the Department of Teaching Media at Southampton University). A study (Charlton *et al.*, 1986) shows that a pupil's hair loss is a problem to teachers as well as to pupils. Not surprisingly, it seems that the pupils who make the best adjustment to a full return to school once treatment is finished are those who maintained contact with friends during the treatment period. One mother said that while the effects of chemother-apy do disappear, the baldness remains for a length of time as a contin-ual reminder of the disease, and makes it very difficult for that child to be treated normally. Eventually the hair does grow back, but sometimes changes in its quality or colour.

The development of teeth can be disturbed. Cataracts, which may be treatable, frequently form on the eyes; 50 per cent have to be repaired surgically. Late neurological damage after BMT in children may result from viral infections, and from certain chemotherapy drugs (Bender-Götze, 1991). Late pulmonary complications contribute to morbidity after BMT in children, and obstructive lung disorders may develop up to 3 years after BMT. Cardiac, renal, and liver functions may also be impaired.

> These (physiological) sequelae are of major significance for chil-dren who should, therefore, have life-long follow-up. Serial assessment of growth and development, endocrine function, respiratory and cardiac function, renal and liver toxicity, ophthal-mologic and neurological examination is essential.

Last, but not least, is the increased risk of secondary cancer, thought to be due to radiation therapy, chemotherapy, and genetic cancer syndromes.

The foregoing complications, including the necessity of repeated hospital check-ups and tests, convey the emotional burden of living with these added difficulties, which would make it hard for any child to feel 'normal'.

Psychological effects of bone-marrow transplantation

Although there are inevitably major psychological effects of BMT, there appears to be a lack of systematic studies on those effects. A pilot study has been undertaken by Pot-Mees and Zeitlin (1987) in London, as a

preliminary to a fuller 3-year study on the psychosocial effects of BMT.
The follow-up has not been traced by the author. However, the pilot
study, which I summarize below, contains some interesting findings.

(Although many of the following findings are predictable, it may be of
interest to link them with the account of Robert's experiences in Part
Two. If so many psychological side-effects are widespread, perhaps they
need to be addressed as part of the overall treatment plan.)

The researchers found that during the pre-admission stage the entire
family was affected from the moment a BMT was proposed. Parents were
'severely distressed' and the majority were depressed. Most experienced
doubt – as part of their difficulty in comprehending the medical details
and the possible side-effects – about this course of treatment throughout
the pre-admission stage. Waiting for the transplant added to their
distress. Among the patient's siblings, blood typing to choose the donor
caused considerable distress; non-donors experienced feelings of relief
as well as rejection; while donors felt pride at having been selected, but
anxiety about the procedures they would have to undergo.

During the transplant stage, not surprisingly, Pot-Mees and Zeitlin
found that the patient's admission to hospital for BMT caused a
complete change in the lifestyle of the whole family. The patients primarily experienced a variety of restrictions: being confined in isolation cubi-
cles, restricted diets and activities, and having little privacy. With the
treatment, the patient's physical appearance changed (loss of hair), as
did their physical and emotional conditions. Side-effects, medical problems, such as graft-versus-host disease (see p. 101), and duration and
intensity of treatment, also affected their emotions.

Generally, the under-5-year-olds tended to become withdrawn and to
regress. Some stopped eating and drinking on their own, lost bladder
and bowel control, lost speech and other skills.

The 5–16-year-olds felt more that living in isolation with almost
constant medical intervention was an intrusion into their privacy and an
attack on their wish to have some control and independence. This often
led to frustration, anger, and clashes with parents and staff over issues of
medication and eating. Apparently, the anger of some children was
directed inward, leading to withdrawal and depression.

Boredom was inevitable. The isolation and side-effects of treatment
led to anxieties in all the children. Most children became over-depen-
dent on their parents, becoming much more anxious if the parents left
the room.

This research then states that 'the patients who deteriorated after the
BMT and finally died usually showed progressive regression and withdrawal. Because of the nature of the problems caused by graft-versus-
host disease, infections, or both, some children had extremely traumatic
medical and psychological experiences before they died, which created
severe guilt feelings in their parents' (p. 79).

Among the effects of the experience on the parents where couples were separated during treatment, the marital relationship was stressed. Not surprisingly, some families experienced increased financial problems. For those parents who stayed in the hospital, most became extremely anxious and distressed at times, and most complained of 'claustrophobic feelings' as well as other psychological complaints.

Many of the siblings developed new behaviour problems, but the distribution of this was, understandably, far greater in the group of donors, as opposed to non-donors.

This pilot-study indicates that BMT temporarily alters the lifestyles and roles of all members of the family, and that further research is needed to ascertain the long-term effects. They recommend that the entire family be assessed – that is, nuclear family plus possibly grand-parents – and monitored in order to evaluate the degree to which the patient's emotional disturbance is reflected in the rest of the family.

These preliminary findings are consistent with other research which states that BMT produces severe psychological disturbance, such as Kamphuis (1979), and Patenaude *et al*. (1979). The latter conclude similarly that BMT 'strains the emotional balance in even previously well-functioning families' and stress the importance of psychological services as part of the team provision.

Gordon (1975), in examining specifically the psychological aspects of isolator therapy in acute leukaemia, suggests that psychological difficulties relate primarily to the stress of adjustment to the diagnosis, but that living in isolation can accentuate the disturbance. Although 'isolator therapy' is more extreme than Robert's isolation situation, the findings would still be relevant. Three decades ago, however, Anna Freud (1965) recognized the psychological meanings for children of isolation: '. . . isolation because of infection gives substance to ever-present fears of being rejected and of being unworthy'.

Atkins and Patenaude (1987) emphasize that as BMT nowadays often necessitates a move to a regional or other distant hospital, this relocation adds to the stress implicit in the transplant. Therefore, they recommend open and frequent communication between medical, psychological, and social services, before, during, and after the transplant period, as well as clear communication with the parents and the mental health professionals to clarify the child's understanding of the complicated procedures and events. If there is not a linking network, differences in technique and approach between what are often three different hospitals leads to mistrust. Finally, they summarize: 'It is important that care-givers from all disciplines and from each institution serve as classifiers and distillers of the transplant experience and as links from one caring hospital staff to another until the patient and family can resume that protective role for themselves' (p. 252).

The traumatic medical and psychological experiences quoted were certainly part of Robert's experience (see Part Two), as well as his mother's subsequent feelings of guilt, as she later conveyed to me. Her guilt covered many areas, including much questioning of what she felt was her less than perfect response to him during illness. She reproached herself for leaving him at all during the final months, saying (unrealistic though this was) that if she had known about the ensuing loss she would have been by his bedside 24 hours a day.

There seemed inadequate communication, too, on the psychosocial side, between their cottage hospital in the North of Scotland, a hospital in the Lowlands where Robert had been for a while, and the hospital in the North of England where he had his transplant. Although some attempt at communication was made between the various social work departments, this was not carried out very effectively. The medical team, of course, had full and detailed communication over the details of his physical condition pre-transplant, and finally a full medical report was sent to the hospitals who knew him, after his death.

Therefore, it seems that as that side of the process indisputably requires full information, not only from a practical point of view but also as a way of learning about the processes and improving research, so the psychological effects need a more thorough monitoring and sharing. The frequent lack of this aspect seems to result from the view that the psychosocial side is not 'a matter of life and death' in the way that the sharing of other information indubitably is. Despite shortages in staffing and funding on the psychosocial side, an enormous effort still needs to be made to keep the network alive. The family and the patient are the centre of this network, and they require sensitive feed-back and contact with all parts of the network at all times.

Psychosocial functioning of children surviving cancer

Before exploring the psychosocial effects specific to cancer, it is important to remember the possible emotional consequences to a child simply of lengthy hospitalization. These have been well documented since Spitz (1945). The early studies by Robertson (e.g. 1952) exemplify the dramatic short-term effects. These prompted the Ministry of Health to recognize the emotional needs of these children in a special report (1959). Isabel Menzies Lyth's paper, *The Psychological Welfare of Children Making Long Stays in Hospital: An Experience in the Art of the Possible* (1982), drawing upon Robertson and Bowlby, sensitively surveys the attachment needs of children and babies in this context. Her suggestions would form a very useful starting-point for both professionals and parents who wish to provide children with the most appropriate care.

Studies by Douglas (1975) show that many brief admissions to hospital, as well as admissions of longer than a week for children under 6 years, were associated with a likelihood of increased emotional problems in later years. However, these findings relate to conditions which had not generally been affected by later, more enlightened approaches to parental visiting and provisions for parents to stay overnight. It is not surprising that a more recent study (Shannon *et al.*,1984) shows that hospital admissions for 6-year-olds do not necessarily lead to subsequent behaviour problems when a progressive paediatric approach is instituted.

However, in Britain, Action for Sick Children (or the National Association for the Welfare of Children in Hospital, as it used to be called) is still striving for these basic tenets of good paediatric practice, which have, after all, been recommended for nearly 40 years. In 1982, a NAWCH survey showed that only half the wards in Britain to which children were admitted had appropriate settings – that is, for example, facilities for parents to be accommodated at night. Their 1988 campaign was called 'Room for Parents': an attempt to focus public consciousness on the need for making room on the wards for parents to share the nursing, as well as room in everyone's hearts and minds for more than formal facilities for visiting ill children. In 1991, the Department of Health *Guidelines for the Welfare of Children and Young People in Hospital* (HMSO) states that:

> A cardinal principle of hospital services for children is complete ease of access to the child by his or her parents . . . This is not a luxury. It is now . . . accepted that the care and comfort of parents for a child is fundamental to the care and treatment of children in hospital.

Yet, in 1995, these cardinal principles are far from being observed throughout the country. The increasing cuts in the National Health Service have eroded efforts to improve facilities; increased poverty and social problems in Britain have led to more families finding the financial and emotional burden of a very ill child very hard to bear. In this present climate nurses and junior doctors often suffer from low morale, overwork, over-crowding on wards, and staff shortages. When they are then presented with families suffering hardship, their own unmet needs are aroused. As they are actually overstretched, they are less resourceful (literally and emotionally) in spending time with children and parents themselves, or facilitating and encouraging parents to stay with children. All these factors compound the actual stress of the illness.

Age seems relevant to the impact of distressing procedures: children under 7 years appear to be most susceptible to painful medical procedures (Jay *et al.*, 1983). Habituation usually takes place, but takes longer for younger children. However, it would be interesting to study whether overall becoming 'habituated' to something unpleasant really is a healthy response! Moreover, there is still the widespread belief (among some professionals and parents) that children should not cry or show distress. One piece of recent research (Manne *et al.*, 1992) shows that children's crying is not reduced by adults' explanations, and erroneously advocates that therefore children should be distracted. Of course, in allowing children to cry, the quality of the adults' responses to the crying would be important. Children would need to feel that their cries were heard and, hopefully, understood. That implies adults' abilities to bear both the child's distress and their own infantile feelings which are aroused by the situation.

Not surprisingly, many studies of the psychosocial functioning of children surviving childhood cancer show that they are at an increased risk of developing emotional problems: O'Malley *et al.* (1979) and Koocher and O'Malley (1981) found that the majority of these children develop at least mild psychiatric symptoms, such as depression, extreme mood changes, anxiety, and low self-esteem. However, in differentiating between the well-adjusted and maladjusted survivors, some of the positive variables appear to be a short course of treatment, no recurrence of the disease, a family which communicates openly and is supportive, an early diagnosis, and the onset of the disease at a young age (Koocher *et al.*, 1980). This better adjustment among young children seems to relate to the resilience of younger children (Rutter, 1980) as well as to the fact that the study included types of cancer predominantly found in early childhood that have a good prognosis if detected early. Therefore, although there certainly is an increased risk of children with cancer developing emotional problems, a foundation of good psychological health in the child and in the family would of course help to mitigate this.

Participation in school during treatment, where possible, sustains hope by providing normality, continuity, and a belief that they will carry on living. However, it appears that teachers need help from professionals (such as hospital teachers, psychologists, psychotherapists, or nurses, who are involved in the hospital treatment) in understanding the implications of the disease as well as their own fears which the illness arouses. Despite the improved cure rate, associations with death prevail. A recent study in the United States of America (Katz *et al.*,1992) recommends school reintegration intervention from the time of diagnosis. This involves supportive counselling, educational presentations, consistent liaison between the school and hospital, and follow-ups after the child has finished treatment. One possible positive outcome is that children who have had cancer were rated by their teachers as being more competent socially (Sanger *et al.*, 1991). However, this may be attributable to social competence acting as a protective factor against the stress of cancer, as has been suggested by Garmezy *et al* (1984) in their study of children facing stressful life-events. In other words, this ability to elicit social support could be adaptive, or it could be a defence – a pseudo-maturity – to mask underlying distress.

Not surprisingly one of the key factors in assessing psychological distress among cancer patients' parents is the amount of social support (Speechley and Noh, 1992). This determines the extent to which the strain associated with being a parent of a child surviving cancer induces adverse psychological consequences. Therefore, the provision of support after cessation of treatment seems important.

A 1991 (Hobart Davies *et al.*) study, which compares self-reports of parenting practices from parents of children with cancer with those of a matched control group, did not find the noticeable differences that professionals involved had predicted. This may be because the parents were generally observed at times of crisis or stress, and perhaps settled into a more normal pattern later. Interestingly, the only noticeable difficulties that parents of cancer children faced were disease-related anxieties. In other words, their anxieties had not percolated through to general problems in parenting.

Siblings of children with life-threatening illnesses show more disturbance than the actual patient in some studies (Cairns *et al.*, 1979; Spinetta, 1981). The obvious problem here is that the siblings can be easily overlooked while the ill child receives all the attention: both as the focus of anxiety as well as, possibly, being the one who is over-indulged. Lansdown and Goldman (1988) offer suggestions on the handling of siblings: in particular they firmly state that the siblings' tendency to feel guilty that they have caused the illness through hasty words and aggressive impulses needs to be acknowledged and addressed.

As stated in a survey of the literature on the psychosocial long-term sequelae of childhood cancer by Van Dongen-Melman and Sanders-Woudstra (1986), there appears to be an emphasis on the impact of loss, separation, and anticipatory mourning, while scant attention has been paid to the implications of *living* with a life-threatening illness. They suggest that 'a child who will die of cancer will also *live* with illness', while at the same time issues concerning loss, anticipatory mourning, loss of self-esteem, and loss of control over daily living need further research and understanding.

In describing children as 'survivors', we still cannot be sure at which point they are no longer more likely to have a recurrence or a related medical problem than the general population. As chemotherapy has only been used extensively relatively recently, there are as yet few studies on 'late deaths', which occur over a span of 20–25 years post-diagnosis (Hawkins *et al.*, 1990). An interesting finding, however, is that there appears to be a threefold increase in the number of deaths from accidents in survivors of tumours of the central nervous system than expected in the general population (Hawkins *et al.*, 1990). This could be due to intellectual or sensory impairment, as the authors suggest. Perhaps emotional disturbance is also a factor in patients being at risk by not taking care, or being unconsciously self-destructive.

Chapter Twelve
After the death of a child

Why should a dog, a horse, a rat, have life,
And thou no breath at all? Thou'lt come no more,
Never, never, never, never, never!

King Lear

Thus King Lear rails against the untimely death of his daughter, Cordelia. He seems momentarily in touch with the finality and reality of her death, and then, almost immediately, he dies too. This may be partly explained by his considerable age, but it serves to illustrate a parent's outrage, despair, and lack of purpose in living, upon the death of his or her own child.

Dora Black emphasizes the need for families to have support after a death. She states (personal communication), 'I like working with the whole family whenever I can, and I'm very keen to see them after a death – to be available. Of course that's very difficult if the family live far from the hospital.' She continues on a more personal level:

What I do with friends who have been bereaved is to drop them a card often, saying 'Thinking of you' – because you *do* think of people often and it's always appreciated. One of the problems that people have in our society is knowing quite what to say. There is still the situation that people report, of people crossing over to the other side of the road, to avoid the bereaved person.

Olivia Cox (1988), whose 2-year-old daughter died of leukaemia, writes of exactly the same experience:

Some would cross the street rather than face our pain and though I hold no blame for these people, there were times when such actions compounded my feelings of isolation to unbearable limits.

She continues to describe her struggle during the fatal illness, 'At some of these times there was even an effort on my part to deny the hurt rather than court further rejections.' She writes that she did not want answers, 'just the silent expression of empathy, and perhaps the comfort of a hug'.

Parents of deceased children report significantly more symptoms related to anxiety, depression, and somatization (Miles, 1985; Moore *et al.*, 1988) and these symptoms are more marked in mothers than in fathers (Rando, 1983). As many studies on grief work show, there is no 'normal' 12-month period for working through the loss, and frequently the process takes years.

In an interesting study of 49 families where a child had died of cancer (McClowry *et al.*, 1987), the authors discovered an 'empty space' phenomenon – a sense of emptiness. They found three different patterns of grieving: 'getting over it', 'filling the emptiness', and 'keeping the connection'. This last pattern seems in some families very linked to 'filling the emptiness'. But in other instances, it was a way of keeping a place for the child who had died, even though this was painful. Therefore, it seems a truthful and essential acknowledgement. Whether or not a family continued to experience an empty space was associated with their willingness or ability 'to get over it' or 'fill the emptiness'. Those who did neither continued to feel an 'empty space' for approximately 8 years. Those who 'filled the emptiness' still experienced an 'empty space' from time to time. However, their efforts to 'fill the emptiness' dominated their lives. On the other hand, those who aimed 'to get over it' viewed the death as a past event, which did not influence their current lives in a major way.

However, the limitations of this research are that there is no attention to the families' unconscious processes. For example, would their dreams contain images of the child who died? And, have they truly internalized valued aspects of the dead child, so that they can indeed move on with the loved lost person established within their inner world? It seems that the families who 'kept a connection' were probably closest to this. I am reminded of a boy who underwent an amputation for cancer, and said 'I get so fed up when teachers want me to be happy all the time. Of course there's sadness. There'll always be sadness.'

Sister Frances Dominica, whose hospice, Helen House, encourages bereaved families to remain in contact for as long as they need, says (personal communication):

> We find that, after the death of a child, the first 2 years are hell for the parents. People don't allow you anything like a long enough time to grieve. Many people think in terms of weeks, or 'After three months you surely ought to be back to normal'. Almost without exception we have found that our families fare worse in the second year than they do in the first. Into the third year the

majority do definitely show signs of having made some sort of adjustment. No way can you claim that they've got over it, *because they never do get over it*. Into the third year many of the families have found a different way of living, accepting the fact that their child has died, and that they've got to make some sort of life – facing the reality of that. But of course there are many individuals, and whole families, where that doesn't apply actually, and it's going to be much, much longer. Sometimes the marriage breaks down, or the surviving siblings show signs of disturbed behaviour long after the 2 years. You can *expect* it for 2 years, but after that you hope that they would have been able to adjust. There are always exceptions.

It's interesting – every year we keep a weekend when we do not accept routine bookings here: we keep the house empty if we can, and we invite all our bereaved families back. At least half of them come. It was quite touching to hear the parents of the very first child who died here, 12 years ago, say how much it means to them that somebody still recognizes that they are bereaved. A lot of people they spend time with now don't even know that she existed. It's important to them that there are some people who still remember.

The contact with the bereaved families is informal – we don't run groups. We have had, from time to time, a little self-help group that's met here for a series of sessions, but the catchment area is difficult, as relatively few of the families are sufficiently local – they're from all over the country. We have sometimes told families about 'Compassionate Friends', and some have found that a helpful contact. Fathers in particular find groups difficult – they don't talk so readily as the mothers may. Contact with another family further on in their bereavement can be a great comfort. Parents have also found that being able to read about the experience of other people helps, because it offers a little ray of hope: you have evidence that other people have been through, or are going through, the same kind of hell, and that you're not mad or sick. So often bereaved families say that one way or another they really feel they have been pushed outside of the circle of ordinary human fellowship.

I asked how much this arose out of their own feelings of displacement and collapse, and how much was as a result of society's stigma? Sister Frances replied:

I think to a large extent society is to blame. It is painful how often people avoid meeting, avoid confrontation – you know, the example of a mother going to meet her children from school and the other parents scatter as she approaches. People will talk about anything except the one thing you feel like talking about, which is your child and the loss you are experiencing. And the reluctance to comment on photographs of the child. Again it's dangerous to generalize, but many parents actually do want to talk about their child, or relive memories even if it does become very emotional. It is because of this tremendous need that they often find that other bereaved parents are the most useful group.

In discussing attitudes to death, Sister Frances commented:

> I think that funeral directors often have got an awful lot to answer for, and yet they are presumably doing what they feel the public is demanding of them. We've had parents in very real distress, because, without being consulted, the undertakers have sometimes embalmed a child, plastered the child in make-up, done all sorts of things to hide the truth. To me that's conniving with the generally held view that the more you pretend, the more you deceive, and the faster you get on with life and get the distress out of the way, the better.
>
> We had parents here quite recently – one child had died 10 months ago, the other died 2 weeks ago – and that's not unusual; we have quite a lot of families losing two or more children. We weren't really involved in the first funeral because we'd only just met the family, and it was all done at home, but when the second little girl died, it all spilt out that they had a horrendous idea of what had to happen the moment the child died: she had to be taken away, her orifices packed, and the cheeks filled out, and make-up applied, making her unrecognizable, and therefore they shouldn't see their child afterwards. We wondered, 'Whatever is this?!' This resulted from the experience they'd had last year, where the funeral directors had said that all these things had to be done to the child, and that, as she wouldn't look at all like her, they really recommended that nobody should see her afterwards. We tried to say that that just wasn't right, and it needn't be like that. They could stay here with her after she had died, as long as they wished. If they wanted to they could wash her and dress her in the clothes they would choose. They could do everything for her and she could then lie in our 'little room' until the day of the funeral. They could go in and out as often as they wished – and the relief! You know, they've talked about it since: the contrast, how bitter they are that it happened so badly the first time. But funeral directors, presumably, are only doing what they feel the public is asking of them.

I discussed with Sister Frances how, as we often find, loss can rekindle earlier losses, and thus the impact of earlier losses is reworked, and I wondered how this continuous process affected those so frequently exposed to death at Helen House? Sister Frances:

We do experience this here, because you've no sooner started to grieve for one child then another child that you love dies – so much unfinished mourning. I find sometimes at the funeral of, for example, an old person with whom I may not have been very emotionally involved, I suddenly experience an enormous well of emotion, out of all proportion to the grief I am actually feeling for this individual, and it's just the unresolved grief from previous bereavements.

I wonder sometimes about Third World countries, where death is so much more commonplace, with children dying like flies of gastro-enteritis or measles or malnutrition, and how often, particularly in Islamic society, the phrase you hear is 'It is God's will'. There you are allowed a limited period of grief – 40 days and then no more. I wonder whether when the death of children is so much more commonplace, the bereavement doesn't go as deep, or whether the limited time-period initiates and in a way brings about a more speedy process, because it is recognized and accepted. And what about their expectations? I mean they are almost bound to expect that some of their children will not survive childhood, aren't they? And does that make it easier? I do not know.

We discussed those families whose grief does not really seem to be resolving itself after 2 or 3 years, and where they return to Helen House in a distraught state. Sister Frances:

Sometimes, if it really isn't working out, they will be referred for professional help. I don't scorn professional help at all, but I think we refer people too readily in the very early stages for professional counselling or therapy. However, one example of where it was very good was where the mother actually started going to therapy a year before her child died, so that she could anticipate the grieving, and then carried on for a year afterwards. That was a marvellous example of good use of therapy.

But I think we too readily turn to experts, because we live in a society which feels we need experts for everything, and where the rest of us easily feel deskilled. There's a failure to recognize that 90 per cent of what a bereaved person needs is a fellow human to be alongside, not with lots of good advice, not using professional skills, but just ready to listen and absorb. People don't want to be told what to do, or how they should be managing their lives or their grief, do they? So I think, give it time, and then if things

really clearly are not coming right, they should seek good professional help. Again we are at a disadvantage because of our large
catchment area, and limited number of links with therapists or
counsellors with whom we have had personal contact. I can think
of three or four parents who really continue to suffer severe
bereavement problems several years on. Whether anybody would
actually be able to help, I don't know. I think we need to recognize, don't we, that for some individuals it is not actually going to
work out. I remember a child psychiatrist saying to us, 'You will,
sooner or later, have a parent who will commit suicide, and the
most important thing is that you don't feel guilty. You cannot be
responsible for another person's life. You can help along the line
and do your best, but you are not responsible.'

Effects on siblings

All infants and children inevitably experience loss (through weaning,
separations, frustration). Some of this loss is in the child's external life,
some in phantasy. For example, a child can imagine that its mother will
never reappear or is dead, when faced with a separation or in response
to the child's aggressive impulses. The child is capable of responding
with feelings of grief, and experiencing the processes of mourning
(Klein, 1940; Erikson, 1950; Bowlby, 1960) as part of normal development.

As Klein explains (drawing upon Freud): the child inevitably experiences states of mind that are similar to the mourning of the adult, and
this is revived whenever loss and grief are experienced in adult life. She
terms this sense of loss and grief the 'depressive position' (as explained
in Chapter 1). Part of the emotional 'work' that the child carries out
when negotiating the depressive position – which is never ultimately
resolved or finally worked through but is a state to which the infant, the
child, and the adult, episodically return – is reality testing. In other
words, as the child's inner world, when faced with loss, feels in grave
danger of disintegrating, he gradually realizes that his destructive phantasies have not succeeded in destroying the 'breast' or the mother (for
example, she returns to him after absence) and his despair at the apparent damage is mitigated by his loving impulses and attempts to repair.
Thus, a gradual distinction between the vicissitudes of the infant's internal world and the external world emerges. Clearly, the way in which the
infant negotiates these early experiences will have inevitable repercus-
sions on his later emotional life.

Therefore, a major event, such as the death of a sibling, and the
extent to which the child can deal with it, would clearly depend, among
other things, on earlier experiences that are re-evoked. There is a

considerable body of evidence to suggest that psychiatric disorder is significantly more common in bereaved children, both during childhood and in adult life (Black, 1978, 1989), and in the siblings of children who have died (Pettle and Lansdown, 1986). In this latter study of 28 children whose brother or sister had died of cancer between 18 and 30 months previously, the majority were found to have behavioural and emotional difficulties. Low self-esteem was found to be very common and was not restricted to those with other emotional problems. The dead sibling was, in these cases, often idealized, thus making it seemingly impossible for the surviving sibling to measure up to the dead one. Self-esteem seemed to relate to the length of the patient's illness – the longer the illness, the greater the self-esteem. This is probably a reflection of parents' greater opportunity to adjust to their own forthcoming loss, and then being able to help their healthy children.

The authors of this study acknowledge that the numbers involved were small, thus making generalizations difficult. Nevertheless, they feel that there were sufficient indicators to suggest that, as they studied children who had been bereaved more than 2 years previously, there were indications that even greater difficulties were experienced in the first year. They suggest that self-esteem is enhanced by the surviving child having experienced all or some of these events: participating in the patient's care – for example, having a helpful role in caring for the sibling; regular hospital visits; being told that death is the likely outcome; having the opportunity to say 'goodbye' near the time of death; being with the rest of the family on the day of the funeral and, possibly, attending the service; being allowed to keep some of the dead child's possessions; and previously having experienced the death of a relative or pet.

There were two further experiences that are of questionable benefit. These are: the sibling dying at home, and seeing the body. Further studies need to be made before these can be truly evaluated. But, as Pettle and Lansdown (1986) state, 'Excluding children from information seems to be unsuccessful in reducing their pain, as clearly they sense that something is seriously amiss, and in the absence of age-appropriate explanations, are prone to fantasize.'

Many siblings of dying children convey ambivalence about the amount of parental attention focused on the ill child (*I'd Rather Stay at Home*, Southampton University film, 1986). The infantile part of the surviving child feels jealous and resentful, and this is sometimes complicated by guilt that their own feelings of rivalry and hate have successfully, possibly magically, brought about this illness. The well child may feel that their own safety is threatened by the event: if it could happen to my brother/sister, what is to stop it happening to me? This could be felt to be as a result of the expectation of retaliation or retribution for destructive fantasies, or that the well child identifies closely with the dying or dead child. Young children may perceive their parents as being unable to protect any of their children.

There seem to be sufficient indicators of potential emotional disturbance, over and above the normal process of grief and mourning, in siblings that would warrant early skilled intervention. A grieving parent would probably not be the best person to help the bereaved child. If psychotherapy is available, it would be an opportunity for skilled interpretation of bereaved siblings' sense of abandonment, jealousy, and anger, through the re-experiencing of separation and loss within the transference, evoked by the ending of sessions and the eventual cessation of therapy. Thus, the struggles would become more conscious, and their unconscious power to affect behaviour and emotions in some of the ways indicated would be lessened.

On a more positive note, although many siblings report feeling 'left out', they also often describe the experience as bringing family members closer together. This feeling is often also mentioned by parents, who, while acknowledging the considerable stress, observe that it can ultimately strengthen marriages and bring families closer (see *I'd Rather Stay at Home*). Ailsa Fabian's (1988) book *The Daniel Diary*, a well-written account of her young son's response to the death of his older sister, gives insight into a young child's struggles to come to terms with this death. Daniel, not quite 3 years old, shows curiosity and determination to understand the truth.

Staff involvement and staff support

Professionals working with terminally ill children face severe psychological stress. Unlike caring for individuals whose lives are not terminal, these caregivers have to face the reality that, despite their efforts, these patients will die. They have various ways of responding to this work situation. Some shut themselves off emotionally, so that it is 'just another job', and therefore they do not feel so buffeted or upset by the work. Some become so caught up in the distress that the part of their careers spent in this speciality is inevitably limited, they suffer from 'burn-out', and usually leave this area altogether. These are usually people who are unable to express their feelings about treating life-threatening illness (Slaby and Glicksman, 1985). Others find sufficient support from colleagues, supervisors, and/or families to enable them to feel adequately supported, understood, and therefore able to continue. Similar to this last category are those who balance their professional life by working part of the time in less distressing work.

The ways in which nurses cope with stress and anxiety in a hospital setting have been analysed in Isabel Menzies Lyth's seminal paper, 'The functioning of social systems as a defence against anxiety' (1959) (see Appendix 3 for a summary). Her findings can be, and have been, usefully applied to many other institutional settings. Although she was writing 35 years ago, much of her thinking is still apt today. This is because hospital management and organization has not basically altered, and, in many ways, neither have the roles of nurses. However, an important and developing part of the teaching programme for student nurses in many teaching hospitals includes the opportunity to discuss feelings about death and dying. Nurses, if part of a coordinated multidisciplinary team, realize that they do not have to be the sole providers of psychosocial support for their patients. Training in how to work as a team is increasingly being recognized as a necessary part of managing a patient with a life-threatening illness.

I found the hospital staff I spoke to had their own perspectives on these issues. Sister Jordan (quoted earlier), in talking about a death on a paediatric ward and the response of the nurses, says (personal communication):

> First of all we have to remember the student nurses. Although they are at the end of their second year, paediatrics is a speciality, and many of them have never seen a dead person, never mind a dead child. So for them it's a very big ordeal, very traumatic. Their experience is only 8 weeks on this ward, so in a way you would think they don't get as involved – but they do, in fact, a lot of the students do, and for them it's difficult. And we do try, on the same day as a death occurs, to get them together and talk about death and dying in children, but it's not always possible. We bring them in here (sister's office) or in the treatment room, and sit and talk about it. I allow them to talk, and then I say what I feel about it. If it's still haunting them, they could bring it up in the monthly support group for student nurses.

This sister then described how doctors can become upset and may cry:

> . . . and that's where you get the situation where we, as sisters, are comforting the doctors, because they feel that they've got nobody to talk to. Remember, we're working with an academic department, where it's all go, go, go, treat, treat, treat, and, as you know, we still have a way to go to get them to understand when not to treat these children, and let them die with dignity, and let mum cuddle them.

She summarized the problem of whether or not staff should be allowed to cry:

> As far as not getting involved – that goes back to when I started – I mean I've been nursing 23 years, and when I started to nurse you

were never allowed to cry. You were never allowed to get emotionally involved with your patients, but, I'm glad to say, particularly in paediatrics, that's now something that isn't frowned upon. Nursing children on a general ward in a general hospital, you tend to find that your managers (because they're not involved, and they only visit the ward) are the ones who say 'Pull yourself together and don't cry'. Over my 8 years here of nursing these children, and with the many deaths that I've been involved in, many of the parents *do* say that to see the nurses crying makes them feel better.

I asked her how she understood that? She continued:

We understand that they know that we have cared for their child and that we are sorry that unfortunately the treatment that we had couldn't save them. They appreciate our involvement.

However, these foregoing comments regarding 'managers' reflect the findings of Menzies Lyth cited earlier, in relation to the 'stiff-upper-lip' ethos.

Sister Jordan described the extent to which she becomes involved with her patients, and talked about one little girl whom she says she will never forget:

She was 12 months old when she was diagnosed as having myeloid leukaemia. She was in with us for something like 8 months, and she was absolutely delicious, and there was no way that she was anybody else's baby but mine! Her mum and I, we had this 'deal' that when mum wasn't there, I was her 'mum'. She was a delight to nurse. This poor little baby was put through all this treatment, Hickman lines, having all these drugs, and so on. She would have been 2 on the Thursday, but she actually died on the Tuesday morning. It was a shock for us, never mind the parents. Even though we know that these children are going to die, it was still a shock, because we are carried along on this wave of 'It'll be all right, of course we can treat', and she died.

But what happened was that Mum went home that night, for the first time in many months, and at 7.10 in the morning, I was just leaving to come to work and the phone was ringing, and we'd got the house alarm on, so it would have meant undoing the alarm which would make me a bit more late, so we just ignored that phone call. My husband dropped me off at the hospital, and I was walking through the ground floor and I saw the mum and dad coming toward me, and she grabbed hold of me and burst into tears and said 'She's dead'. For me, even though I knew she was going to die, it was just awful.

I laid her out, and put her in this little dress, and I took her down to the mortuary. Unfortunately, during that weekend there was a fire and we'd had two children brought in to Accident and Emergency, dead, as well as another child, and as they were going down the porter said 'Ooh, sister, you know three other children died this weekend'. I remember saying 'This one is so precious, don't tell me about any other child who's died'. Because it's a little one, you're carrying her down in your arms, and putting her into the mortuary and leaving her there.

Then of course because we knew this family they asked me if I would go to the funeral. Well, oh dear, that was absolutely traumatic, and I remember going home and for about 4 days I kept saying to my husband, 'Why did the baby die?' I was very upset, and then what actually helped was her mum: she was able to ring me up, and she'd say to me, 'Look, you know, one day's good and one day isn't, but I'm all right and I'm going to have another baby.' She did have another baby, and was very worried about that baby, but he had a blood test, and was all right. Since then she's had another one, and she's moved to Devon, and they have rebuilt their lives quite nicely. But in that room, Room 8, if you look on the door, there's still all these little stickers, from this little baby, and her name, we stuck them on. And you know, that's just one . . .

That was 6 years ago, and she still seems to feel raw.

She then described how her work with families involved much more than conventional nursing – for example, after a child had died of leukaemia, she took the parents down to the room where the body was laid out, and described this scene:

Clare's mum touched her, and she exclaimed 'Oh my God, she's so cold!' And I thought, 'Oh gosh, that's something we forget, don't we?' In the midst of all their grief, we just take the child and put them in the fridge, and of course they're going to be cold. For the mum, to see and feel that – to see Clare lying there, and just to touch her, she couldn't believe how cold she was. I very gently had to say, 'Sylvie, this is what happens'. From then on it got worse, because I had to change the child – the mum insisted I put her in a new track-suit – put her back, and then of course one grandma faints, somebody else was screaming. Eventually I got them all sorted out, back up here on the ward, and then I have to take the brother, Clare's uncle, down to get the death certificate, because none of them were in any fit state whatsoever to go. That is a horrendous experience. I mean, I'd known Clare for about 5 years, and this final thing, for parents, I think is absolutely awful, although the people down there at the Registry Offffice try to be nice, under the circumstances.

She acknowledged the difficulty in knowing when to cut off from the families, where she feels torn between helping them and leading her own life:

It's difficult, because I find that I want to go, and I want to help them, but I also think I've got my own life to lead. On my days off I've got this to do, and that to do, and to have to say 'Yes, Sylvie, I'll come and see you', when I've only got one day off. I think to myself, why do I say it? Why do I say 'I'm going to go', when I know very well I've got this to do, that to do. So I've got to ring up and say 'Look, I'm awfully sorry, but would you mind . . .' And then last time I saw her I said 'I'll give you a ring', but I haven't, and I feel guilty. Now, when I've got a number of days off I'll ring her up.

It must be very hard, I suggested, because she needed time to switch off and get away from all this. Sister Jordan agreed:

Oh yes, where I found it hard was one time, before, when Clare had relapsed, and they sent her home, before she came into hospital and died. Her parents said 'Come round and see Clare'. So I think it was after an early shift that I went round there. I found it particularly painful to go into their playroom, with this little girl and her friend from next door, and they were playing Children's Trivial Pursuit. They were just so lovely, and I thought, 'Oh dear, for the parents it must be soul-destroying, to be sitting, just waiting and watching that little life – you know – go.'

She clearly felt that this visit to the child at home put her more in touch with the parents' plight, and yet overall in a way that she valued rather than avoided. I asked her if in fact she thought she was more open to painful feelings than most people in her profession? She replied: 'I think maybe I'm more open than most, but I think there's a lot more that are – certainly in paediatrics. You can't look after children and not become involved, you can't.' And this is after 18 years of working in paediatrics, and 23 years of nursing. She added:

I've worked at Great Ormond Street and Guy's, and very special-ized places where we've had some quite horrendous deaths as well. What makes me want to carry on is working with this team of haematologists, now that we are offering about a 75 per cent cure for lymphoblastic (not as much for myeloid) leukaemia. But in the 8 years I've been here, the changes in the treatment and the new drugs are so impressive, and they are so dedicated, that if there is going to be a cure for leukaemia, I feel that they deserve to find it here.

She acknowledged that she felt carried along by the dynamic spirit of the department and by its medical successes, and that if leukaemia was still in its earlier less treatable stages she would find it much harder to continue in this work. Moreover, as it is a mixed paediatric ward, where many children come in and get better and go home, a balance is kept.

She wondered whether her degree of involvement meant that she was over-identified with her patients, rather than simply feeling empathetic, but then concluded that working with these children led to her valuing her own life, as well as her own problems then becoming insignificant by comparison.

Speaking from the viewpoint of her work in a children's hospice, Sister Frances Dominica described the support needed for staff:

I suppose we need different levels of support and ways of recharging our batteries. Every week from just before Helen House opened, we have had a staff support group, which meets for an hour and is normally facilitated by a consultant child psychiatrist. This is an opportunity for everyone and anyone on the team to share whatever they feel is appropriate, and it's interesting how, to begin with, it was almost always focused on a child or children. In time it became concerned with the families, and how the families were or were not coping, and only after that did it feel safe enough for members of the team to express how they were feeling and reacting, and what the experience was doing to them.

We also have a professional person who is available once a week for individuals to talk to. Some people have found that useful. Then it comes down to the individual discovering what he or she finds most helpful. It may be an understanding spouse, although many people have found that people who are not actually experiencing the day-to-day happenings at Helen House are limited in the support they can offer. However compassionate and understanding they try to be, it's not the same as talking to somebody who's actually here. Some people rely on their religious faith; some have activities and hobbies. I myself find it helpful to go away three or four times a year and be quite alone for a few days: to listen to lovely music, or to walk. It's the withdrawing and solitude, I think, that I find most helpful.

I asked her if she was then cutting off, or, in fact, going over and digesting the experience. She replied that it was more the latter:

. . . because you are experiencing one major grief after another. People sometimes say to us 'How do you remain emotionally uninvolved?' Well, it's a non-question, isn't it. You don't. You become very involved, or you couldn't do the job. In a setting like this, the families really do seem to adopt you as part of their family; they'll select their own people, on the team, as their 'specials', so there's strength in that, in that you're not always the key person.

So you do not decide who the key worker is, I asked, they choose you? Sister Frances replied:

We try to let them do that, without realizing what they're doing. That person becomes the 'contact' person, and then there's a back-up person. But that doesn't eliminate the other members of the team: anybody and everybody is involved. It happens naturally that people gravitate towards certain people, I think. Sometimes it's the child who says, 'I want to be looked after by so-and-so', so we encourage that. A recent study of staff stress discovered without doubt that the greatest support came from informal mutual support within the team. Many members of the team have worked together for a number of years. They know each other very well indeed, and have learnt to recognize each other's signs of stress and distress. You learn to know who benefits from hugs and who best benefits from space.

This degree of emotional involvement recalls that of the hospital sister cited earlier. It seems that both respond to the challenge of the daily confrontation with the reality that some of their patients will die. However, while the hospital sister needs the balance of less seriously ill patients and medical treatment breakthroughs, Sister Frances may be more able to face the existential reality because of the support of her religious beliefs. The mutual support from the care team, which Sister Frances values, also seems to be the most usual avenue of support for professionals in hospital settings.

In time it is possible for some of the raw feelings of loss and hopelessness to alter. In the mourning process the person who has died almost miraculously ceases to cause a wounding feeling, or to be an external presence that is missing, and instead there evolves a warmer sense of their becoming, paradoxically, more present, and a part of the bereaved person: of being alive in memory. In psychoanalytic terms, they have been internalized or integrated, and have become an alive person in the bereaved's inner world, and a part of their personality.

Some of this process is conveyed in this extract from Wordsworth's *Tintern Abbey*:

And now, with gleams of half-extinguished thought,
With many recognitions dim and faint,
And somewhat of a sad perplexity,
The picture of the mind revives again:
While here I stand, not only with the sense
Of pleasure, but with pleasing thoughts
That in this moment there is life and food
For future years . . .

Epilogue

As long as I live I shall probably grieve, even if time makes it more gentle, less frequent. But in death and grief, because there is pain, therefore I know there is life, and life is change and I must set some limit or I shall nibble at these thoughts and feelings for the rest of my life.

Mary Jones (1988)

The little boy whom I have described in detail still has an important place in my mind. It was perhaps his tenacity, and his ability to endure, often stoically, days and nights of torturous treatment and illness, that I remember above all as his main characteristics. He 'held on' to life as long as he could, surviving several crises. Although I did not know him prior to his last illness, I feel that in health he must have been a passionate child, with a great zest for life, and with an ability to form strong relationships. Even on the brink of death he seemed – for some of the time – steeped in life.

In working with this particular child I had to bear in mind his parents' views about illness and death. I felt that I had to try to use the parents' basic strengths, directly, or through Peter, the social worker. My work was inevitably tempered by the extent to which the parents could adjust to his imminent death. Nevertheless, the resourcefulness of Robert's mother was truly impressive. Working with people who are dying is always salutary: it puts into perspective (albeit temporarily) other worries, leading to more tolerance of these difficulties.

Now, reflecting on this experience, the question of the moral and ethical efficacy of keeping someone alive under these conditions arises once more. Most parents *do* opt for the fight for life for their child, even if the chances of success are very slim. Occasionally, some children manage to find a way of conveying to their parents that they do not want to continue with the ordeal. Some parents respect this, and allow the child to die peacefully, preferably in its own home.

Over the past 30 years, enormous advances have been made towards increasing the survival of cancer patients. In the mid-1960s, 90 per cent of children diagnosed with the most common form of childhood cancer (acute lymphoblastic leukaemia) died within 3 years. Today, approximately 75 per cent of children treated survive 3–5 years after diagnosis without recurrence; the survival rate for AML with the most recent treatment can allow us to push up the traditional 30–55 per cent. Long-term cure is not necessarily the outcome, even if remission is achieved. Overall, 63 per cent of children with cancer can expect to reach long-term remission (Stiller, 1994).

Robert's prognosis was much more pessimistic, especially with the lack of an appropriate sibling donor. For some doctors, a sense of involvement is maintained in treating people with terminal illness, such as cancer, through the developments in research. As these developments become more successful, so the doctor's task in relation to individual patients becomes less grim. One medical oncologist, Dr Maurice Slevin (1994), believes that cancer is under-treated, not over-treated: 'Cancer makes people feel sick and can cause severe pain, shortness of breath and loss of weight. If you give chemotherapy and the side-effects are less than the symptoms, overall the patient benefits.'

Nevertheless, some doctors still tend to give the parents a prognosis weighted towards a hopeful outcome, rather than the full truth – however bleak – of the situation. There is a possibility that a 'hopeful' (more optimistic than the truth), or censored diagnosis, could have a benevolent effect. Doctors quite often talk about a 5–10 per cent 'response rate'. Whilst this refers to the percentage of cancers that shrink by half or more during treatment, the patient or parents may think that this percentage refers to cure – not remission. It is here that I feel that this 'kindness' towards the family (or fear of being the harbinger of bad news?) is doing a disservice to the whole process of attempting to arrive at the most appropriate decision and of knowing where they stand.

As I mentioned in Chapter 7, Robert's parents probably were not told the full truth about his chances of survival. However, if there is a foundation of truth, those involved can of course view this basic truth according to their own bias. For example, one 13-year-old boy, when told he had a 30 per cent chance of survival, was sure that he would be 'one of the lucky ones'. A bone-marrow transplant may lead to remission, but remission can only be assessed retrospectively, as it is impossible to tell if a few leukaemic cells remain in the body after treatment. Facing a relapse is often worse than facing the original diagnosis, because a relapse suggests that the doctors may not be able to cure the patient (see Dr Anne Kilby's comments, Chapter 4). There is also the memory of unpleasant treatments and side-effects that the patient then knows he will have to endure again.

Untreated acute leukaemia would bring an inevitably premature death. The choice, then, of a mismatch bone-marrow transplant is taking the risk of making that life even shorter, and of a possibly more troubled death. The months of possible 'tortures' and of isolation are part of the price to pay for the possibility of an extra lease of life. These are the factors to be taken into consideration by the parents and by the medical team, and were explored more fully in Chapters 10 and 11.

It is worth asking whether the cases where the child is treated beyond what appears to be the bounds of humanity, where 'torturous' treatment is given even when there is a very small chance of success, are partly symptoms of a lack of an effective multi-disciplinary team. (Depending on the resources available, a paediatric multi-disciplinary team can include all or some of these people: doctors, nurses, teachers, physio-therapists, occupational therapists, social workers, clergy, psychologists, child psychotherapists, psychiatrists, play specialists, nursery nurses, health visitors, speech therapists, and community nurses. It is unlikely that anaesthetists, radiotherapists, and other specialists would be involved in the regular discussion of the psychosocial aspects of the child – although that would be desirable.) In other words, a decision to treat may, on occasion, indicate a more or less unilateral decision on the part of the consultant.

My hypothesis is that in a divided team where, for example, the nurses (and child psychiatrist, child psychotherapist or psychologist if there is one) are in touch with and are carrying the child's suffering, the doctors in charge of the physical care may not be. The latter may be aware of 'improvements' in the patient, such as a rise in the platelet level, while the patient's overall condition and level of discomfort may be appalling. Thus, they may be only taking into account the patient's physical condition, and not the emotional side. This pattern is not inevitable; of course the team can be split in other ways. The function of team meetings is for all these differing views of the patient to be pooled, discussed, and, bearing in mind the parents' wishes (and of course, if possible, the child's), for an informed decision about further treatment to be constantly reviewed. The differing members of the care team would still 'carry' different functions, and this is intrinsically useful and spares individuals from a possibly too onerous task. But these parts of a whole do need to be able to come togther to discuss the various aspects, in a way that is ultimately humane for the patient. However, all this takes time; people need to value the time spent thinking together as a team for this function not to be eroded by other duties. Hospital doctors in Britain are notoriously over-worked and under considerable stress, so it seems that practical considerations do often prevent them from contributing equally to the psychosocial aspects of the team. This dilemma exacerbates whatever splits are present in the team. Neverthe-less, it is an ethical question as to whether doctors should, or could, or want to shift from their position of prime decision-makers to one where they are more a part of a homogeneous team.

A switch to terminal care does not preclude the care-givers being alert to the possibility of sudden recovery. Just as our ancestors were often fearful of being buried alive (Puckle, 1926), so some people nowadays may feel that, in *allowing* someone to die, any diversion from the path towards death will not be noticed or tolerated.

As there is always uncertainty as to when death will occur, each day can become meaningful and precious if valued in its own right. The focus for patient and family, therefore, can become short-term, or immediate. A patient, or his family, who is not told as much as possible of the reality – however stark – of the situation can feel cheated of the lost opportunity to use the available time constructively. Elinor, a 17-year-old girl, at the stage of various treatments not working, said 'I need to know if I'm dying so that I can begin living.' It is important, in dealing with the dying, that we do not forget that life, even a drastically shortened life, can be worth living, and that remissions, if not miracles, do occur. And just as every child has a right to whatever medical care is available, so it is every dying child's right to have emotional care and support, including the right to express every sort of feeling.

We all have to face death, as part of life. It is particularly difficult in our society not to see the death of a child as a failure, a breakdown in our attempt to control the forces of mind and body, to equate health with goodness and correct living and illness and death with evil. For those not having to face death and dying as part of their work, or a life-threatening illness in someone close, death can be denied until the day it comes. This may successfully avoid conscious anxieties, but may disturb us more deeply than a more open acknowledgement of our mortality. For example, illness affects most of us at some time. This unpredictable experience – which stirs up associations with death – can be deeply unsettling.

However, those working with the dying, those who face the death of one they love, and those who survive a life-threatening illness, often find that they gain insight into parts of their psyche that previously were inaccessible; that they can emerge strengthened, 'a sadder and a wiser man' as Coleridge put it in *The Ancient Mariner*, aware of their own vulnerability and mortality, and therefore their own humanity.

A 13-year-old boy who had had bone cancer and an amputation of his leg, said, a year later: 'How fragile life is, and dumb, and stupid, what's the point.' He momentarily curled up, talked about death being an easy way out, but then, 'I think life mustn't be wasted . . . Some people talk about an afterlife. I don't believe in that. I think you only get one chance.' It is this awareness of our own fragility and that of others that can actually enhance, strengthen, and enable us to continue to be sensitive to our patients or our loved ones, for we are not then putting so much of our energy into denial.

'Crisis' means 'time of danger' and it also means 'turning-point'. A crisis in both nuances is what the patient facing death experiences, and is something those close to the patient are also capable of going through. 'The helper and the helped are in a partnership, both often changed by the experience,' as Derek Nuttall, an ex-Director of CRUSE, said at a conference on 'Bereavement: Grief and Loss' (Association of Child Psychology and Psychiatry, 1988). There is the danger of a frightening or lonely experience, or the possibility of a turning-point, leading to decisive change and development, for both the dying and the carers.

Within the concept of wholeness there is without doubt a place for death alongside life. If we see, feel, and dwell only upon life, we shall, strangely, not be truly living. To come up against the death of a child forces us to re-evaluate our lives, and thus perhaps become more aware of what it is to be alive.

A 17-year-old dying young woman, Elinor (mentioned on the previous page), showed me this passage:

> If we can live with the knowledge that death is our constant companion, travelling on our 'left shoulder', then death can become . . . our 'ally', still fearsome but continually a source of wise counsel. With death's counsel, the constant awareness of the limit of our time to live and love, we can be guided to make the best use of our time and live life to the fullest . . . When we shy away from death, the ever-changing nature of things, we inevitably shy away from life.
>
> M. Scott Peck (1990), pp. 142–3

Appendix I
Analysis of Robert's drawings

I was fortunate to have the opportunity to show Robert's drawings (see p. 20) to Dr Mary Sue Moore, a psychotherapist and psychologist who has carried out considerable research into children's drawings. She gave her comments before I had told her many details, other than the child's age, sex, and the fact that he had a terminal illness. This was in order for us to test whether her observations could be appropriately applied. She clarified my understanding of them considerably.

Moore stated that the first picture we draw in any particular period of time carries the strongest projection of ourself. She commented that the figure in this first drawing has what is sometimes called a 'refrigerator' body: it is squarish in shape, has no shoulders, and is without feet, and the body goes off the bottom of the page. She said that this kind of body is drawn by children from many sub-groups, but frequently the main experience that they have had has been a traumatic physical experience: for example, children with chronic medical conditions where they have had repeated intrusive operations. The child is warding off any sensations to the body by drawing the body as if it is just a block. (Other physical traumas, such as sexual abuse, may also lead to this type of depiction [Moore, 1994b].)

Moore expressed interest in the fact that the head is connected directly to the body without any neck. She says that this is typical for young children, but it also indicates that the child has little cognitive ability to distance himself psychologically from the events that he has experienced, whether internal or external. 'Therefore, his impulses are probably strongly felt by him,' she says. He does not have the ability that, say, a 9- or 10-year-old child has to *think* about things, and thus separate himself from his impulses and the reality of the life experiences.

Moore then commented on the drawing of birds in the sky, with a heavy layer of sky across it. 'Clouds, rain, snow, and birds have all been interpreted variously to represent a sense of oppression from the environment, from above. This can be interpreted as parental or authority figures to whom the child is closely attached, who are watching over, but also oppressively involved in, the child's life.'

She added that it was very significant that he had placed the sun directly over the figure. Moore referred to research carried out by Mary Main (Berkeley, USA), who found that this positioning frequently occurred where a close family member had died but the loss was unmourned and unresolved and was still actively felt; then the child often drew a sun over that member of the family. She wondered, therefore, about this positioning (which is not the more typical placing of the sun, in a corner of the picture) over the only figure in the picture and suggests that he himself feels at risk of dying, or is dying.

Moore noticed the little stick-like arms: 'Those are arms that are not particularly useful. Children who have an active sense of control over their environment draw two-dimensional arms – not just one line – which are usually connected to a shoulder. We have our sense of power in our shoulders. So I guess he does not feel very powerful.'

When looking at the second picture, Moore commented that it was striking that the leaves of the plants stretch upwards. Apparently, in the research on the drawings of terminally ill children (Bach, 1969), the leaves of plants often reach upward in some sense of growth. In this research, the number of plants represented was often significant in relation to the duration of the illness or the number of months of life left. Moore observes that he has overlapped himself with one of the plants, so we may wonder what he is saying about his life, his years, his experience of growing.

She continued:

> Another conspicuous feature is that although the figure still has the same little helpless arms, these are reaching up. A very young child does these asking-for-help, comfort, needing-to-be-picked-up arms. It's a much more dependent stance. If you put yourself in the position of the child in the drawing, you can see how it feels.
>
> I would say that the first figure represents more an attempt to be grown up, to stand up to things, to present himself with intact defences. My guess is that when he drew this second figure, more of his feelings were showing, about wishing he could be held or comforted.

Moore pointed out that in this picture, in contrast to the first one, he has shown his legs touching the ground, so that some part of him which is a 'whole, longing, connected self' is being shown. He shows this figure as wearing clothes – unlike the first one, which is a non-sexual rendering.

Both drawings, Moore felt, are inappropriately immature for a 7-year-old child, and would be more characteristic of a 4-and-a-half-year-old or a 5-year-old. Therefore she wondered at what age the child had had traumatic experiences, and whether something had occurred between the age of 3 and 5 which had fixed his emotional development.

Another point to notice, Moore said, is the positioning of figures on the page. The first drawing shows the figure more or less centrally positioned, and, therefore, suggests the present or the here-and-now, while the second shows the figure far over to the right. This is generally assumed to be a looking toward or thinking about the future. Therefore, this suggests that it is more about how he sees himself henceforth, rather than now.

At this point, I gave Mary Sue Moore details of Robert and of my contact with him, including a description of his physical condition. This led Moore to feel that the first drawing conveyed that he had lost a sense of his body: it is swathed in something like a heavy garment. His swollen purple body may have led him to lose a sense of his actual skin, as a container for his body. We agreed that the diagnosis and the ensuing invasive and pervasive treatments that he had undergone could indeed have led to the lack of emotional development that Moore had speculated.

We discussed the positioning of the figure in the second drawing in the light of the seriousness of the illness perhaps having a full impact on him between the ages of 6 and 7, and how this figure seems to depict both himself and me. Thus, from his comments, it seems that I am this figure, but that it embodies both me and himself identifying with me. Therein, there is a feeling that there is a future, but it is a very short one – only two more trees. Feeling that this was a reflection of the work I was doing with him, Moore said, 'There's a real self here that's identifying with you in a positive way.'

She agreed with my thoughts about a fantasy of heaven Robert may have had: feeling that this positive reaching upwards may have indicated a hopefulness towards something that could only be better than that which he was currently experiencing.

Finally, Moore pointed out that it has been observed in the drawing of dying children that a halo is often depicted – and we both felt this first drawing could indeed convey a halo.

Appendix II
Extracts from the
Nuremberg Code (1947)

1. The voluntary consent of the human subject is absolutely essential . . . there should be made known to him, the nature, duration . . . all inconveniences and hazards reasonably to be expected; and the effects upon his health or person which may possibly come from his participation in the experiment.

   The duty and responsibility for ascertaining the quality of the consent rests upon each individual who initiates, directs . . . It is a personal duty and responsibility which may not be delegated . . .

6. The degree of risk to be taken should never exceed that determined by the humanitarian importance of the problem to be solved by the experiment.

9. During the course of the experiment the human subject should be at liberty to bring the experiment to an end if he has reached the physical or mental state where continuation . . . seems to him to be impossible.

10. During the course of the experiment the scientist in charge must be prepared to terminate the experiment at any stage, if he has probable cause to believe . . . that a continuation . . . is likely to result in injury, disability, or death . . .

Appendix III
Note on Isabel Menzies Lyth's 'The functioning of social systems as a defence against anxiety' (1959)

This is a summary of a process one sees at work in hospital work with children. Menzies Lyth describes the ways in which nurses are confronted with death and suffering, as well as distasteful and distressing tasks, far more than one would ordinarily come across. They are confronted by opposing sets of feelings in their work: pity, compassion, and love versus hatred and resentment of the patients who arouse these strong feelings. These powerful feelings reflect primitive phantasies (in other words, unconscious phantasies) which are in everyone, relating to infancy. These phantasies are around feelings of omnipotence: where the infant feels that his loving impulses can be life-giving while his aggressive impulses are capable of killing. Understandably, then, the infant's inner world is peopled by damaged, injured, or dead objects (see reference to Witham's paper, p. 14), as well as loved objects and loving feelings.

The stress that a nurse then feels, the argument continues, is influenced by her own inner world and elements remaining from infancy. Unconsciously she will respond in part at least according to her unconscious phantasies. Similarly, patients and their families have an inner world which may well be characterized by violent phantasies with which the adult is not normally in touch. The overt distress or subtle messages from patients or relatives therefore increase the nurses' stress, possibly at an unconscious level. Menzies Lyth summarizes this dilemma thus: 'By the nature of her profession the nurse is at considerable risk of being flooded by intense and unmanageable anxiety.'

She then proceeds to describe the ways in which the hospital situation protects the nurse from this anxiety. This is, for example, through splitting the nurses' duties between several patients, through moving nurses from ward to ward, through depersonalizing the patients, through an expectation of professional and emotional detachment, and through performing ritualized tasks.

Thus, this 'social defence system', as Menzies Lyth calls it (following

Jaques, 1955), helps the individual to avoid anxiety, uncertainty, and guilt. As the social system sufficiently matches the individual psychic defence system of the nurses, both continue to support each other through a continuous process of projection and introjection. Menzies Lyth writes that this situation does not facilitate growth or maturation in the nurses, and may partly account for the high level of wastage in the profession.

In Noreen Ramsay's interesting observational study of a hospice, 'Sitting close to death' (in press, 1995, for Group Analysis), the institution's specific defences against anxiety and death emerge. The difficulties in staying with those anxieties, rather than being busy, are brought out. See also Dartington, 'Where angels fear to tread: idealism, despondency and inhibition of thought in hospital nursing' (1994).

Glossary

Some medical and psychoanalytic terms used in this book

acute: coming sharply to a crisis.

benign: a lump in the body which does not invade the surrounding tissues nor travel to other parts of the body; not malignant.

biopsy: examination of small piece of tissue from the body; removal of such tissue.

chemotherapy: treatment of disease using drugs or chemicals.

chronic: lingering, lasting, constant.

cytotoxic: cell poisoning.

decathect: (psychoanalytic term) to withdraw the investment of energy, or interest, in *external objects*.

denial: (psychoanalytic term) defence mechanism by which either some aspect of the self is denied, or some painful experience is denied.

dysfunction: not functioning properly.

ego: (psychoanalytic term) the part of the self, or psychic apparatus, which is organized; that which may 'be called reason and common sense, in contrast to the id, which contains the passions . . .' (Freud, 1923).

external object: (psychoanalytic term) person or thing which is recognized by the subject as being external to himself – 'out there' – as opposed to objects which have been introjected into the ego.

haematology: study of, or science of, the blood.

identification: (psychoanalytic term) process by which a person either borrows his identity from someone else, or extends his identity into someone else, or confuses or fuses his identity with someone else.

internal objects: (psychoanalytic term) mental processes which are located in an inner, or psychical, space, in contrast to their 'external' equivalents; images occurring in phantasies which are felt to be real.

maladaptive: faulty adaptation to, or interaction with, environment.

217

malignant: a cancer that grows and can travel to other parts of the body.

neuroblastoma: malignant neoplasm, or new growth of abnormal tissue, characterized by immature nerve cells.

object: (psychoanalytic term) person or thing to which feeling or action is directed; that to which subject relates.

oedema: swelling caused by fluid retention.

oncology: the study and treatment of cancer.

palliative: that which serves to alleviate, or bring relief to, disease, without curing. See p. 86 and p. 88.

phantasy (and fantasy): see 'Note on conventions', p. xiv.

platelet: a very small cell in the blood, essential for the clotting of blood.

projection: (psychoanalytic term) process by which specific impulses, aspects of the self, wishes, or *internal objects* are imagined to be located in someone else. This is usually preceded by denial that this aspect is felt by the person who projects.

projective identification: (psychoanalytic term) 'part of the self and internal objects are split off and projected into the external object, which then becomes possessed by, controlled and identified with the projected parts' (Segal, 1973, p. 27).

radiotherapy: treatment of disease by radiation; that is, by electromagnetic waves of energy.

respite care: complementary, flexible care in the home or home-from-home setting with appropriate medical and nursing support, offering parents or carers an interval of relief.

reintrojection: (psychoanalytic term) process by which feelings which had been projected into an *external object* (and which may have been thus modified) are then taken back into the psyche; that which has been reintrojected becomes an *internal object*.

renal: of the kidney.

splitting: (psychoanalytic term) both *ego* and *object* can be split; in splitting of the object, the two parts are typically perceived as 'good' and 'bad'.

tissue-type: mass of cells of one kind.

transference: (psychoanalytic term) process by which a patient displaces on to the therapist feelings which derive from earlier relationships (see p. 75 for a fuller explanation).

tumour: lump, growth, or swelling in any part of the body; can be malignant or benign.

venesection: surgical blood-letting by the opening of a vein.

venous: of the blood vessels.

Useful addresses

The Brain Tumor Charity (formerly Samantha Dickson Brain Tumor Trust)
Largest dedicated brain tumor charity in UK with highest level of laboratory
based brain tumor research in the country.
www.braintumortrust.co.uk

Cancer Research UK
UK's leading charity dedicated to cancer research
Information
0207 242 0200
www.cancerresearchuk.org

Charlie's Challenge
Raises money to finance research into brain tumors.
www.charlieschallenge.com

The Children's Cancer and Leukemia Group (CCLG)
National professional body responsible for the organization of the treatment
and management of children with cancer.
Coordination of national and international clinical trials, including biological studies.
National cancer registration and provision of information for patients and
families.
0116 249 4460
info@cclg.org.uk

Children's Cancer Support Group
Offers advice and support to families and relatives of children with various
forms of cancer. Based in N.W. of U.K.
0151 523 8886
www.chicsonline.org

Children with Cancer UK
Research; innovative welfare projects; raising awareness.
0207 404 0808
info@childrenwithcancer.org.uk

The Compassionate Friends
Supporting bereaved parents and their families after a child dies.
0845 1232304
www.tcf.org.uk

Cruse Bereavement Care
Telephone helpline, as well as face-to-face support.
Branches across Britain.
0844 4779400
helpline@cruse.org.uk

Jimmyteens
A collection of video diaries, animations, and other creative recordings, made by young cancer patients about their cancer journeys.
www.jimmyteens.tv

CLIC Sargent for Children with Cancer
Help and support for parents, young people, children, and professionals.
0300 330 0803
www.clicsargent.org.uk

Macmillan Cancer Support (includes children)
Practical, medical, emotional and financial support, and campaigns for better cancer care.
0808 808 0000
www.macmillan.org.uk

Noah's Ark Children's Hospice
Practical and emotional support for life-limited children and their families in North London and south Hertfordshire.
0208 449 8877
Noahsarkhospice.org.uk

Rainbow Trust Children's Charity
Emotional and practical support to families who have a child with a life-threatening illness.
01372 363438
enquiries@rainbowtrust.org.uk

The Neuroblastoma Society
Raises funds for British research into the disease
www.nsoc.co.uk

BOOKS FOR YOUNG CHILDREN

'Althea' (1981). *Going into Hospital.* London: Dinosaur Publications (Collins).
'Althea' (1991). *I have Cancer.* London: Dinosaur Publications (Collins).
'Althea' (2001). *When Uncle Bob Died: Talking It Through.* London: Dinosaur Publications (Collins).
Bruna, Dick. (2003). *Miffy in Hospital.* London: Egmont.
Burningham, J. (2003). *Granpa.* London: Cape.
Marleau, E. (2010). *My First Visit to the Hospital.* London: Quarto Publishing.
Sam, J. (2011). *I have Cancer.* ('Perfect Paperback'.) Mustang, Oklahoma: Tate Publishing & Enterprises.
Snell, N. (1984). *Emma's Cat Dies.* London: Puffin.
Stickney, D. (1984). *Waterbugs and Drangonflies. Explaining Death to Young Children.* Cleveland, Ohio: Pilgrim Press.

BOOKS FOR CHILDREN AGED 7–11 YEARS

Viorst, J. (1987). *The Tenth Good Thing about Barney.* London: Collins.
Walker, Alice. (1988). *To Hell with Dying.* London: Hodder & Stoughton.
White, E.B. (2003). *Charlotte's Web.* London: Puffin.

BOOKS FOR CHILDREN IN BOTH GROUPS ABOVE

Durant, A. (2004). *Always and Forever.* (Illustrator Debi Gliori.) London: Picture Corgi.
Mellonie, B. and Ingpen, R. (1983). *Beginnings and Endings with Lifetimes in Between.* Surrey: Paper Tiger, Dragon's World.
Varley, S. (2013). *Badger's Parting Gifts.* Atlanta, Georgia: Anderson Press.

BOOKS FOR OLDER CHILDREN

Lewis, C.S. (1966). *A Grief Observed.* London: Faber.
Little, J. (1985). *Mama's Going to Buy You a Mockingbird.* New York: Viking Children's Books.
Rosen, M. (2011). *Michael Rosen's Sad Book.* (Illustrator Quentin Blake.) London: Walker Books.
Salten, F. (2011). *Bambi.* Read Books.

References

Adams-Greenly M. (1991). Psychological assessment and intervention at initial diagnosis. *Pediatrician* 18: 3–10

Ahmedzai S. (1993). The medicalisation of dying – a doctor's view. In: D. Clark (Ed.) *The Future of Palliative Care*. Buckingham: Open University Press.

Alderson P. (1990). *Choosing for Children – parents' consent to surgery*. Oxford: Oxford University Press.

Alderson P. (1993). *Children's Consent to Surgery*. Buckingham: Open University Press.

Alexander I, Alderstein A. (1958). Affective responses to the concept of death in a population of children and early adolescents. *Journal of Genetic Psychology* 93: 167–77.

Alvarez A. (1974). *The Savage God*. Harmondsworth: Penguin.

Anthony E, Koupernik C. (1973). *The Child in his Family: The Impact of Disease and Death*. Vol. 2. New York: Wiley.

Anthony S. (1973). *The Discovery of Death in Childhood and After*. Harmondsworth: Penguin.

Anthony Z, Bhana K. (1989–1990). An exploratory study of Muslim girls' understanding of death. *Omega Journal of Death and Dying* 19 (3): 215–27.

Aries P. (1974). *Western Attitudes toward Death*. Baltimore, MD; London: Johns Hopkins University Press.

Atkin M. (1981). Fatal illness: how does the family cope? *Nursing* (March).

Atkins D, Patenaude A. (1987). Psychosocial preparation and followup for paediatric bone marrow transplant patients. *American Journal of Orthopsychiatry* 57: 246–52.

Bach S. (1969). *Spontaneous Paintings of Severely Ill Patients: A Contribution to Psychosomatic Medicine*. Basle, Switzerland: JR Geigy.

Baldwin J. (1963). *The Fire Next Time*. Harmondsworth: Penguin.

Bender-Götze C. (1991). Late effects of allogenic bone marrow transplantation in children. *Pediatrician* 18: 71–5.

Berger J. (1984). *And Our Faces, My Heart, Brief as Photos*. London: Writers & Readers.

Berger J. (1988). My mother's secrets. *New Statesman & Society* 10 June.

Bergmann T. (1965). *Children in the Hospital*. New York: International Universities Press.

Bettelheim B. (1967). *The Empty Fortress*. New York: Free Press.

Bick E. (1967). The experience of the skin in early object relations. In: M. Harris Williams (Ed.) *Collected Papers of Martha Harris and Esther Bick*. Strath Tay, Perthshire: Clunie.

Bion W. (1962). *Learning from Experience*. New York: Jason Aronson.

Bion W. (1984). *Second Thoughts*. London: Maresfield Reprints/Karnac.

Black D. (1978). The bereaved child. *Journal of Child Psychology and Psychiatry* 19: 287–92.

Black D. (1989). Life-threatening illness, children, and family therapy. *Journal of Family Therapy* 11: 81–101.

Black D, Hardoff D, Nelki J. (1989). Educating medical students about death and dying. *Archives of Diseases in Childhood* 64: 750–3.

Bloom A. (1988). My country childhood. *Country Living* May.

Bluebond-Langner M. (1978). *The Private Worlds of Dying Children*. Princeton, NJ: Princeton University Press.

Bowlby J. (1960). Grief and mourning in infancy and early childhood. *Psychoanalytic Study of the Child*, vol. 15 London: Hogarth, pp. 9–52.

Bowlby J. (1973). *Attachment*, Vol. I. Attachment and Loss. London: Hogarth.

Bowlby J. (1979). On knowing what you are not supposed to know and feeling what you are not supposed to feel. *Canadian Journal of Psychiatry* 24 (5): 403–8.

Bowlby J, Robertson J, Rosenbluth D. (1952). A two-year-old goes to hospital. *Psychoanalytic Study of the Child*, vol. 12 London: Hogarth, pp. 88–90.

Bozeman M, Orbach C, Sutherland A. (1955). Psychological impact of cancer and its treatment, III: The adaptation of mothers to threatened loss of children through leukaemia. Part I. *Cancer* 8: 1–19.

Brindle D. (1988). Terminally ill 'put off death' for a festival. *Guardian* 23 September.

Brown H, Kelly, M. (1976). Stages of bone marrow transplantation: a psychiatric perspective. *Psychosomatic Medicine* 38 (6): 339–446.

Burton L. (Ed.) (1974). *Care of the Child Facing Death*. London: Routledge & Kegan Paul.

Cairns N, Clark G, Smith S, Lansky, S. (1979). Adaption of siblings to childhood malignancy. *Journal of Paediatrics* 95: 484–7.

Candy-Gibbs S, Sharp KC, Petrum C. (1984–1985). The effects of age, object, and cultural /religious background on children's concepts of death. *Omega Journal of Death and Dying* 15(4): 329–46.

Cannadine D. (1981). War and death, grief and mourning in modern Britain. In: J. Whaley (Ed.) *Mirrors of Mortality: Studies in the Social History of Death*. London: Europa.

Chambers T. (1987). Hospices for children? *British Medical Journal* 294: 1309–10.

Charlton A, Pearson D, Morris-Jones P. (1986). Children's return to school after treatment for solid tumours. *Social Science Medicine* 12: 1337–46.

Chesler M, Barbarin O. (1987). *Childhood Cancer and the Family*. New York: Brunner/Mazel.

Chesler M, Paris J, Barbarin O. (1986). 'Telling' the child with cancer: parental choices to share information with ill children. *Journal of Paediatric Psychology* 11 (4): 497–516.

Childers P, Wimmer M. (1971). The concept of death in early childhood. *Child Development* 42: 1299–1301.

Chodoff P, Friedman S, Hamburg D. (1964). Stress, defenses, and coping behaviour: observations in parents of children with malignant diseases. *American Journal of Psychiatry* 120: 743–9.

Claflin C, Barbarin O. (1991). Does 'telling' less protect more? Relationships among age, information disclosure, and what children with cancer see and feel. *Journal of Pediatric Psychology* 16 (2): 169–91.

Clunies-Ross C, Lansdown R. (1988). Concepts of death, illness and isolation found in children with leukaemia. *Child: care, health and development* 14: 373–86.

Coetzee JM. (1994). *The Master of Petersburg*. London: Secker.

Corr C, McNeil J. (Eds) (1986). *Adolescence and Death*. NewYork: Springer.

Corr C, Corr D. (Eds) (1985). *Hospice Approaches to Pediatric Care*. New York: Springer.

Cousens P, Waters B, Said J, Stevens M. (1988). Cognitive effects of cranial irradiation in leukaemia: a survey and meta-analysis. *Journal of Child Psychology and Psychiatry* 29 (6): 839–52.

Cox O. (1988). *Sunday's Child*. Bath: Ashgrove Press.

Crispell K, Gomez C. (1987). Proper care for the dying a critical public issue. *Journal of Medical Ethics* 13: 74–80.

Dartington A. (1994). Where angels fear to tread: idealism, despondency and inhibition of thought in hospital nursing. In: A. Obholzer and V.Z. Roberts (Eds) *The Unconscious at Work* London: Routledge. pp 101–109.

Davies R, Quinlan D, McKegney F, Kimball C. (1973). Organic factors and psychological adjustment in advanced cancer patients. *Psychosomatic Medicine* 35 (6): 464–71.

Debuskey M. (Ed.) (1970). Orchestration of care. In: *The Chronically Ill Child and his Family*. Springfield, IL: Charles Thomas.

De Creamer W. (1983). A crosscultural perspective on personhood. *Milbank Memorial Fund* 61: 19–34.

Detwiler DA. (1981). The positive function of denial. *Journal of Paediatrics* 99: 401–2.

Dominica F. (1987). Reflections on death in childhood. *British Medical Journal* 294: 108–10.

Douglas J. (1975). Early hospital admissions and later disturbances of behaviour and learning. *Developmental Medicine and Child Neurology* 17: 456–80.

Dufour D. (1989). Home or hospital care for the child with end-stage cancer: effects on the family. *Issues in Comprehensive Paediatric Nursing* 12: 371–83.

Dunkel-Schetter C, Wortman C. (1982). The interpersonal dynamics of cancer problems in social relationships and their impact on the patient. In: H. Friedman and M. Di Matteo (Eds) *Interpersonal Issues in Health Care*. New York: Academic Press.

Eiser C. (1985). *The Psychology of Childhood Illness*. New York: Springer-Verlag.

Eissler KR. (1955). *The Psychiatrist and the Dying Patient*. New York: International Universities Press.

Eliot TS. (1944). *The Four Quartets*. London: Faber.

Elliot M. (1981). Parent care. In: E. Kübler-Ross (Ed.) *Living with Death and Dying*. London: Souvenir Press.

Erikson E. (1950). *Childhood and Society*. New York: Norton.

Escher M. (1961). *The Graphic Work*. London: Pan/Ballantine.

Fabian A. (1988). *The Daniel Diary*. London: Grafton Books.

Feifel H. (1962). Attitudes towards death in some normal and some mentally ill populations. In: H. Feifel (Ed.) *The Meaning of Death*. New York: McGraw-Hill.

Florian V, Kravetz S. (1985). Children's concepts of death – a cross-cultural comparison among Muslims, Druze, Christians, and Jews in Israel. *Journal of Cross-Cultural Psychology* 16 (2) June: 174–89.

Forfar J. (1984). Demography, vital statistics, and the pattern of disease in childhood. In: J. Forfar and G. Arneil (Eds) *Textbook of Paediatrics* (3rd Edition). Edinburgh: Churchill Livingstone.

Freud A. (1952). The role of bodily illness in the mental life of children. *Psychoanalytic Study of the Child*. 7: 69–81.

Freud A. (1965). Children in the hospital. In: *The Writings of Anna Freud*, Vol.V. New York: International Universities Press.

Freud S. (1900). Distortion in dreams. In: J. Strachey (Ed.) *The Standard Edition of the Complete Psychological Works of Sigmund Freud*, 24 vols, 1953–73. London: Hogarth, 4: 134–62.

Freud S. (1905). Fragment of an analysis of a case of hysteria. *S.E.* 7: 3–122.

Freud S. (1915a). Our attitude towards death. *S.E.* 14: 289–300.

Freud S. (1915b). Mourning and melancholia. *S.E.* 14: 237–60.

Freud S. (1920). Beyond the pleasure principle. *S.E.* 18: 7–63.

Freud S. (1920a). A psychogenesis of a case of homosexuality in a woman. *S.E.* 18: 145–72.

Freud S. (1920b). Letter to Ferenczi, February 4, in M. Schur (1972) *Freud: Living and Dying*. London: Hogarth.

Freud S. (1923). The ego and the id. *S.E.* 19: 3–66.

Freud S. (1929). Letter to Ludwig Binswanger. In: E. Freud (Ed.) *The Letters of Sigmund Freud 1873–1939*. London: Hogarth/Institute of Psycho-Analysis, p. 386 (1970).

Freud S. (1938). An outline of psychoanalyis. *S.E.* 23, chs II, VII, VIII.

Fromm E. (1974). *The Anatomy of Human Destructiveness*. London: Cape.

Furman E. (1974). *A Child's Parent Dies*. New Haven, CT: Yale University Press.

Furman E., (1984). Helping children cope with dying. *Journal of Child Psychotherapy* 10 (2): 151–7.

Gaes J. (1987). *My book for kids with Cansur (sic)* Aberdeen and S. Dakota: Melius & Peterson.

Garmezy N, Masten A, Tellegan A. (1984). The study of stress and competence in children. *Child Development* 55: 97–111.

Geist R. (1979). Onset of chronic illness in children and adolescents: psychotherapeutic and consultative intervention. *American Journal of Orthopsychiatry* 49(1): 4–23.

Gibran K. (1926). *The Prophet*. London: Pan, 1980.

Glaser B, Strauss A. (1963). *Awareness of Dying*. Chicago: Altline.

Gordon A. (1975). Psychological aspects of isolator therapy in acute leukaemia. *British Journal of Psychiatry* 127: 588–90.

Gorer G. (1965). *Death, Grief and Mourning in Contemporary Britain*. London: Cresset Press.

Greenacre P. (1980). Infant reactions to restraint. In: *Trauma, Growth and Personality*. New York: International Universities Press.

Hageboeck H. (1962). Tragic silence. *New York Sunday Times Magazine*, 5 August.

Hawkins M. (1989). Long term survival and cure after childhood cancer. *Archives of Disease in Childhood* 64: 798–807.

Hawkins M, Kingston J, Kinnier Wilson L. (1990). Late deaths after treatment for childhood cancer. *Archives of Disease in Childhood* 65: 1356–63.

Hippocrates (Translated by WHS Jones) *The Loeb Classical Library*, Vol. 1, 299–332. Cambridge, Mass: Harvard University Press (1962).

Hobart Davies W, Noll R, De Stefano L, Bukowski W, Kulkarni R. (1991). Differences in the child–rearing practices of parents of children with cancer and controls: the perspectives of parents and professionals. *Journal of Pediatric Psychology* 16 (3): 295–306.

Hoffman I, Futterman E. (1971). Coping with waiting: psychiatric intervention and study in the waiting room of a paediatric oncology unit. *Comprehensive Psychiatry* 12: 67–81.

Holmes H, Holmes F. (1975). After ten years, what are the handicaps and life styles of children treated for cancer? *Clinical Pediatrics* 14: 819–23.

Howell D. (1967). A child dies. *Hospital Topics* February.

Hughes P, Lieberman S. (1990). Troubled parents: vulnerability and stress in childhood cancer. *British Journal of Medical Psychology* 63: 53–64. In *Collected Papers: Through Paediatrics to Psychoanalysis*. London: Tavistock, 1958.

Isaacs S. (1952). The nature and function of phantasy. In: M. Klein and J. Riviere (Eds) *Developments in Psycho-Analysis*. London: Hogarth.

Jamison R, Lewis S, Burish T. (1986). Co-operation with treatment in adolescent cancer patients. *Journal of Adolescent Health Care* 7: 162–7

Janssen Y. (1983). Early awareness of death in normal development. *Infant Mental Health Journal* 4 (2): 95–103.

Jaques E. (1955). Social systems as a defence against persecutory and depressive anxiety. In: M. Klein, P. Heimann and R. Money-Kyrle (Eds) *New Directions in Psycho-Analysis*. London: Tavistock.

Jay S, Ozolins M, Elliott H, Caldwell S. (1983). Assessment of children's distress during painful medical procedures. Health Psychology 2 (2): 133–147.

Johnson F, Rudolph L, Hartman J. (1979). Helping the family cope with childhood cancer. *Psychosomatics* 20: 241–51.

Jones M. (1988). *Secret Flowers: Mourning and Adaptation to Loss*. London: Women's Press.

Judd D. (1988). The hollow laugh: an account of the first six months of therapy with a brain-damaged boy. *Journal of Child Psychotherapy* 14 (2): 79–92.

Judd D. (1994). Life-threatening illness as psychic trauma: psychotherapy with adolescent cancer patients. In: A. Erskine and D. Judd (Eds) *The Imaginative Body – psychodynamic therapy in health care*. London: Whurr.

Kahana R. (1972). Personality and response to physical illness. *Archives of Psychosomatic Medicine* 8: 42–62.

Kamphuis R. (1979). Psychological and ethical considerations in the use of germ-free treatment. In: Fleidner *et al.* (Eds) *Clinical and Experimental Gnotobiotic*. Stuttgart: Fischer Verlag.

Kane B. (1979). Children's concepts of death. *Journal of Genetic Psychology* 134: 141–53.

Kastenbaum R. (1981). *Death, Society, and Human Experience* (2nd edn). St Louis, MO: Mosby.

Kastenbaum R. (1982). Dying is healthy and death a bureaucrat: our fantasy machine is alive and well. In: M. Di Matteo and H. Freidman (Eds) *Interpersonal Personal Issues in Health Care*. San Diego: Academic Press.

Katz E, Varni J, Rubenstein C, Blew A, Hubert N. (1992). Teacher, parent, and child evaluative ratings of a school reintegration intervention for children with newly diagnosed cancer. *Children's Health Care* 21 (2): 69–75.

Kaufman C, Harbeck R, Olsen R, Nitschke R. (1992). The availability of psychosocial interventions to children with cancer and their families. *Children's Health Care* 21 (1): 21–5.

Keats J. (1817). Letter to his brothers George and Tom, April. In: M. B. Forman (Ed.) *Letters*. Oxford: Oxford University Press (1952).

Kendrick C, Culling J, Oakhill T, Mott M. (1986). Children's understanding of their illness and its treatment within a paediatric oncology unit. *Association of Child Psychology and Psychiatry Newsletter* 8(2): 16–20.

Keniston K. (1967). The medical student. *Yale Journal of Biological Medicine* 39: 346

Khan M. (1986). The concept of cumulative trauma. In: G. Kohon (Ed.) *The British School of Psychoanalysis - the Independent Tradition*. London: Free Association Books.

Kinlen L. (1988). Evidence for an infective cause of childhood leukaemia: a comparison of a Scottish new town with nuclear reprocessing sites in Britain. *Lancet* ii: 1323–7.

Kinlen L, O'Brien F, Clarke K, Balkwill A, Matthews F. (1993). Rural population mixing and childhood leukaemia: effects of the North Sea oil industry in Scotland, including the area near Dounreay nuclear site. *British Medical Journal* 306: 743–8.

Klein M. (1932). Preface to 1st edition,*The Psycho-Analysis of Children*. London: Hogarth (1949) pp. 7–10.

Klein M. (1937). Love, guilt and reparation. In: *Love, Guilt and Reparation and Other Works*. London: Hogarth (1975).

Klein M. (1940). Mourning and its relation to manic-depressive states. In: *Love, Guilt and Reparation and Other Works*. London: Hogarth (1975).

Klein M. (1946). Notes on some schizoid mechanisms. In: *Envy and Gratitude*. London: Hogarth (1975).

Klein M. (1949). The relation between obsessional neurosis and the early stages of the super-ego. In: *The Psycho-Analysis of Children*. London: Hogarth (1975), pp. 149 –75.

Klein M. (1952). The origins of transference. In: *Envy and Gratitude*. London: Hogarth (1975).

Kohlberg L. (1976). Moral stages and moralisation: the cognitive-developmental approach. In: T. Lickona (Ed.) *Moral Development and Behaviour: Theory, Research and Social Issue*. New York: Holt, Rinehart & Winston.

Kohut H. (1977). *The Restoration of the Self*. New York: International Universities Press.

Koocher G, O'Malley J. (1981). *The Damocles Syndrome*. New York: McGraw-Hill.

Koocher G., O'Malley J, Janis L, Foster D. (1980). Psychological adjustment among paediatric survivors. *Journal Child Psychology and Psychiatry* 21: 163–73.

Koocher G, Sallan S. (1978). Paediatric oncology. In: P. Magrab (Ed.) *Psychological Management of Pediatric Problems* Vol. I, *Early Life Conditions and Chronic Disease*. Baltimore, MD: University Park Press.

Kübler-Ross E. (1970). *On Death and Dying*. New York: Macmillan.

Kübler-Ross E. (1975). *Death: The Final Stage of Growth*. Englewood Cliffs, NJ: Prentice-Hall

Kübler-Ross E. (1983). *On Children and Death*. London: Macmillan.

Kübler-Ross E. (1987). *Living with Death and Dying*. London: Souvenir Press.

Lamerton R. (1973). *Care of the Dying*. London: Priory Press.

Lansdown R. (1980). *More than Sympathy: the Everyday Needs of Sick and Handicapped Children*. London: Tavistock.

Lansdown R. (1987). The development of the concept of death and its relationship to communicating with dying children. In: E. Karas (Ed.) *Current Issues in Clinical Psychology*. London: Plenum.

Lansdown R, Goldman A. (1988). The psychological care of children with malignant disease. *Journal of Child Psychology and Psychiatry* 29: 555–67.

Lansky S. (1974). Childhood leukaemia – the psychiatrist as a member of the oncology team. *Journal of American Academy of Child Psychiatry* 13: 499–508.

Lansky S, Cairns N *et al.* (1978). Childhood cancer, parent discord and divorce. *Paediatrics* 62: 184–8.

Lauer M, Camitta B. (1980). Home care for dying children; a nursing model. *Journal of Paediatrics* 97: 1032–5.

Lazarus R. (1976). *Patterns of Adjustment.* New York: McGraw-Hill.

Leikin S. (1981). An ethical issue in pediatric cancer care: nondisclosure of a fatal prognosis. *Pediatric Annals* 10: (10) 37–43.

Levenson P, Copeland D, Morrow J, Pfefferbaum B, Silberberg Y. (1983). Disparities in disease-related perceptions of adolescent cancer patients and their parents. *Journal of Paediatric Psychology* 8: 33–45.

Levine S. (1986). *Who Dies? An Investigation of Conscious Living and Conscious Dying.* Bath: Gateway.

Lewis CS. (1966). *A Grief Observed.* London: Faber.

Likierman M. (1987) The function of anger in human conflict. *International Review of Psycho-Analysis* 14: 143–61.

List M, Ritter-Sterr C, Lansky S. (1991). Cancer during adolescence. *Paediatrician* 18: 32–6.

Liston E. (1975). Education on death and dying: a neglected area in the medical curriculum. *Omega* 6 (3): 193–8.

Mahabeer M. (1980). An investigation of the relationship between certain demographic variables and death anxiety in Indian youth. (Unpublished thesis, University of Durban – Westville, South Africa.)

Manne S, Bakeman R, Jacobson P, Gorfinkle K, Bernstein D, Redd W. (1992). Adult–child interaction during invasive medical procedures. *Health Psychology* 11 (4): 241–9.

Marcus S. (1966). *The Other Victorians.* London: Weidenfeld.

Martin B. (1985). Home care for terminally ill children and their families. In: C. Corr and D. Corr (Eds) *Hospice Approaches to Pediatric Care.* New York: Springer.

Martinson I, Armstrong G *et al.* (1978). Home care for children dying of cancer. *Paediatrics* 62: 106–13.

McClowry E, Davies K, May K., Kulenkamp E, Martinson L. (1987). The empty space phenomenon: the process of grief in the bereaved family. *Death Studies* 361–74.

McCue K. (1980). Preparing children for medical procedures. In: J. Kellerman (Ed.) *Psychological Aspects of Childhood Cancer.* Springfield, IL: CC Thomas.

McKeown T. (1976). *The Modern Rise of Population.* London: Arnold.

McNeill P. (1988). The sociology of health. *New Statesman & Society* 8 July.

McWhirter L, Young V, and Majiery Y. (1983). Belfast children's awareness of violent death. *British Journal of Social Psychology* 22: 81–92.

Menzies Lyth I. (1959). The functioning of social systems as a defence against anxiety. In: *Containing Anxiety in Institutions.* London: Free Association Books (1988) pp. 43–85.

Menzies Lyth I. (1982). *The Psychological Welfare of Children Making Long Stays in Hospital: an Experience in the Art of the Possible.* London: Tavistock Institute of Human Relations Occasional Paper No. 3.

Menzies Lyth I. (1989). The aftermath of disaster. In: *The Dynamics of the Social.* London: Free Association Books.

Miles M. (1985). Emotional symptoms and physical health in bereaved parents. *Nursing Research* 34: 76–81.

Miller P. (1987). Death with dignity and the right to die: sometimes doctors have a duty to hasten death. *Journal of Medical Ethics* 13: 81–5.

Milne R. (1988). Hinkley cancer rate higher. *Guardian* 19 December.

Ministry of Health, Central Health Services Council (1959). *The Welfare of Children in Hospital*. London: HMSO.

Mitchell-Rossdale J. (1988). Tread softly . . . some thoughts on creativity. British Journal of Psychotherapy 2nd Annual Lecture, 23 May.

Moore MS. (1990). Understanding children's drawings: developmental and emotional indicators in children's human figure drawings. *Journal of Educational Therapy* 3(2): 35–47.

Moore MS. (1994a). Reflections of self: the use of drawings in evaluating and treating physically ill children. In: A. Erskine and D. Judd (Eds) *The Imaginative Body – psychodynamic therapy in health care*. London: Whurr.

Moore MS. (1994b). Common charateristics in the drawings of ritually abused children and adults. In: V. Sinason (Ed.) *Treating Survivors of Satanist Abuse*. London: Routledge, pp. 221–41.

Moore I, Gilliss C, Martinson I. (1988). Psychosomatic symptoms in parents two years after the death of a child with cancer. *Nursing Research* 37 (22): 104–7.

Morrisey J. (1963a). A note of interviews with children facing imminent death. *Social Casework* 44: 343–5.

Morrisey J. (1963b). Children's adaptations to fatal illness. *Social Work* 8: 81–8.

Munro A. (1971). *Lives of Girls and Women*. Harmondsworth: Penguin (1982).

Muir L, Notta H. (1993). An Asian mothers' group. *Groupwork* 6 (2): 122–32.

Murphy N. (1992). The physician as artist and guide. *Loss, Grief, and Care* 15–22.

Nagera H. (1970). Children's reaction to the death of important objects: a developmental approach. *Psychoanalytic Study of the Child*. 25: 360–400.

Nagy MH. (1959). The child's view of death. In: H. Feifel (Ed.) *The Meaning of Death*. New York: McGraw-Hill.

Natterson J. (1973). The fear of death in fatally ill children and their parents. In: (Eds) E. Anthony and C. Koupernik *The Child in his Family*, Vol. 2. New York: Wiley.

Natterson J, Knudson A. (1960). Observations concerning fear of death in fatally ill children and their mothers. *Psychosomatic Medicine* 22: 456–65.

Nicholson R. (1986). *Medical Research with Children: Ethics, Law, and Practice*. Oxford: Oxford University Press.

Norton J. (1963). Treatment of a dying patient. *Psychoanalytic Study of the Child*. London: Hogarth 18: 541–60.

O'Malley J, Koocher G, Foster D, Slavin L. (1979). Psychiatric sequelae of surviving childhood cancer. *Orthopsychiatry* 49: 608–16.

Obholzer A. (1994). Managing social anxieties in public sector organisations. In: A. Obholzer and V. Z. Roberts (Eds) *The Unconscious at Work*. London: Routledge. pp. 169–78.

Orbach I. (1988). *Children Who Don't Want to Live*. San Francisco: Jossey-Bass.

Orbach I, Gross Y, Glaubman H, Berman D. (1985). Children's perception of death in humans and animals as a function of age, anxiety and cognitive ability. *Journal of Child Psychology and Psychiatry* 26: 453–63.

Parker M, Mauger D. (1979). *Children with Cancer: A Handbook for Families and Helpers*. London: Cassell.

Parkes CM. (1972). *Bereavement: Studies of Grief in Adult Life*. London: Tavistock.

Parkes CM. (1979). Terminal care: evaluation of in-patient service at St Christopher's Hospice, part I: self-assessments of effects of the service on surviving spouses. *Postgraduate Medical Journal* 55: 523–87.

Patenaude A, Szymanski L, Rappeport J. (1979). Psychosocial costs of bone marrow transplantation in children. *American Journal of Orthopsychiatry* 49 (3): 409–22.

Pettle M, Lansdown R. (1986). Adjustment to the death of a sibling. *Archives of Disease in Childhood* 61: 278–83.

Pfefferbaum B, Lucas R. (1979). Management of acute psychologic problems in paediatric oncology. *General Hospital Psychiatry* 1 (3): 214–19.

Piaget J. (1932). *The Moral Judgement of the Child*. London: Routledge & Kegan Paul.

Piaget J. (1951). *The Child's Conception of the World*. London: Routledge & Kegan Paul.

Pincus L. (1976). *Death and the Family*. London: Faber.

Piontelli A. (1992). *From Fetus to Child*. London: Routledge.

Pot-Mees C, Zeitlin H. (1987). Psychosocial consequences of bone marrow transplantation in children: a preliminary communication. *Journal of Psychosocial Oncology* 5(2): 73–81.

Puckle B. (1926). *Funeral Customs: their Origin and Development*. London: Werner Laurie.

Ramsay N. (in press). Sitting close to death – a ward observation on a palliative care unit. *Group Analysis*.

Rando T. (1983). An investigation of grief and adaptation in parents whose children have died from cancer. *Journal of Pediatric Psychology* 8(1): 3–20.

Rank O. (1929). *The Trauma of Birth*. New York: Harcourt, Brace.

Reilly T, Hasazi J, Bond L. (1983). Children's conception of death and personal mortality. *Journal of Paediatric Psychology* 8(1): 21–31.

Richmond J, Waisman H. (1955). Psychological aspects of management of children with malignant disease. *American Journal of Diseases in Children* 89: 42–7.

Rilke RM. (1914). *Duino Elegies*. London: Chatto (1981).

Robertson J. (1952). Film: *A Two Year-Old Goes to Hospital*. London: Tavistock Child Development Research Unit.

Rochlin G. (1959). The loss complex a contribution to the etiology of depression. *Journal of American Psychoanalytic Association* 7: 299–316.

Rochlin G. (1967). How young children view death and themselves. In: E. Grollman (Ed.) *Explaining Death to Children*. Boston, MA: Beacon.

Rothenberg, M. (1974). Problems posed for staff who care for the child. In: L. Burton, (Ed.) *Care of the Child Facing Death*. London: Routledge & Kegan Paul.

Rutter M.(1980). The long-term effects of early experience. *Developmental Medical Child Neurology* 2: 800–15.

Sadgrove J. (1988). Electricity and cancer. *Guardian* 27 July.

Sanders J, Pritchard S, Mahoney P *et al.* (1986). Growth and development following marrow transplantation for leukaemia. *Blood* 68: 1129–35.

Sanger M, Copeland D, Davidson, E. (1991). Psychosocial adjustment among pediatric cancer patients: a multidimensional assessment. *Journal of Pediatric Psychology* 16(4): 463–74.

Scott Peck M. (1990). *The Road Less Travelled*. London: Arrow.

Segal H. (1973). *Introduction to the Work of Melanie Klein*. London: Hogarth.

Segal H. (1987). Silence is the real crime. *International Review of Psycho-Analysis* 14: 3–12.

Shannon F, Fergusson D, Dimond M. (1984). Early hospital admissions and subsequent behaviour problems in 6 year olds. *Archives of Disease in Childhood* 59: 815–19.

Sigler A. (1970). The leukaemic child and his family: an emotional challenge. In: M.

Debuskey (Ed.) *The Chronically Ill Child and his Family*. Springfield, IL: CC Thomas.

Slaby A, Glicksman A. (1985). *Adapting to Life-Threatening Illness*. New York: Praeger.

Slevin M. (1994). Quoted in C. Read, When is it time to give in to cancer? *The Independent* 15 February.

Solnit A, Green M. (1963). Paediatric management of the dying child, II: a study of the child's reaction to the fear of dying. In: A. Solnit and S. Provence (Eds) *Modern Perspectives in Child Development*. New York: International Universities Press.

Sontag S. (1978). *Illness as Metaphor*. New York: Farrar, Strauss & Giroux.

Souhami R. (1993). Care for the adolescent with cancer. *European Journal of Cancer* (Oxford) 29a: 2215–16.

Speechley K, Noh S. (1992). Surviving childhood cancer, social support, and parents' psychological adjustment. *Journal of Pediatric Psychology* 17 (1): 15–31.

Spinetta J. (1974). The dying child's awareness of death. *Psychology Bulletin* 81 (4): 256–60.

Spinetta J. (1975). Death anxiety in the outpatient leukaemic child. *Paediatrics*, 56 (6): 1034–7.

Spinetta J. (1977). Adjustment in children with cancer. *Journal of Paediatric Psychology* 2 (2): 49–51.

Spinetta J. (1981). The sibling of the child with cancer. In: J. Spinetta and P. Deasy-Spinetta (Eds) *Living With Childhood Cancer*. St Louis, MO: CV Mosby.

Spinetta J. (1982). Behavioural and psychological research in childhood cancer: an overview. *Cancer* 50: 1939–43.

Spinetta J, Deasy-Spinetta P. (Eds) (1981). *Living With Childhood Cancer*. St Louis, MO: CV Mosby.

Spinetta J, Moloney L. (1978). The child with cancer: patterns of communication and denial. *Journal of Consulting & Clinical Psychology* 48: 1540–1.

Spinetta J, Rigler D, Karon M. (1973). Anxiety in the dying child. *Paediatrics* 52 (6): 841–5.

Spinetta J, Rigler D, Karon M. (1974). Personal space as a measure of the dying child's sense of isolation. *Journal of Consulting & Clinical Psychology* 42: 751–6.

Spitz L. (1988). (Nuffield Professor of Paediatric Surgery, Institute of Child Health; Hon. Consultant Surgeon, Great Ormond Street Hospital for Sick Children, London) *Observer Magazine*, 17 July.

Spitz R. (1945). *Hospitalism. Psychoanalytic Study of the Child* 1: 53–74.

Springer K. (1994). Beliefs about illness causality among pre-schoolers with cancer: evidence against immanent justice. *Journal of Pediatric Psychology* 19 (1): 91–101.

Stambrook M, Parker K. (1987). The development of the concept of death in childhood: a review of the literature. *Merrill-Palmer Quarterly* 33 (2): 133–57.

Stannard D. (1977). *The Puritan Way of Death: A Study in Religion, Culture and Social Change*. Oxford: Oxford University Press.

Stedeford A. (1984). *Facing Death: Patients, Families, and Professionals*. London: Heinemann Medical.

Stehbens J, Kisker C, Wilson B. (1983). Achievement and intelligence test-retest performance in paediatric cancer patients at diagnosis and one year later. *Journal of Paediatric Psychology* 8: 47–56.

Stein A, Wooley H. *et al.* (1988). Imparting the diagnosis of life-threatening illness. Paper presented at 60th Annual Meeting, British Paediatric Association, New York.

Stein R, Jessop D. (1984). Does paediatric home care make a difference for children with chronic illness? *Paediatrics* 73: 845–53 (Paediatric Ambulatory Care Treatment Study).

Stiller C. (1994). Population based survival rates for childhood cancer in Britain, 1981–1991. *British Medical Journal* 309: 1612–16.

Stiller C. (1985). Descriptive epidemiology of childhood leukaemia and lymphoma in Great Britain. *Leukaemia Research* 9 (6): 671–4.

Thomas D. (1966). Do not go gentle into that good night. In: *Collected Poems*. London: Dent (1977).

Thomas D. (1966). Death shall have no dominion. In: *Collected Poems*. London: Dent (1977).

Tropauer A *et al.* (1970). Psychological aspects of the care of children with cystic fibrosis. *American Journal of Diseases in Children* 119: 424–32.

Turk J. (1964). Impact of cystic fibrosis on family functioning. *Paediatrics* 34: 67–71.

Twaddle V, Britton P, Craft A, Noble T, Kernahan J. (1983). Intellectual function after treatment for leukaemia or solid tumours. *Archives of Disease in Childhood* 58: 949–52.

Van Dongen-Melman J, Sanders-Woudstra J. (1986). Psychosocial aspects of childhood cancer: a review of the literature. *Journal of Child Psychology and Psychiatry* 27: 145–80.

Vernick J. (1973). Meaningful communication with the fatally ill child. In: E. Anthony and C. Koupernik (Eds) *The Child in his Family* Vol. II. New York:Wiley.

Vernick J, Karon M. (1965). Who's afraid of death on a leukaemia ward? *American Journal of Diseases in Children* 109: 393–7.

Waechter E. (1968). Death anxiety in children with fatal illness. Doctoral dissertation, Stanford University, Ann Arbor, MI: Univ. Microfilms, No. 72–26, 056.

Waechter E. (1971). Children's awareness of fatal illness. *American Journal of Nursing* 71: 1168–72.

Walker G. (1983). The pact: the caretaker-parent/ill child coalition in families with chronic illness. *Family Systems Medicine* 1: 4, 7–29.

Walvin J. (1987). *Victorian Values*. London: Cardinal (Sphere Books).

Watson D, Robinson A, Bailey C. (1981). A reappraisal of routine marrow examination therapy of acute lymphoblastic leukaemia. *Archives of Disease in Childhood* 56: 392–4.

Watson M. (1983). Psychological intervention with cancer patients: a review. *Psychological Medicine* 13: 839–46.

Weil M, Smith M, Khayat D. (1994). Truth-telling to cancer patients in the Western European context. *Psycho-Oncology* 3: 21–6.

Weininger O. (1979). Young children's concepts of dying and dead. *Psychological Reports* 44: 395–407.

Weithorn L, Campbell S. (1982). The competency of children and adolescents to make informed treatment decisions. *Child Development* 53: 1589–98.

Wells R. (1988). *Helping Children Cope with Grief*. London: Sheldon Press.

Wenestam C. (1982). Children's reactions to the word death. Unpublished paper, Dept. of Education, University of Göteborg, Sweden.

Willcock D. (1988).(Producer) *The Facts of Death Film by Everyman*, BBC TV, 15 August.

Williams T. (1957). *Orpheus Descending*. Harmondsworth: Penguin (1976).

Winnicott DW. (1951). Transitional objects and transitional phenomena. In: *Collected Papers: Through Paediatrics to Psychoanalysis*. London: Tavistock (1958).

Winnicott DW. (1954). A primary state of being: pre-primitive stages. In: *Human Nature*. London: Free Association Books (1988).

Winnicott DW. (1962). Ego integration in child development. In: *The Maturational Processes and the Facilitating Environment*. London: Hogarth (1987).

Winnicott DW. (1963). The value of depression. In: *Home is Where We Start From* Harmondsworth: Penguin (1987).

Winnicott DW. (1972). Basis for self in body. *International Journal of Child Psychotherapy* 1 (1): 7–16.

Winnicott DW. (1974). *Playing and Reality*. Harmondsworth: Penguin.

Winnicott DW. (1987). *The Maturational Processes and the Facilitating Environment*. London: Hogarth.

Winnicott DW. (1988). *Human Nature*. London: Free Association Books.

Witham A. (1985). The idealization of dying. *Free Associations* 3: 80–91.

Wölfflin H. (1932) *Principles of Art History*. New York: Dover.

Wolstenholme G, O'Connor M. (Eds) (1964). *Law and Ethics of Transplantation. Ciba Foundation Blueprint*. London: J & A Churchill.

Woolley H, Stein A, Forrest G, Baum J. (1989). Imparting the diagnosis of life threatening illness in children. *British Medical Journal* 17 June, 1623–6.

Yalom I. (1980). *Existential Psychotherapy*. New York: Basic Books.

Yorke C. (1985). Fantasy and the body-mind problem. *Psychoanalytic Study of the Child* 40: 319–28.

Yudkin S. (1967). Children and death. *Lancet* i: 37–41.

Zorza R, Zorza V. (1980). *A Way to Die: Living to the End*. London: Deutsch.

Index